YOU'RE READING THE WRONG WAY!

SPY x FAMILY reads from right to left, starting in the upper-right corner. Japanese is read from right to left, meaning that action, sound effects, and word-balloon order are completely reversed from English order.

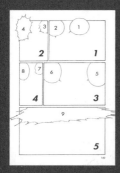

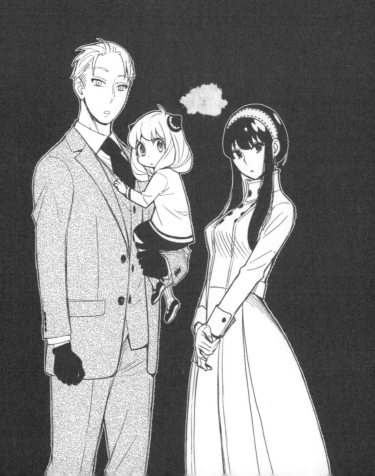

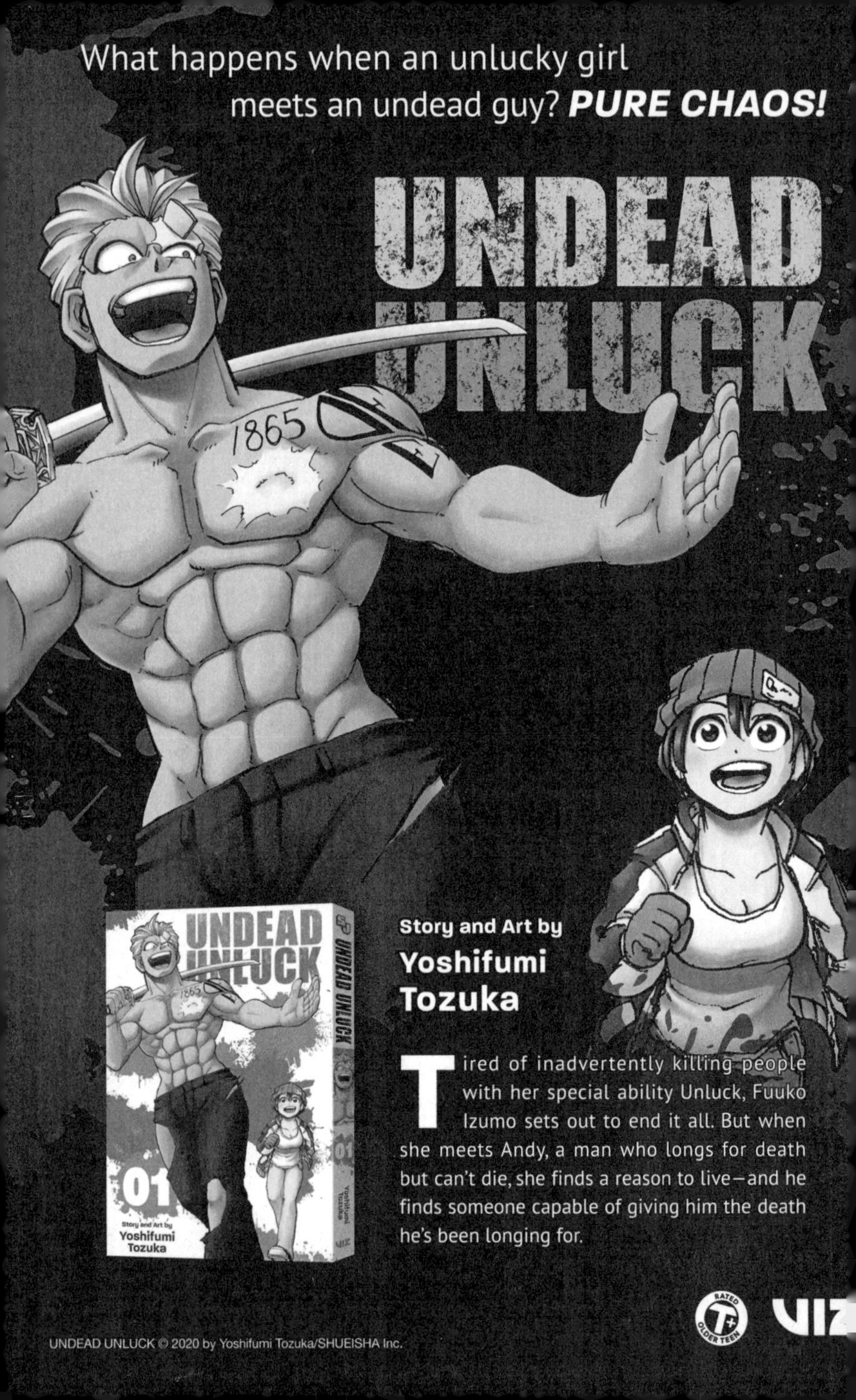
What happens when an unlucky girl meets an undead guy? PURE CHAOS!
UNDEAD UNLUCK
1865
UNDEAD UNLUCK
UNDEAD UNLUCK
01
Story and Art by Yoshifumi Tozuka
Yoshifumi Tozuka
VIZ
Story and Art by
Yoshifumi Tozuka
Tired of inadvertently killing people with her special ability Unluck, Fuuko Izumo sets out to end it all. But when she meets Andy, a man who longs for death but can't die, she finds a reason to live—and he finds someone capable of giving him the death he's been longing for.
RATED T+ OLDER TEEN
VIZ
UNDEAD UNLUCK © 2020 by Yoshifumi Tozuka/SHUEISHA Inc.

SPY×FAMILY 7

SHONEN JUMP Edition

STORY AND ART BY **TATSUYA ENDO**

Translation **CASEY LOE**

Touch-Up Art & Lettering **RINA MAPA**

Design **JIMMY PRESLER**

Editor **JOHN BAE**

SPY x FAMILY © 2019 by Tatsuya Endo
All rights reserved.
First published in Japan in 2019 by SHUEISHA Inc., Tokyo.
English translation rights arranged by SHUEISHA Inc.

The stories, characters, and incidents mentioned in this publication are entirely fictional.

Printed in Italy

Published by VIZ Media, LLC
P.O. Box 77010
San Francisco, CA 94107

10 9 8 7 6 5 4
First printing, April 2022
Fourth printing, May 2022

viz.com

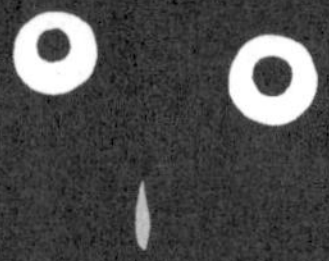

I'm clearly aging.

—TATSUYA ENDO

Tatsuya Endo was born in Ibaraki Prefecture, Japan, on July 23, 1980. He debuted as a manga artist with the one-shot "Seibu Yugi" (Western Game), which ran in the Spring 2000 issue of *Akamaru Jump*. He is the author of *TISTA* and *Gekka Bijin* (Moon Flower Beauty). *Spy x Family* is his first work published in English.

SPY x FAMILY

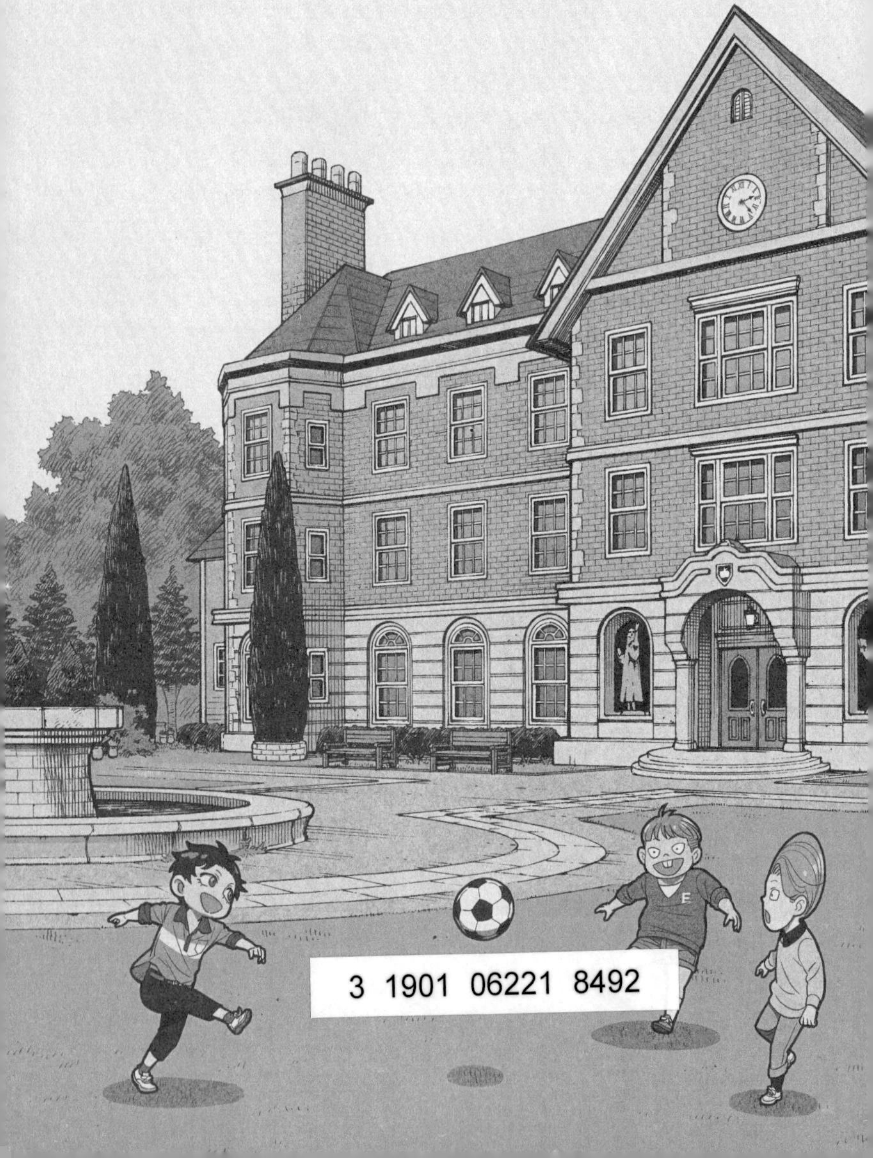

TOP SECRET

(BONUS) LOID'S WEEK IN FASHION

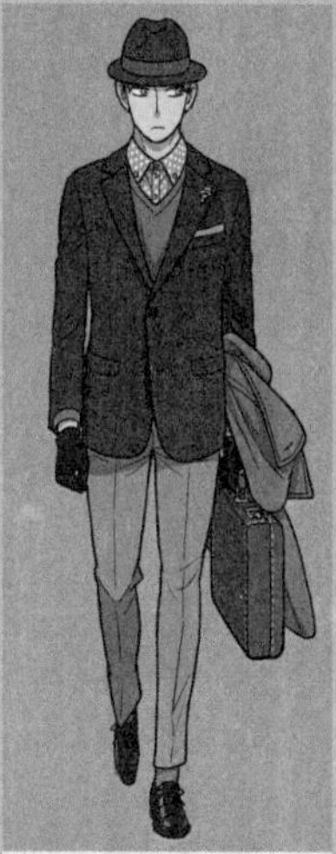

DAY 1
TODAY'S WORK ENSEMBLE HAS AN AUTUMNAL FLAIR. BALANCING SPY WORK AND MY HOSPITAL JOB IS ALWAYS A CHALLENGE.

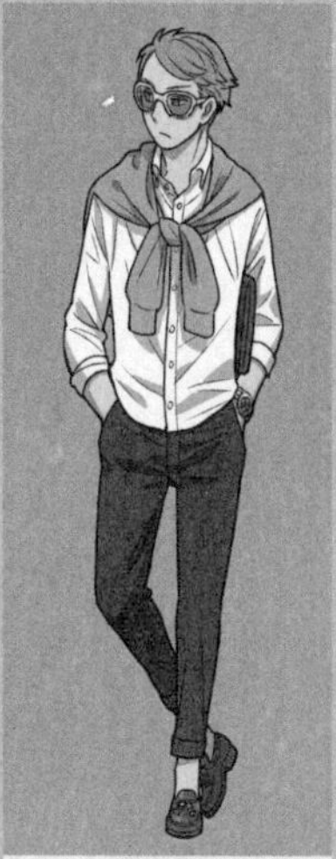

DAY 2
TO SECURE A PARTICULAR PIECE OF FOOTAGE, I'M INFILTRATING A BROADCAST STUDIO AS A TELEVISION DIRECTOR. SIDE MISSIONS LIKE THIS ARE COMMONPLACE.

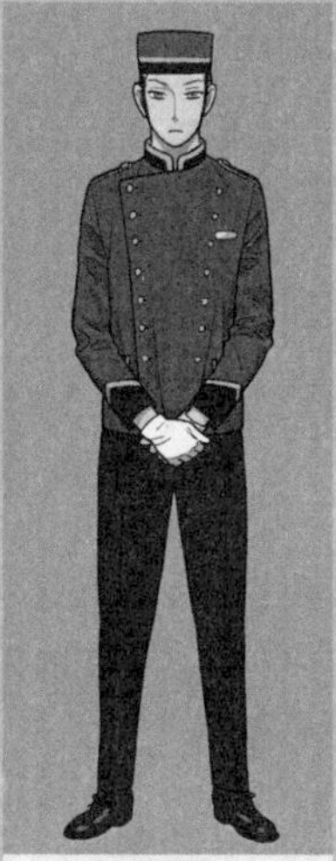

DAY 3
A SECRET MEETING OF POLITICIANS IS BEING HELD TODAY AT A BERLINT HOTEL. I'VE ASSEMBLED THE RIGHT LOOK FOR PLANTING LISTENING DEVICES.

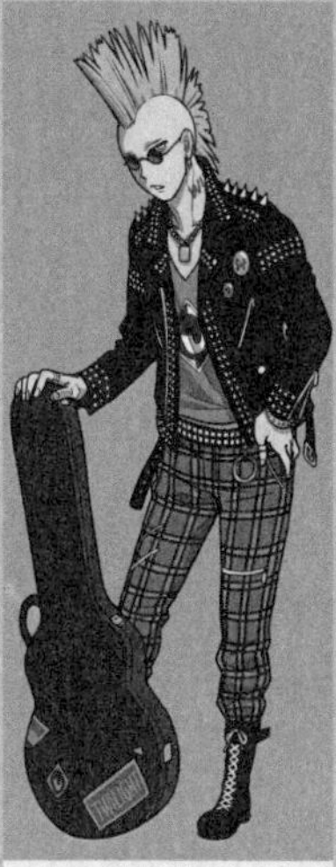

DAY 4
PUNK MUSIC IS BANNED IN OSTANIA, BUT INTEL SUGGESTS THAT THE LEADER OF AN ANTI-GOVERNMENT ORGANIZATION WILL BE ATTENDING AN UNDERGROUND PUNK ROCK FESTIVAL.

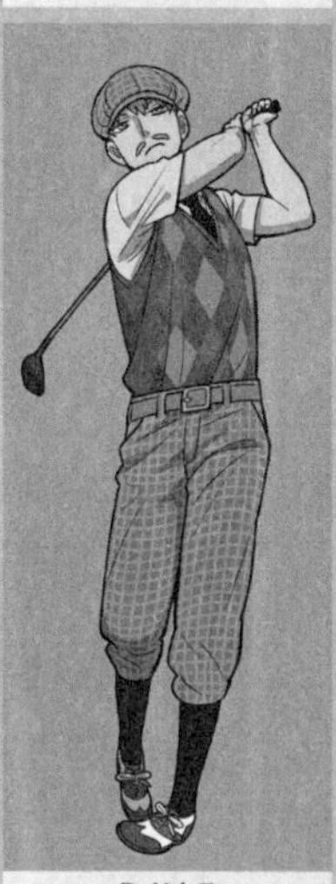

DAY 5
TODAY I'LL BE ATTENDING A GOLF TOURNAMENT FULL OF VIPS. A ROUND OF GOLF AWAY FROM THE BUSTLE OF THE CITY ACTUALLY SOUNDS PRETTY NICE... HAVE I BEEN WORKING TOO MUCH?

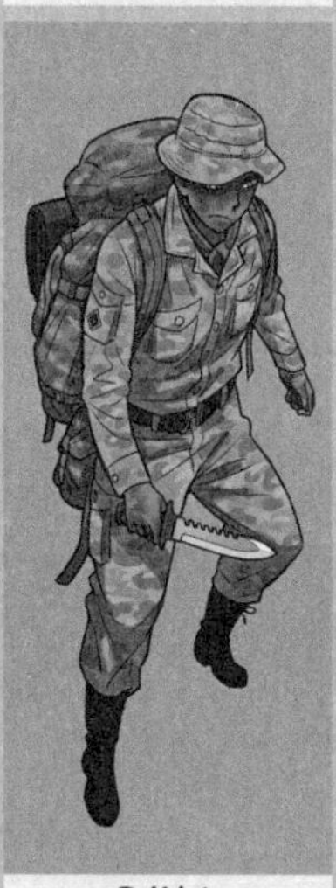

DAY 6
ANYA HAS BEEN BEGGING ME TO TRY GOURMET COCOA, SO I'M VENTURING INTO THE WILDERNESS IN SEARCH OF CACAO BEANS. I'LL DO WHATEVER I MUST FOR OPERATION STRIX!

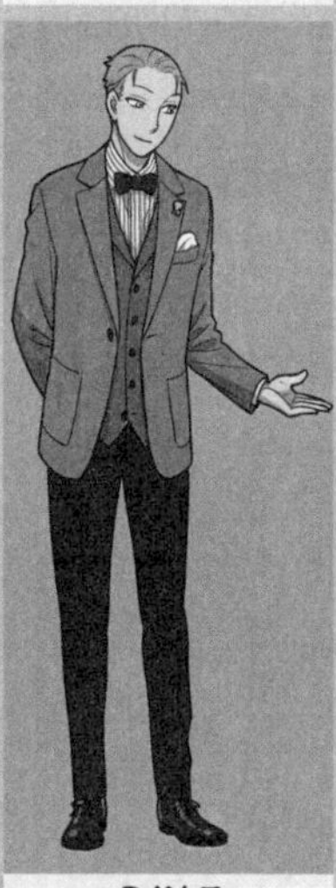

DAY 7
TONIGHT I'LL BE TAKING YOR TO DINNER. "LOID FORGER" NEVER TAKES A DAY OFF. REMEMBER, THIS IS ALL FOR THE SAKE OF WORLD PEACE!

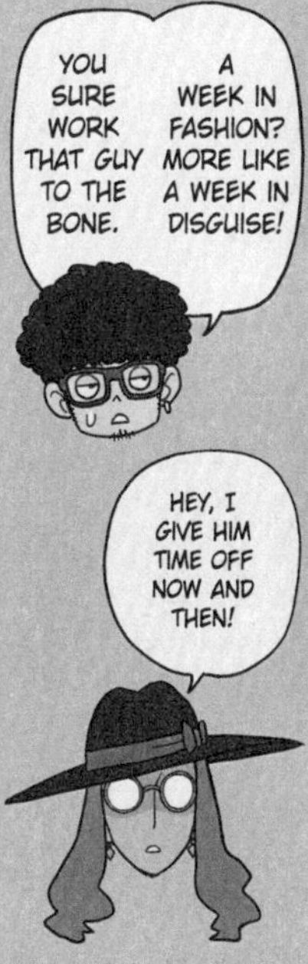
A WEEK IN FASHION? MORE LIKE A WEEK IN DISGUISE!
YOU SURE WORK THAT GUY TO THE BONE.
HEY, I GIVE HIM TIME OFF NOW AND THEN!

7

STORY AND ART BY
TATSUYA ENDO

SPY×FAMILY

SPY×FAMILY CHARACTERS

LOID FORGER

....
ROLE: Husband
....

Known as a skilled psychiatrist, Loid is actually "Twilight," a spy and master of disguise serving the nation of Westalis.

YOR FORGER

....
ROLE: Wife
....

A city hall clerk who also lives a secret life as a talented contract killer. Her code name is "Thorn Princess."

ANYA FORGER

....
ROLE: Daughter
....

Anya is a first grader at the prestigious Eden Academy. A telepath whose abilities were created in an experiment conducted by a certain organization. She can read minds.

BOND FORGER

....
ROLE: Dog
....

Anya's playmate and the family guard dog. As a former military test subject, he can see the future.

MISSION

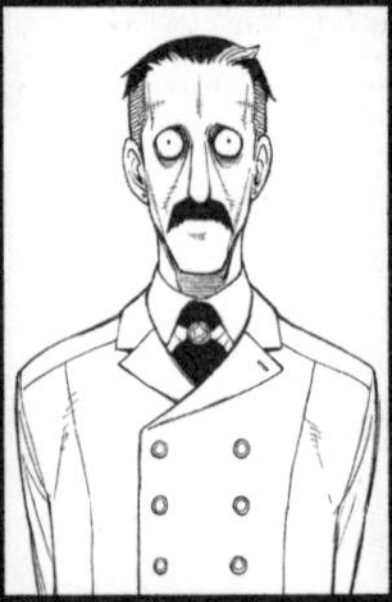

OPERATION STRIX

Spy on Donovan Desmond, a dangerous figure who threatens to disrupt peace between the East and West. Must gain entry into the prestigious Eden Academy to breach the target's inner circle.

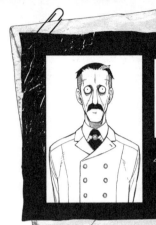

TARGET

DONOVAN DESMOND

The focus of Operation Strix. Chairman of Ostania's National Unity Party.

KEY PEOPLE

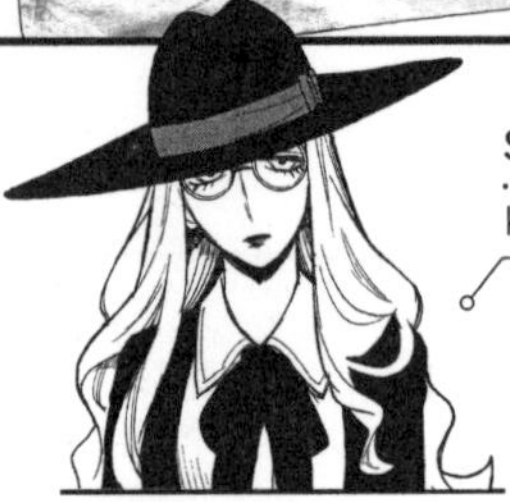

SILVIA SHERWOOD

Handler for Westalis's intelligence agency.

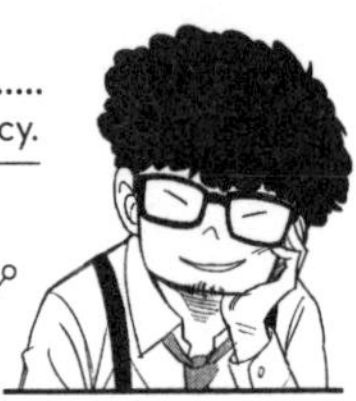

FRANKY

Intelligence asset who works with Twilight.

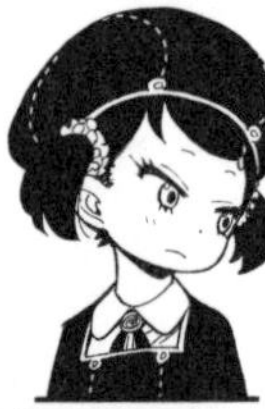

BECKY BLACKWELL

Anya's friend.

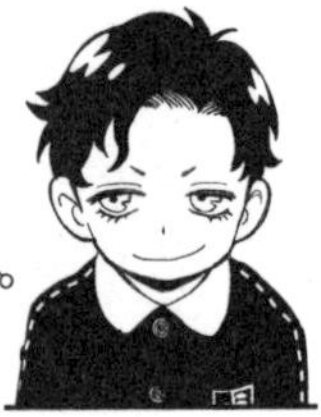

DAMIAN DESMOND

Second son of Donovan Desmond.

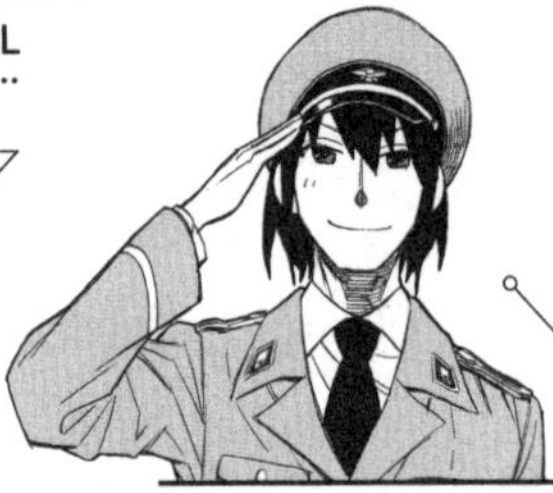

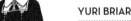

YURI BRIAR

Yor's younger brother, a secret police officer.

STORY

Westalis secret agent Twilight receives orders to uncover the plans of Donovan Desmond, the warmongering chairman of Ostania's National Unity Party. To do so, Twilight must pose as Loid Forger, create a fake family, and enroll his child at the prestigious Eden Academy. However, by sheer coincidence, the daughter he selects from an orphanage is secretly a telepath! Also, the woman who agrees to be in a sham marriage with him is secretly an assassin! While concealing their true identities from one another, the three now find themselves living together as a family.

Twilight teams up with fellow agent Nightfall and the two successfully complete their mission. In seeking to claim the role of Twilight's wife for herself, Nightfall challenges Yor to a tennis match, but the agent loses decisively. Meanwhile, Eden Academy is about to hold a get-together for elite students and their parents. Can Twilight exploit a planned meeting between Donovan Desmond and his son Damian in order to get closer to his target?

CONTENTS

SPY×FAMILY 7

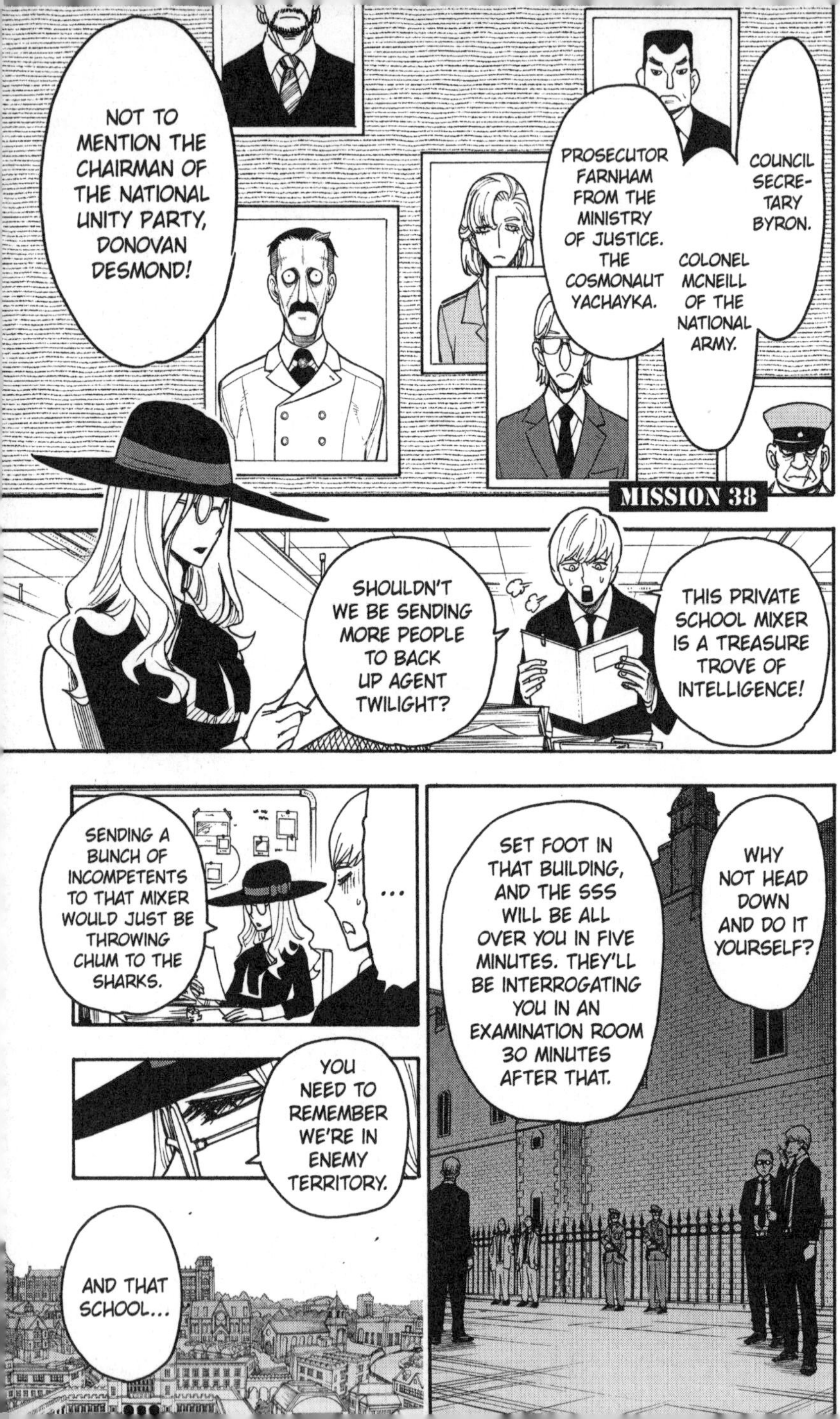
COUNCIL SECRETARY BYRON.
PROSECUTOR FARNHAM FROM THE MINISTRY OF JUSTICE. THE COSMONAUT YACHAYKA.
COLONEL MCNEILL OF THE NATIONAL ARMY.
NOT TO MENTION THE CHAIRMAN OF THE NATIONAL UNITY PARTY, DONOVAN DESMOND!
MISSION 38
THIS PRIVATE SCHOOL MIXER IS A TREASURE TROVE OF INTELLIGENCE!
SHOULDN'T WE BE SENDING MORE PEOPLE TO BACK UP AGENT TWILIGHT?
WHY NOT HEAD DOWN AND DO IT YOURSELF?
SET FOOT IN THAT BUILDING, AND THE SSS WILL BE ALL OVER YOU IN FIVE MINUTES. THEY'LL BE INTERROGATING YOU IN AN EXAMINATION ROOM 30 MINUTES AFTER THAT.
...
SENDING A BUNCH OF INCOMPETENTS TO THAT MIXER WOULD JUST BE THROWING CHUM TO THE SHARKS.
YOU NEED TO REMEMBER WE'RE IN ENEMY TERRITORY.
AND THAT SCHOOL...

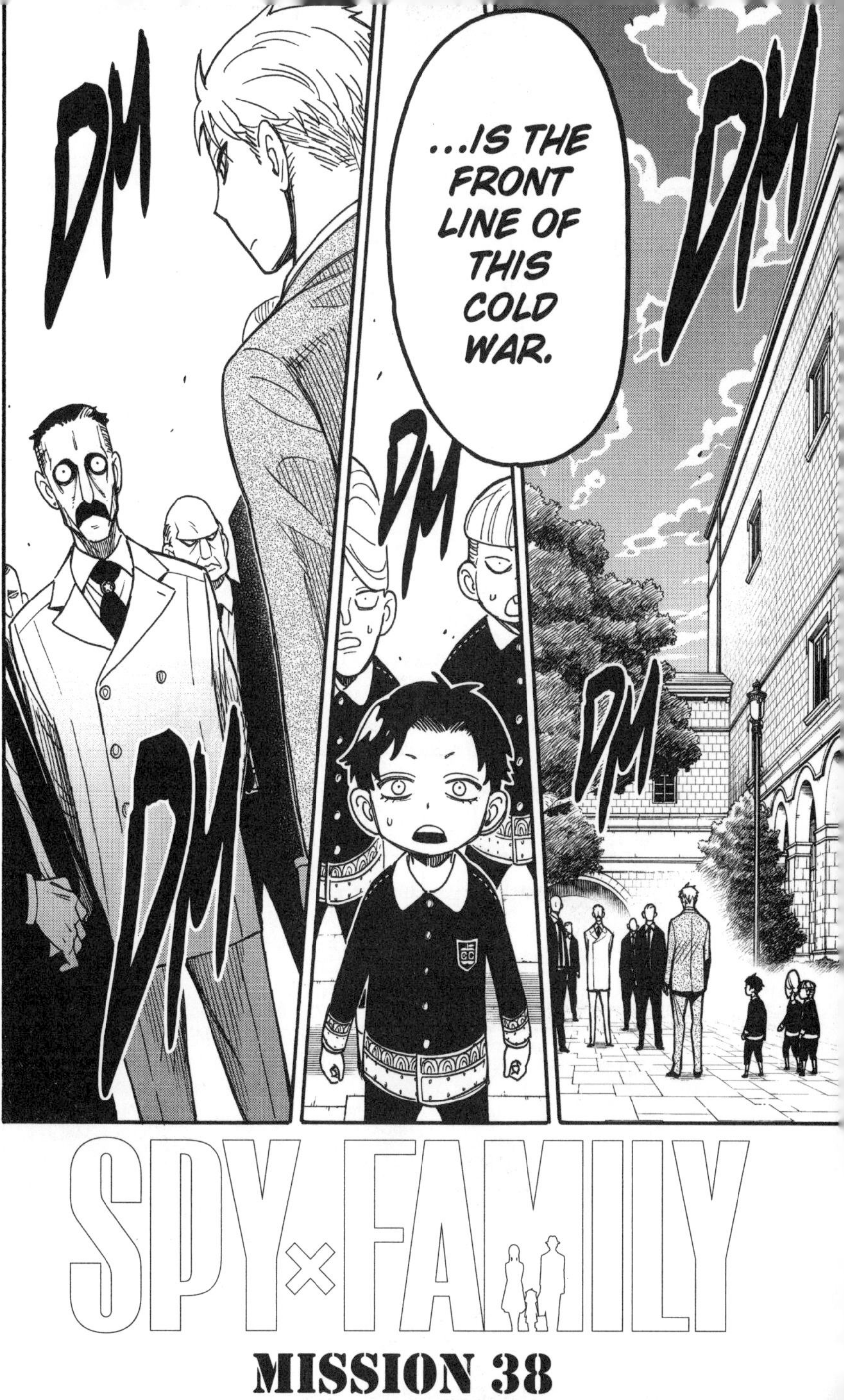
DM
DM
...IS THE FRONT LINE OF THIS COLD WAR.
DM
DM
DM

SPY×FAMILY

MISSION 38

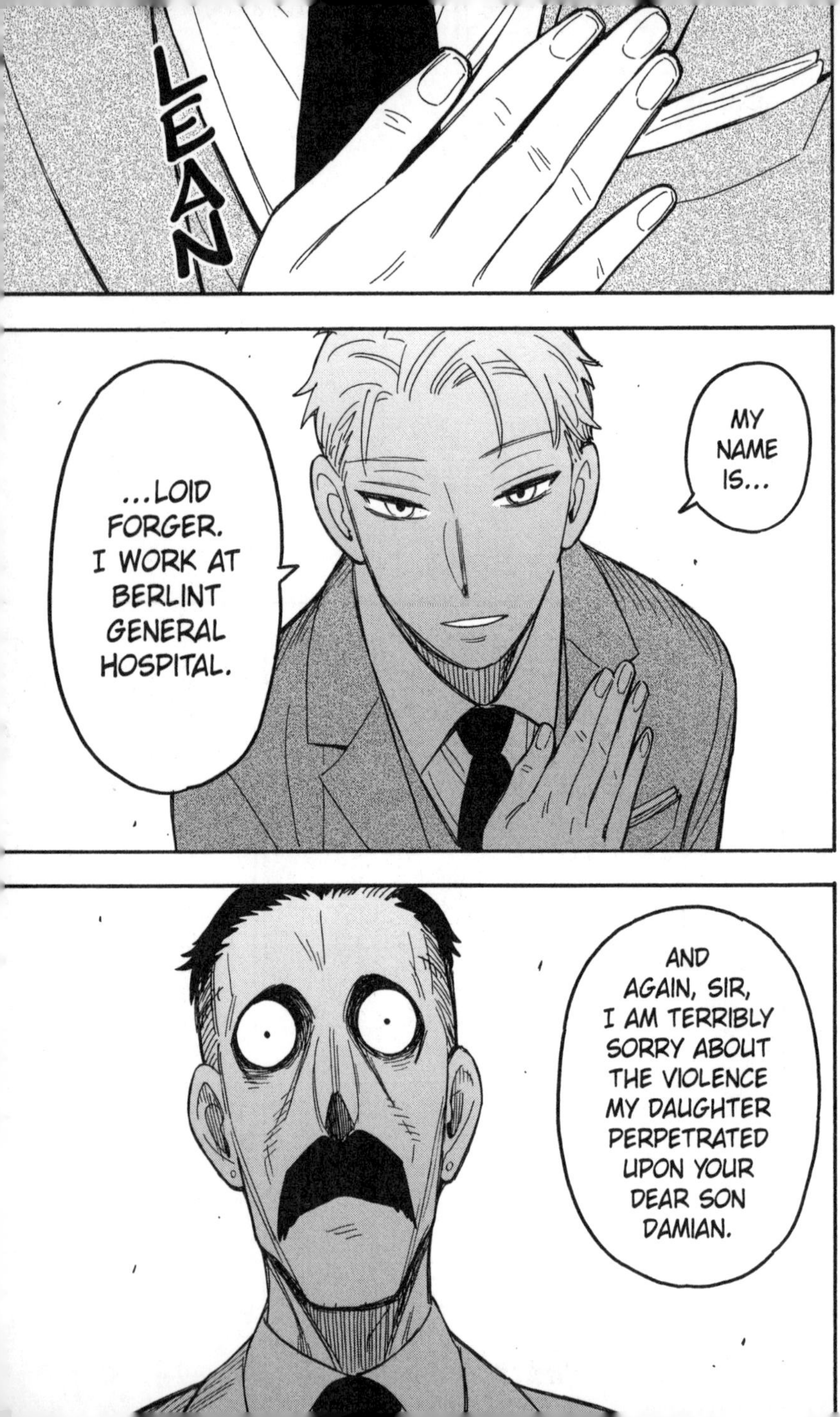
LEAN
MY NAME IS...
...LOID FORGER. I WORK AT BERLINT GENERAL HOSPITAL.
AND AGAIN, SIR, I AM TERRIBLY SORRY ABOUT THE VIOLENCE MY DAUGHTER PERPETRATED UPON YOUR DEAR SON DAMIAN.

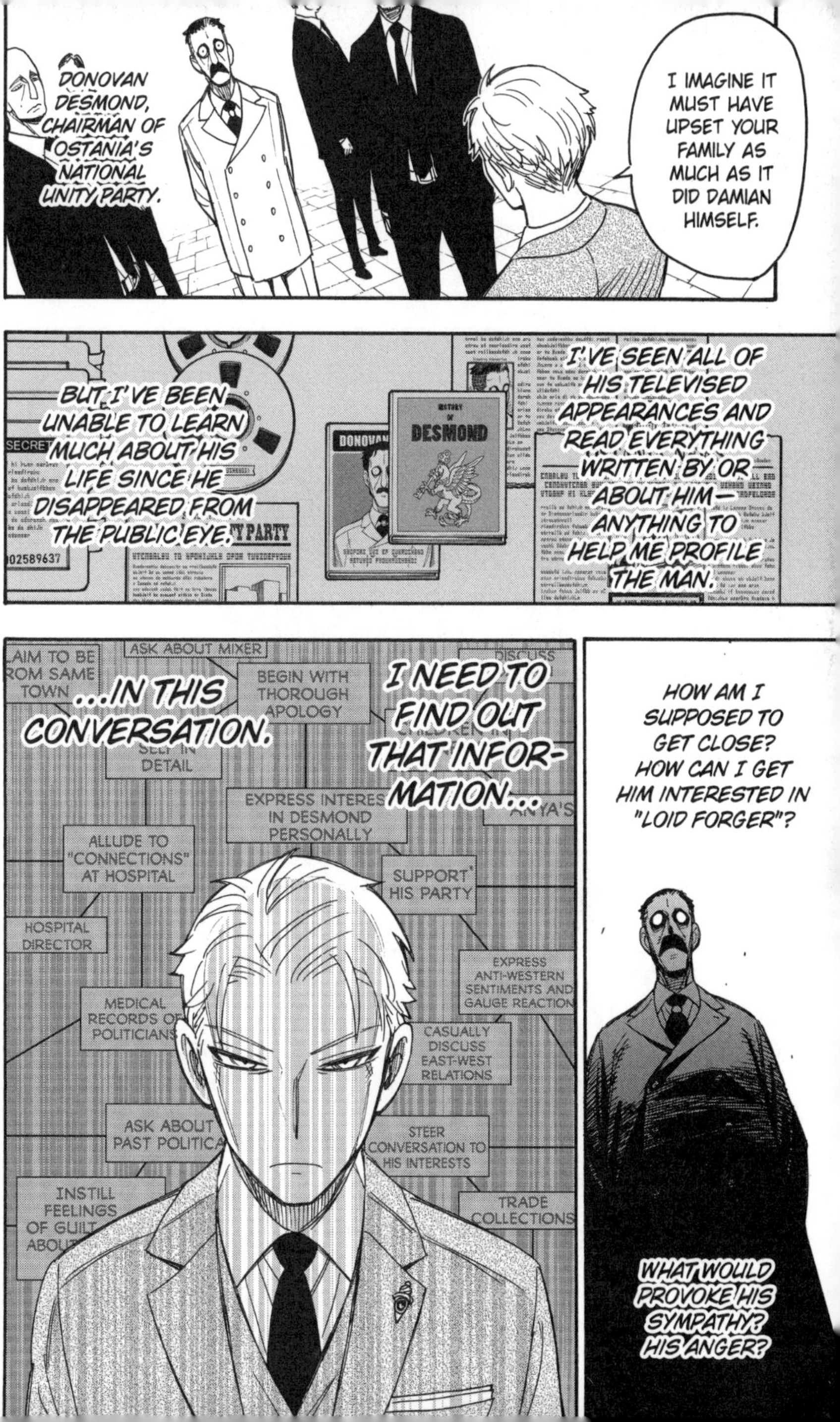

I IMAGINE IT MUST HAVE UPSET YOUR FAMILY AS MUCH AS IT DID DAMIAN HIMSELF.
DONOVAN DESMOND, CHAIRMAN OF OSTANIA'S NATIONAL UNITY PARTY.
I'VE SEEN ALL OF HIS TELEVISED APPEARANCES AND READ EVERYTHING WRITTEN BY OR ABOUT HIM—ANYTHING TO HELP ME PROFILE THE MAN.
DESMOND
DONOVAN
SECRET
BUT I'VE BEEN UNABLE TO LEARN MUCH ABOUT HIS LIFE SINCE HE DISAPPEARED FROM THE PUBLIC EYE.
HOW AM I SUPPOSED TO GET CLOSE? HOW CAN I GET HIM INTERESTED IN "LOID FORGER"?
WHAT WOULD PROVOKE HIS SYMPATHY? HIS ANGER?
I NEED TO FIND OUT THAT INFORMATION...
...IN THIS CONVERSATION.
ASK ABOUT MIXER
BEGIN WITH THOROUGH APOLOGY
ALLUDE TO "CONNECTIONS" AT HOSPITAL
SUPPORT HIS PARTY
HOSPITAL DIRECTOR
EXPRESS ANTI-WESTERN SENTIMENTS AND GAUGE REACTION
CASUALLY DISCUSS EAST-WEST RELATIONS
STEER CONVERSATION TO HIS INTERESTS
TRADE COLLECTIONS

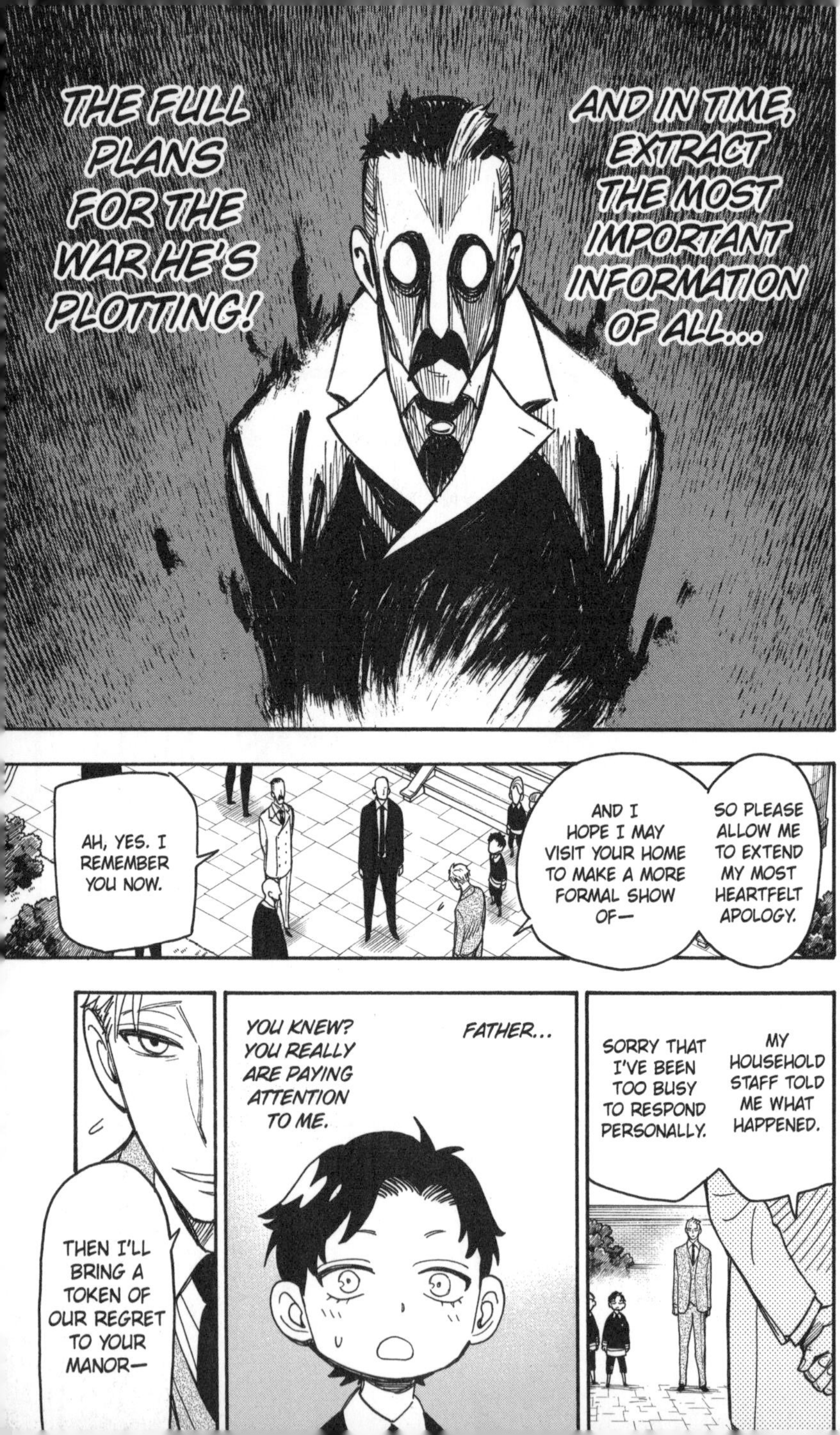
AND IN TIME, EXTRACT THE MOST IMPORTANT INFORMATION OF ALL...
THE FULL PLANS FOR THE WAR HE'S PLOTTING!
SO PLEASE ALLOW ME TO EXTEND MY MOST HEARTFELT APOLOGY.
AND I HOPE I MAY VISIT YOUR HOME TO MAKE A MORE FORMAL SHOW OF—
AH, YES. I REMEMBER YOU NOW.
MY HOUSEHOLD STAFF TOLD ME WHAT HAPPENED.
SORRY THAT I'VE BEEN TOO BUSY TO RESPOND PERSONALLY.
FATHER...
YOU KNEW? YOU REALLY ARE PAYING ATTENTION TO ME.
THEN I'LL BRING A TOKEN OF OUR REGRET TO YOUR MANOR—

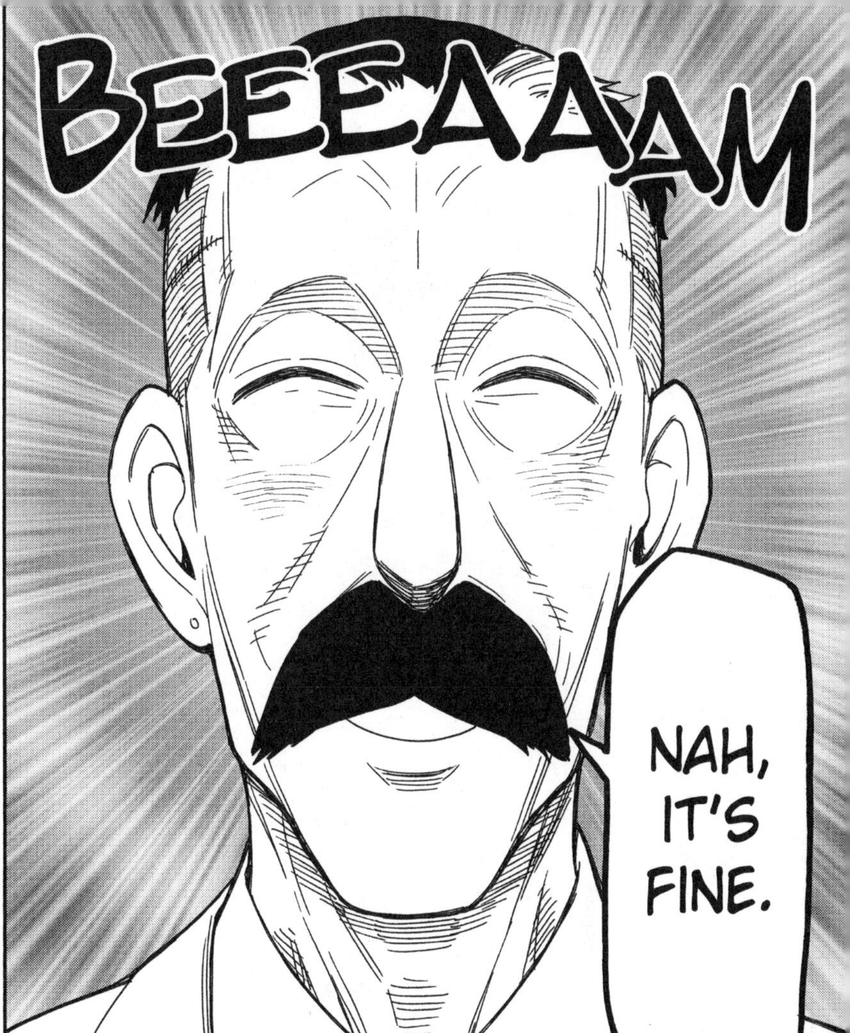
BEEEAAAM
NAH, IT'S FINE.
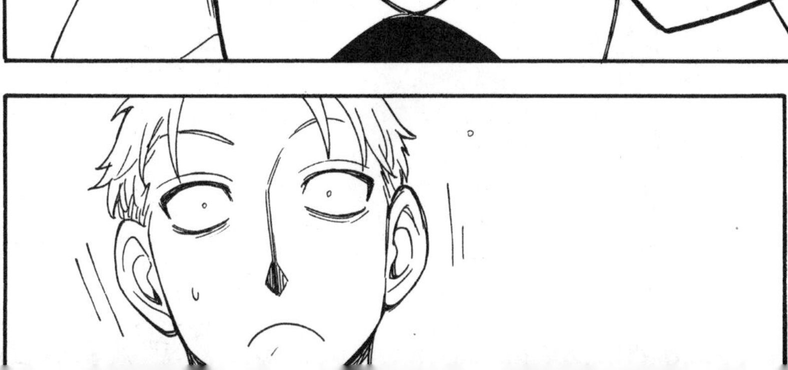

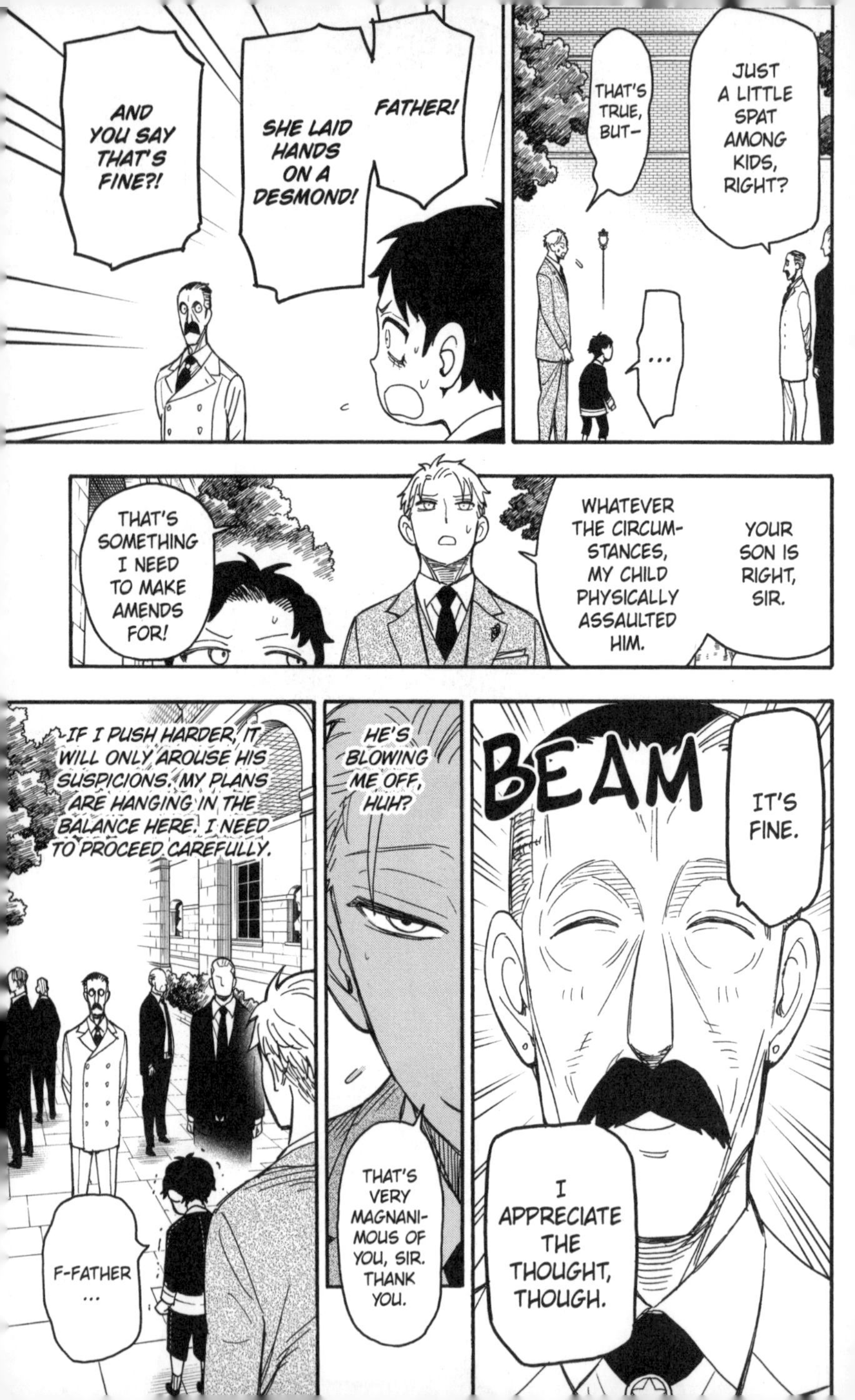
JUST A LITTLE SPAT AMONG KIDS, RIGHT?
THAT'S TRUE, BUT—
...
FATHER!
SHE LAID HANDS ON A DESMOND!
AND YOU SAY THAT'S FINE?!
YOUR SON IS RIGHT, SIR.
WHATEVER THE CIRCUM-STANCES, MY CHILD PHYSICALLY ASSAULTED HIM.
THAT'S SOMETHING I NEED TO MAKE AMENDS FOR!
BEAM
IT'S FINE.
I APPRECIATE THE THOUGHT, THOUGH.
HE'S BLOWING ME OFF, HUH?
THAT'S VERY MAGNANI-MOUS OF YOU, SIR. THANK YOU.
IF I PUSH HARDER, IT WILL ONLY AROUSE HIS SUSPICIONS. MY PLANS ARE HANGING IN THE BALANCE HERE. I NEED TO PROCEED CAREFULLY.
F-FATHER ...

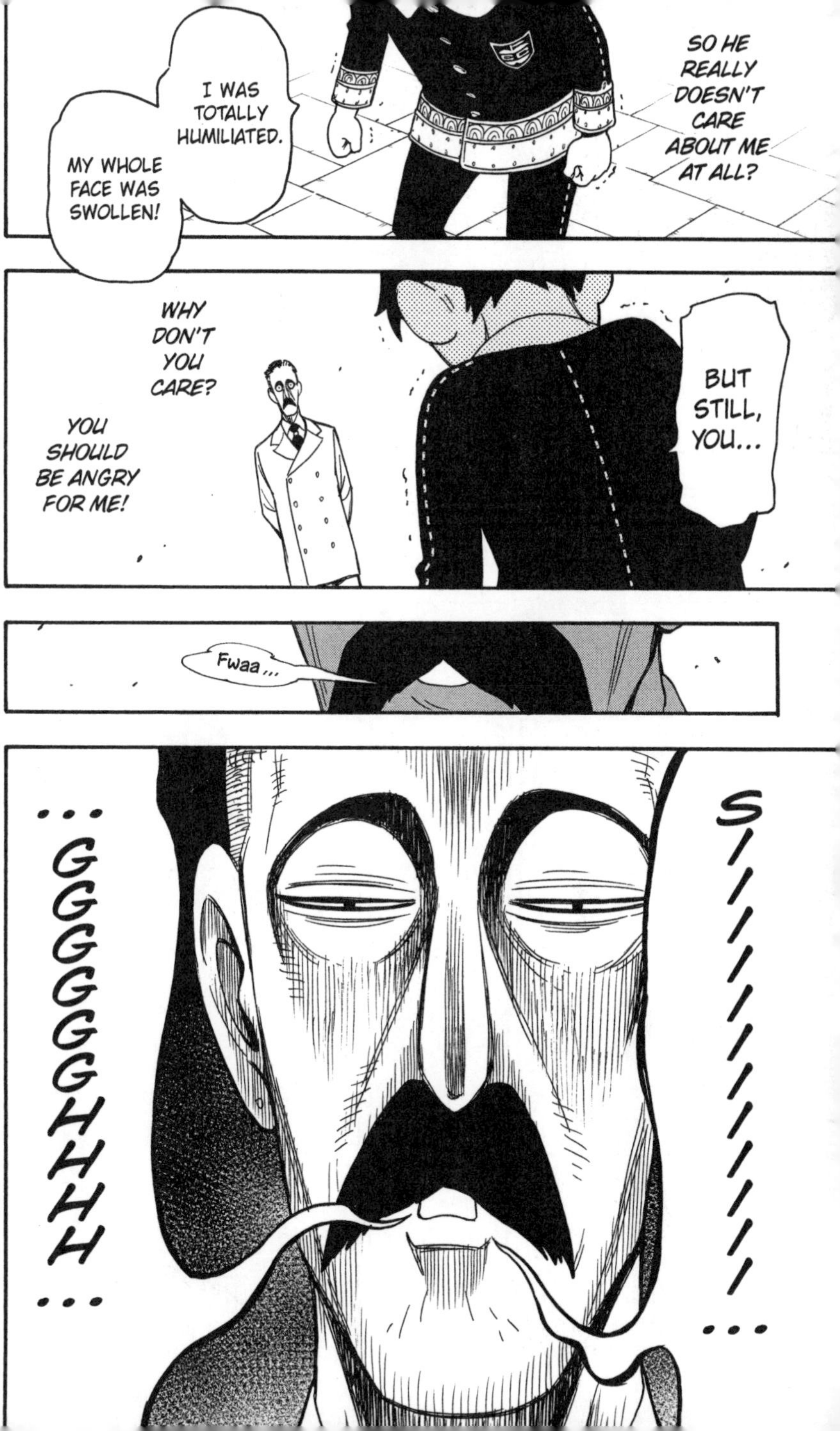
SO HE REALLY DOESN'T CARE ABOUT ME AT ALL?
I WAS TOTALLY HUMILIATED.
MY WHOLE FACE WAS SWOLLEN!
BUT STILL, YOU...
WHY DON'T YOU CARE?
YOU SHOULD BE ANGRY FOR ME!
Fwaa...
SIIIIIIIIIIIIII...
...GGGGGGHHHHH...

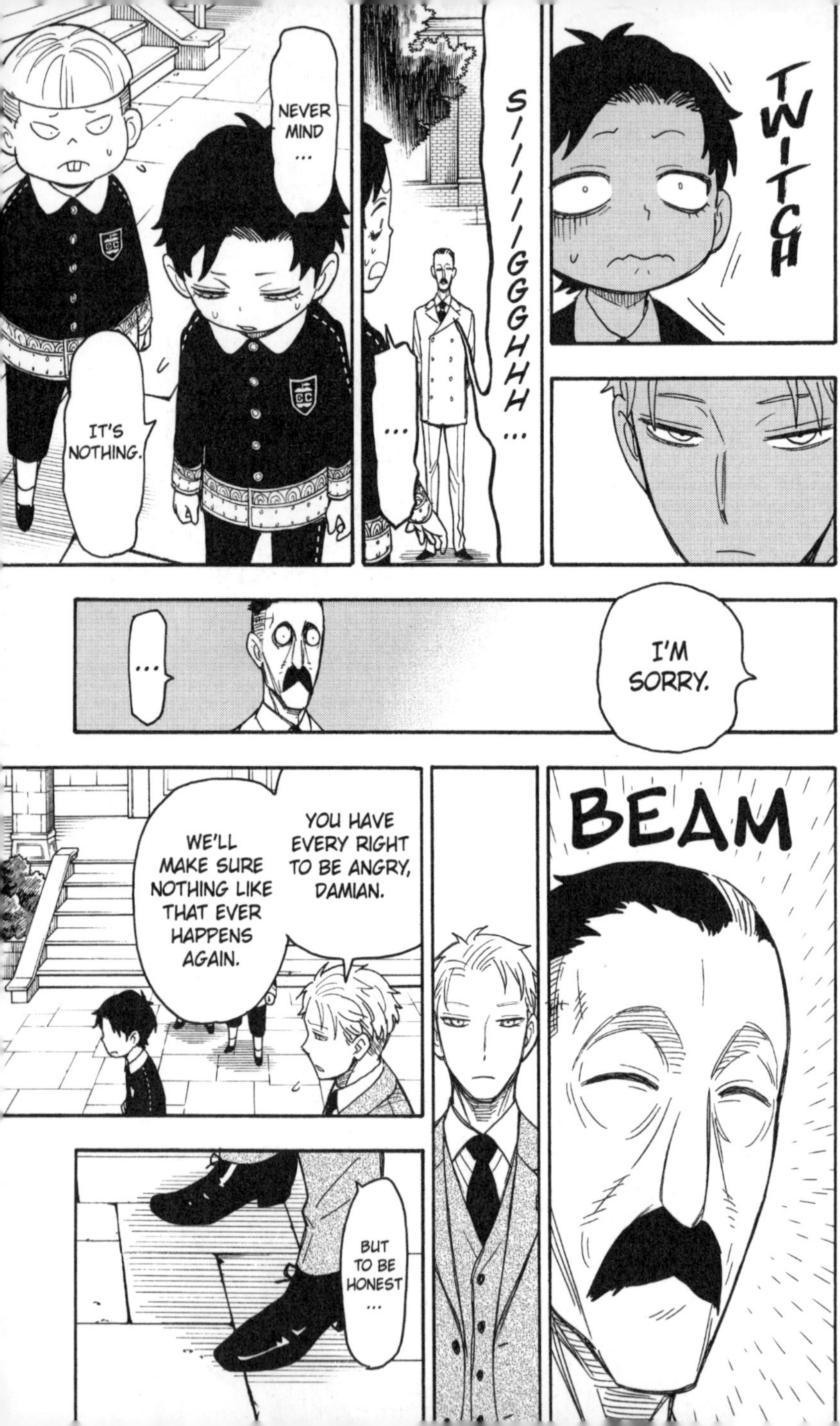
TWITCH
S//////GGGHHH...
...
NEVER MIND ...
IT'S NOTHING.
I'M SORRY.
...
BEAM
YOU HAVE EVERY RIGHT TO BE ANGRY, DAMIAN.
WE'LL MAKE SURE NOTHING LIKE THAT EVER HAPPENS AGAIN.
BUT TO BE HONEST ...

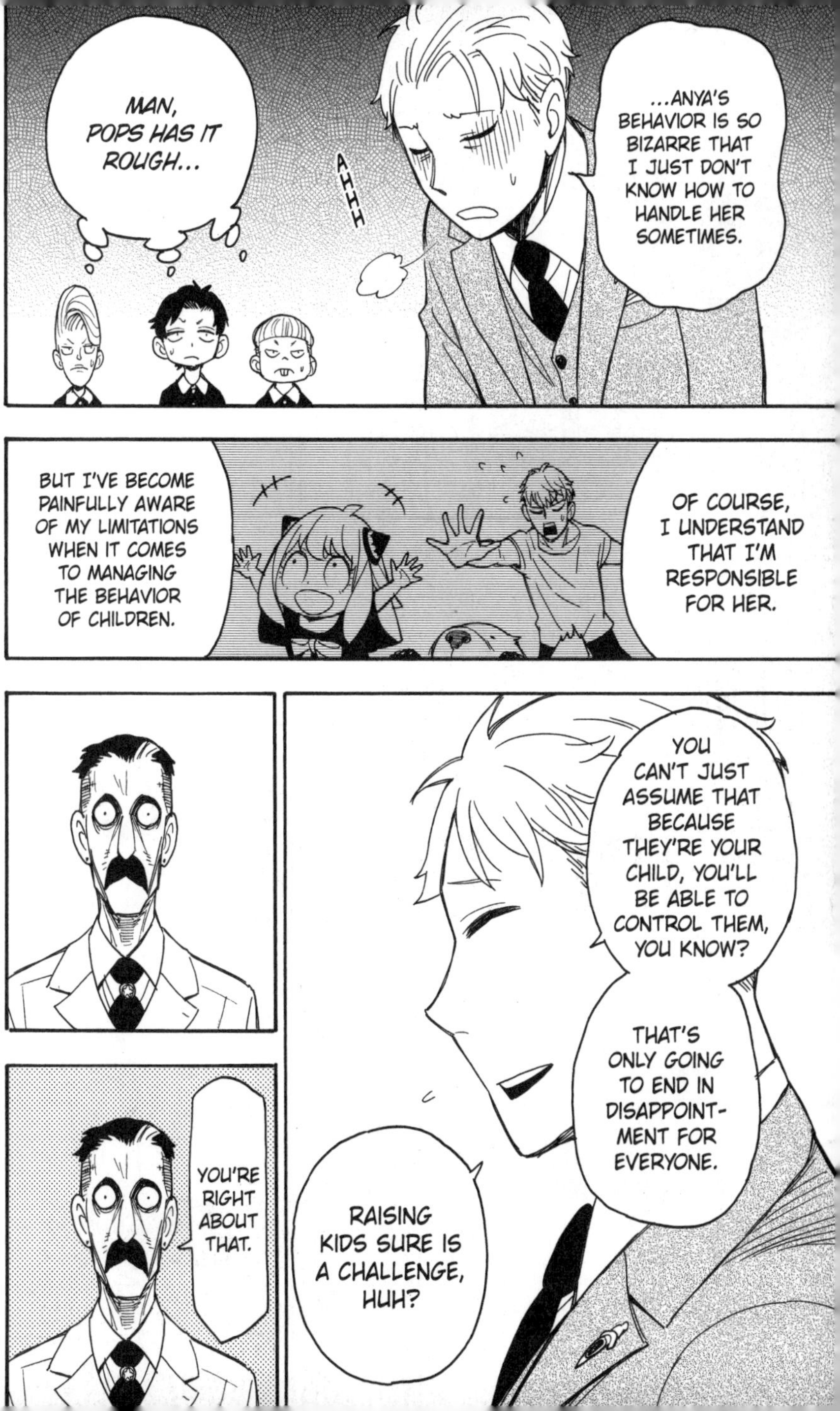
...ANYA'S BEHAVIOR IS SO BIZARRE THAT I JUST DON'T KNOW HOW TO HANDLE HER SOMETIMES.
AHHHH
MAN, POPS HAS IT ROUGH...
OF COURSE, I UNDERSTAND THAT I'M RESPONSIBLE FOR HER.
BUT I'VE BECOME PAINFULLY AWARE OF MY LIMITATIONS WHEN IT COMES TO MANAGING THE BEHAVIOR OF CHILDREN.
YOU CAN'T JUST ASSUME THAT BECAUSE THEY'RE YOUR CHILD, YOU'LL BE ABLE TO CONTROL THEM, YOU KNOW?
THAT'S ONLY GOING TO END IN DISAPPOINTMENT FOR EVERYONE.
RAISING KIDS SURE IS A CHALLENGE, HUH?
YOU'RE RIGHT ABOUT THAT.

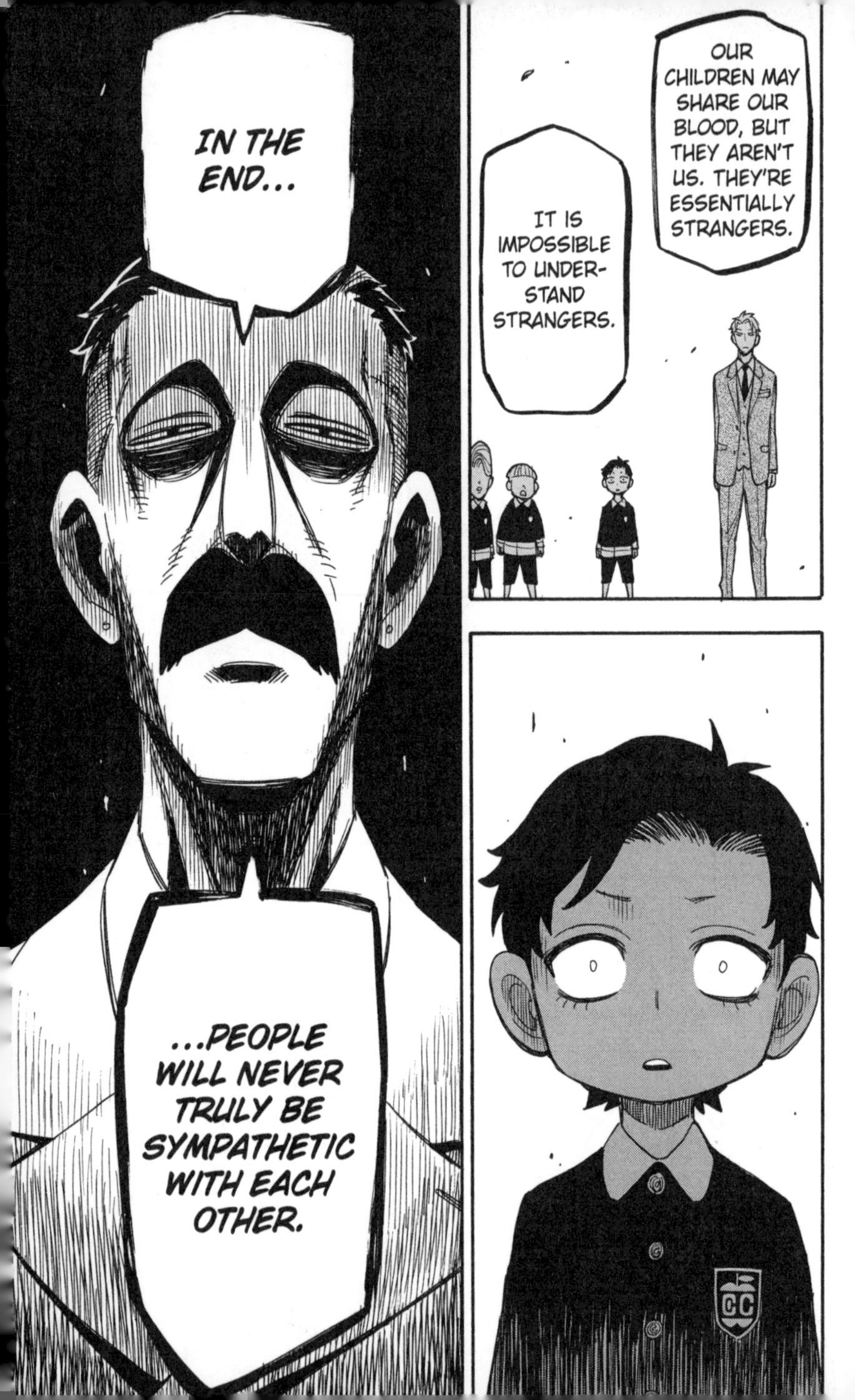
OUR CHILDREN MAY SHARE OUR BLOOD, BUT THEY AREN'T US. THEY'RE ESSENTIALLY STRANGERS.
IT IS IMPOSSIBLE TO UNDER-STAND STRANGERS.
IN THE END...
...PEOPLE WILL NEVER TRULY BE SYMPATHETIC WITH EACH OTHER.

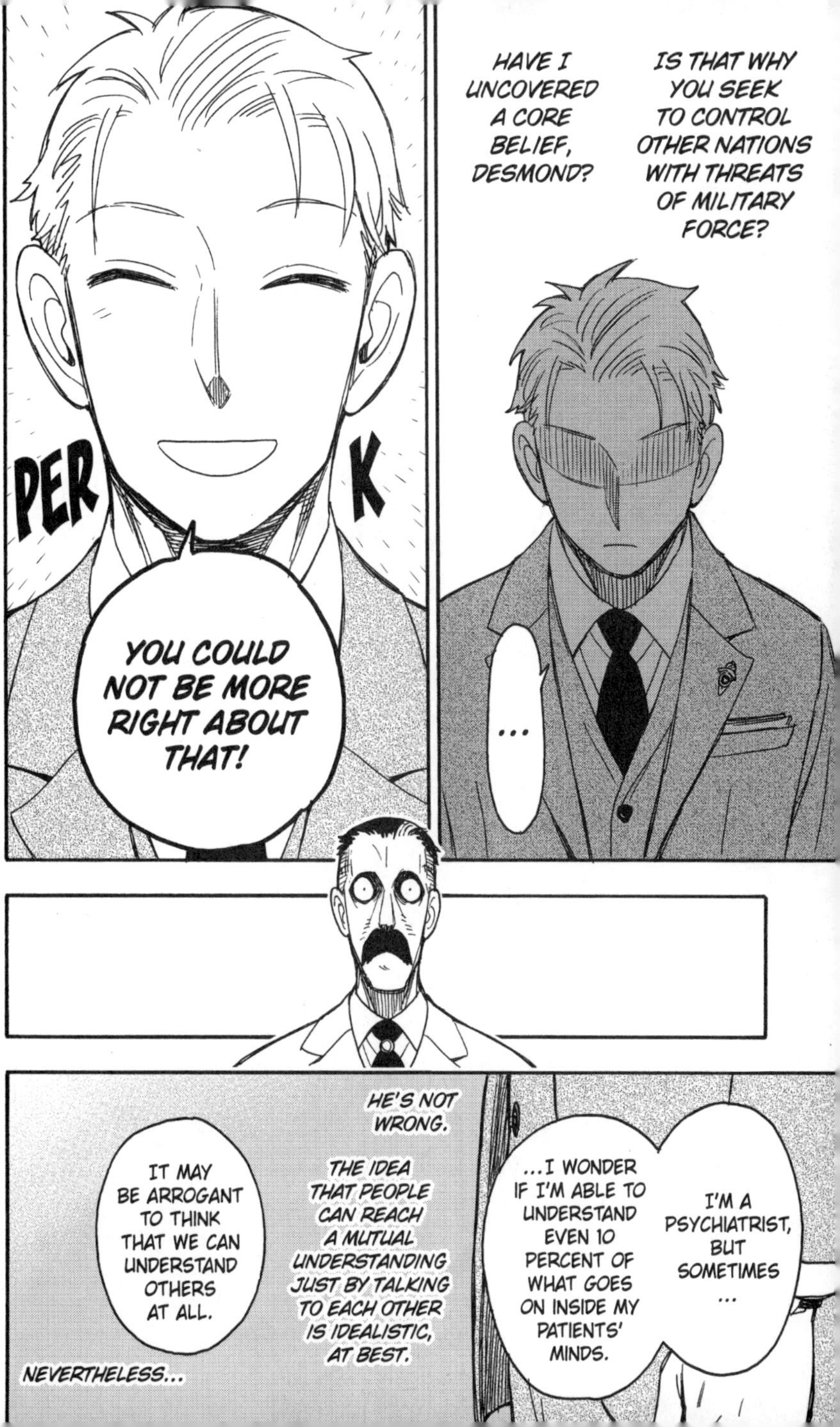
IS THAT WHY YOU SEEK TO CONTROL OTHER NATIONS WITH THREATS OF MILITARY FORCE?
HAVE I UNCOVERED A CORE BELIEF, DESMOND?
...
PERK
YOU COULD NOT BE MORE RIGHT ABOUT THAT!
I'M A PSYCHIATRIST, BUT SOMETIMES...
...I WONDER IF I'M ABLE TO UNDERSTAND EVEN 10 PERCENT OF WHAT GOES ON INSIDE MY PATIENTS' MINDS.
HE'S NOT WRONG.
THE IDEA THAT PEOPLE CAN REACH A MUTUAL UNDERSTANDING JUST BY TALKING TO EACH OTHER IS IDEALISTIC, AT BEST.
IT MAY BE ARROGANT TO THINK THAT WE CAN UNDERSTAND OTHERS AT ALL.
NEVERTHELESS...

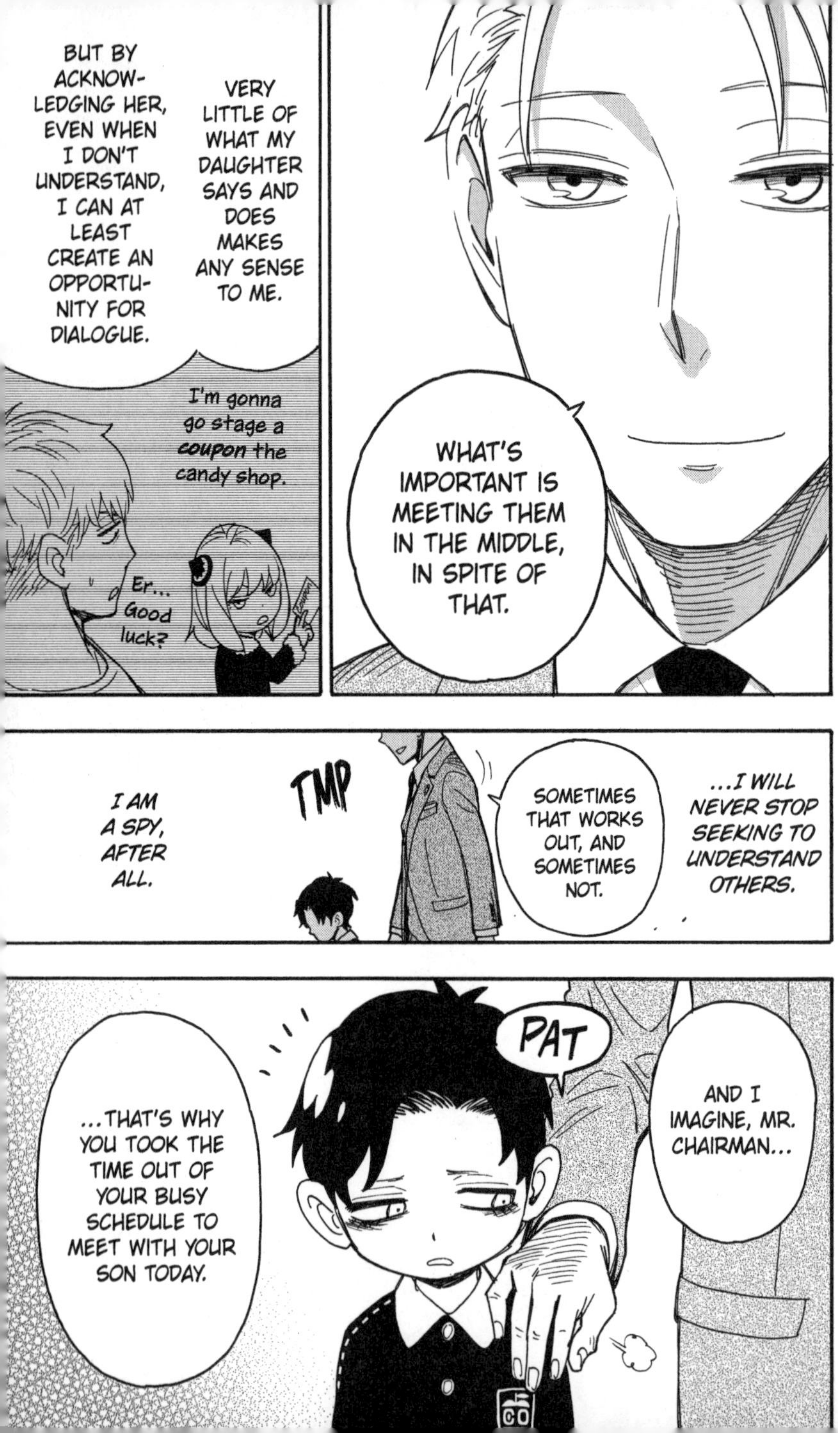
WHAT'S IMPORTANT IS MEETING THEM IN THE MIDDLE, IN SPITE OF THAT.
VERY LITTLE OF WHAT MY DAUGHTER SAYS AND DOES MAKES ANY SENSE TO ME.
BUT BY ACKNOWLEDGING HER, EVEN WHEN I DON'T UNDERSTAND, I CAN AT LEAST CREATE AN OPPORTUNITY FOR DIALOGUE.
I'm gonna go stage a **coupon** the candy shop.
Er... Good luck?
...I WILL NEVER STOP SEEKING TO UNDERSTAND OTHERS.
SOMETIMES THAT WORKS OUT, AND SOMETIMES NOT.
TMP
I AM A SPY, AFTER ALL.
AND I IMAGINE, MR. CHAIRMAN...
PAT
...THAT'S WHY YOU TOOK THE TIME OUT OF YOUR BUSY SCHEDULE TO MEET WITH YOUR SON TODAY.

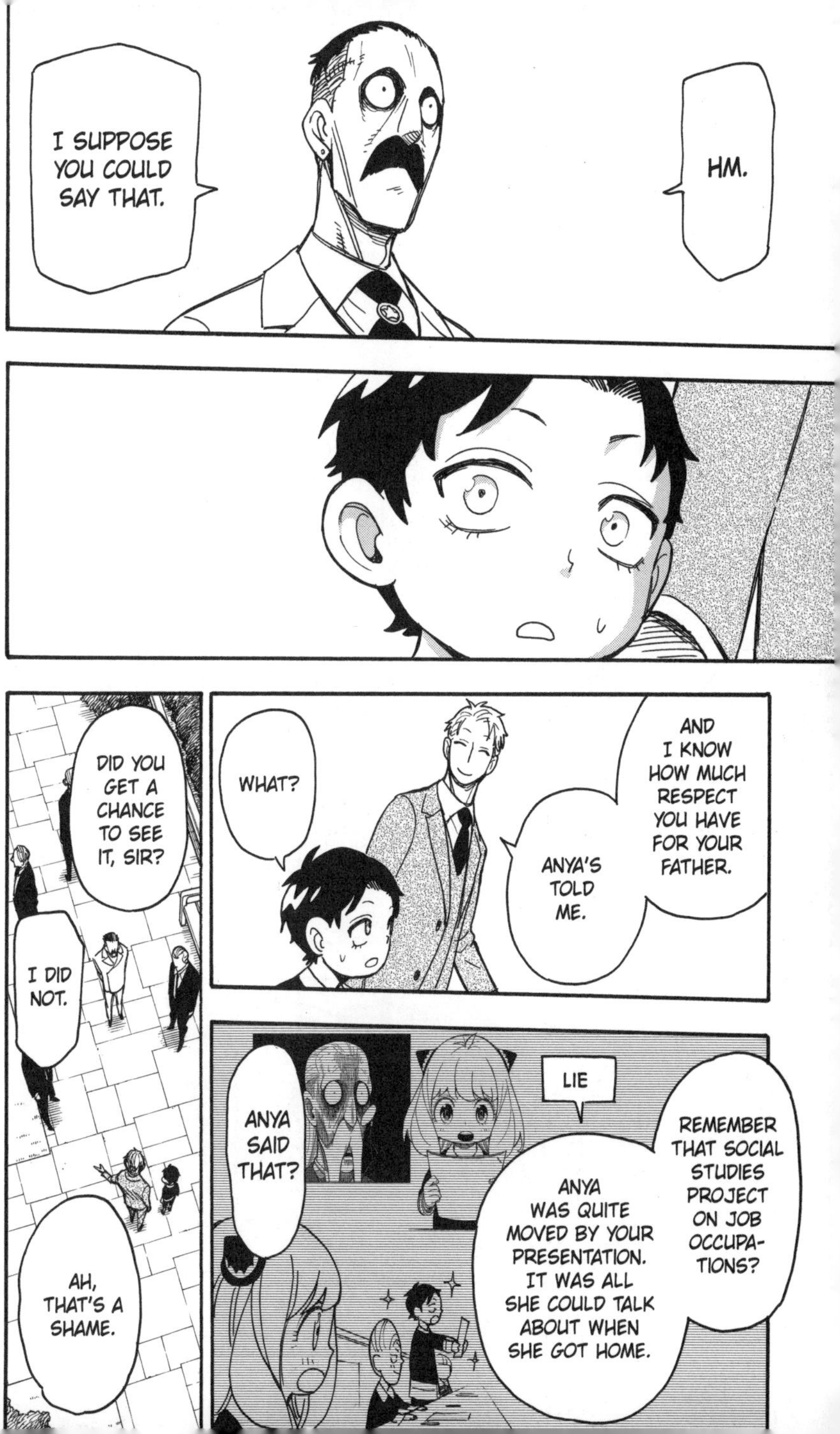
HM.
I SUPPOSE YOU COULD SAY THAT.
AND I KNOW HOW MUCH RESPECT YOU HAVE FOR YOUR FATHER.
ANYA'S TOLD ME.
WHAT?
REMEMBER THAT SOCIAL STUDIES PROJECT ON JOB OCCUPA-TIONS?
LIE
ANYA WAS QUITE MOVED BY YOUR PRESENTATION. IT WAS ALL SHE COULD TALK ABOUT WHEN SHE GOT HOME.
ANYA SAID THAT?
DID YOU GET A CHANCE TO SEE IT, SIR?
I DID NOT.
AH, THAT'S A SHAME.

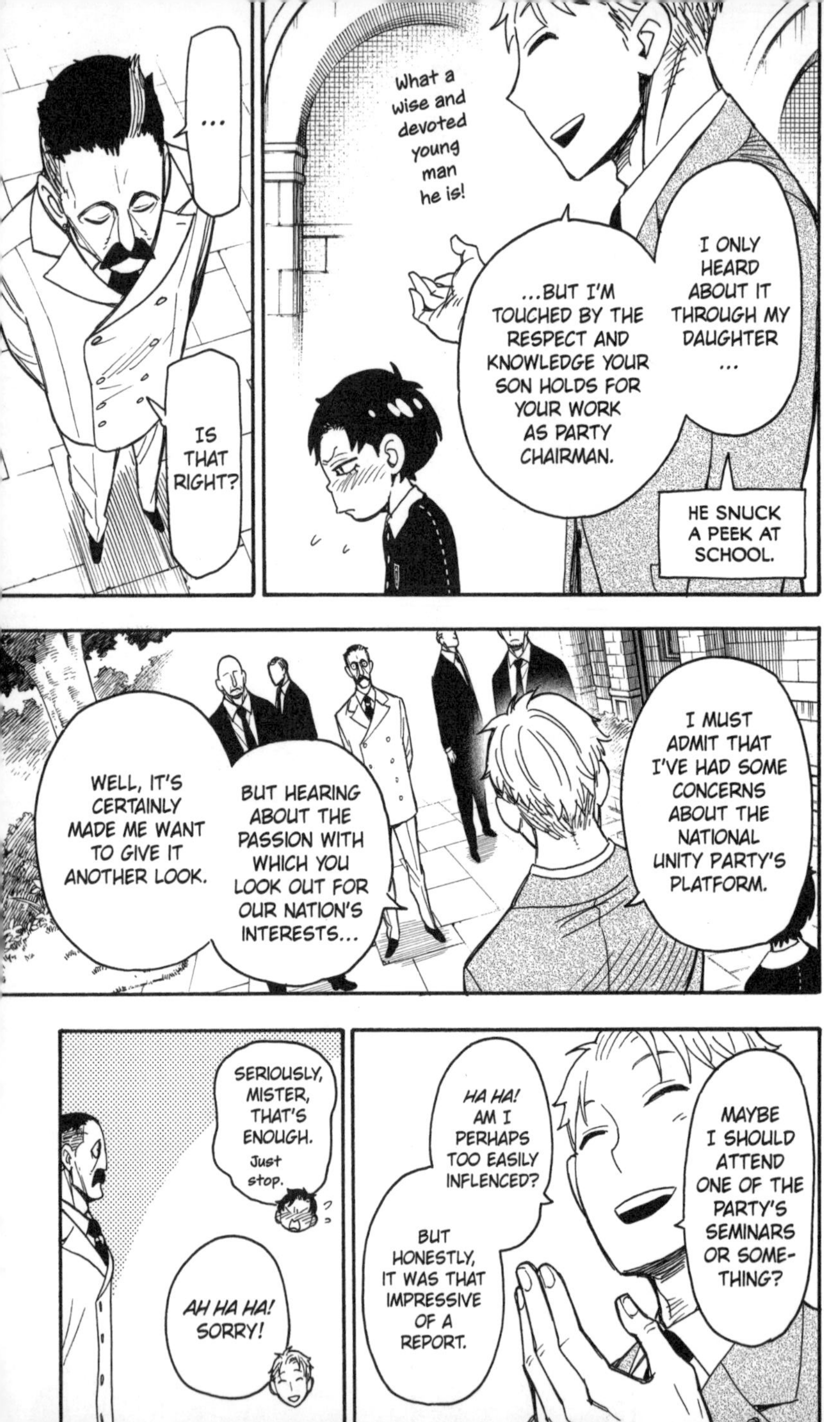
I ONLY HEARD ABOUT IT THROUGH MY DAUGHTER...
...BUT I'M TOUCHED BY THE RESPECT AND KNOWLEDGE YOUR SON HOLDS FOR YOUR WORK AS PARTY CHAIRMAN.
What a wise and devoted young man he is!
HE SNUCK A PEEK AT SCHOOL.
...
IS THAT RIGHT?
I MUST ADMIT THAT I'VE HAD SOME CONCERNS ABOUT THE NATIONAL UNITY PARTY'S PLATFORM.
BUT HEARING ABOUT THE PASSION WITH WHICH YOU LOOK OUT FOR OUR NATION'S INTERESTS...
WELL, IT'S CERTAINLY MADE ME WANT TO GIVE IT ANOTHER LOOK.
MAYBE I SHOULD ATTEND ONE OF THE PARTY'S SEMINARS OR SOME-THING?
HA HA! AM I PERHAPS TOO EASILY INFLENCED?
BUT HONESTLY, IT WAS THAT IMPRESSIVE OF A REPORT.
SERIOUSLY, MISTER, THAT'S ENOUGH.
Just stop.
AH HA HA! SORRY!

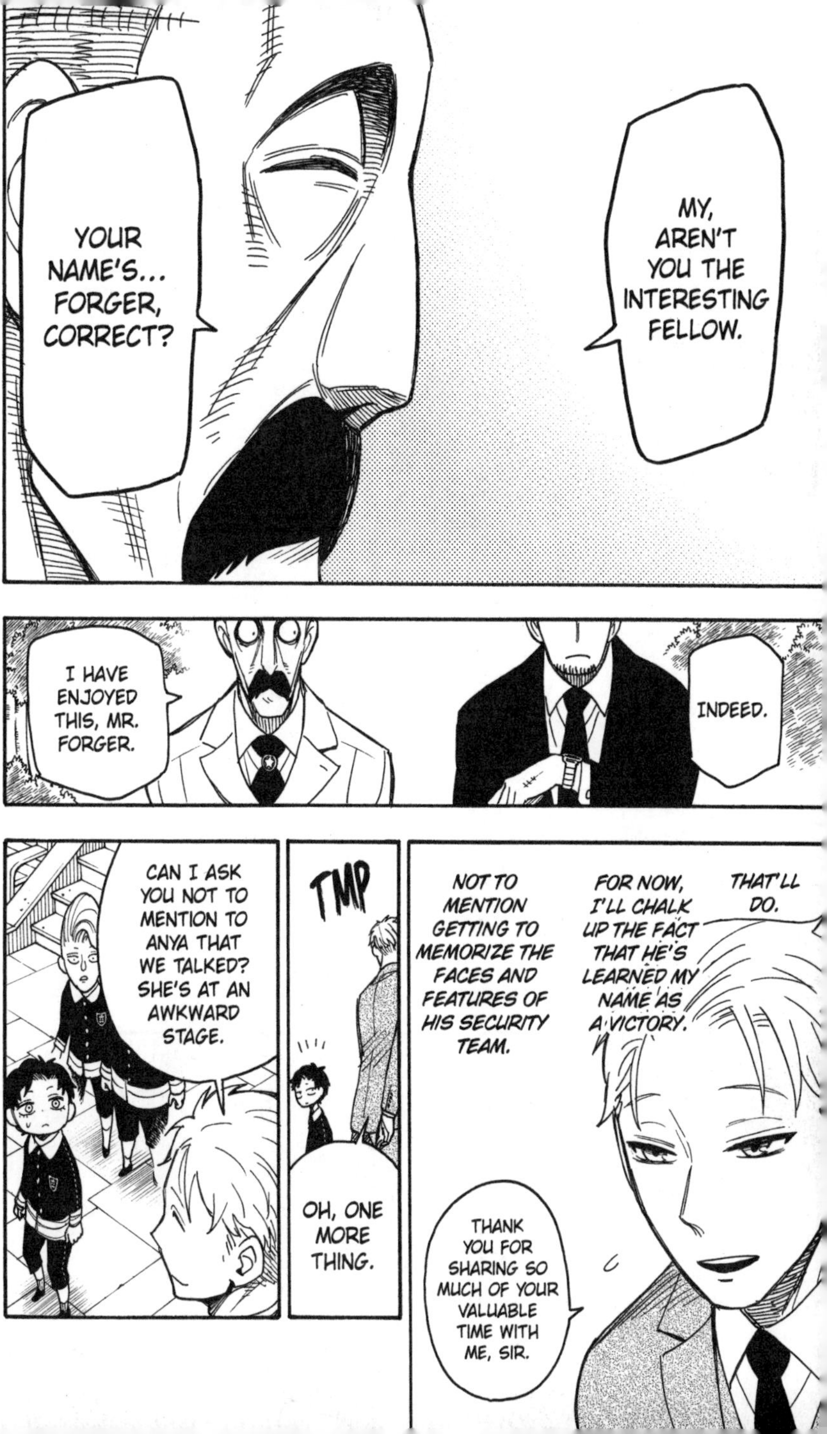
MY, AREN'T YOU THE INTERESTING FELLOW.
YOUR NAME'S... FORGER, CORRECT?
INDEED.
I HAVE ENJOYED THIS, MR. FORGER.
THAT'LL DO.
FOR NOW, I'LL CHALK UP THE FACT THAT HE'S LEARNED MY NAME AS A VICTORY.
NOT TO MENTION GETTING TO MEMORIZE THE FACES AND FEATURES OF HIS SECURITY TEAM.
THANK YOU FOR SHARING SO MUCH OF YOUR VALUABLE TIME WITH ME, SIR.
TMP
OH, ONE MORE THING.
CAN I ASK YOU NOT TO MENTION TO ANYA THAT WE TALKED? SHE'S AT AN AWKWARD STAGE.

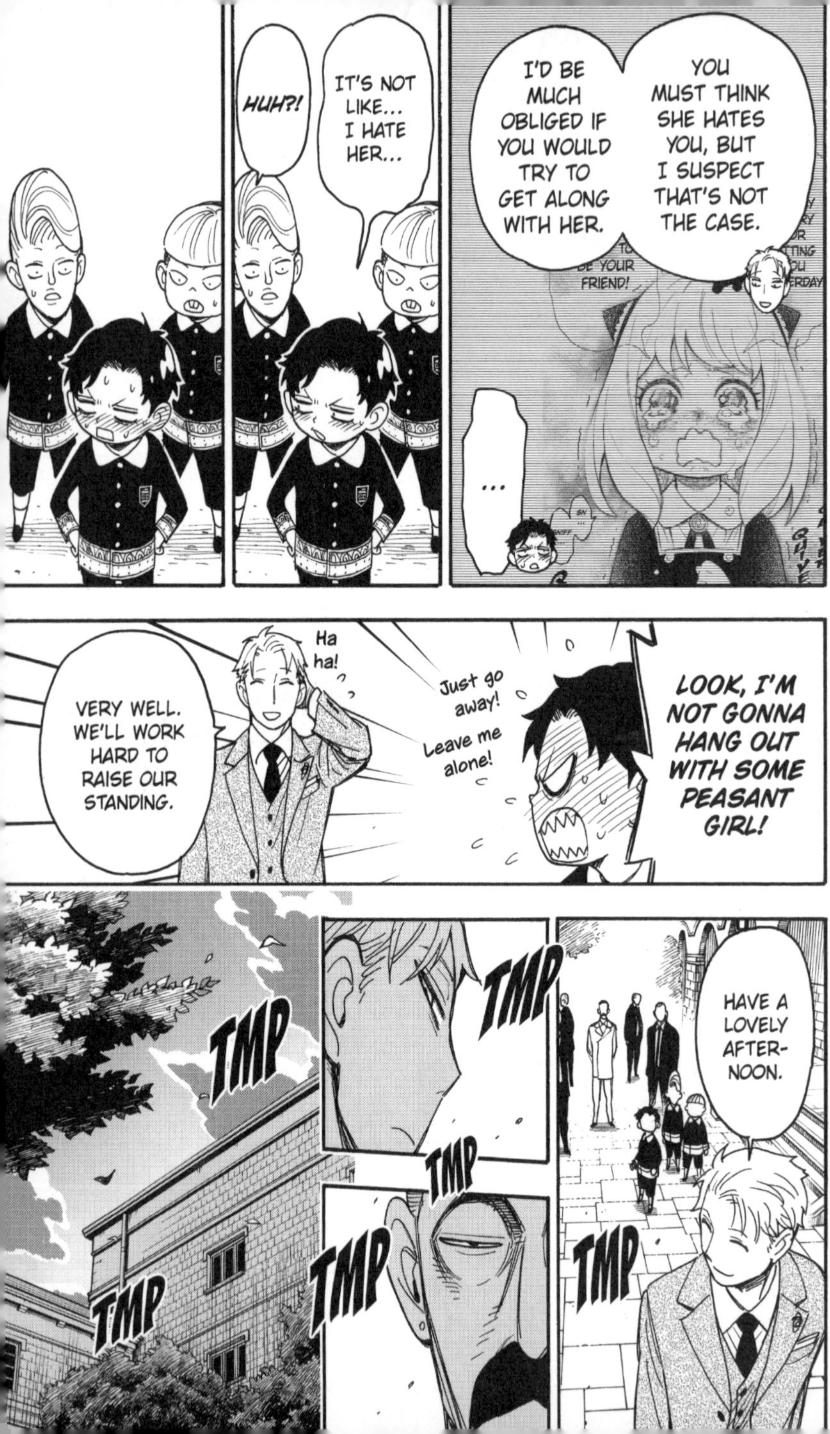
YOU MUST THINK SHE HATES YOU, BUT I SUSPECT THAT'S NOT THE CASE.
I'D BE MUCH OBLIGED IF YOU WOULD TRY TO GET ALONG WITH HER.
...
IT'S NOT LIKE... I HATE HER...
HUH?!
LOOK, I'M NOT GONNA HANG OUT WITH SOME PEASANT GIRL!
Just go away! Leave me alone!
Ha ha!
VERY WELL. WE'LL WORK HARD TO RAISE OUR STANDING.
HAVE A LOVELY AFTER-NOON.
TMP
TMP
TMP
TMP
TMP
TMP

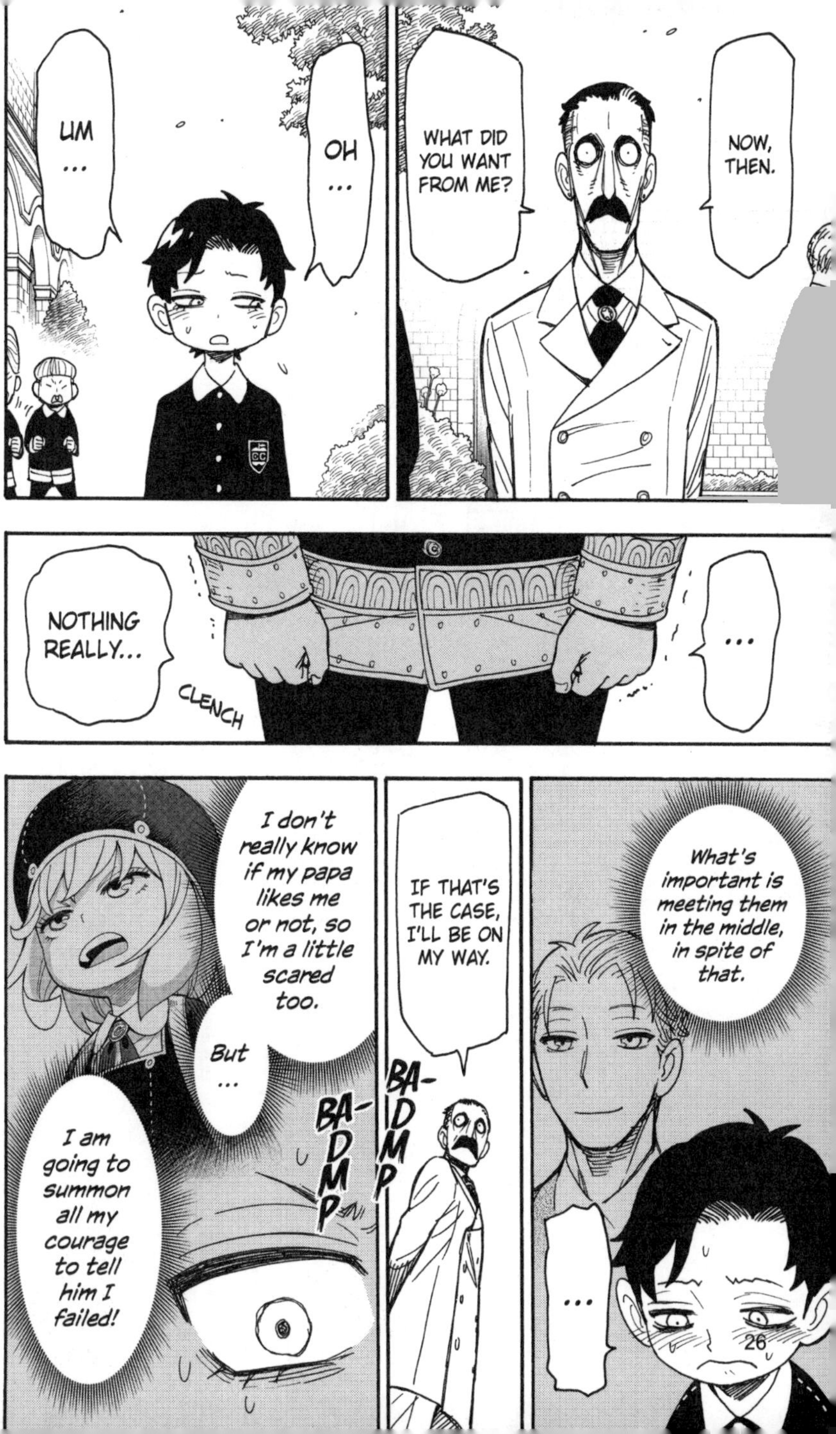
NOW, THEN.
WHAT DID YOU WANT FROM ME?
OH ...
UM ...
...
NOTHING REALLY...
CLENCH
What's important is meeting them in the middle, in spite of that.
...
IF THAT'S THE CASE, I'LL BE ON MY WAY.
BA-DMP
I don't really know if my papa likes me or not, so I'm a little scared too.
But ...
I am going to summon all my courage to tell him I failed!
BA-DMP

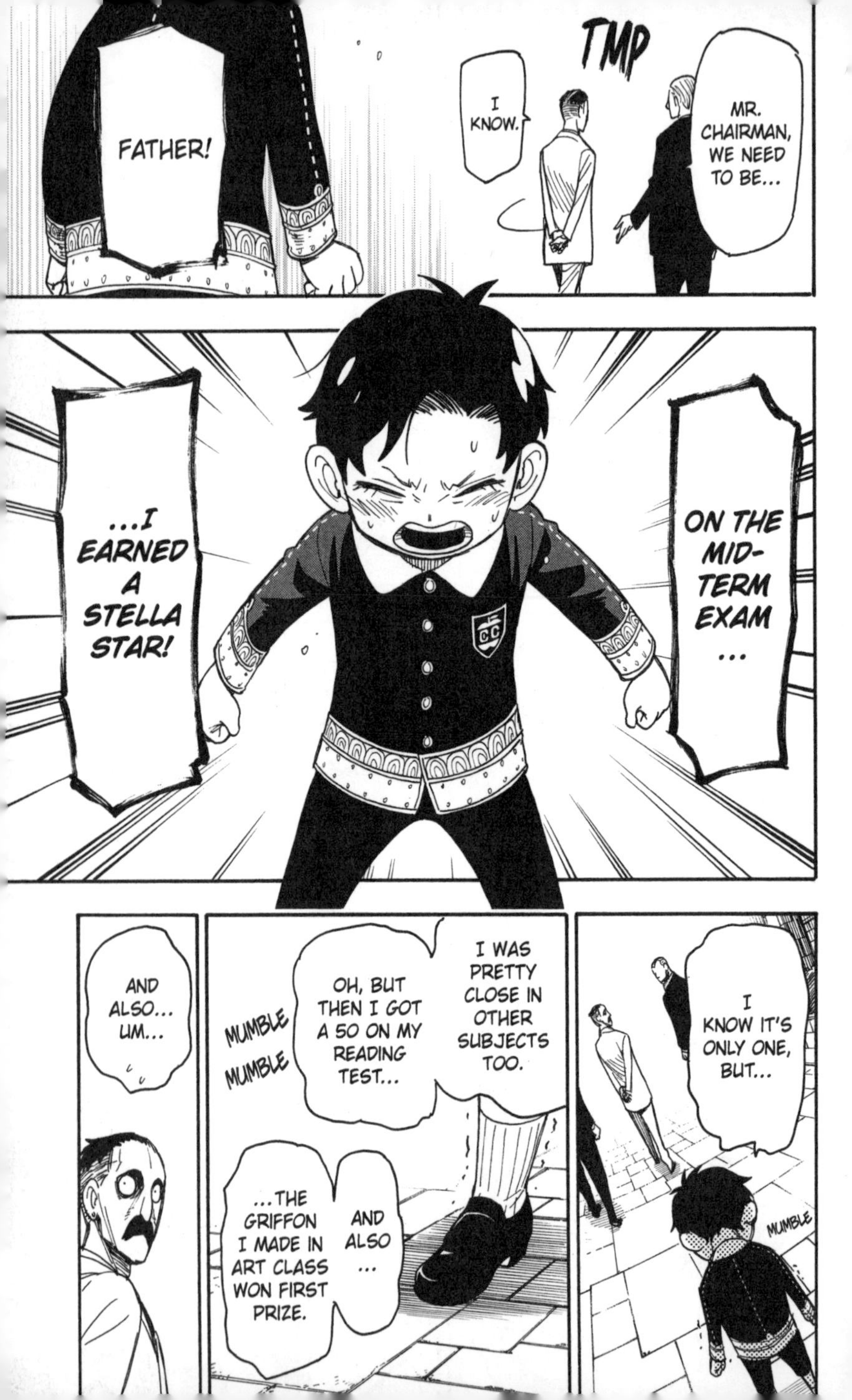
TMP
MR. CHAIRMAN, WE NEED TO BE...
I KNOW.
FATHER!
ON THE MID-TERM EXAM...
...I EARNED A STELLA STAR!
I KNOW IT'S ONLY ONE, BUT...
MUMBLE
I WAS PRETTY CLOSE IN OTHER SUBJECTS TOO.
OH, BUT THEN I GOT A 50 ON MY READING TEST...
MUMBLE MUMBLE
AND ALSO...
...THE GRIFFON I MADE IN ART CLASS WON FIRST PRIZE.
AND ALSO... UM...

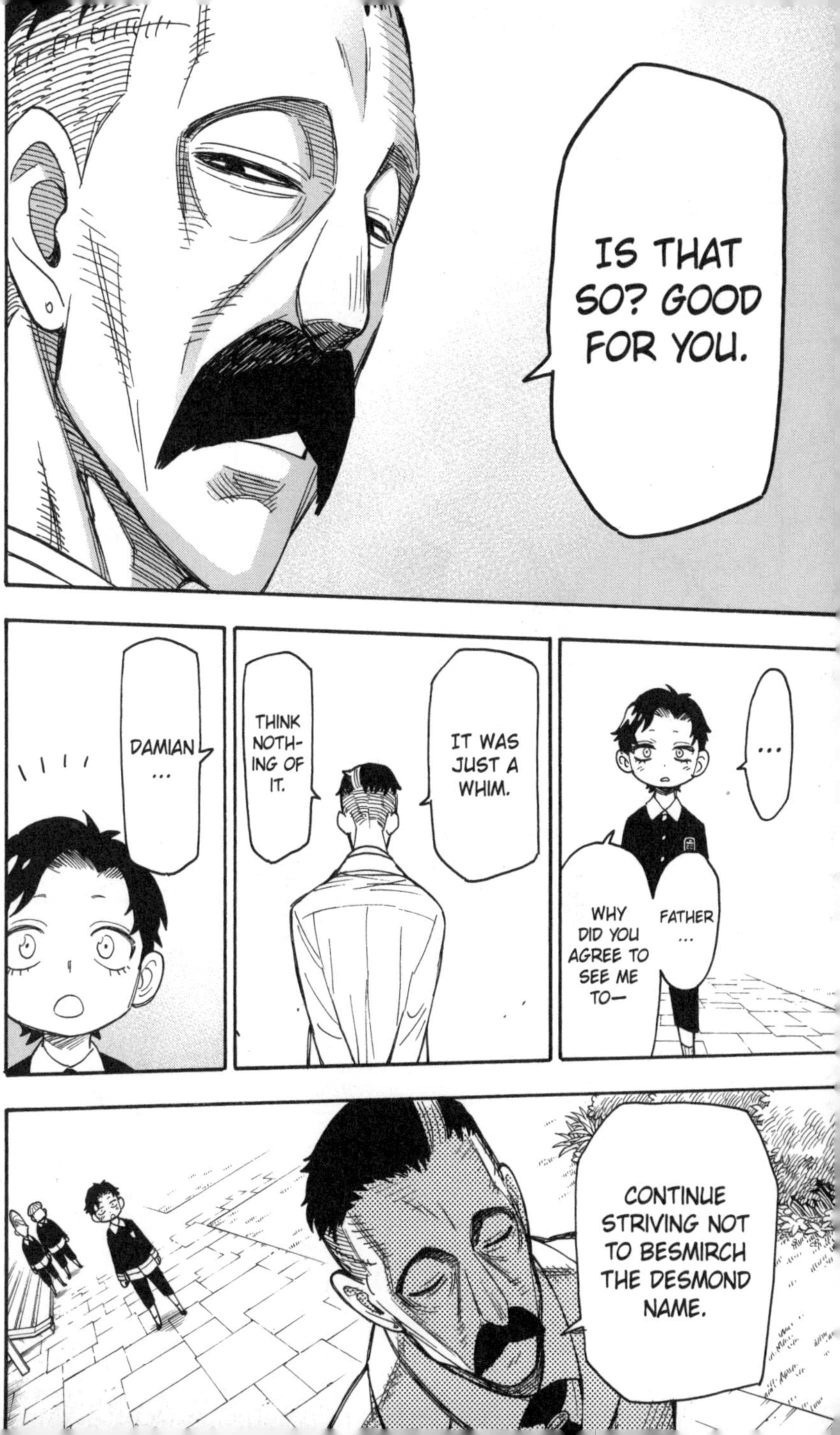
IS THAT SO? GOOD FOR YOU.
...
FATHER...
WHY DID YOU AGREE TO SEE ME TO—
IT WAS JUST A WHIM.
THINK NOTH-ING OF IT.
DAMIAN...
CONTINUE STRIVING NOT TO BESMIRCH THE DESMOND NAME.

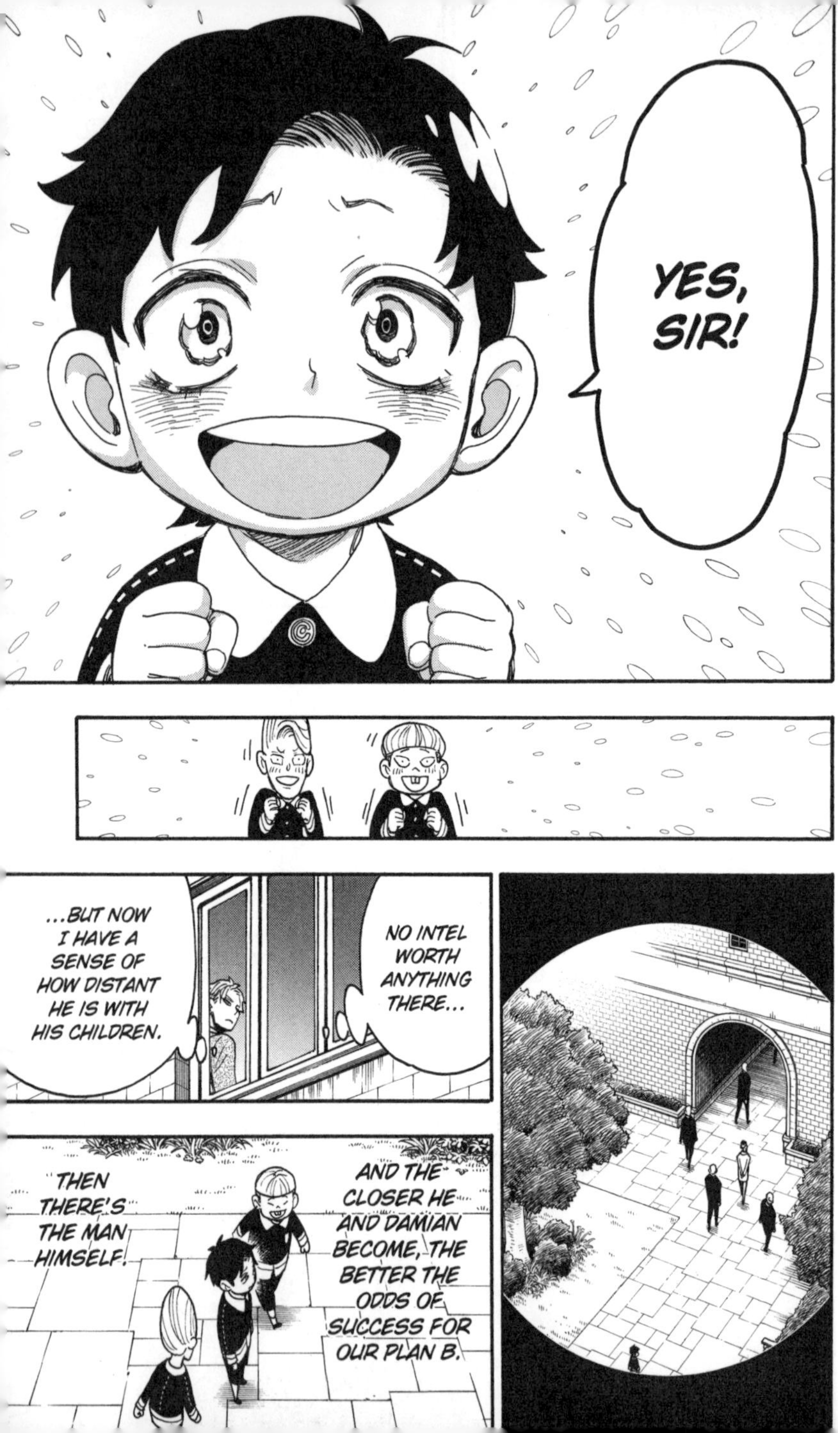
YES, SIR!
NO INTEL WORTH ANYTHING THERE...
...BUT NOW I HAVE A SENSE OF HOW DISTANT HE IS WITH HIS CHILDREN.
THEN THERE'S THE MAN HIMSELF.
AND THE CLOSER HE AND DAMIAN BECOME, THE BETTER THE ODDS OF SUCCESS FOR OUR PLAN B.

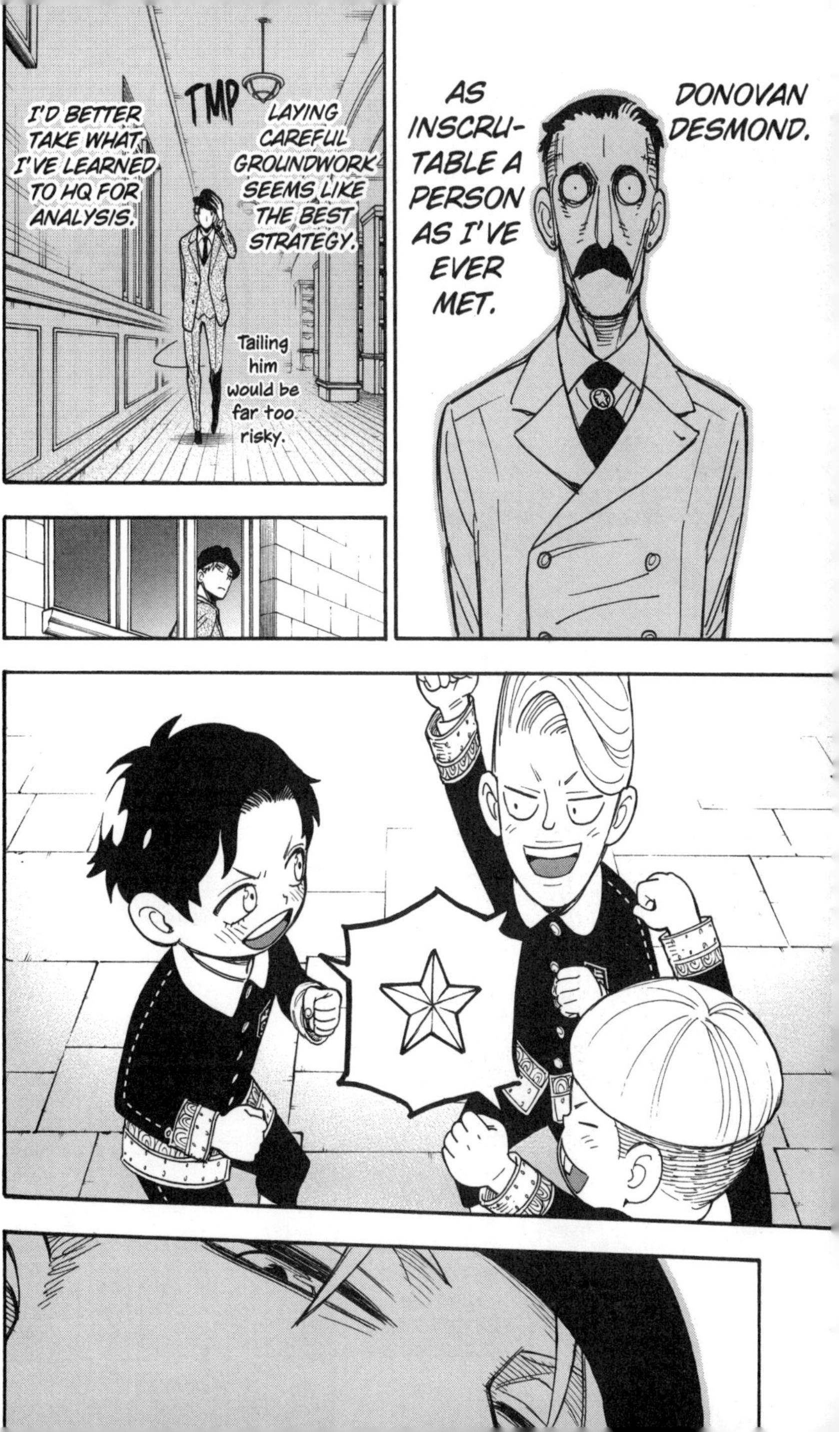
DONOVAN DESMOND.
AS INSCRUTABLE A PERSON AS I'VE EVER MET.
LAYING CAREFUL GROUNDWORK SEEMS LIKE THE BEST STRATEGY.
TMP
I'D BETTER TAKE WHAT I'VE LEARNED TO HQ FOR ANALYSIS.
Tailing him would be far too risky.

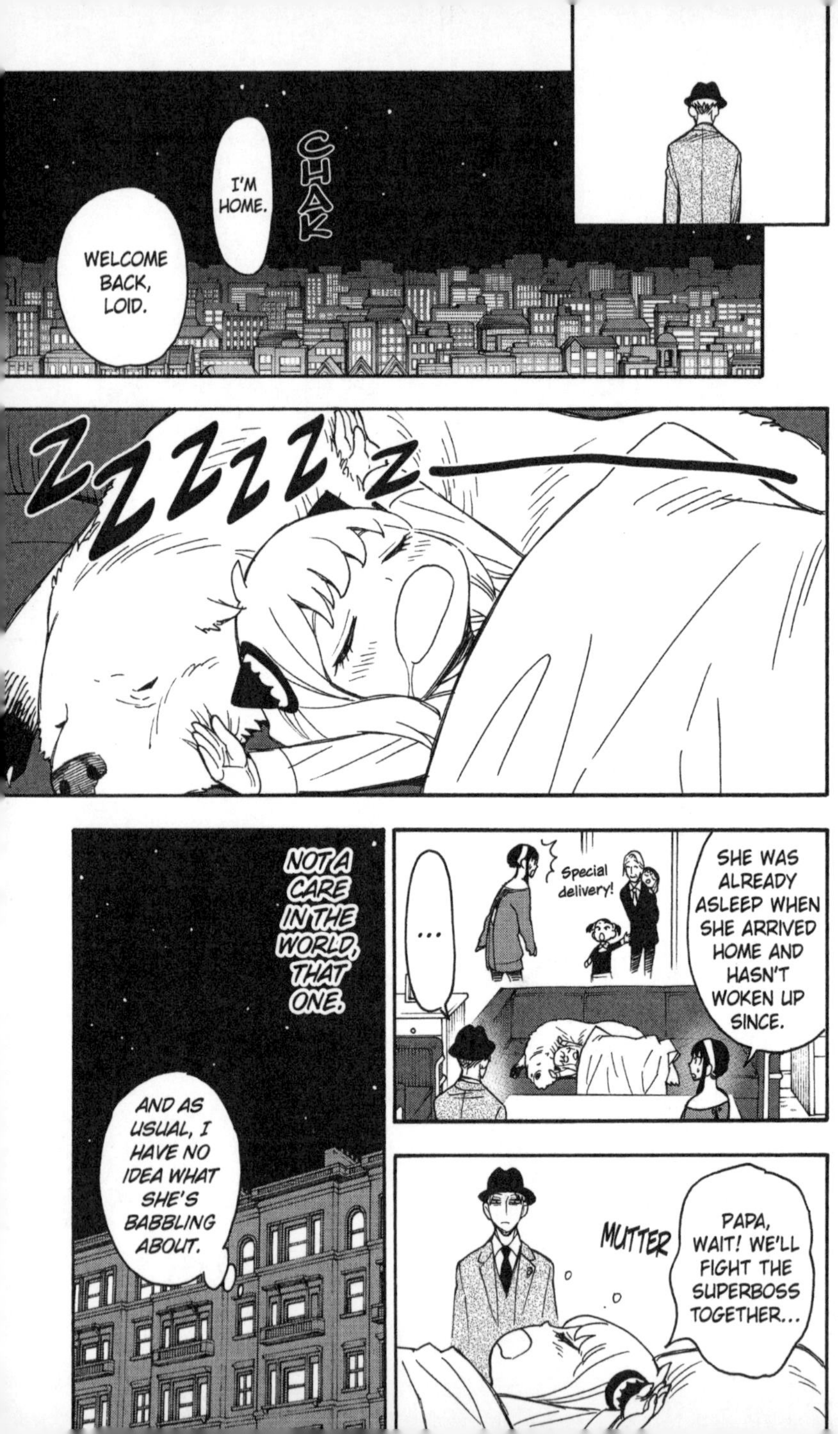
CHAK
I'M HOME.
WELCOME BACK, LOID.
ZZZZZZZ—
SHE WAS ALREADY ASLEEP WHEN SHE ARRIVED HOME AND HASN'T WOKEN UP SINCE.
Special delivery!
...
PAPA, WAIT! WE'LL FIGHT THE SUPERBOSS TOGETHER...
MUTTER
NOT A CARE IN THE WORLD, THAT ONE.
AND AS USUAL, I HAVE NO IDEA WHAT SHE'S BABBLING ABOUT.

SPY×FAMILY

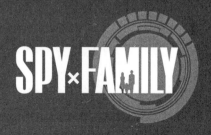

MISSION 39

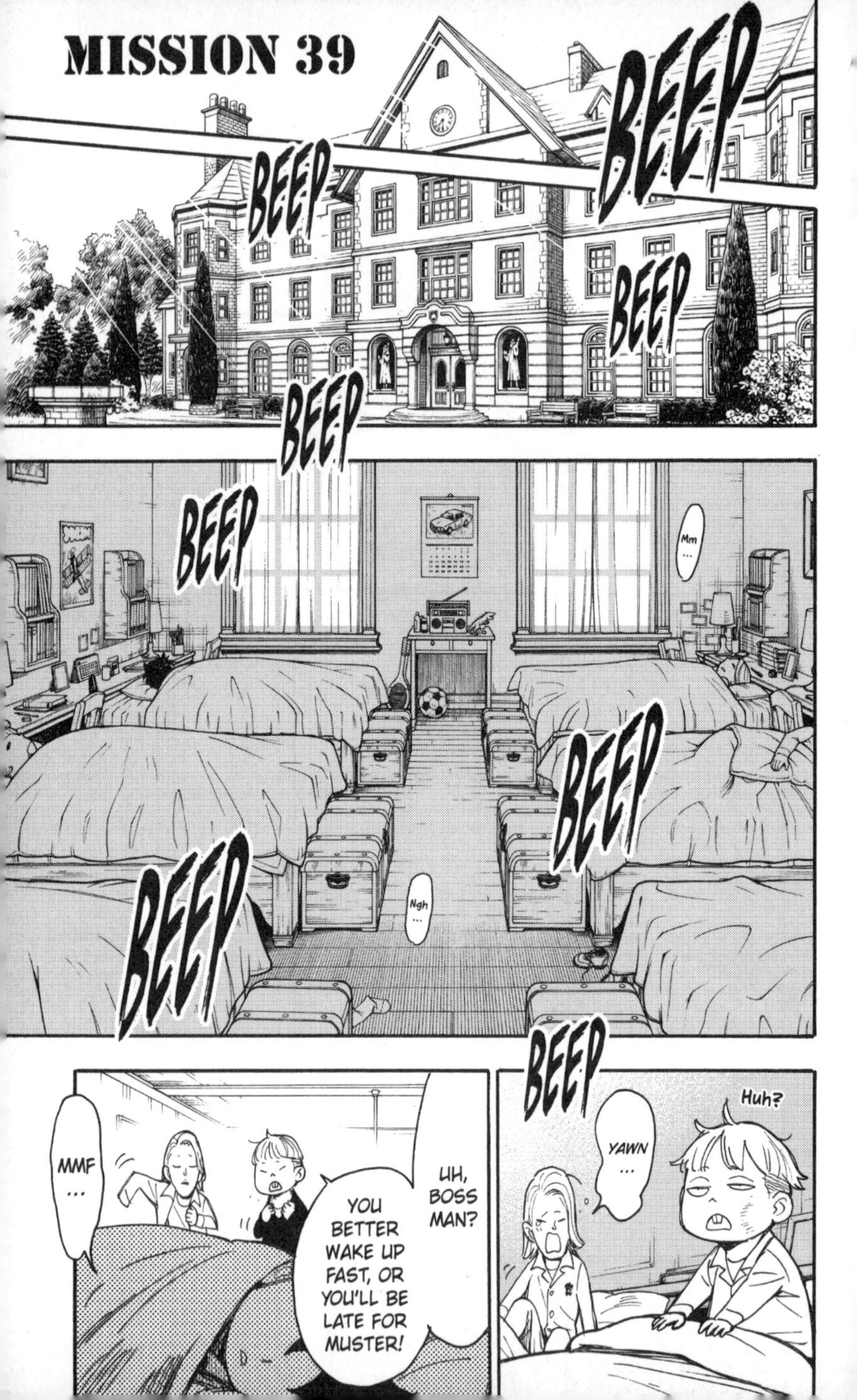
BEEP
BEEP
BEEP
BEEP
BEEP
Mm ...
BEEP
BEEP
Ngh ...
BEEP
Huh?
YAWN ...
UH, BOSS MAN?
YOU BETTER WAKE UP FAST, OR YOU'LL BE LATE FOR MUSTER!
MMF ...

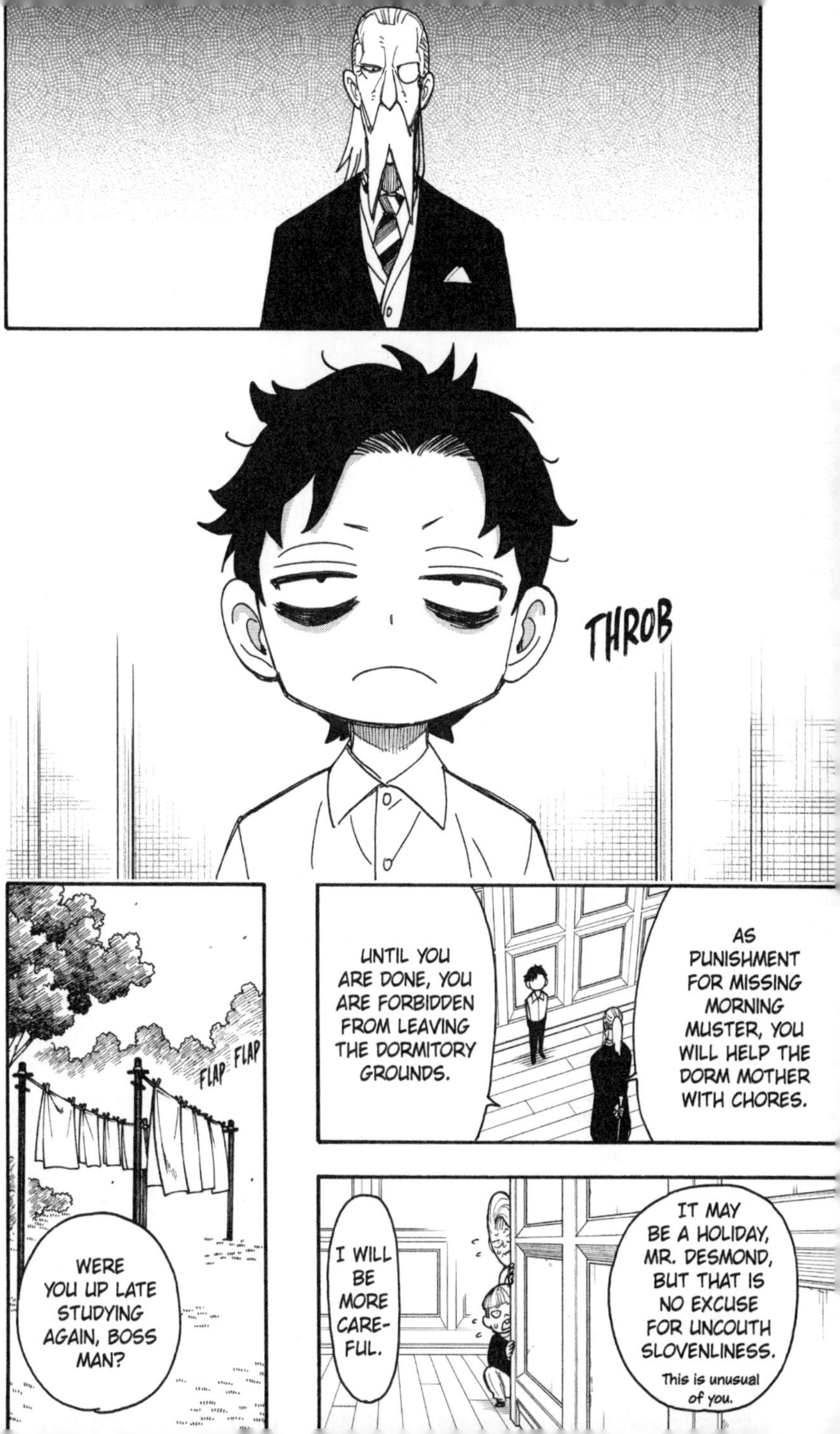
THROB
AS PUNISHMENT FOR MISSING MORNING MUSTER, YOU WILL HELP THE DORM MOTHER WITH CHORES.
UNTIL YOU ARE DONE, YOU ARE FORBIDDEN FROM LEAVING THE DORMITORY GROUNDS.
IT MAY BE A HOLIDAY, MR. DESMOND, BUT THAT IS NO EXCUSE FOR UNCOUTH SLOVENLINESS.
This is unusual of you.
I WILL BE MORE CARE-FUL.
FLAP FLAP
WERE YOU UP LATE STUDYING AGAIN, BOSS MAN?

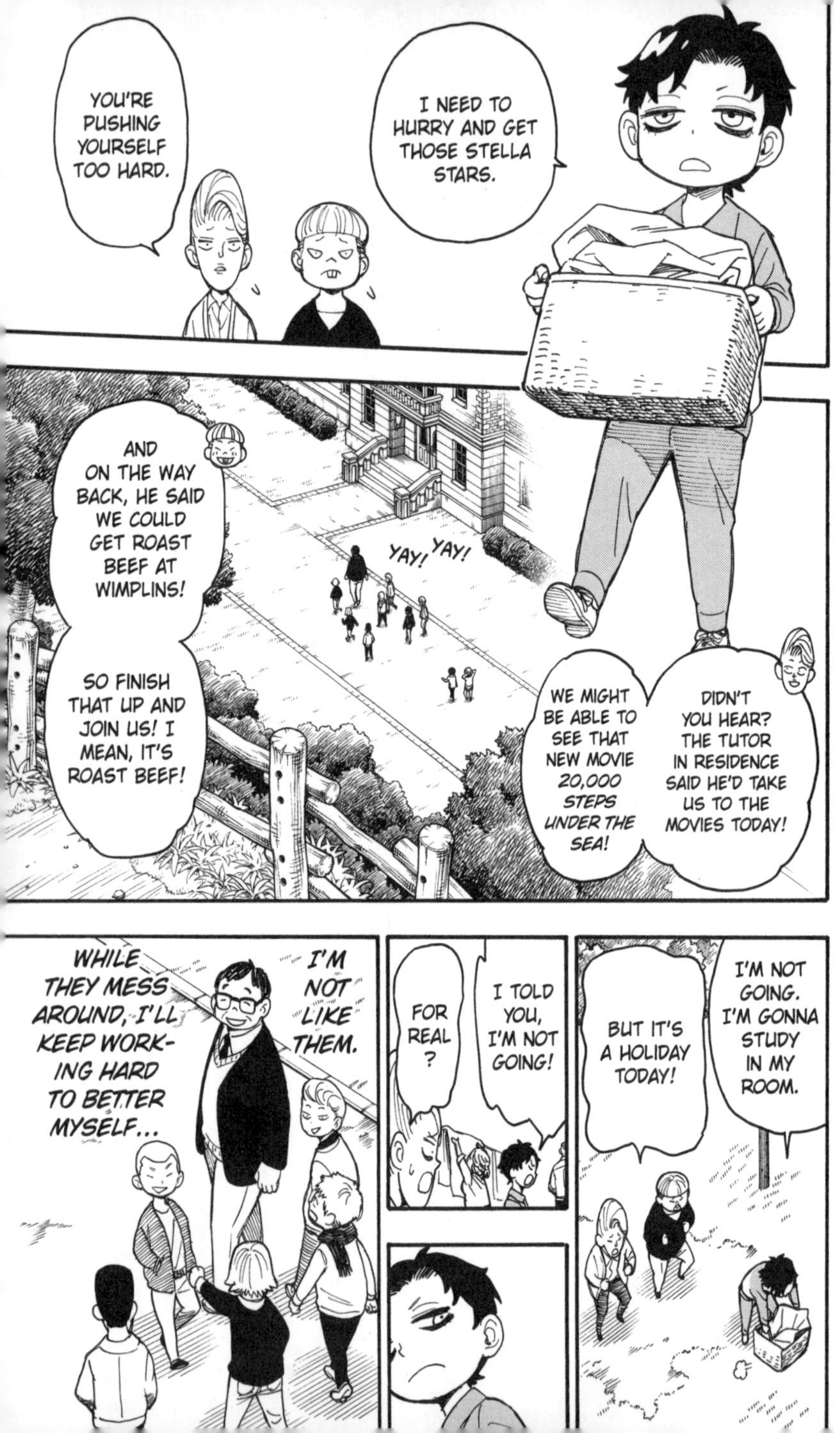
I NEED TO HURRY AND GET THOSE STELLA STARS.
YOU'RE PUSHING YOURSELF TOO HARD.
DIDN'T YOU HEAR? THE TUTOR IN RESIDENCE SAID HE'D TAKE US TO THE MOVIES TODAY!
WE MIGHT BE ABLE TO SEE THAT NEW MOVIE 20,000 STEPS UNDER THE SEA!
YAY! YAY!
AND ON THE WAY BACK, HE SAID WE COULD GET ROAST BEEF AT WIMPLINS!
SO FINISH THAT UP AND JOIN US! I MEAN, IT'S ROAST BEEF!
I'M NOT GOING. I'M GONNA STUDY IN MY ROOM.
BUT IT'S A HOLIDAY TODAY!
I TOLD YOU, I'M NOT GOING!
FOR REAL?
I'M NOT LIKE THEM.
WHILE THEY MESS AROUND, I'LL KEEP WORKING HARD TO BETTER MYSELF...

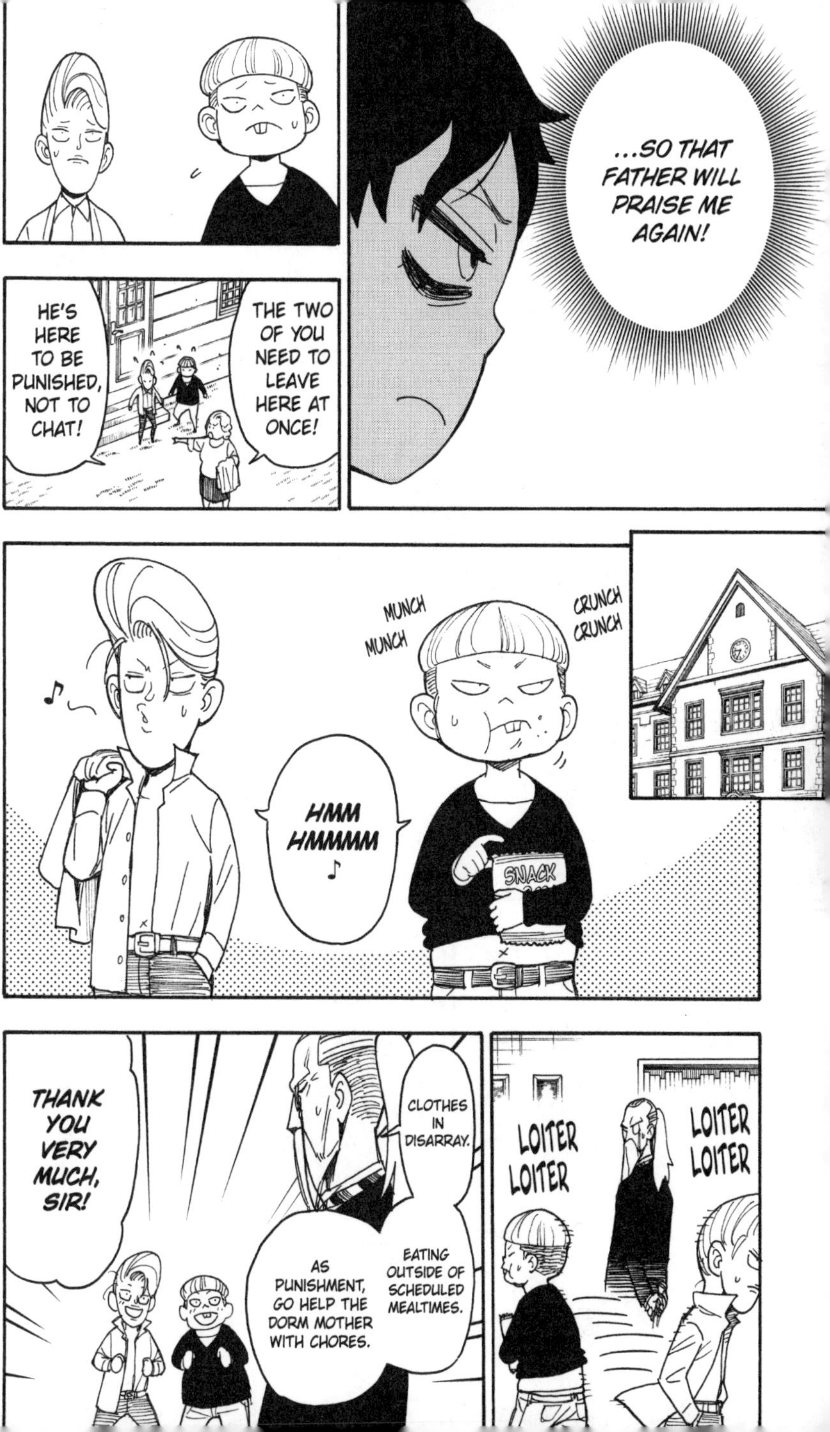
...SO THAT FATHER WILL PRAISE ME AGAIN!
THE TWO OF YOU NEED TO LEAVE HERE AT ONCE!
HE'S HERE TO BE PUNISHED, NOT TO CHAT!
CRUNCH CRUNCH
MUNCH MUNCH
HMM HMMMMM ♪
SNACK
LOITER LOITER
LOITER LOITER
CLOTHES IN DISARRAY.
EATING OUTSIDE OF SCHEDULED MEALTIMES.
AS PUNISHMENT, GO HELP THE DORM MOTHER WITH CHORES.
THANK YOU VERY MUCH, SIR!

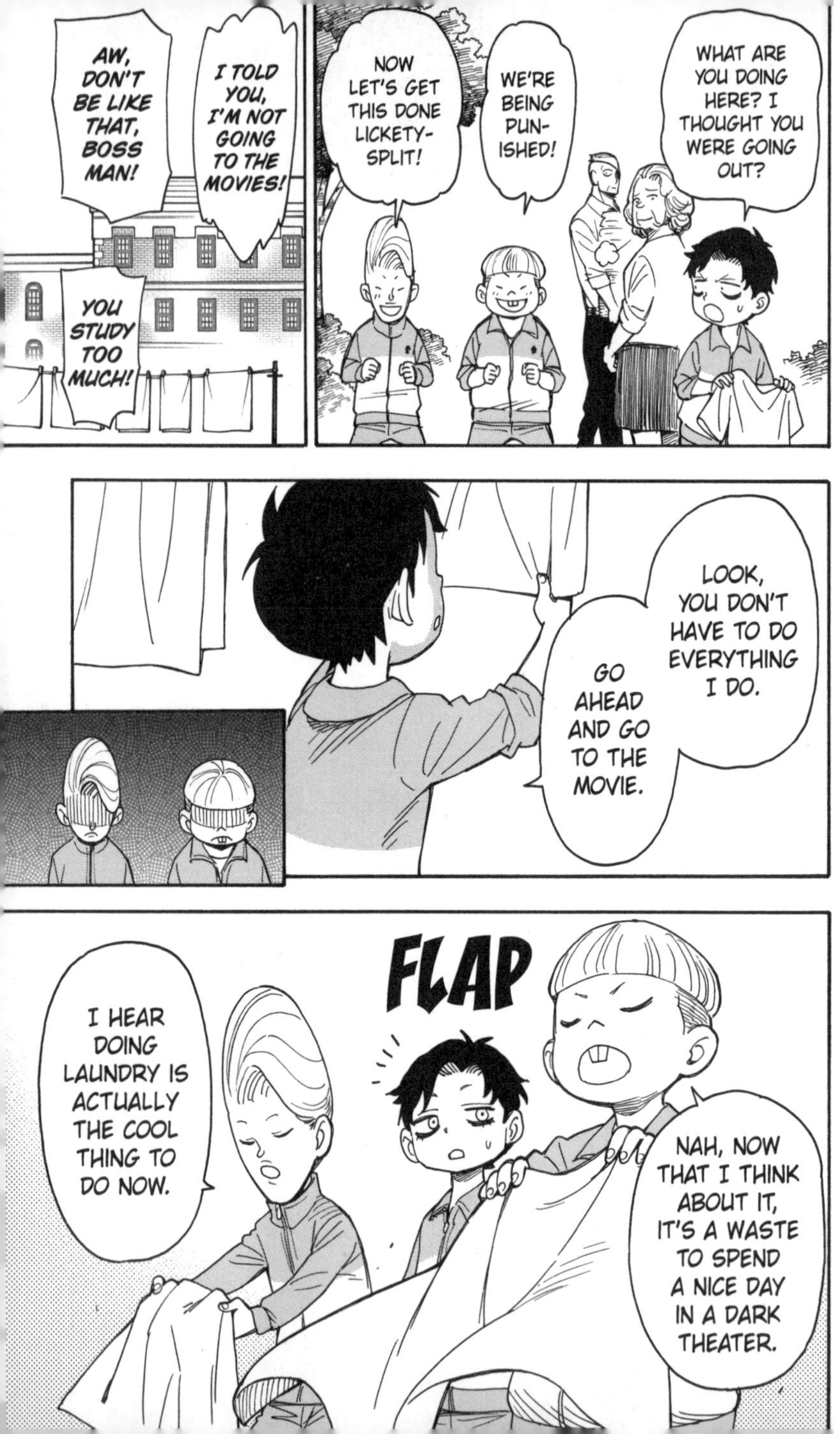
WHAT ARE YOU DOING HERE? I THOUGHT YOU WERE GOING OUT?
WE'RE BEING PUN-ISHED!
NOW LET'S GET THIS DONE LICKETY-SPLIT!
I TOLD YOU, I'M NOT GOING TO THE MOVIES!
AW, DON'T BE LIKE THAT, BOSS MAN!
YOU STUDY TOO MUCH!
LOOK, YOU DON'T HAVE TO DO EVERYTHING I DO.
GO AHEAD AND GO TO THE MOVIE.
FLAP
NAH, NOW THAT I THINK ABOUT IT, IT'S A WASTE TO SPEND A NICE DAY IN A DARK THEATER.
I HEAR DOING LAUNDRY IS ACTUALLY THE COOL THING TO DO NOW.

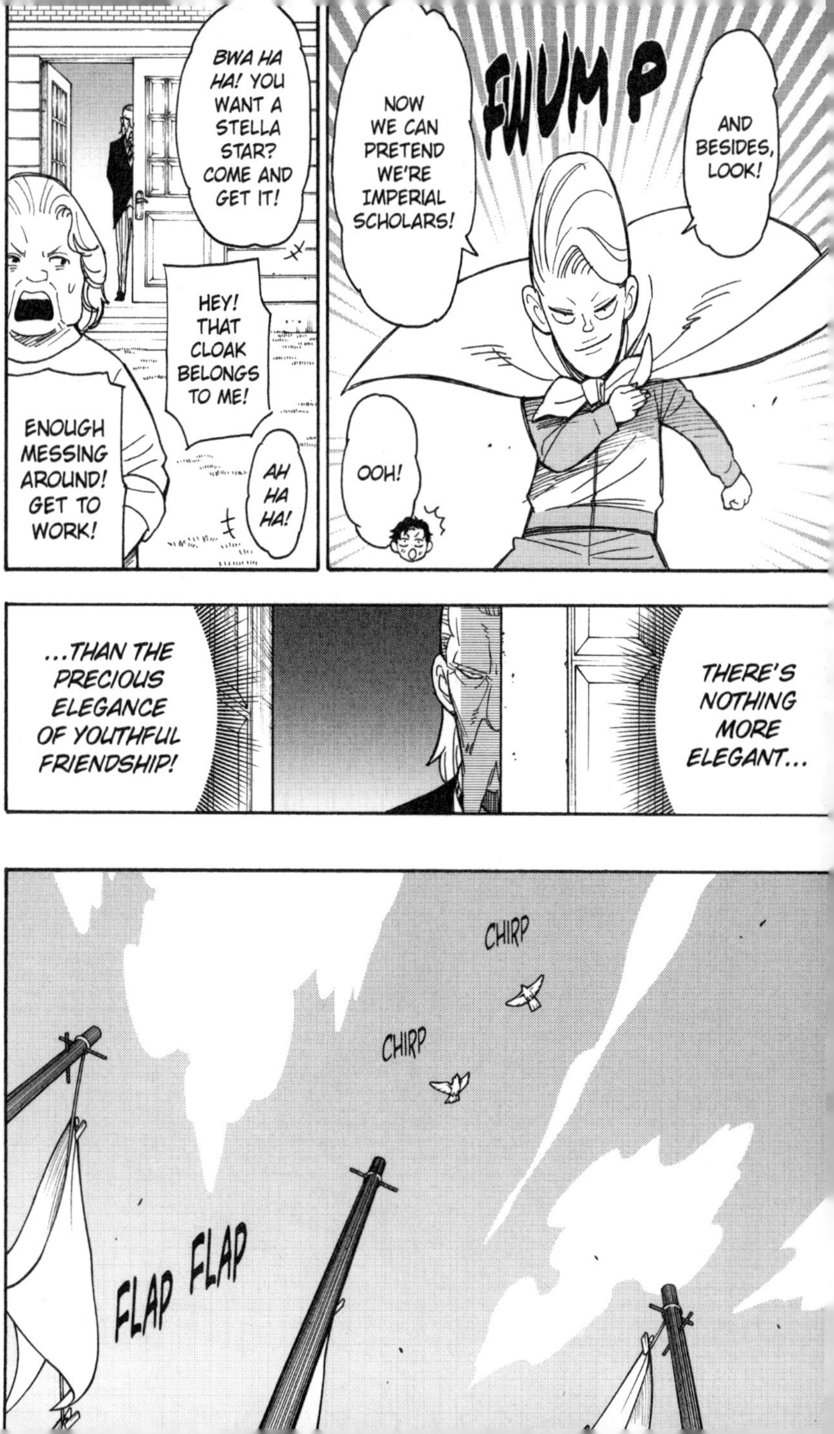
FWUMP
AND BESIDES, LOOK!
NOW WE CAN PRETEND WE'RE IMPERIAL SCHOLARS!
OOH!
BWA HA HA! YOU WANT A STELLA STAR? COME AND GET IT!
HEY! THAT CLOAK BELONGS TO ME!
AH HA HA!
ENOUGH MESSING AROUND! GET TO WORK!
THERE'S NOTHING MORE ELEGANT...
...THAN THE PRECIOUS ELEGANCE OF YOUTHFUL FRIENDSHIP!
CHIRP
CHIRP
FLAP FLAP

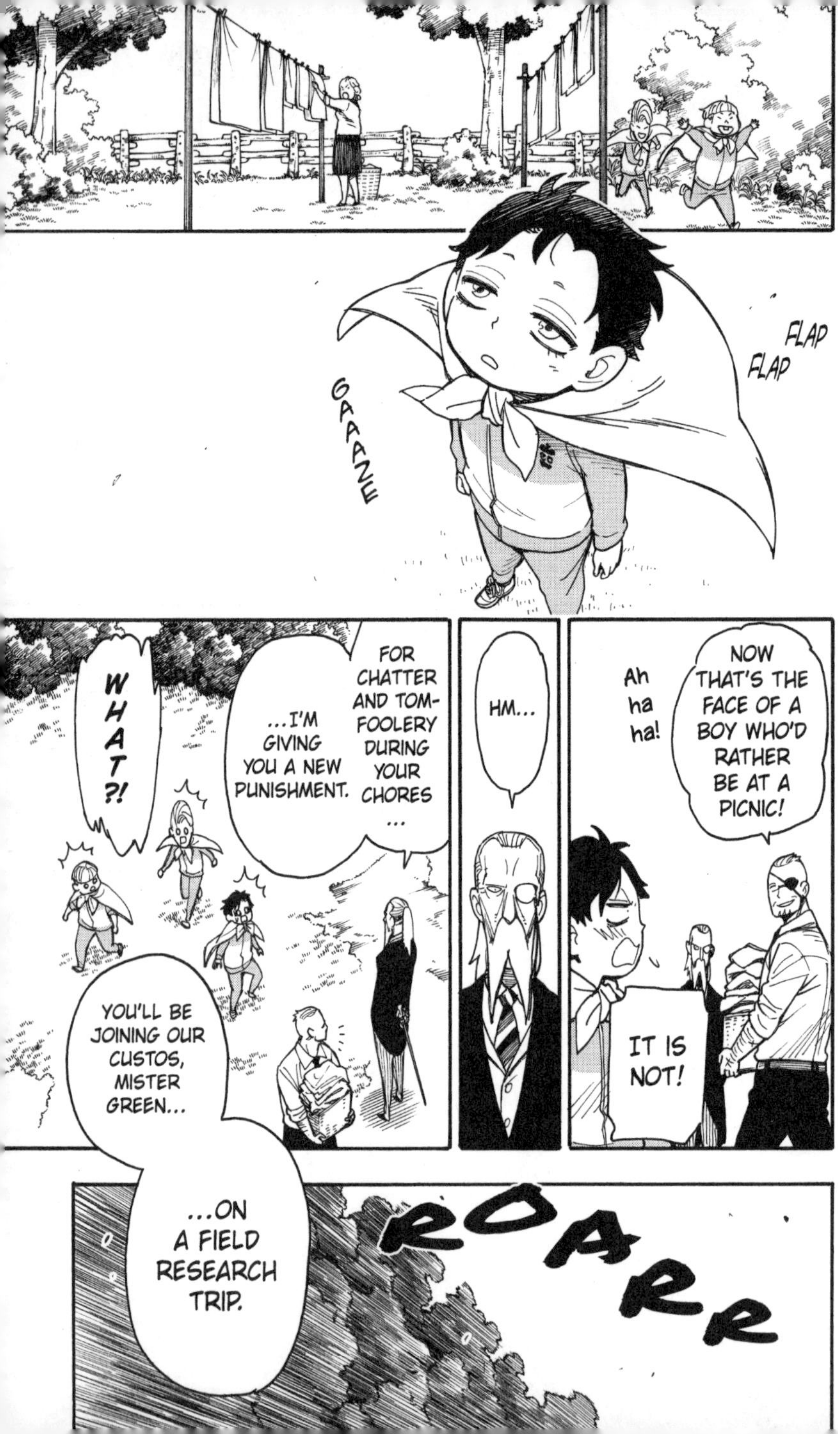
FLAP FLAP
GAAAAZE
NOW THAT'S THE FACE OF A BOY WHO'D RATHER BE AT A PICNIC!
Ah ha ha!
IT IS NOT!
HM...
FOR CHATTER AND TOM-FOOLERY DURING YOUR CHORES...
...I'M GIVING YOU A NEW PUNISHMENT.
WHAT?!
YOU'LL BE JOINING OUR CUSTOS, MISTER GREEN...
...ON A FIELD RESEARCH TRIP.
ROARR

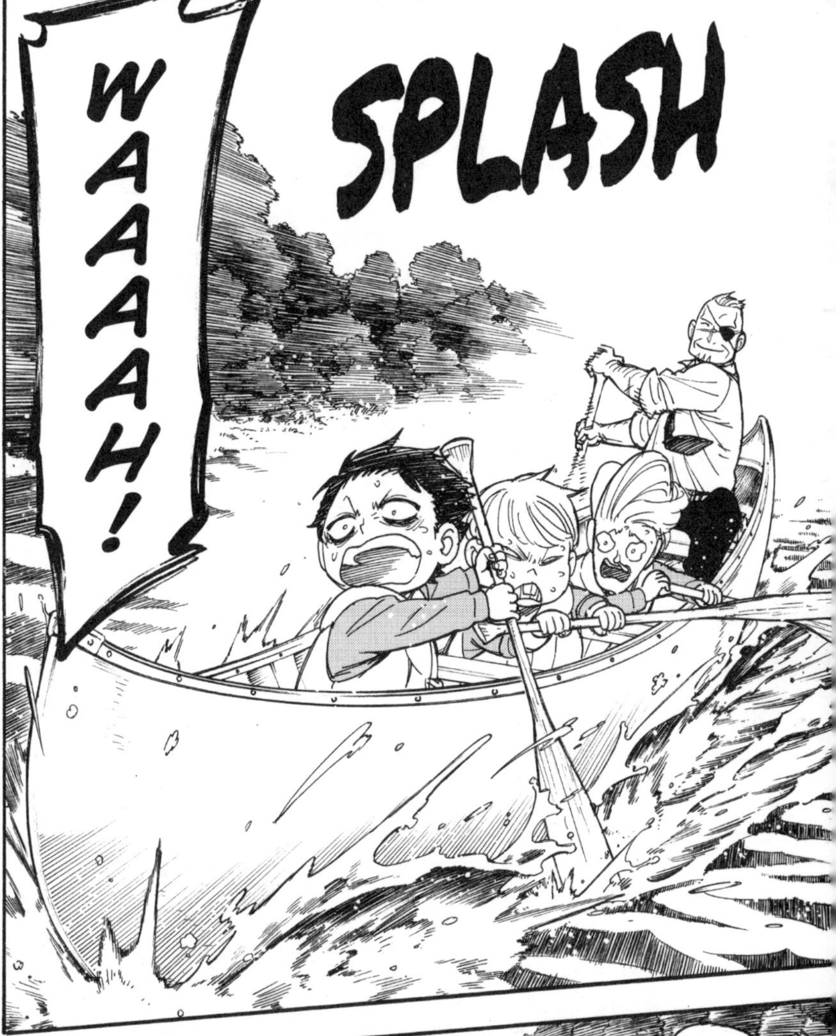
SPLASH
WAAAAH!

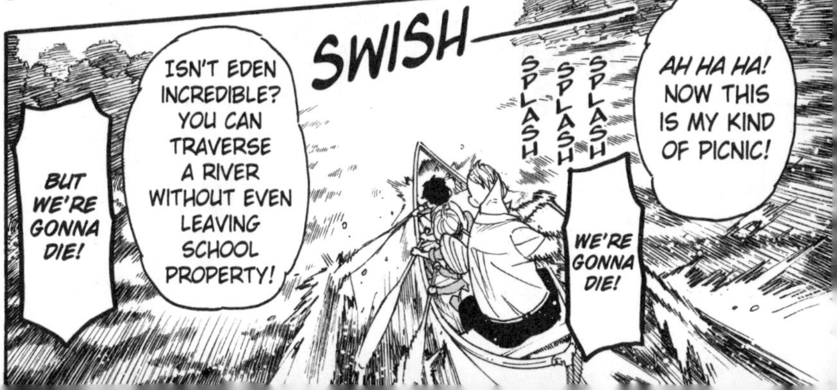
AH HA HA! NOW THIS IS MY KIND OF PICNIC!
SPLASH SPLASH SPLASH
WE'RE GONNA DIE!
SWISH
ISN'T EDEN INCREDIBLE? YOU CAN TRAVERSE A RIVER WITHOUT EVEN LEAVING SCHOOL PROPERTY!
BUT WE'RE GONNA DIE!

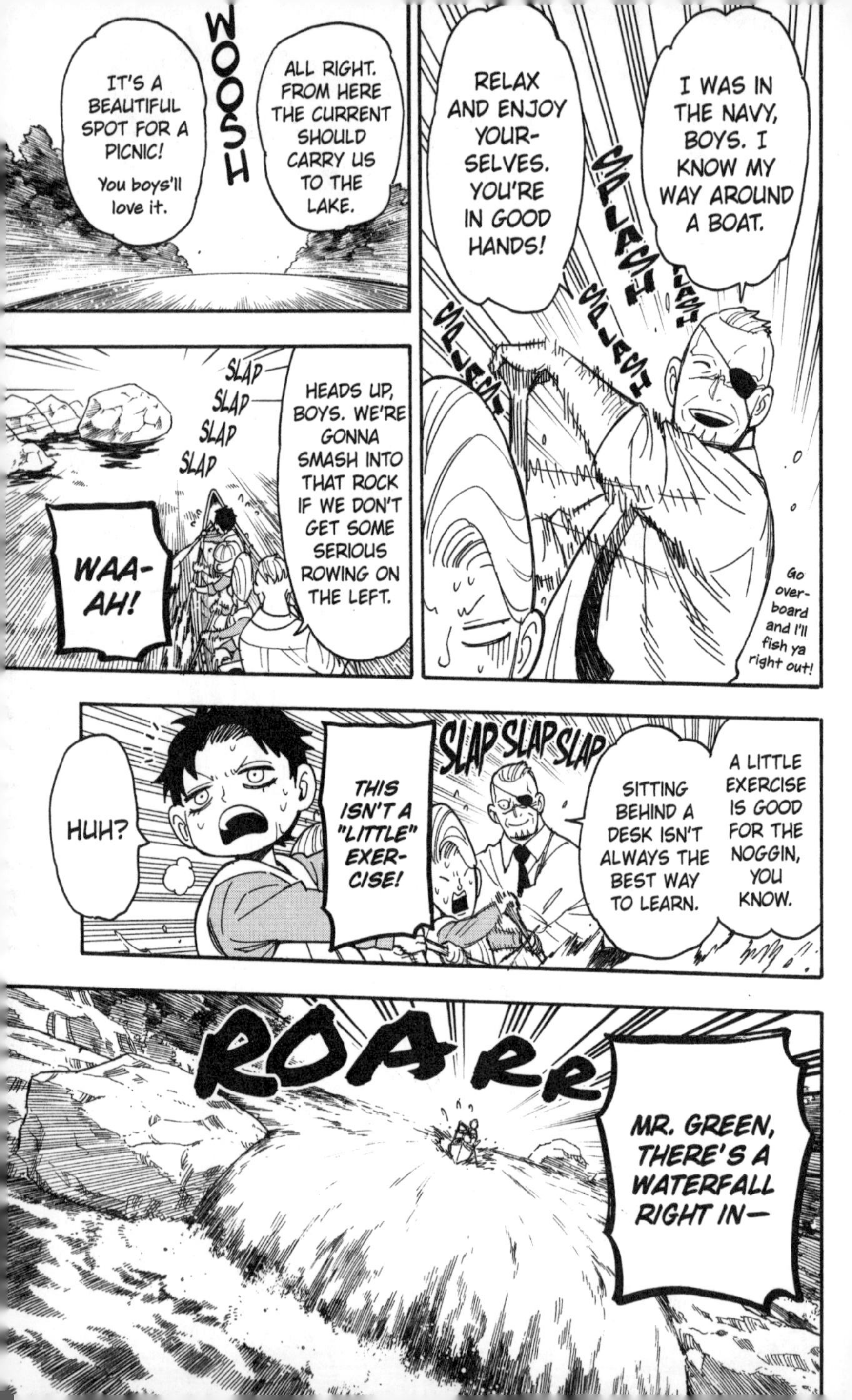
I WAS IN THE NAVY, BOYS. I KNOW MY WAY AROUND A BOAT.
RELAX AND ENJOY YOURSELVES. YOU'RE IN GOOD HANDS!
SPLASH SPLASH SPLASH SPLASH
Go overboard and I'll fish ya right out!
ALL RIGHT. FROM HERE THE CURRENT SHOULD CARRY US TO THE LAKE.
WOOSH
IT'S A BEAUTIFUL SPOT FOR A PICNIC!
You boys'll love it.
HEADS UP, BOYS. WE'RE GONNA SMASH INTO THAT ROCK IF WE DON'T GET SOME SERIOUS ROWING ON THE LEFT.
SLAP SLAP SLAP SLAP
WAA-AH!
A LITTLE EXERCISE IS GOOD FOR THE NOGGIN, YOU KNOW.
SITTING BEHIND A DESK ISN'T ALWAYS THE BEST WAY TO LEARN.
SLAP SLAP SLAP
THIS ISN'T A "LITTLE" EXERCISE!
HUH?
MR. GREEN, THERE'S A WATERFALL RIGHT IN—
ROARR

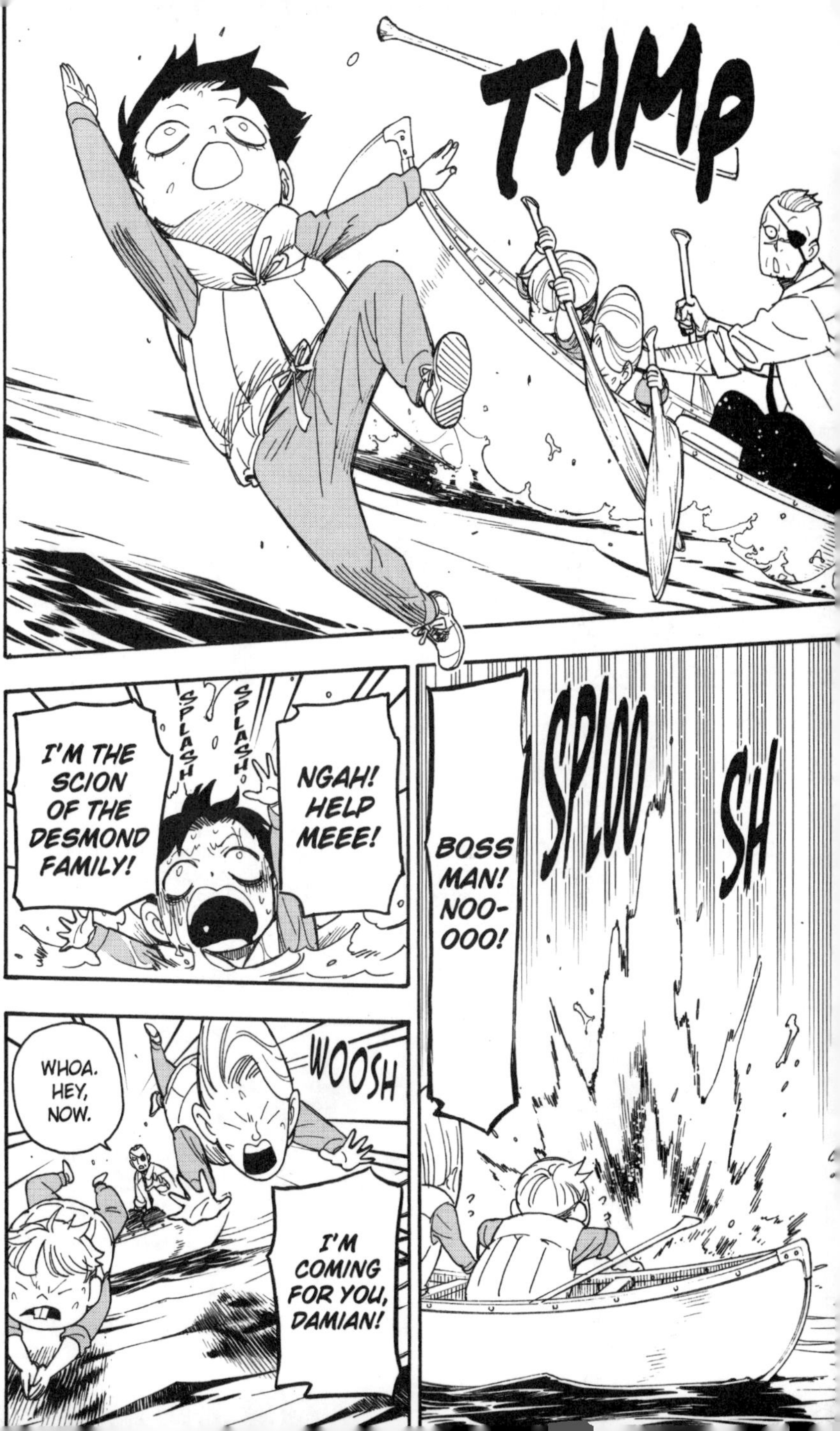
THMP
SPLOOOSH
BOSS MAN! NOO-OOO!
SPLASH SPLASH
NGAH! HELP MEEE!
I'M THE SCION OF THE DESMOND FAMILY!
WOOSH
WHOA. HEY, NOW.
I'M COMING FOR YOU, DAMIAN!

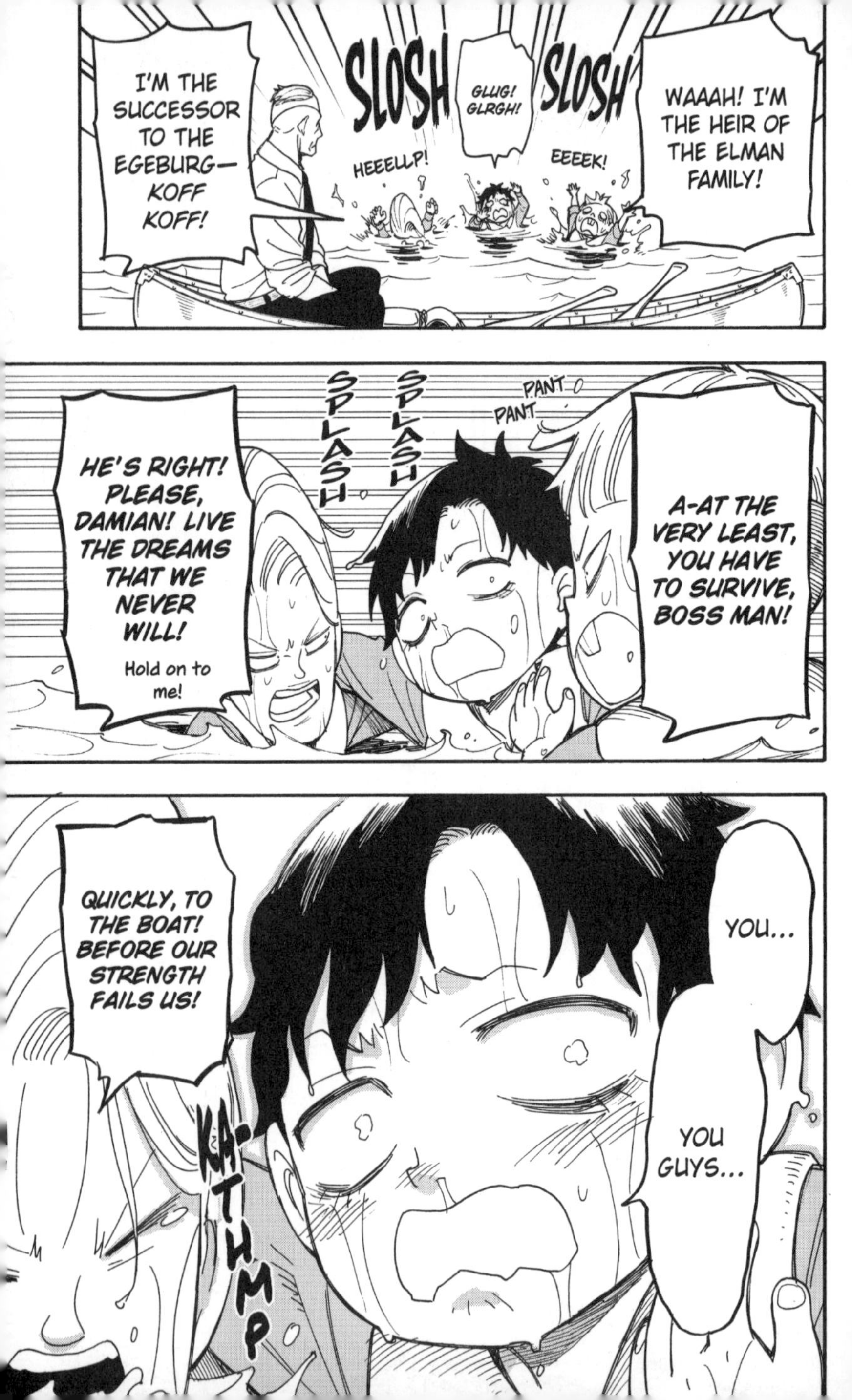
WAAAH! I'M THE HEIR OF THE ELMAN FAMILY!
SLOSH
EEEEK!
GLUG! GLRGH!
SLOSH
HEEELLP!
I'M THE SUCCESSOR TO THE EGEBURG— KOFF KOFF!
A-AT THE VERY LEAST, YOU HAVE TO SURVIVE, BOSS MAN!
PANT PANT
SPLASH SPLASH
HE'S RIGHT! PLEASE, DAMIAN! LIVE THE DREAMS THAT WE NEVER WILL!
Hold on to me!
YOU...
YOU GUYS...
QUICKLY, TO THE BOAT! BEFORE OUR STRENGTH FAILS US!
KA-THUMP

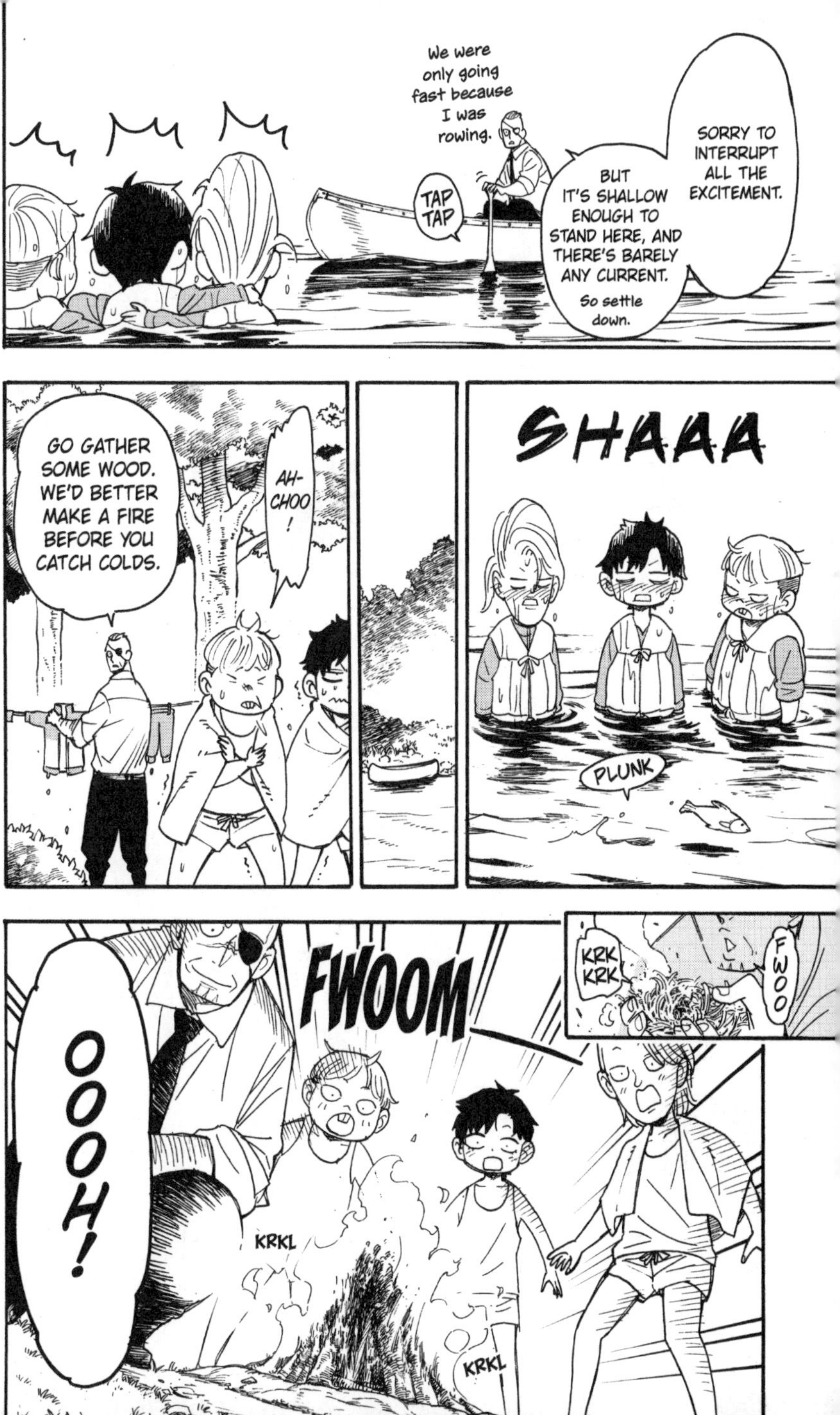
SORRY TO INTERRUPT ALL THE EXCITEMENT.
BUT IT'S SHALLOW ENOUGH TO STAND HERE, AND THERE'S BARELY ANY CURRENT.
So settle down.
We were only going fast because I was rowing.
TAP TAP
SHAAA
PLUNK
AH-CHOO!
GO GATHER SOME WOOD. WE'D BETTER MAKE A FIRE BEFORE YOU CATCH COLDS.
FWOO
KRK KRK
FWOOM
OOOOH!
KRKL
KRKL

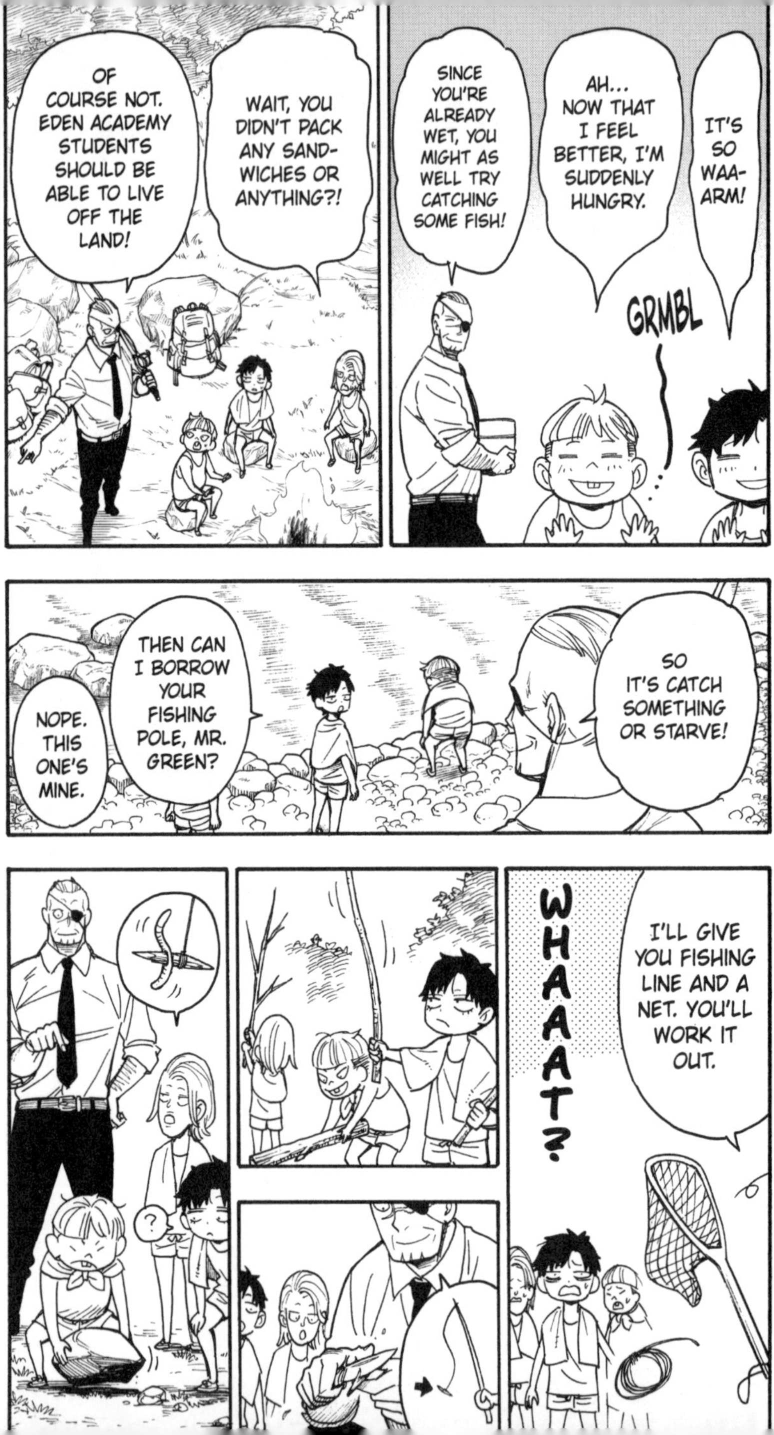
IT'S SO WAA-ARM!
AH... NOW THAT I FEEL BETTER, I'M SUDDENLY HUNGRY.
GRMBL
SINCE YOU'RE ALREADY WET, YOU MIGHT AS WELL TRY CATCHING SOME FISH!
WAIT, YOU DIDN'T PACK ANY SAND-WICHES OR ANYTHING?!
OF COURSE NOT. EDEN ACADEMY STUDENTS SHOULD BE ABLE TO LIVE OFF THE LAND!
SO IT'S CATCH SOMETHING OR STARVE!
THEN CAN I BORROW YOUR FISHING POLE, MR. GREEN?
NOPE. THIS ONE'S MINE.
I'LL GIVE YOU FISHING LINE AND A NET. YOU'LL WORK IT OUT.
WHAAAAT?
?

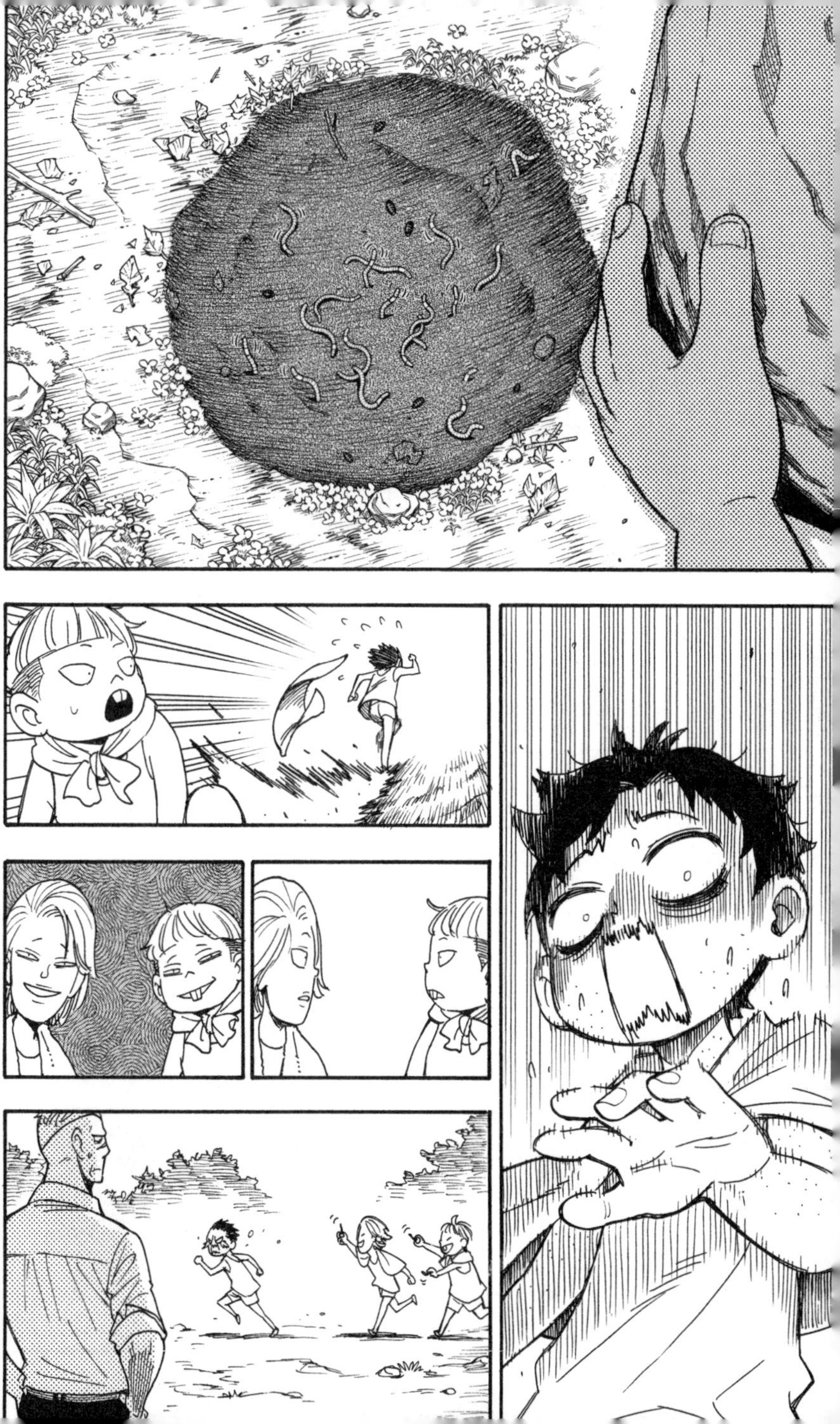

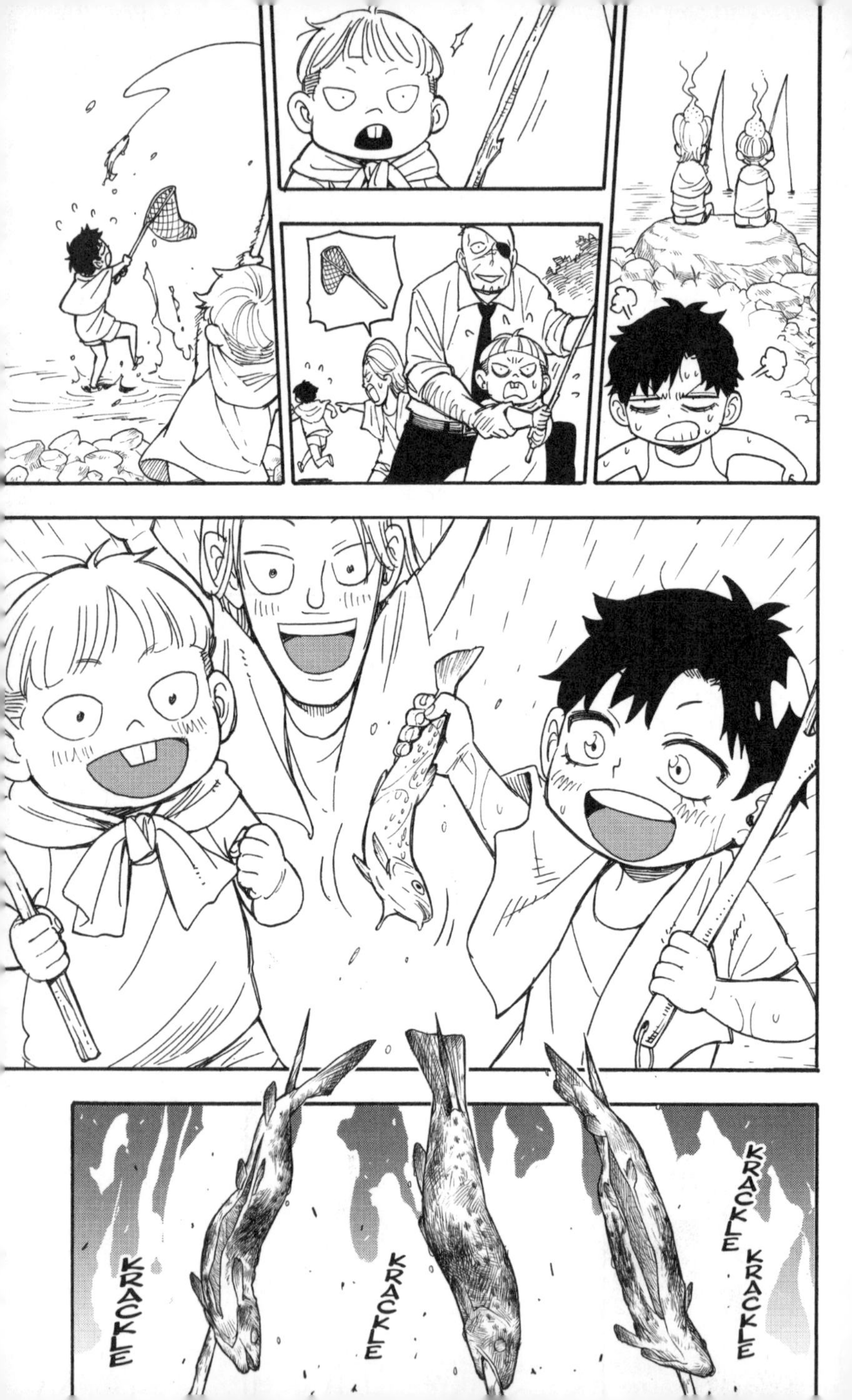
KRACKLE
KRACKLE
KRACKLE
KRACKLE

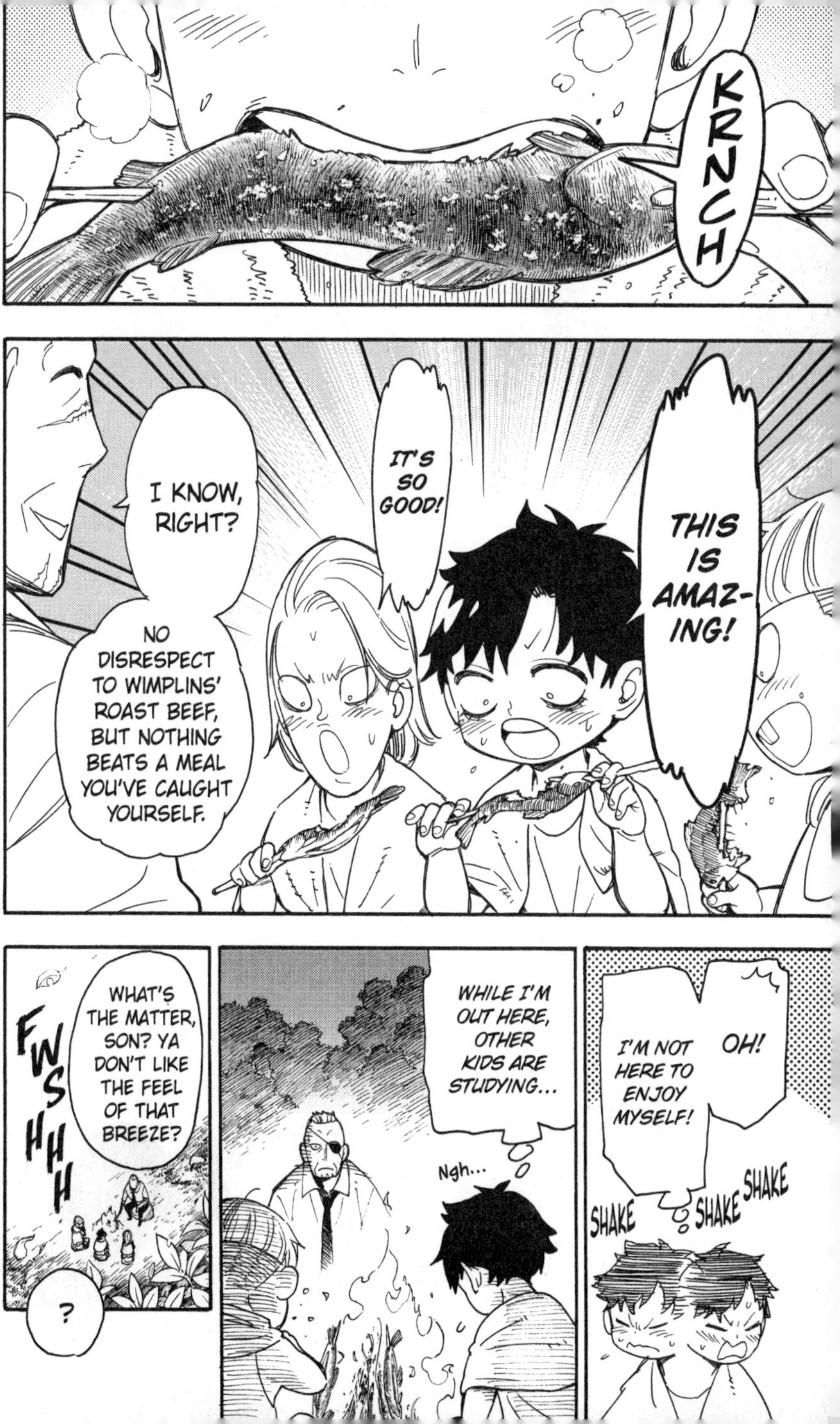
KRNCH
THIS IS AMAZING!
IT'S SO GOOD!
I KNOW, RIGHT?
NO DISRESPECT TO WIMPLINS' ROAST BEEF, BUT NOTHING BEATS A MEAL YOU'VE CAUGHT YOURSELF.
OH!
I'M NOT HERE TO ENJOY MYSELF!
SHAKE SHAKE SHAKE
WHILE I'M OUT HERE, OTHER KIDS ARE STUDYING...
Ngh...
WHAT'S THE MATTER, SON? YA DON'T LIKE THE FEEL OF THAT BREEZE?
FWSHHH
?

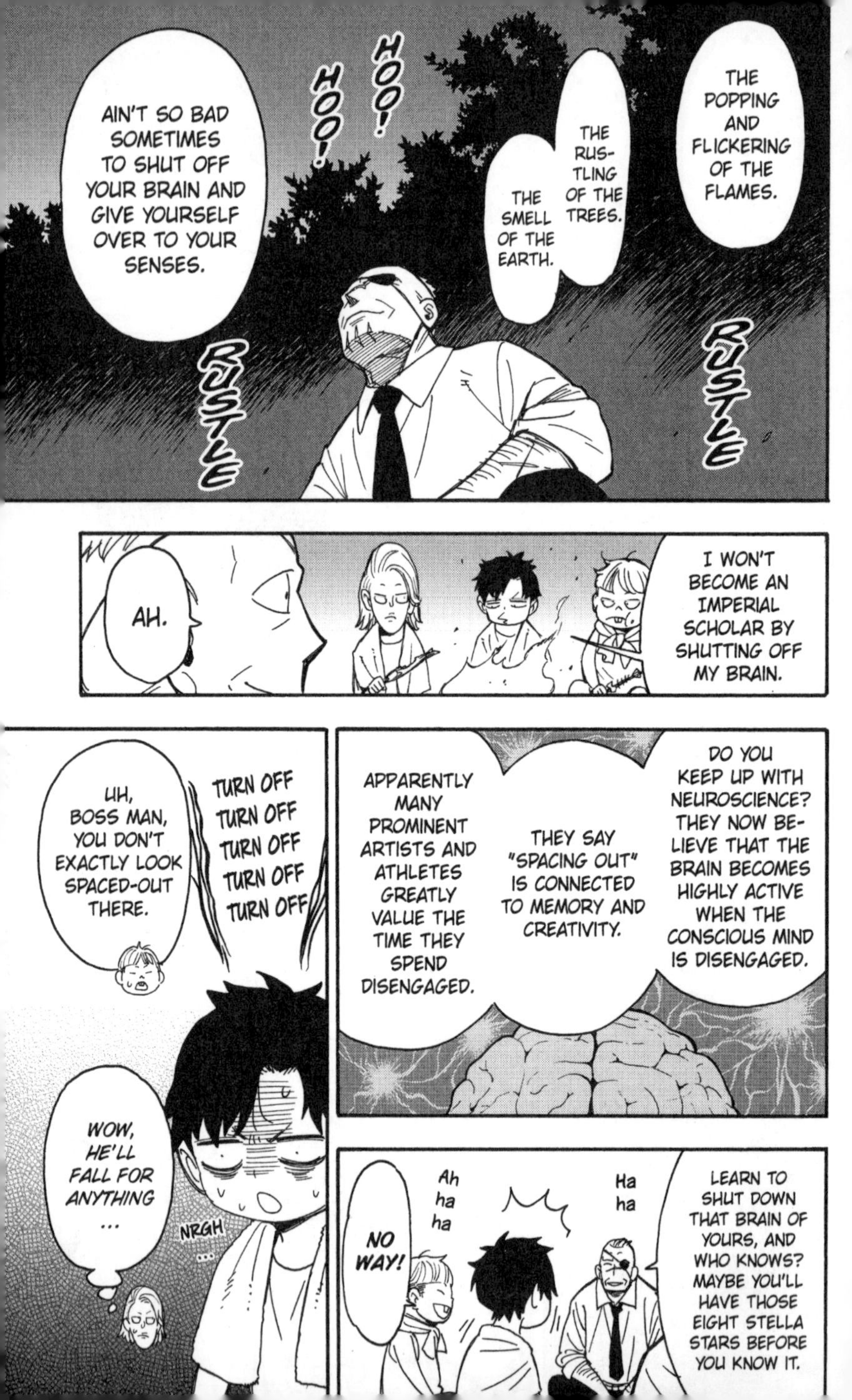
THE POPPING AND FLICKERING OF THE FLAMES.
THE RUS-TLING OF THE TREES.
THE SMELL OF THE EARTH.
HOO! HOO!
AIN'T SO BAD SOMETIMES TO SHUT OFF YOUR BRAIN AND GIVE YOURSELF OVER TO YOUR SENSES.
RUSTLE
RUSTLE
I WON'T BECOME AN IMPERIAL SCHOLAR BY SHUTTING OFF MY BRAIN.
AH.
DO YOU KEEP UP WITH NEUROSCIENCE? THEY NOW BE-LIEVE THAT THE BRAIN BECOMES HIGHLY ACTIVE WHEN THE CONSCIOUS MIND IS DISENGAGED.
THEY SAY "SPACING OUT" IS CONNECTED TO MEMORY AND CREATIVITY.
APPARENTLY MANY PROMINENT ARTISTS AND ATHLETES GREATLY VALUE THE TIME THEY SPEND DISENGAGED.
LEARN TO SHUT DOWN THAT BRAIN OF YOURS, AND WHO KNOWS? MAYBE YOU'LL HAVE THOSE EIGHT STELLA STARS BEFORE YOU KNOW IT.
Ha ha
Ah ha ha
NO WAY!
TURN OFF TURN OFF TURN OFF TURN OFF TURN OFF
UH, BOSS MAN, YOU DON'T EXACTLY LOOK SPACED-OUT THERE.
WOW, HE'LL FALL FOR ANYTHING...
NRGH...

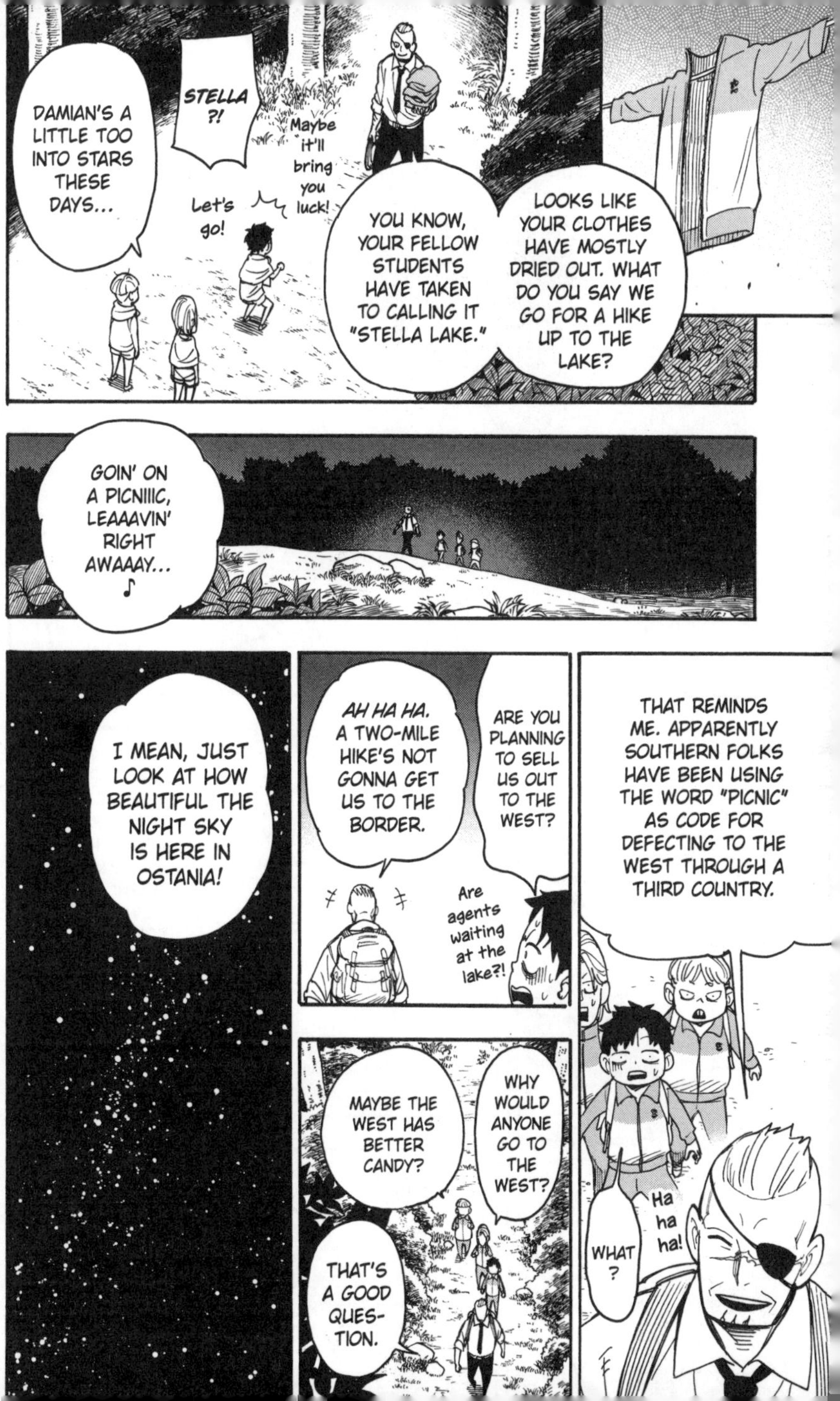
LOOKS LIKE YOUR CLOTHES HAVE MOSTLY DRIED OUT. WHAT DO YOU SAY WE GO FOR A HIKE UP TO THE LAKE?
YOU KNOW, YOUR FELLOW STUDENTS HAVE TAKEN TO CALLING IT "STELLA LAKE."
Maybe it'll bring you luck!
STELLA?!
Let's go!
DAMIAN'S A LITTLE TOO INTO STARS THESE DAYS...
GOIN' ON A PICNIIIC, LEAAAVIN' RIGHT AWAAAY... ♪
THAT REMINDS ME. APPARENTLY SOUTHERN FOLKS HAVE BEEN USING THE WORD "PICNIC" AS CODE FOR DEFECTING TO THE WEST THROUGH A THIRD COUNTRY.
Ha ha ha!
WHAT?
ARE YOU PLANNING TO SELL US OUT TO THE WEST?
Are agents waiting at the lake?!
AH HA HA. A TWO-MILE HIKE'S NOT GONNA GET US TO THE BORDER.
WHY WOULD ANYONE GO TO THE WEST?
MAYBE THE WEST HAS BETTER CANDY?
THAT'S A GOOD QUES-TION.
I MEAN, JUST LOOK AT HOW BEAUTIFUL THE NIGHT SKY IS HERE IN OSTANIA!

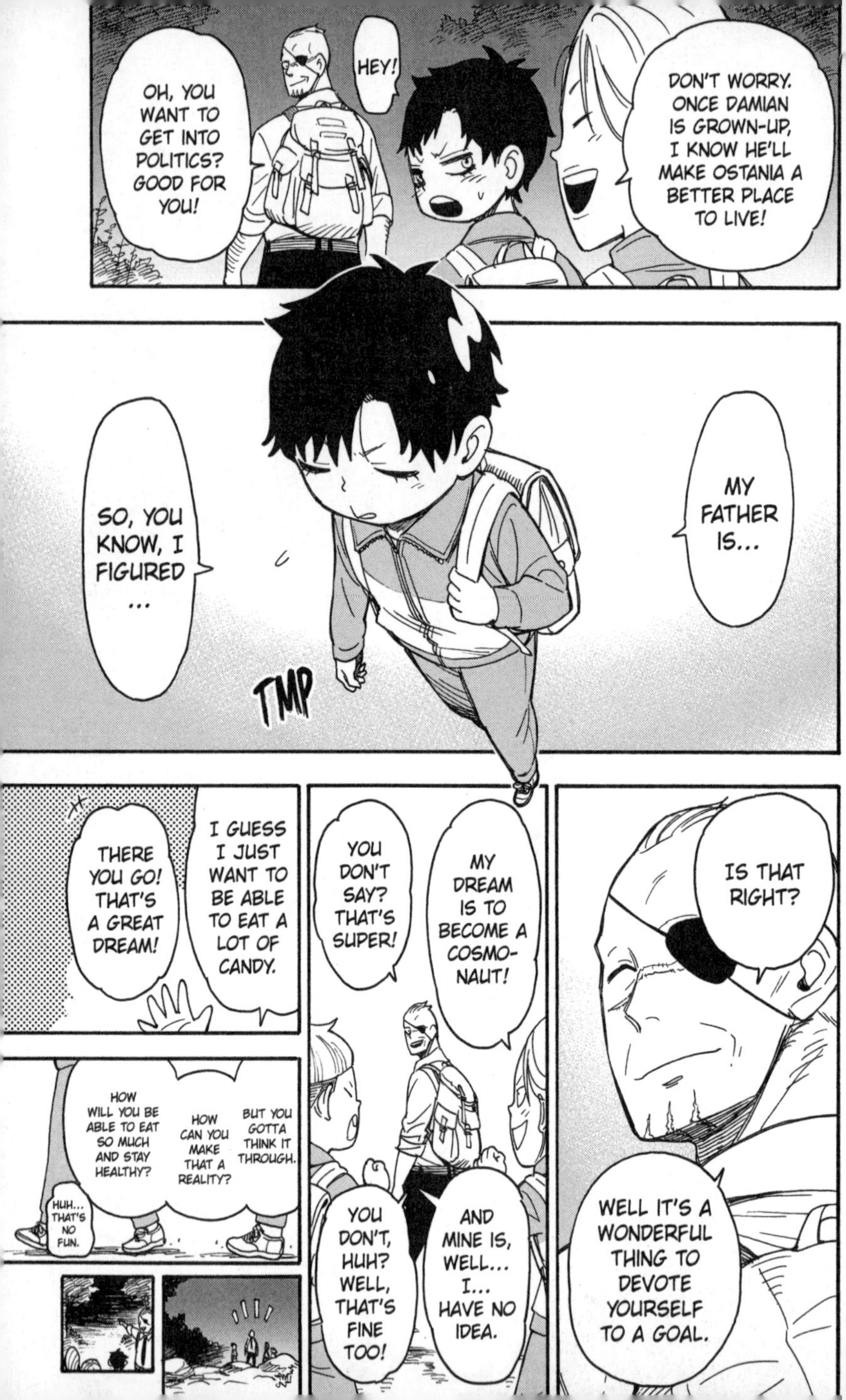
DON'T WORRY. ONCE DAMIAN IS GROWN-UP, I KNOW HE'LL MAKE OSTANIA A BETTER PLACE TO LIVE!
HEY!
OH, YOU WANT TO GET INTO POLITICS? GOOD FOR YOU!
MY FATHER IS...
SO, YOU KNOW, I FIGURED...
TMP
IS THAT RIGHT?
WELL IT'S A WONDERFUL THING TO DEVOTE YOURSELF TO A GOAL.
MY DREAM IS TO BECOME A COSMO-NAUT!
YOU DON'T SAY? THAT'S SUPER!
AND MINE IS, WELL... I... HAVE NO IDEA.
YOU DON'T, HUH? WELL, THAT'S FINE TOO!
I GUESS I JUST WANT TO BE ABLE TO EAT A LOT OF CANDY.
THERE YOU GO! THAT'S A GREAT DREAM!
BUT YOU GOTTA THINK IT THROUGH.
HOW CAN YOU MAKE THAT A REALITY?
HOW WILL YOU BE ABLE TO EAT SO MUCH AND STAY HEALTHY?
HUH... THAT'S NO FUN.

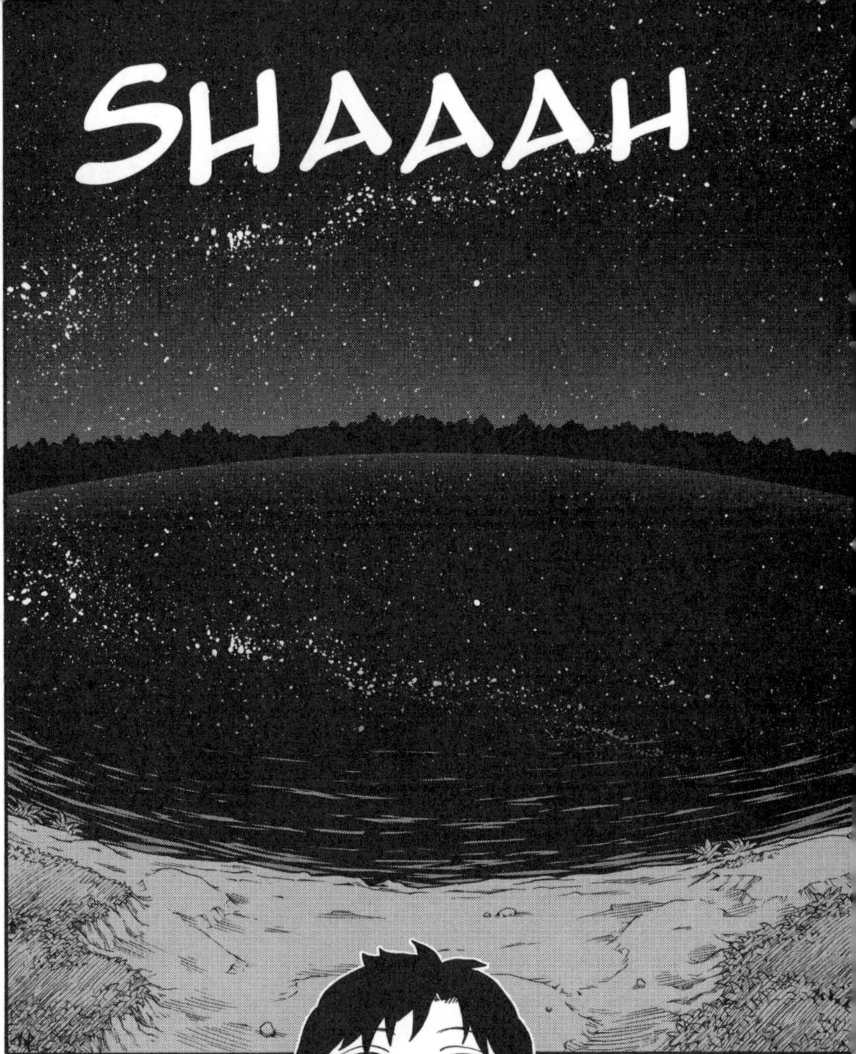
SHAAAH
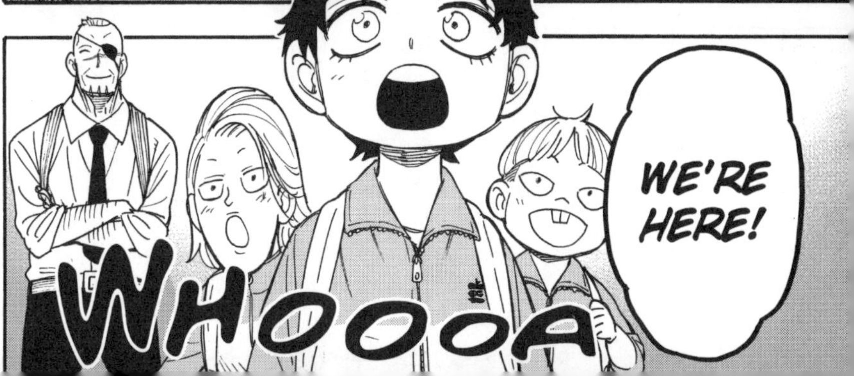
WE'RE HERE!
WHOOOA

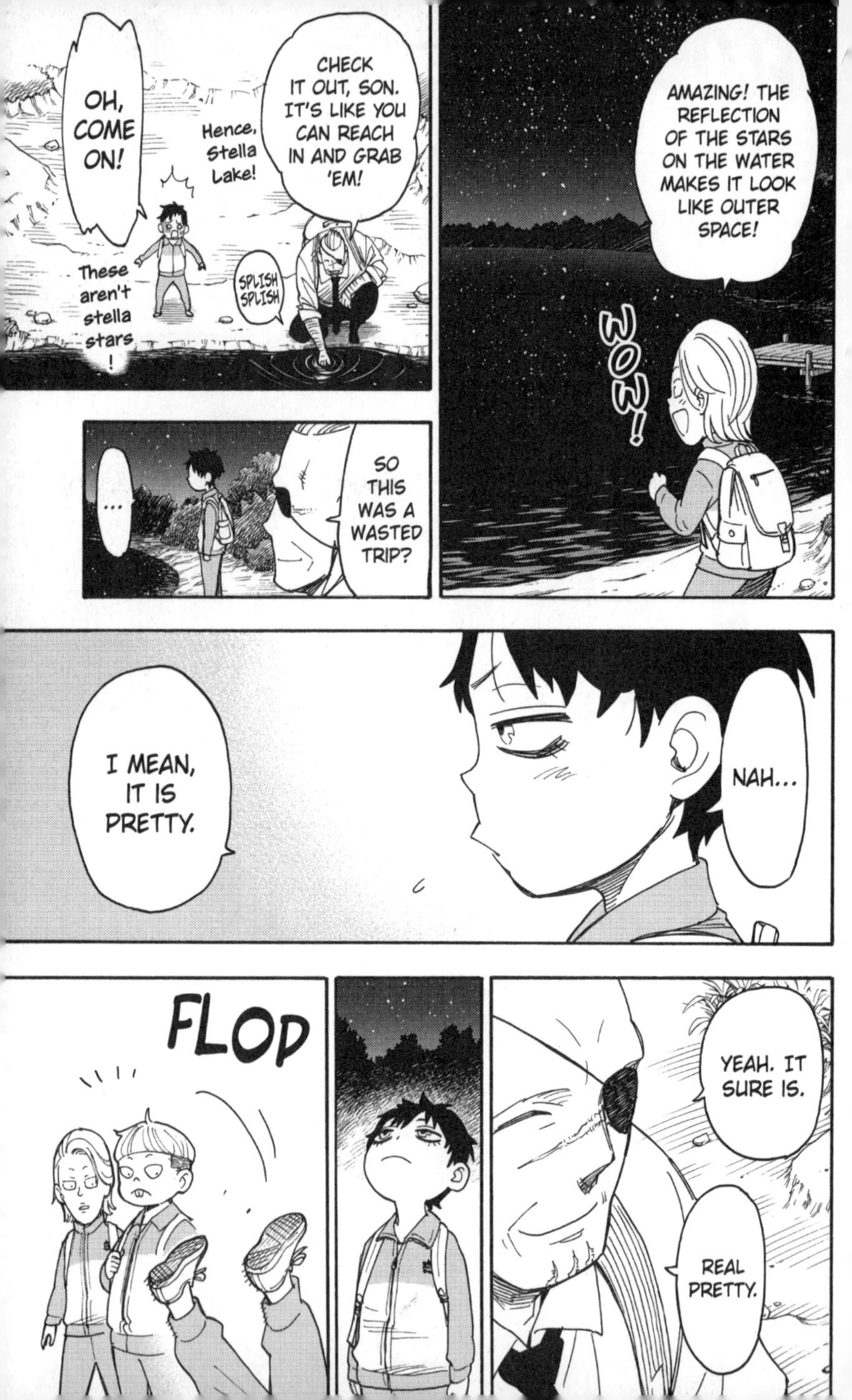
AMAZING! THE REFLECTION OF THE STARS ON THE WATER MAKES IT LOOK LIKE OUTER SPACE!
WOW!
CHECK IT OUT, SON. IT'S LIKE YOU CAN REACH IN AND GRAB 'EM!
Hence, Stella Lake!
SPLISH SPLISH
OH, COME ON!
These aren't stella stars!
SO THIS WAS A WASTED TRIP?
...
NAH...
I MEAN, IT IS PRETTY.
YEAH. IT SURE IS.
REAL PRETTY.
FLOP

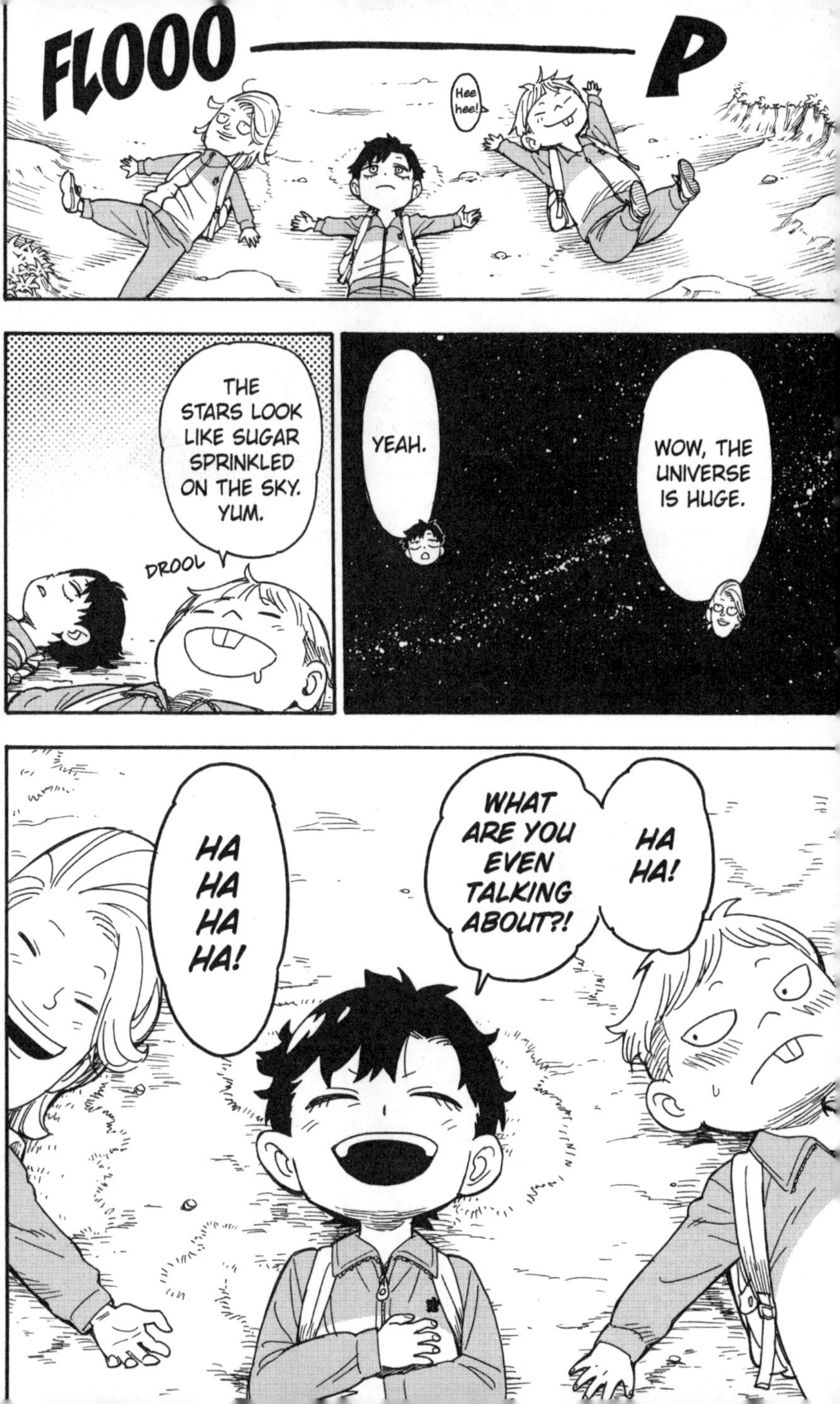
FLOOO—P
Hee hee!
WOW, THE UNIVERSE IS HUGE.
YEAH.
THE STARS LOOK LIKE SUGAR SPRINKLED ON THE SKY. YUM.
DROOL
HA HA!
WHAT ARE YOU EVEN TALKING ABOUT?!
HA HA HA HA!

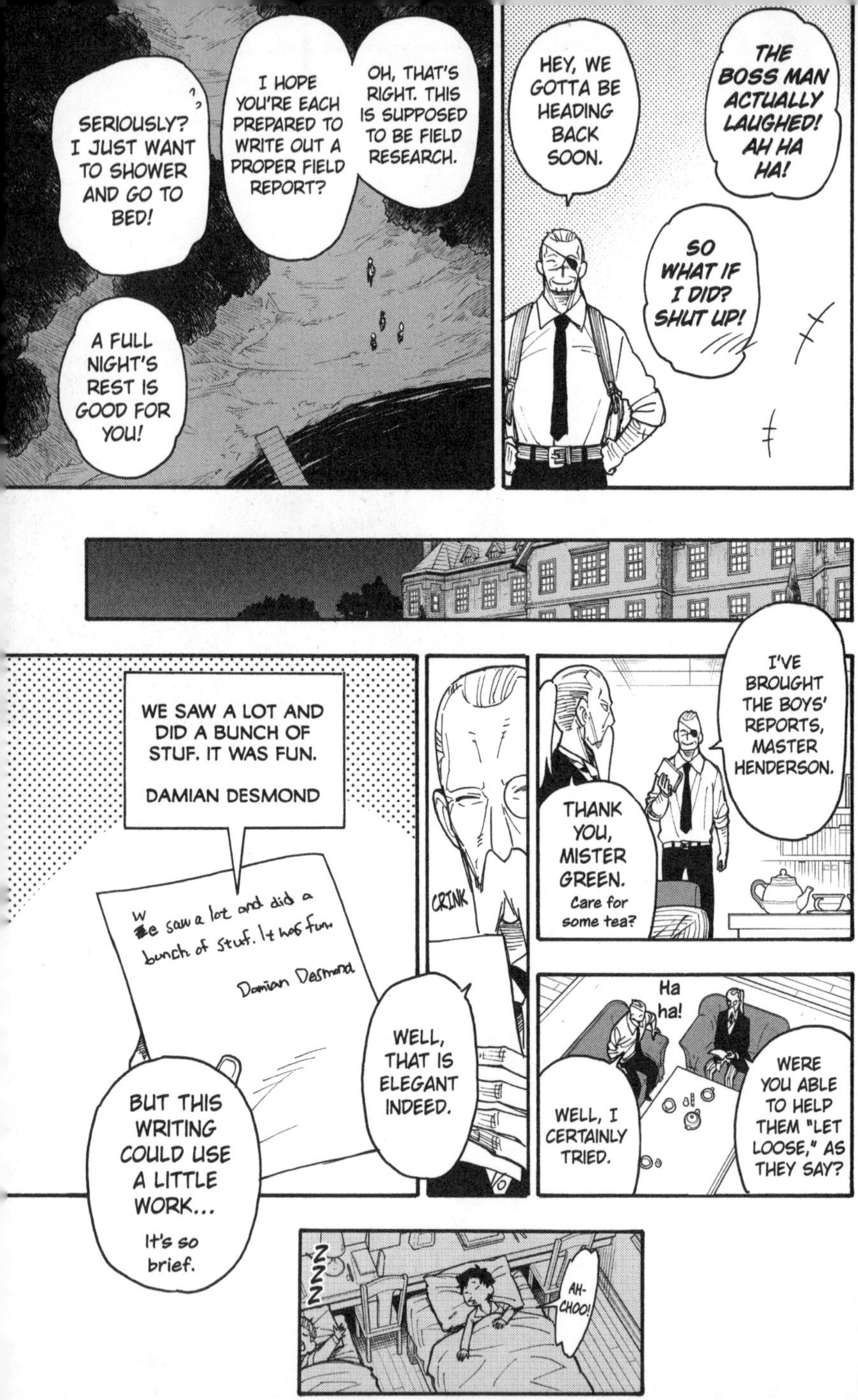
THE BOSS MAN ACTUALLY LAUGHED! AH HA HA!
SO WHAT IF I DID? SHUT UP!
HEY, WE GOTTA BE HEADING BACK SOON.
OH, THAT'S RIGHT. THIS IS SUPPOSED TO BE FIELD RESEARCH.
I HOPE YOU'RE EACH PREPARED TO WRITE OUT A PROPER FIELD REPORT?
SERIOUSLY? I JUST WANT TO SHOWER AND GO TO BED!
A FULL NIGHT'S REST IS GOOD FOR YOU!
I'VE BROUGHT THE BOYS' REPORTS, MASTER HENDERSON.
THANK YOU, MISTER GREEN.
Care for some tea?
Ha ha!
WERE YOU ABLE TO HELP THEM "LET LOOSE," AS THEY SAY?
WELL, I CERTAINLY TRIED.
CRINK
WELL, THAT IS ELEGANT INDEED.
WE SAW A LOT AND DID A BUNCH OF STUF. IT WAS FUN.
DAMIAN DESMOND
We saw a lot and did a bunch of stuf. It was fun.
Damian Desmond
BUT THIS WRITING COULD USE A LITTLE WORK...
It's so brief.
ZZZ
AH-CHOO!

SPY×FAMILY

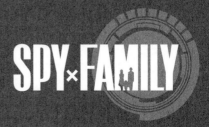

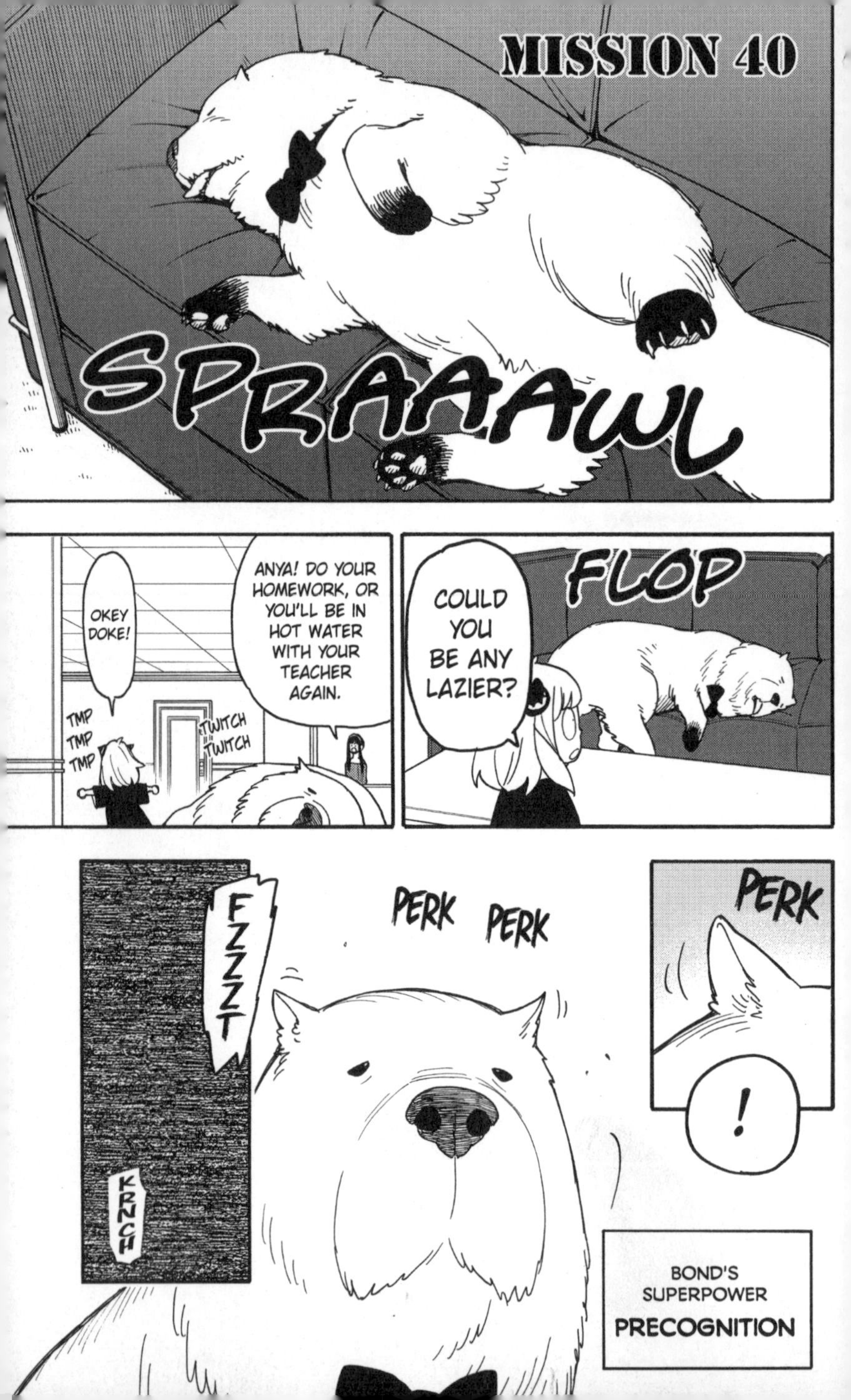
MISSION 40
SPRAAAWL
FLOP
COULD YOU BE ANY LAZIER?
ANYA! DO YOUR HOMEWORK, OR YOU'LL BE IN HOT WATER WITH YOUR TEACHER AGAIN.
OKEY DOKE!
TWITCH TWITCH
TMP TMP TMP
PERK
!
PERK PERK
FZZZT
KRNCH
BOND'S SUPERPOWER
PRECOGNITION

FZZ...

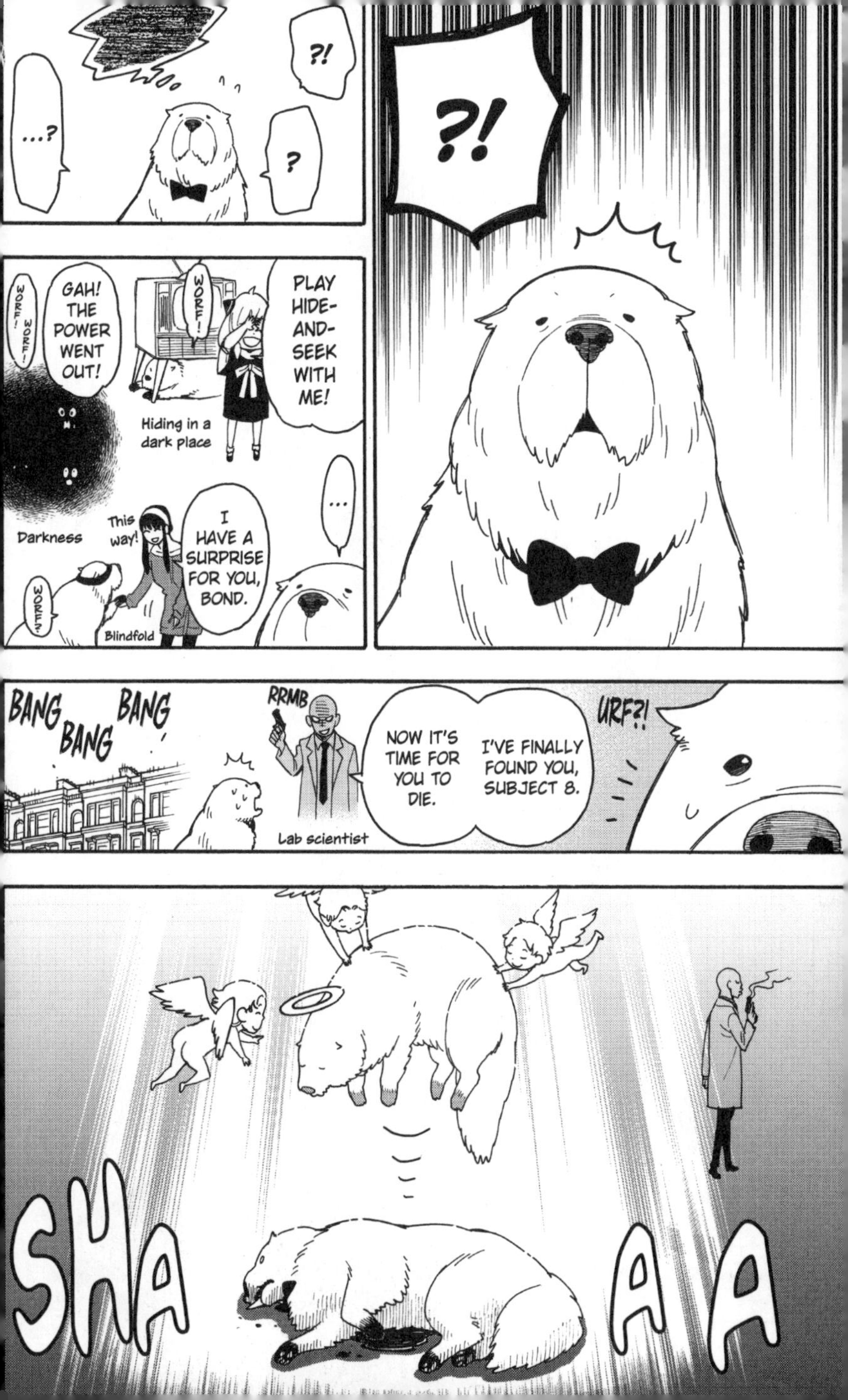
?!
?!
?
...?
PLAY HIDE-AND-SEEK WITH ME!
WORF!
Hiding in a dark place
GAH! THE POWER WENT OUT!
WORF! WORF!
...
I HAVE A SURPRISE FOR YOU, BOND.
This way!
Darkness
WORF?
Blindfold
URF?!
I'VE FINALLY FOUND YOU, SUBJECT 8.
NOW IT'S TIME FOR YOU TO DIE.
RRMB
Lab scientist
BANG
BANG
BANG
SHAAAA

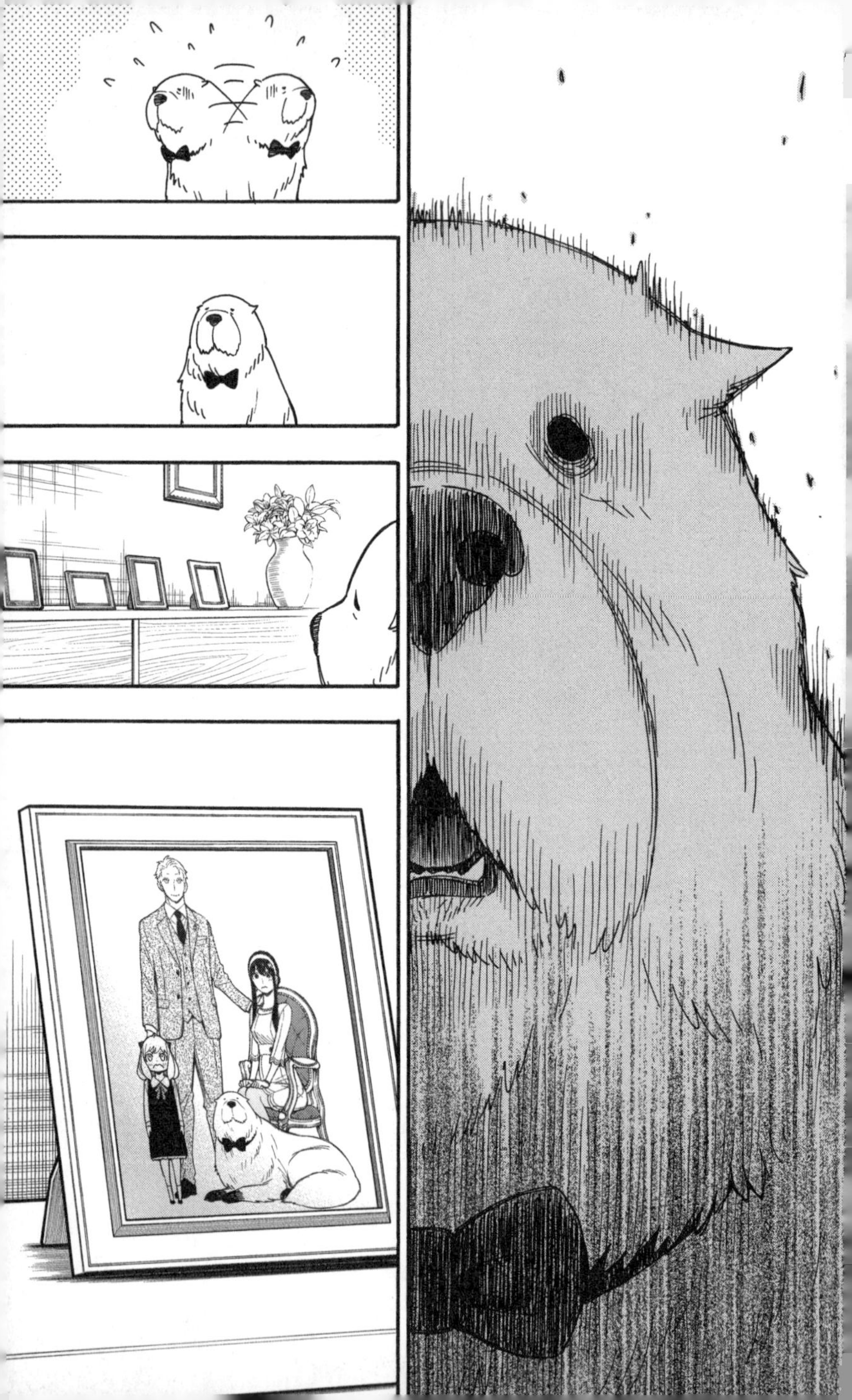

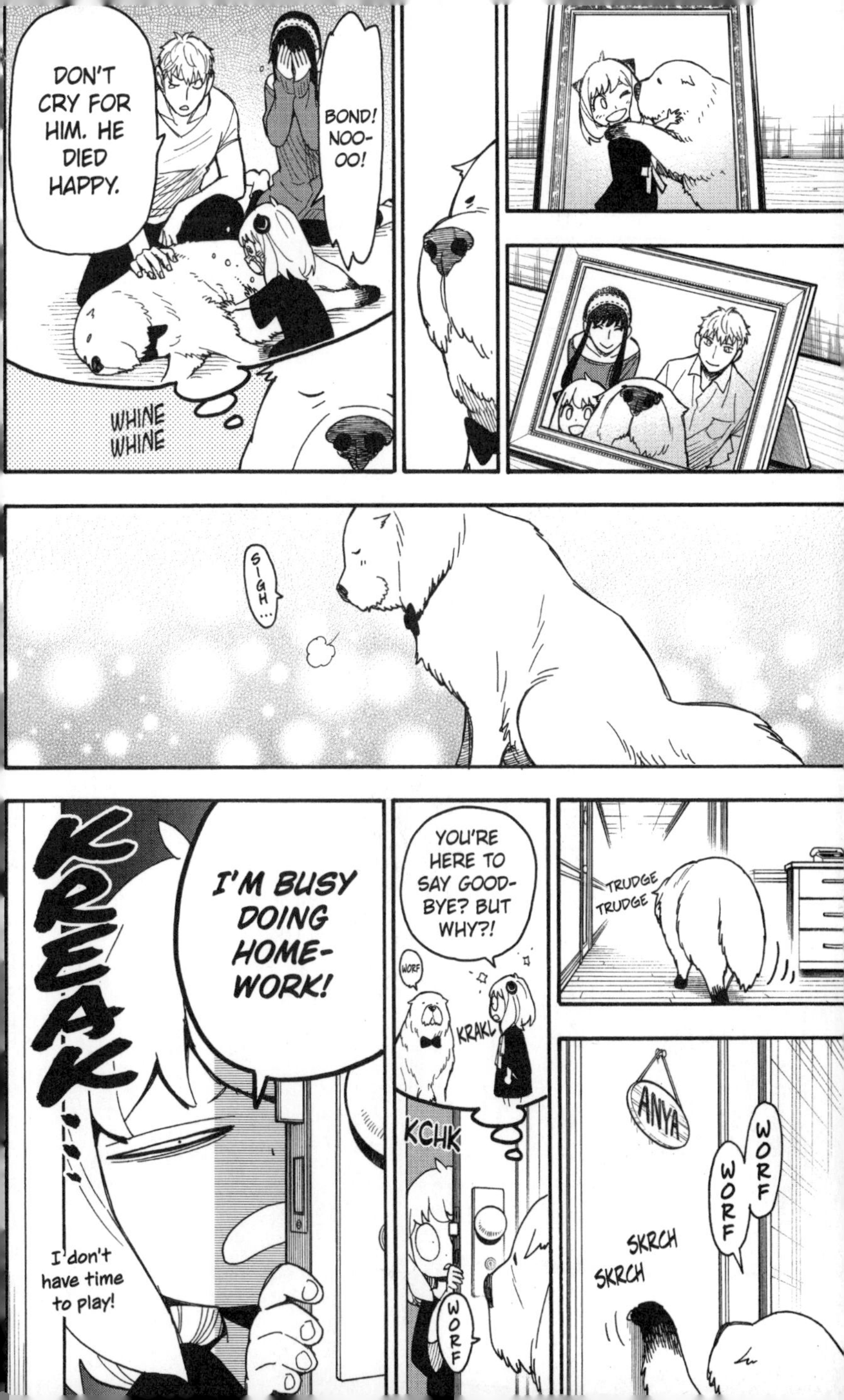

BOND! NOOO-OO!
DON'T CRY FOR HIM. HE DIED HAPPY.
WHINE WHINE
SIGH...
TRUDGE TRUDGE
ANYA
WORF
WORF
SKRCH SKRCH
YOU'RE HERE TO SAY GOOD-BYE? BUT WHY?!
WORF
KRAKL
KCHK
WORF
I'M BUSY DOING HOME-WORK!
KREAK...
I don't have time to play!

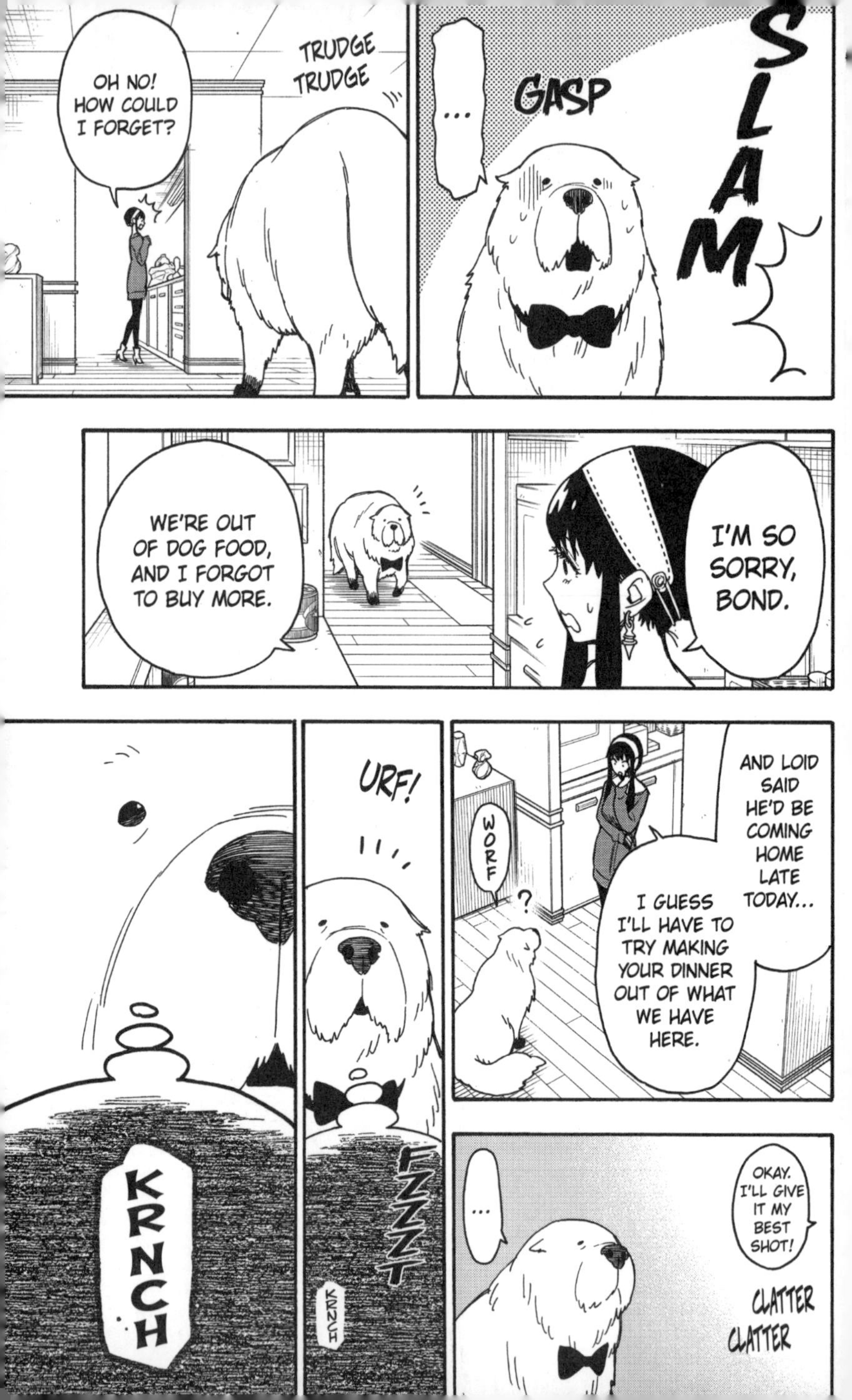
SLAM
...
GASP
TRUDGE TRUDGE
OH NO! HOW COULD I FORGET?
I'M SO SORRY, BOND.
WE'RE OUT OF DOG FOOD, AND I FORGOT TO BUY MORE.
AND LOID SAID HE'D BE COMING HOME LATE TODAY...
I GUESS I'LL HAVE TO TRY MAKING YOUR DINNER OUT OF WHAT WE HAVE HERE.
WORF
?
OKAY. I'LL GIVE IT MY BEST SHOT!
...
CLATTER CLATTER
URF!
FZZZT
KRNCH
KRNCH

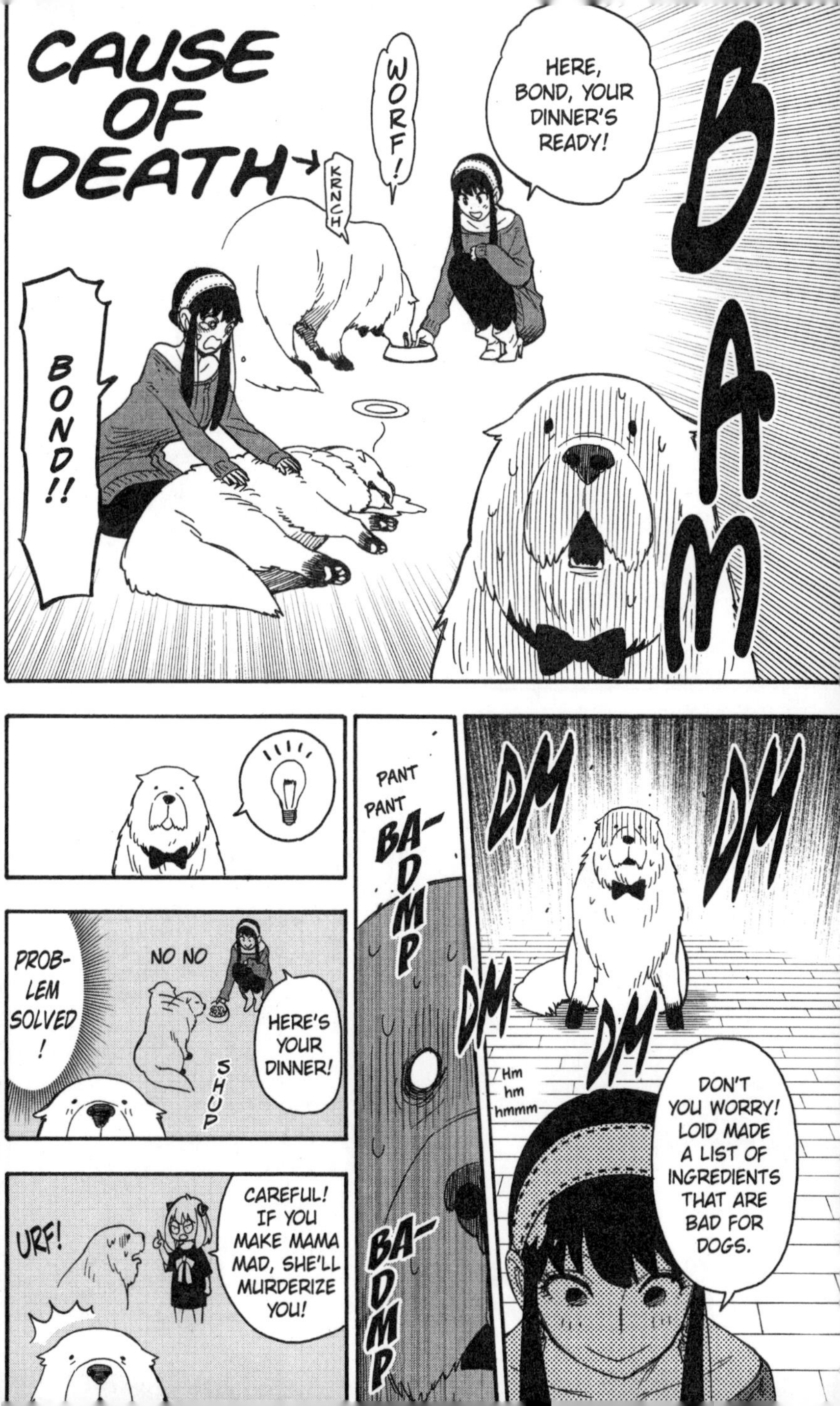
BAM
HERE, BOND, YOUR DINNER'S READY!
WORF!
KRNCH
CAUSE OF DEATH
BOND!!
DM DM
DM DM
DM
DM
DON'T YOU WORRY! LOID MADE A LIST OF INGREDIENTS THAT ARE BAD FOR DOGS.
Hm hm hmmm
PANT PANT
BA-DMP
BA-DMP
PROB-LEM SOLVED!
NO NO
HERE'S YOUR DINNER!
SHUP
CAREFUL! IF YOU MAKE MAMA MAD, SHE'LL MURDERIZE YOU!
URF!

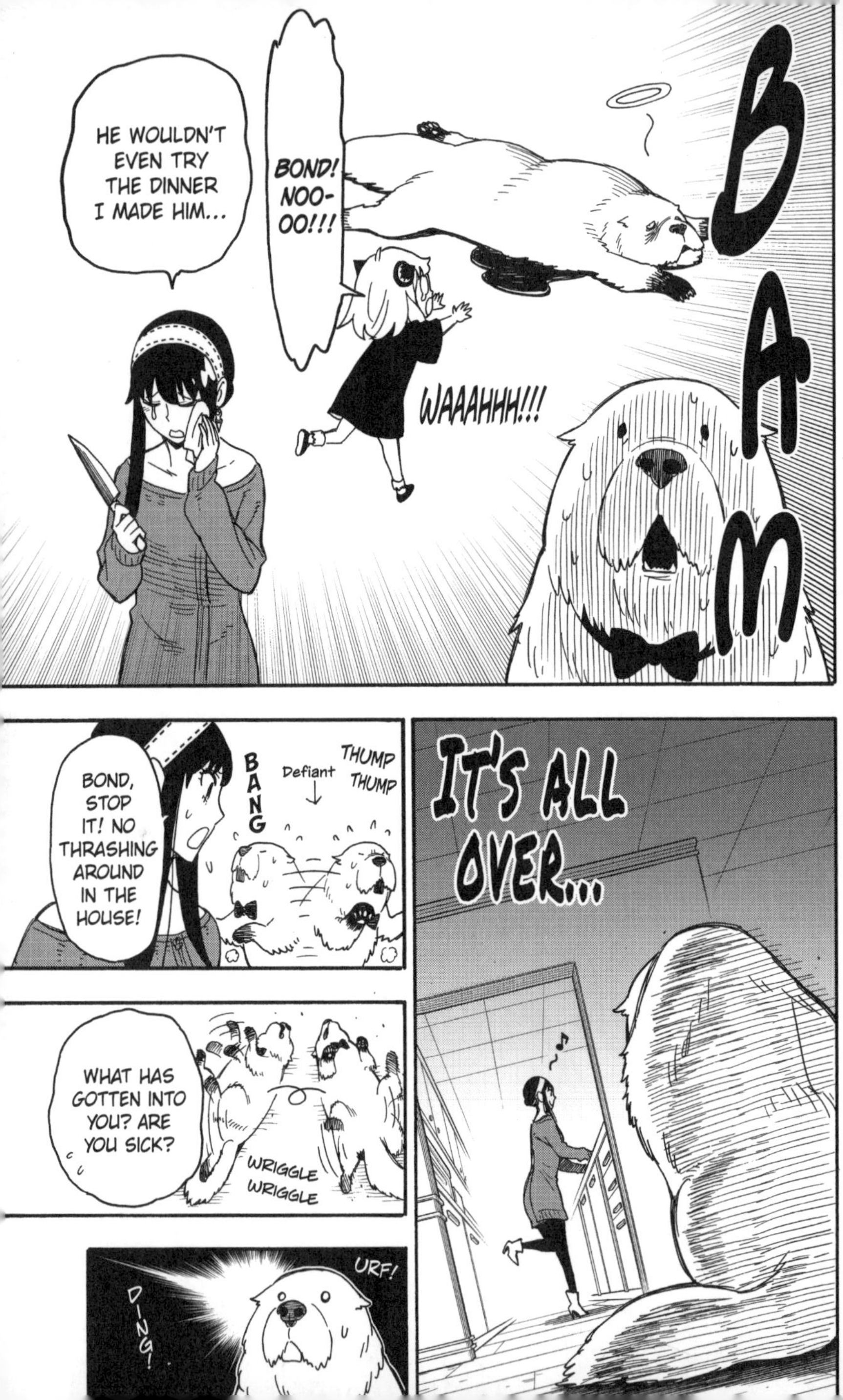
BAM
BOND! NOO-OO!!!
WAAAHHH!!!
HE WOULDN'T EVEN TRY THE DINNER I MADE HIM...
IT'S ALL OVER...
THUMP THUMP
BANG
Defiant
BOND, STOP IT! NO THRASHING AROUND IN THE HOUSE!
WHAT HAS GOTTEN INTO YOU? ARE YOU SICK?
WRIGGLE WRIGGLE
URF!
DING!

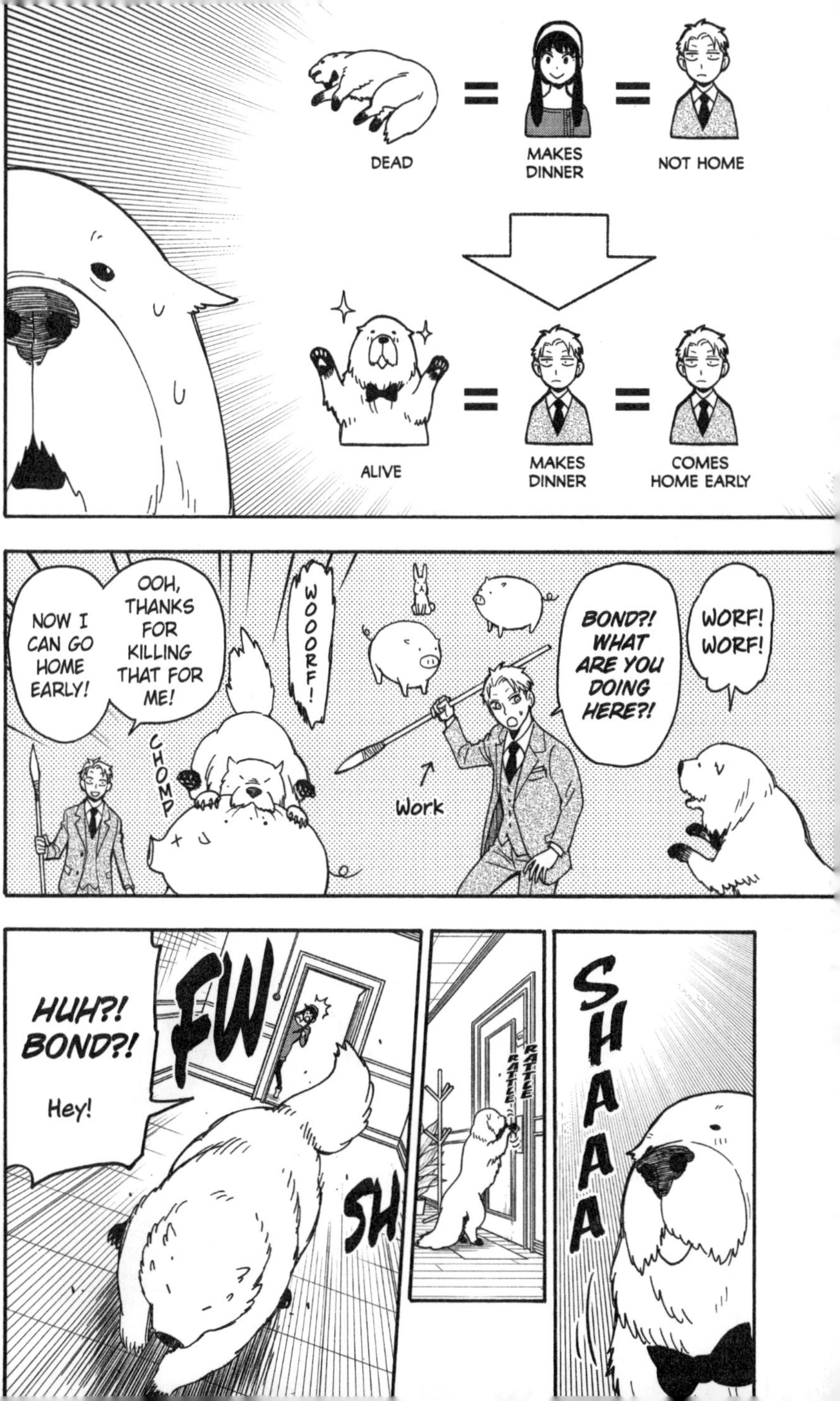
DEAD
MAKES DINNER
NOT HOME
ALIVE
MAKES DINNER
COMES HOME EARLY
WORF! WORF!
BOND?! WHAT ARE YOU DOING HERE?!
Work
WOOOORF!
CHOMP
OOH, THANKS FOR KILLING THAT FOR ME!
NOW I CAN GO HOME EARLY!
SHAAAA
RATTLE
RATTLE
FW
HUH?! BOND?!
Hey!
SH

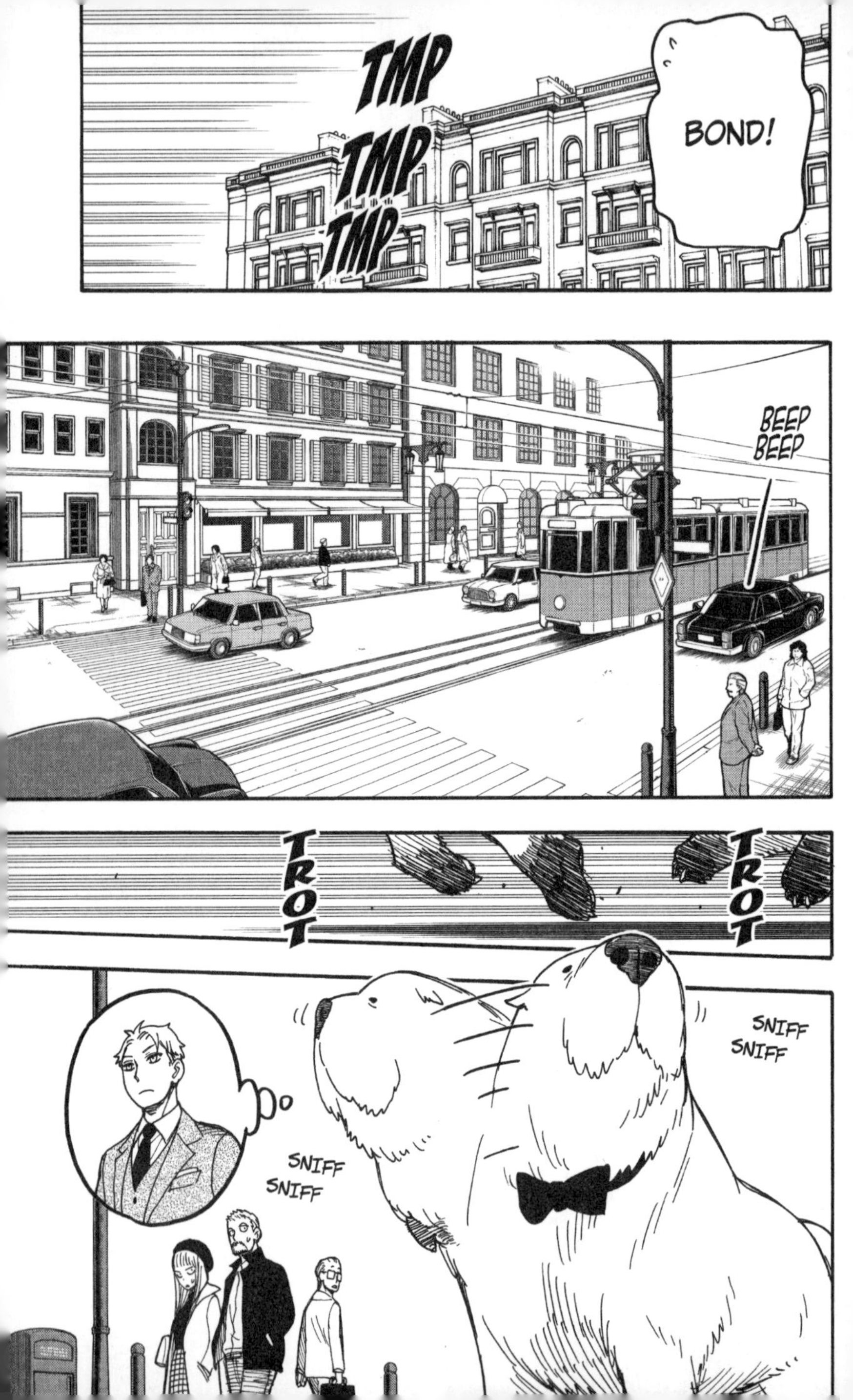
BOND!
TMP TMP TMP
BEEP BEEP
TROT TROT
SNIFF SNIFF
SNIFF SNIFF

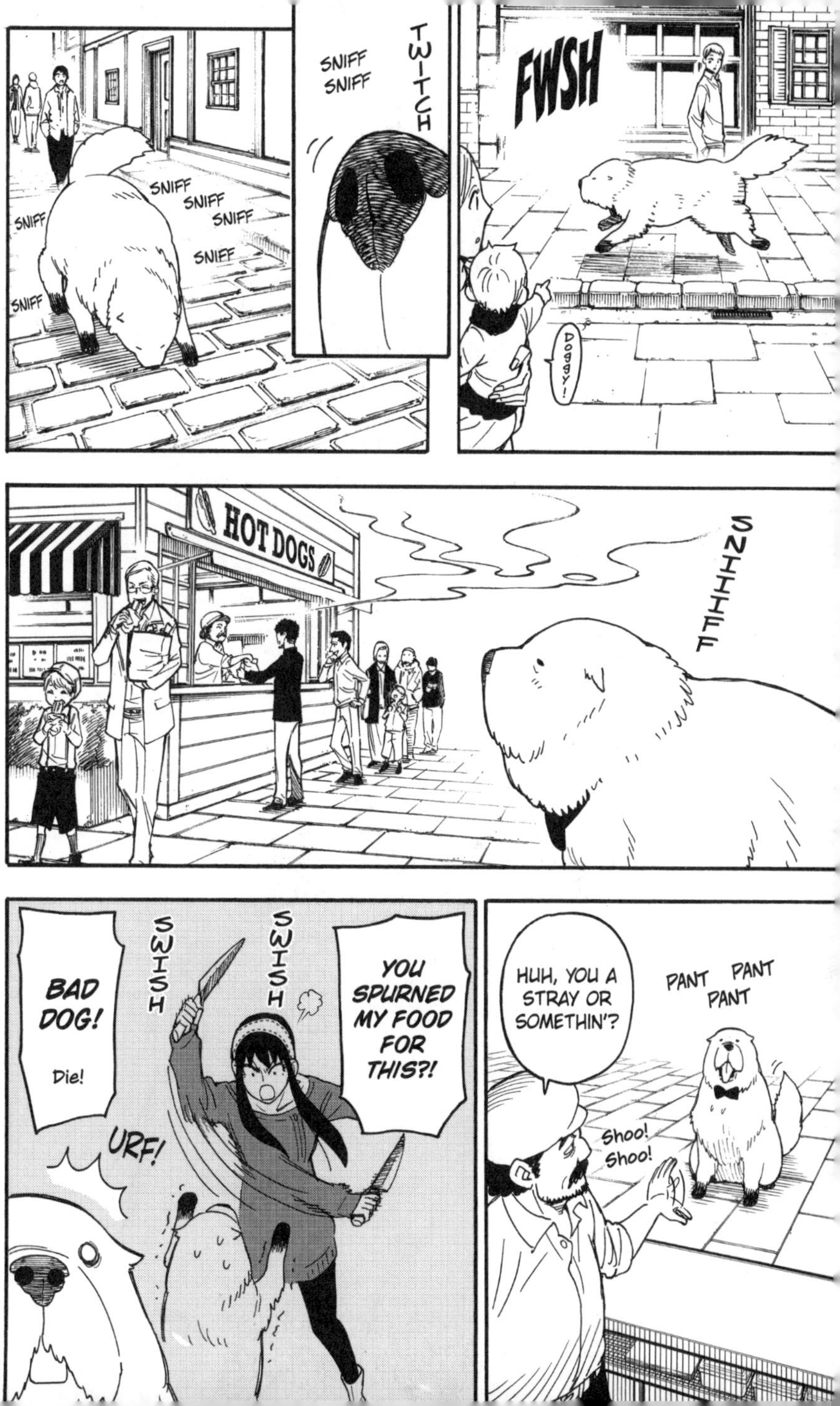
FWSH
Doggy!
SNIFF SNIFF
TWITCH
SNIFF
SNIFF
SNIFF
SNIFF
SNIFF
SNIFF
HOT DOGS
SNIIIFF
HUH, YOU A STRAY OR SOMETHIN'?
PANT PANT PANT
Shoo! Shoo!
YOU SPURNED MY FOOD FOR THIS?!
SWISH
SWISH
BAD DOG!
Die!
URF!

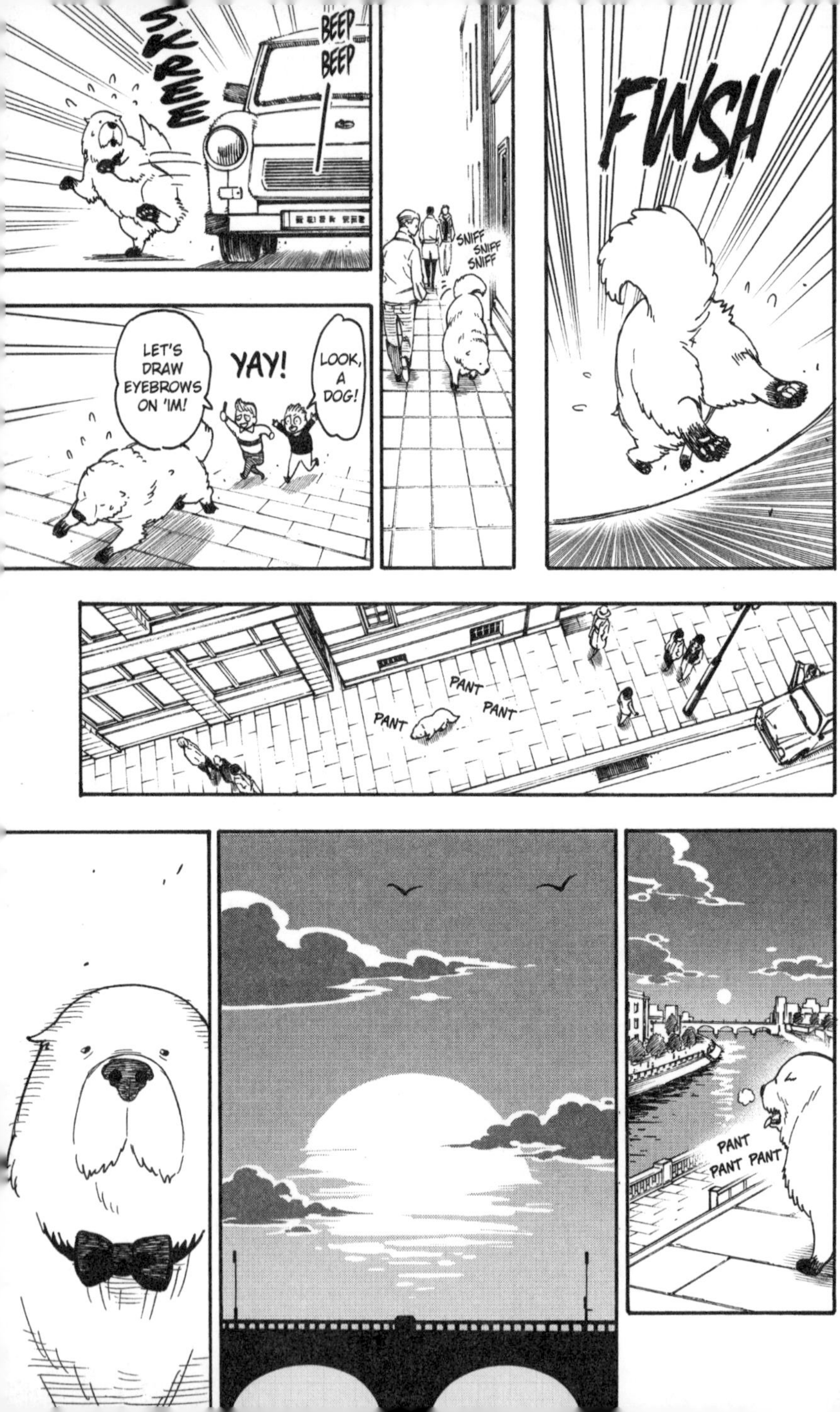
FWSH
SNIFF SNIFF SNIFF
BEEP BEEP
SKREE
LOOK, A DOG!
YAY!
LET'S DRAW EYEBROWS ON 'IM!
PANT PANT
PANT
PANT PANT PANT

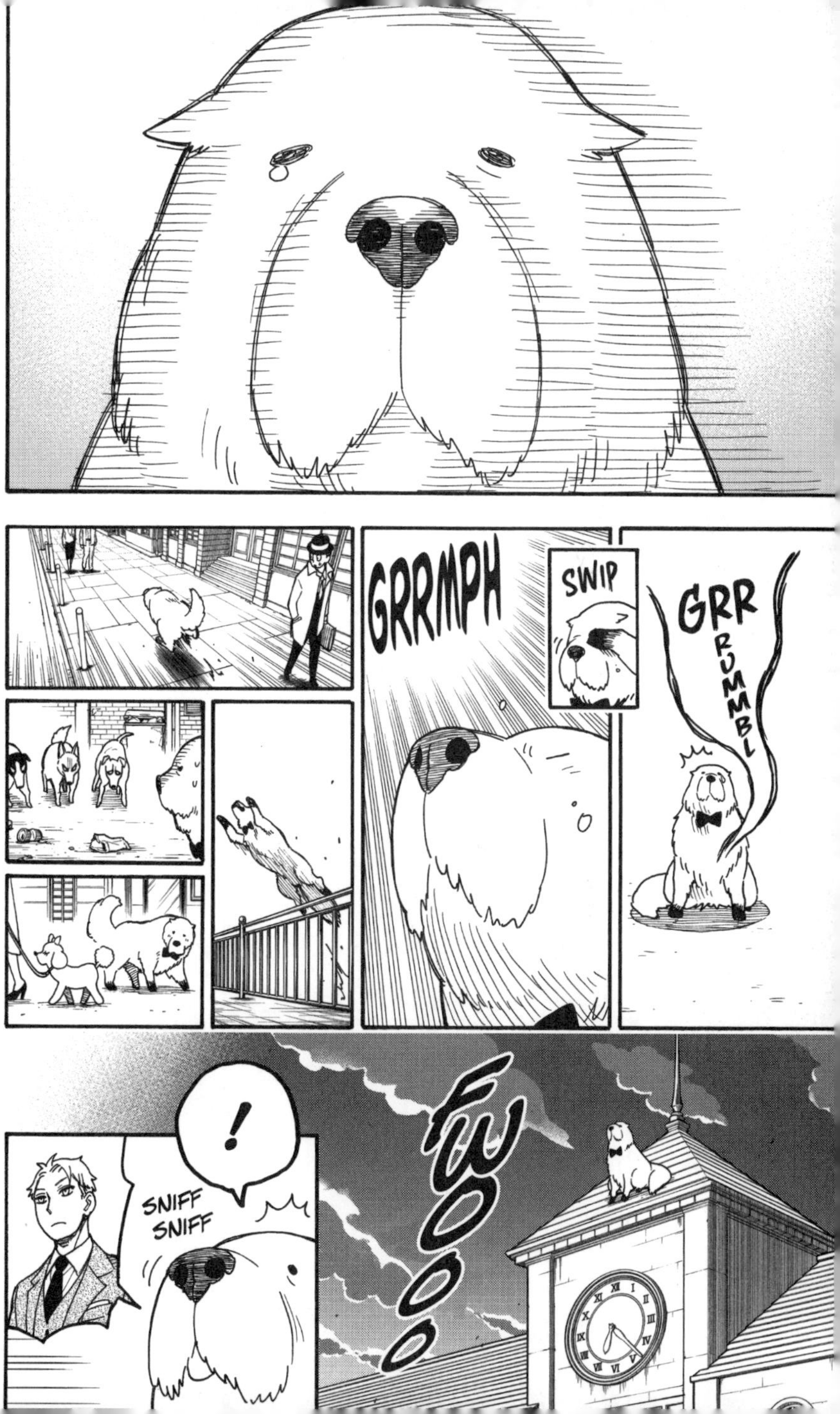
GRR
RUMMBL
SWIP
GRRMPH
FWOOOOO
!
SNIFF SNIFF

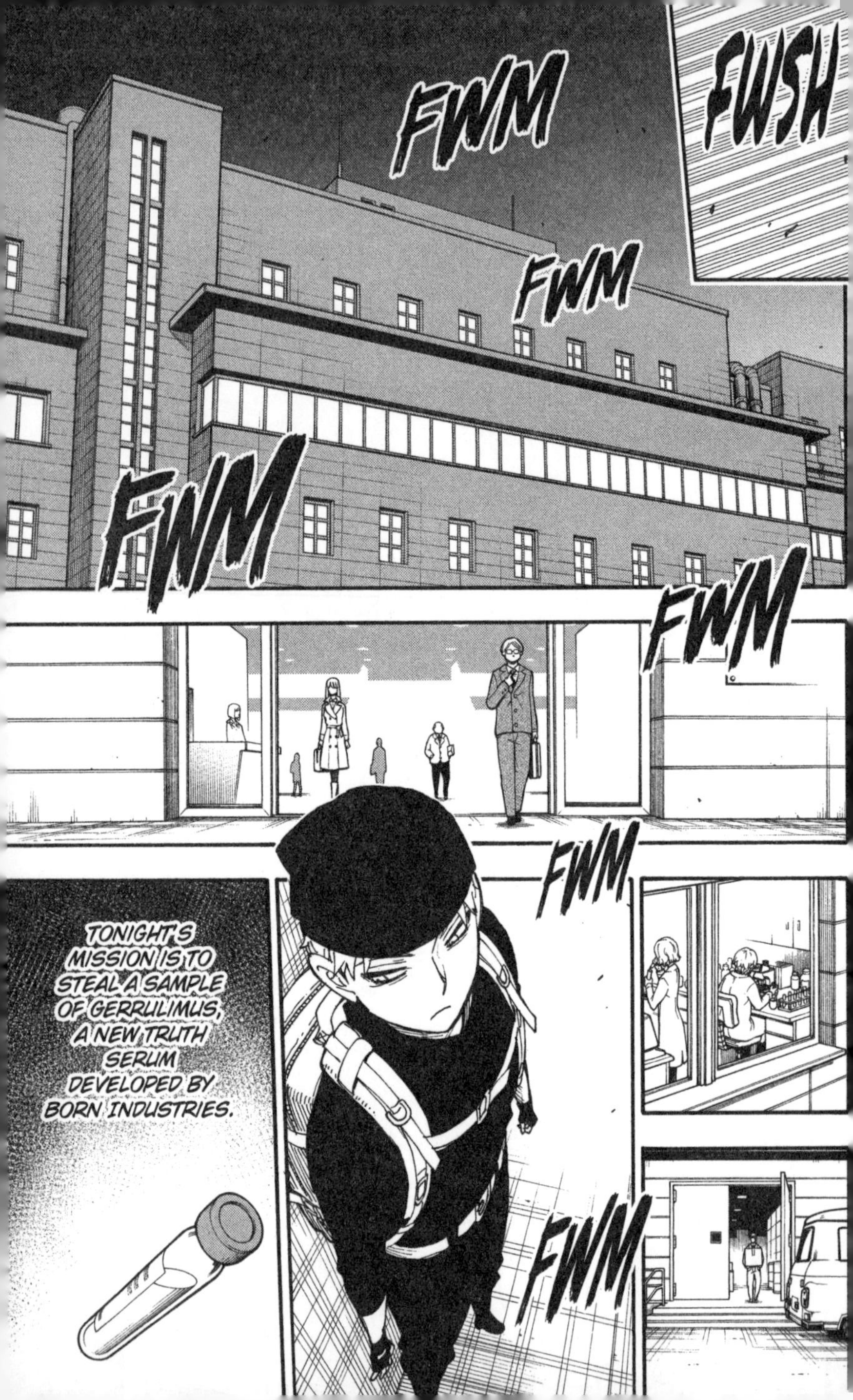
FWSH
FWM
FWM
FWM
FWM
FWM
FWM
TONIGHT'S MISSION IS TO STEAL A SAMPLE OF GERRULIMUS, A NEW TRUTH SERUM DEVELOPED BY BORN INDUSTRIES.

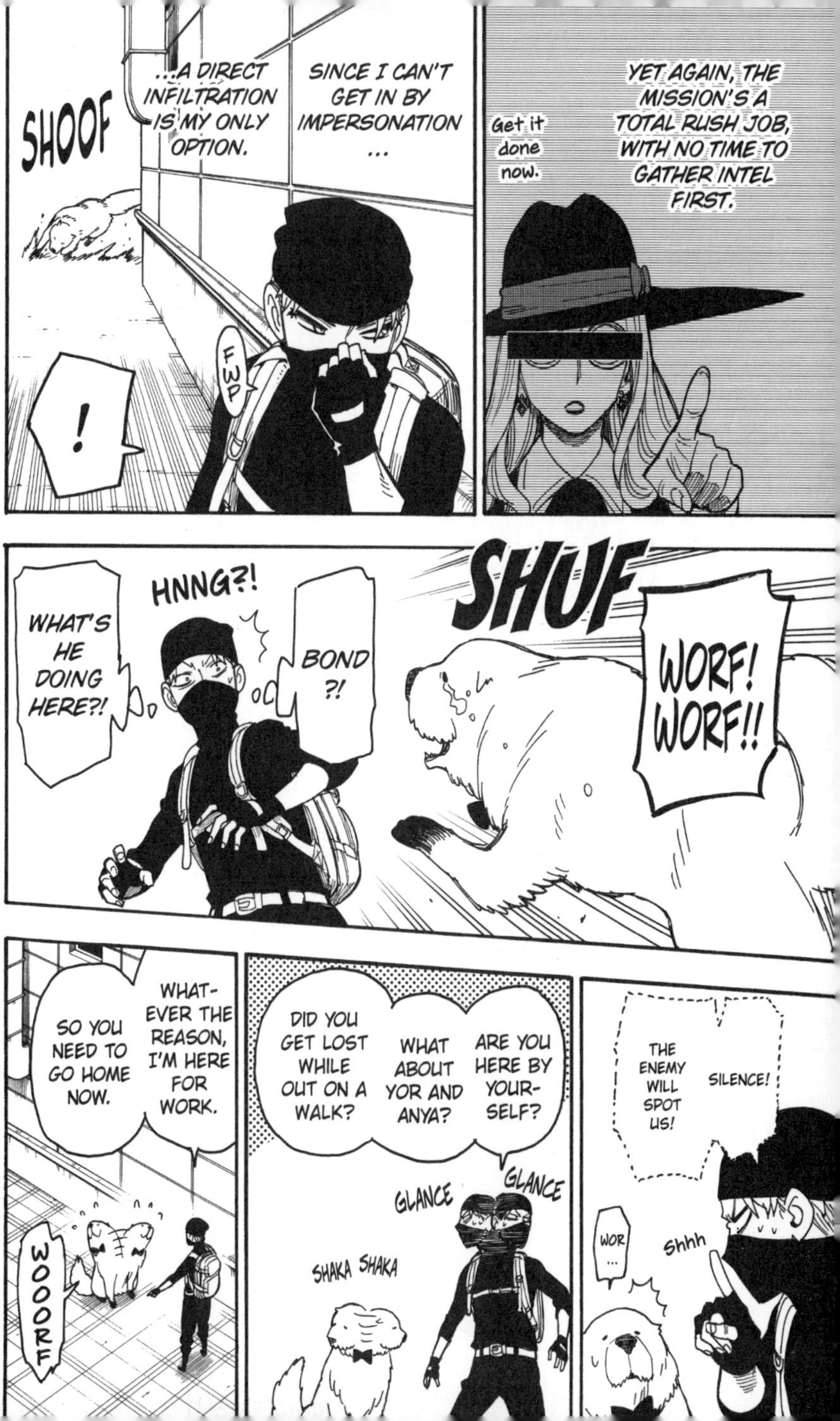
YET AGAIN, THE MISSION'S A TOTAL RUSH JOB, WITH NO TIME TO GATHER INTEL FIRST.
Get it done now.
SINCE I CAN'T GET IN BY IMPERSONATION ...
...A DIRECT INFILTRATION IS MY ONLY OPTION.
SHOOF
FWP
!
SHUF
WORF! WORF!!
BOND ?!
HNNG?!
WHAT'S HE DOING HERE?!
SILENCE!
THE ENEMY WILL SPOT US!
WOR ...
Shhh
ARE YOU HERE BY YOURSELF?
WHAT ABOUT YOR AND ANYA?
DID YOU GET LOST WHILE OUT ON A WALK?
GLANCE
GLANCE
SHAKA SHAKA
WHATEVER THE REASON, I'M HERE FOR WORK.
SO YOU NEED TO GO HOME NOW.
WOOOORF

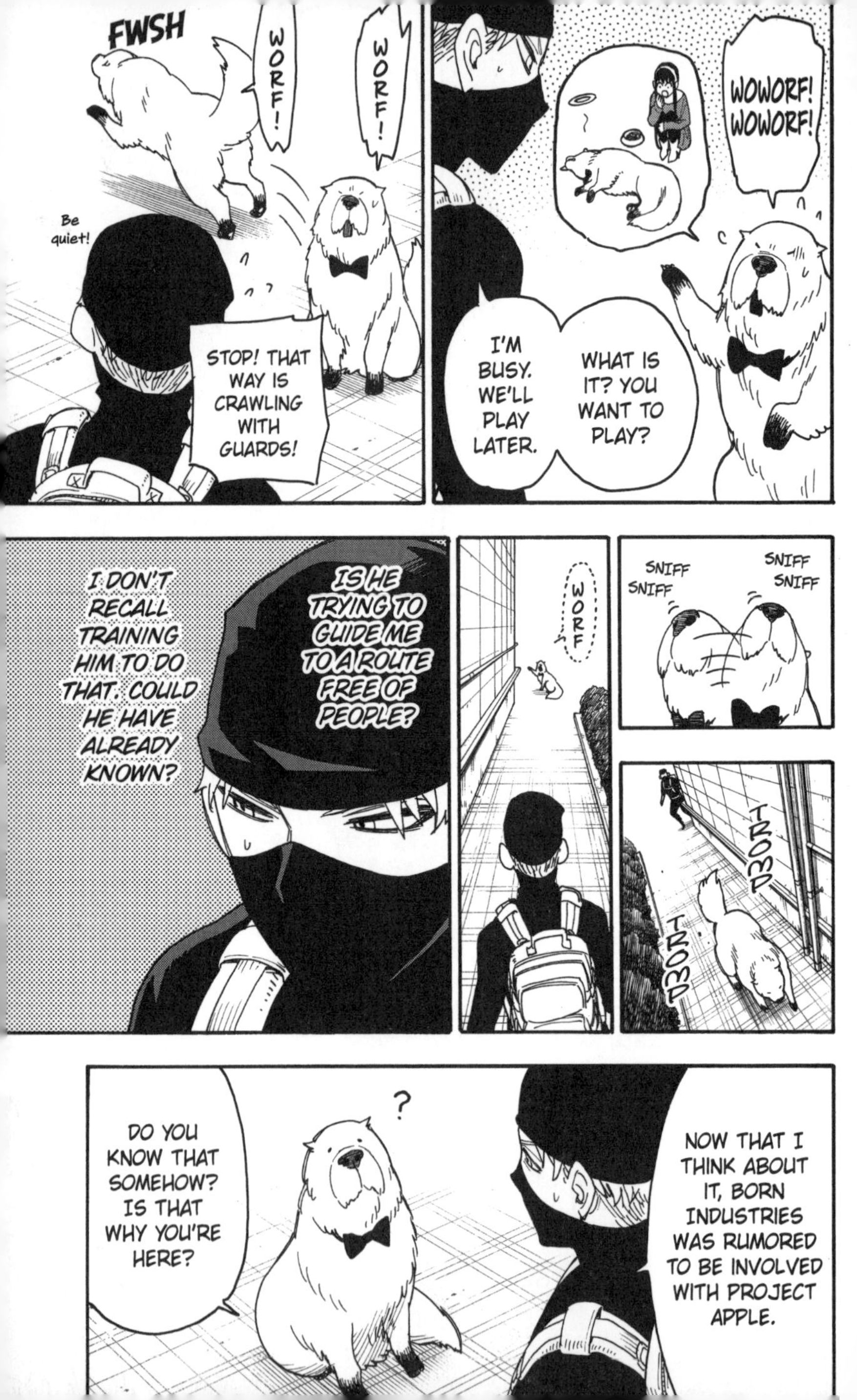
WOWORF! WOWORF!
WHAT IS IT? YOU WANT TO PLAY?
I'M BUSY. WE'LL PLAY LATER.
WORF!
WORF!
FWSH
Be quiet!
STOP! THAT WAY IS CRAWLING WITH GUARDS!
SNIFF SNIFF
SNIFF SNIFF
TROMP
TROMP
WORF
IS HE TRYING TO GUIDE ME TO A ROUTE FREE OF PEOPLE?
I DON'T RECALL TRAINING HIM TO DO THAT. COULD HE HAVE ALREADY KNOWN?
NOW THAT I THINK ABOUT IT, BORN INDUSTRIES WAS RUMORED TO BE INVOLVED WITH PROJECT APPLE.
?
DO YOU KNOW THAT SOMEHOW? IS THAT WHY YOU'RE HERE?

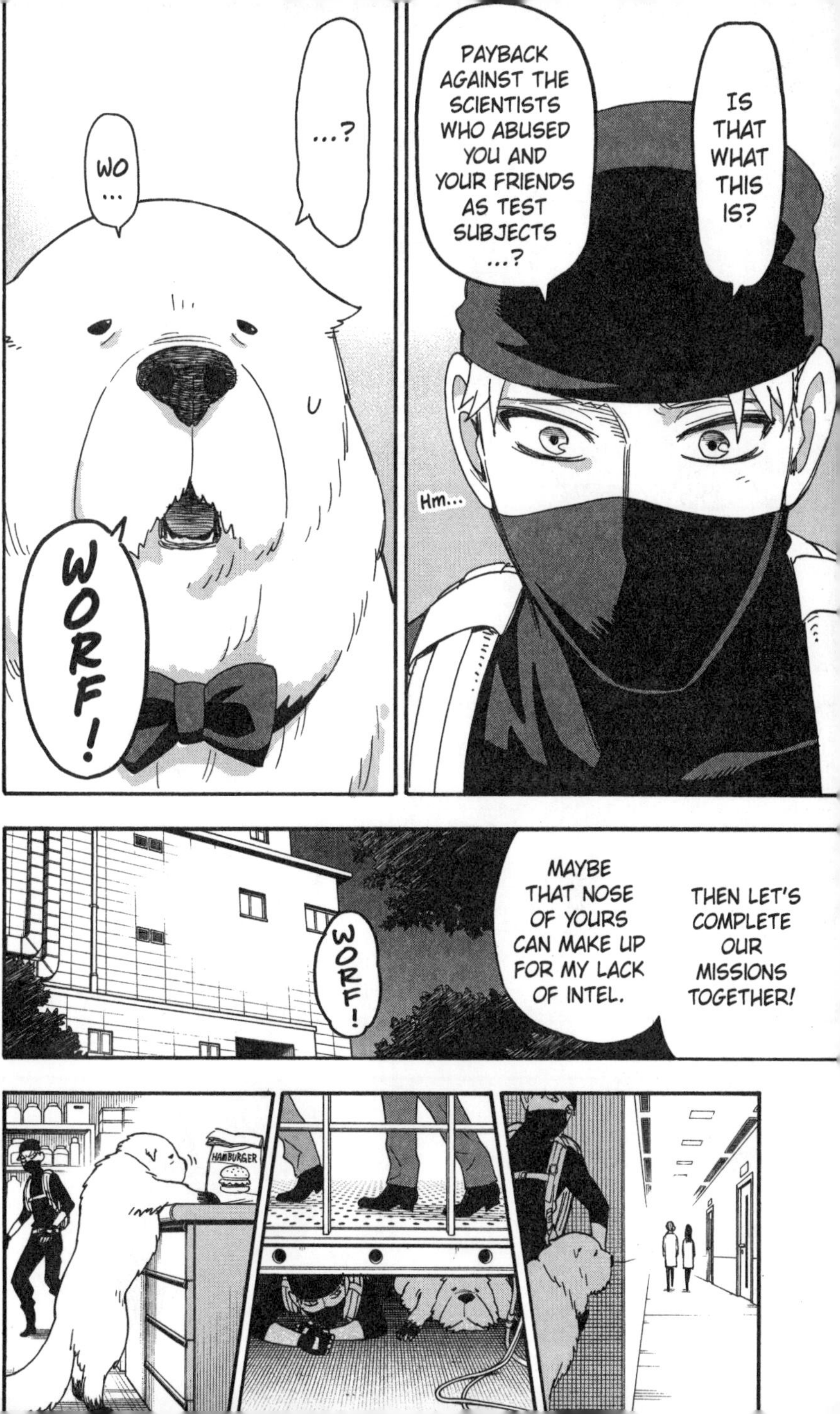
IS THAT WHAT THIS IS?
PAYBACK AGAINST THE SCIENTISTS WHO ABUSED YOU AND YOUR FRIENDS AS TEST SUBJECTS ...?
Hm...
...?
WO ...
WORF!
THEN LET'S COMPLETE OUR MISSIONS TOGETHER!
MAYBE THAT NOSE OF YOURS CAN MAKE UP FOR MY LACK OF INTEL.
WORF!
HAMBURGER

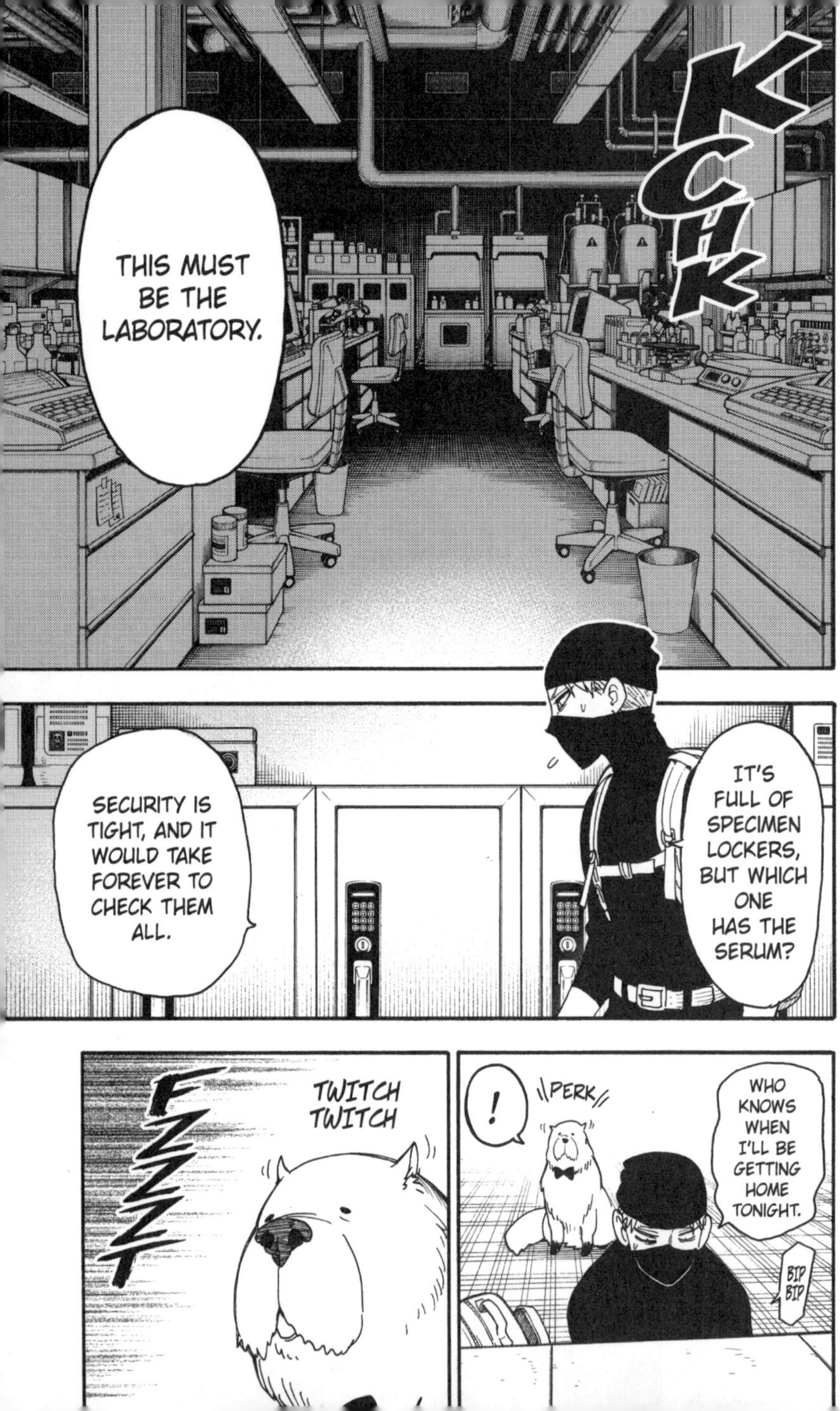
KCHK
THIS MUST BE THE LABORATORY.
IT'S FULL OF SPECIMEN LOCKERS, BUT WHICH ONE HAS THE SERUM?
SECURITY IS TIGHT, AND IT WOULD TAKE FOREVER TO CHECK THEM ALL.
WHO KNOWS WHEN I'LL BE GETTING HOME TONIGHT.
PERK
!
BIP BIP
TWITCH TWITCH
FZZZT

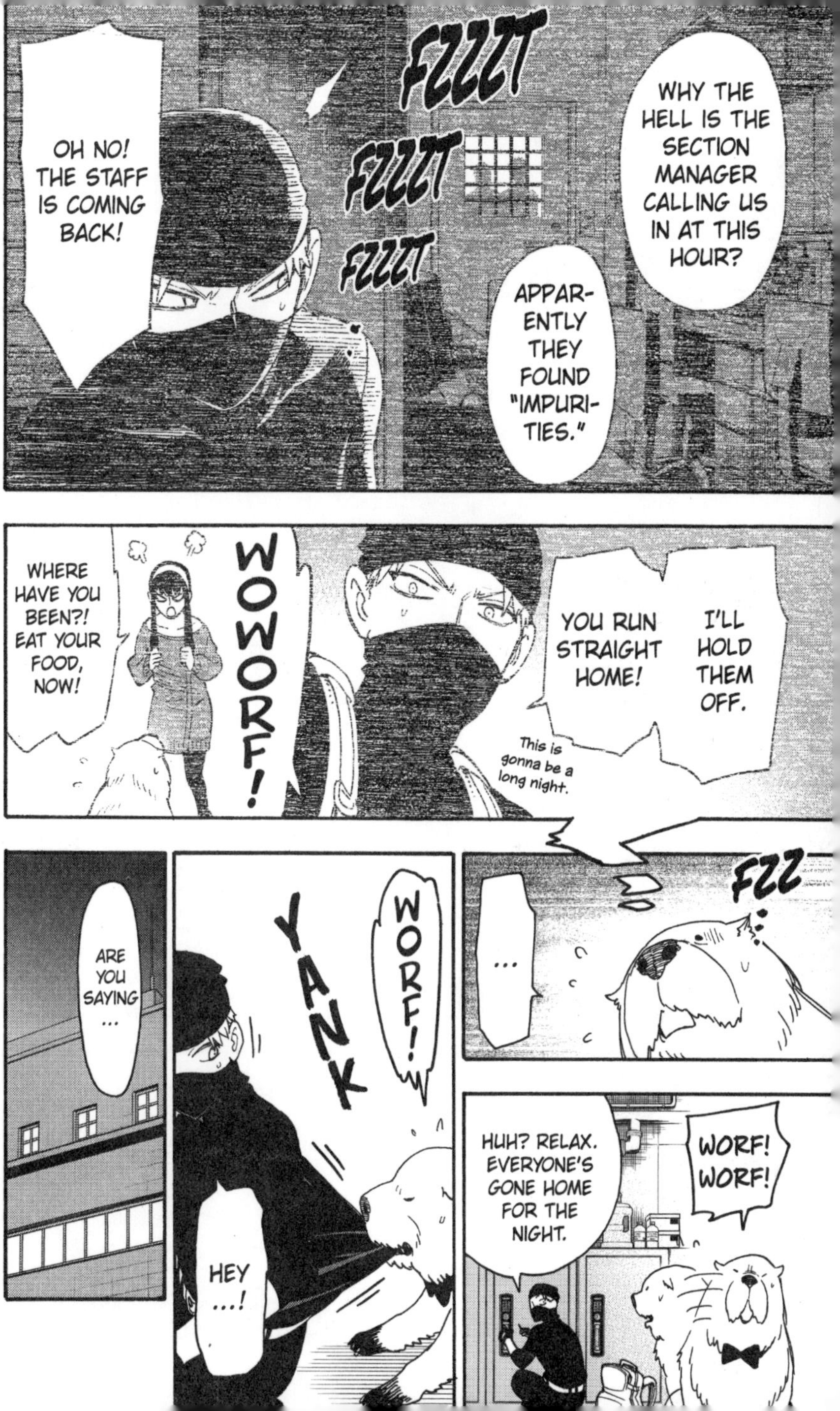
WHY THE HELL IS THE SECTION MANAGER CALLING US IN AT THIS HOUR?
APPARENTLY THEY FOUND "IMPURITIES."
FZZZT
FZZZT
FZZZT
OH NO! THE STAFF IS COMING BACK!
I'LL HOLD THEM OFF.
YOU RUN STRAIGHT HOME!
This is gonna be a long night.
WOWORF!
WHERE HAVE YOU BEEN?! EAT YOUR FOOD, NOW!
FZZ
...
WORF! WORF!
HUH? RELAX. EVERYONE'S GONE HOME FOR THE NIGHT.
WORF!
YANK
HEY ...!
ARE YOU SAYING ...

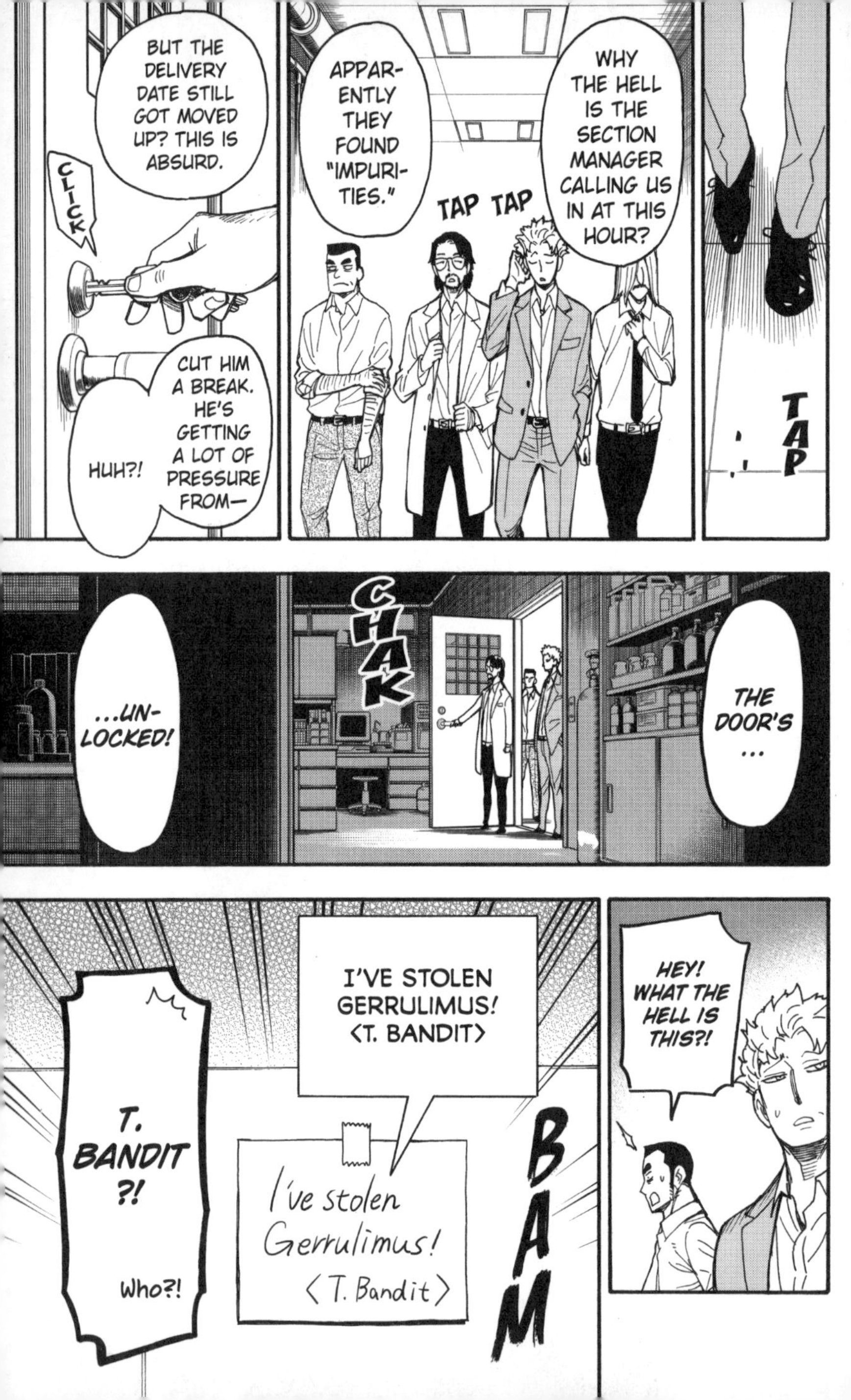
TAP
WHY THE HELL IS THE SECTION MANAGER CALLING US IN AT THIS HOUR?
APPARENTLY THEY FOUND "IMPURITIES."
TAP TAP
BUT THE DELIVERY DATE STILL GOT MOVED UP? THIS IS ABSURD.
CLICK
CUT HIM A BREAK. HE'S GETTING A LOT OF PRESSURE FROM—
HUH?!
THE DOOR'S...
CHAK
...UNLOCKED!
HEY! WHAT THE HELL IS THIS?!
I'VE STOLEN GERRULIMUS! <T. BANDIT>
BAM
I've stolen Gerrulimus! <T. Bandit>
T. BANDIT?!
Who?!

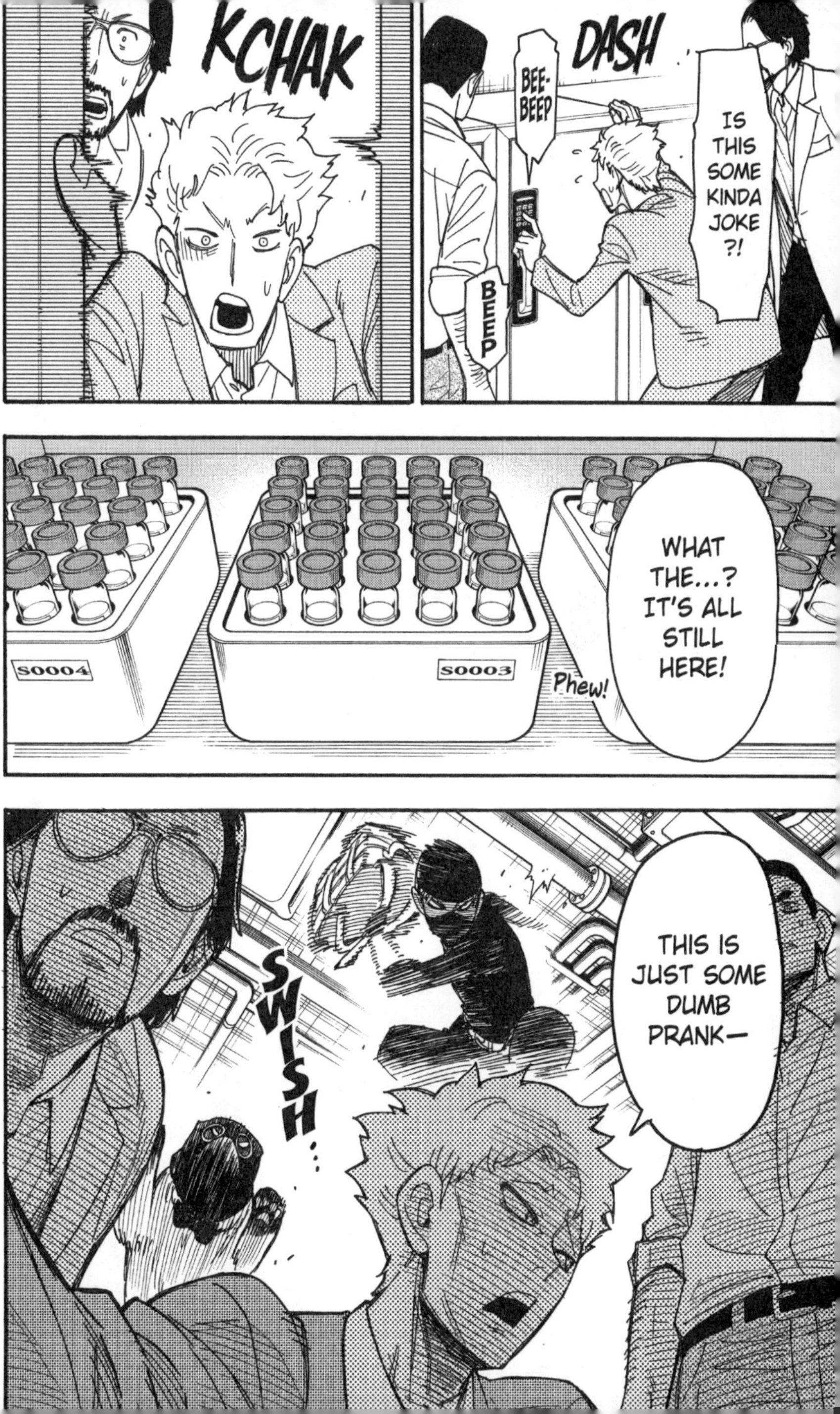
IS THIS SOME KINDA JOKE?!
DASH
BEE-BEEP
BEEP
KCHAK
WHAT THE...? IT'S ALL STILL HERE!
Phew!
S0003
S0004
THIS IS JUST SOME DUMB PRANK—
SWISH...

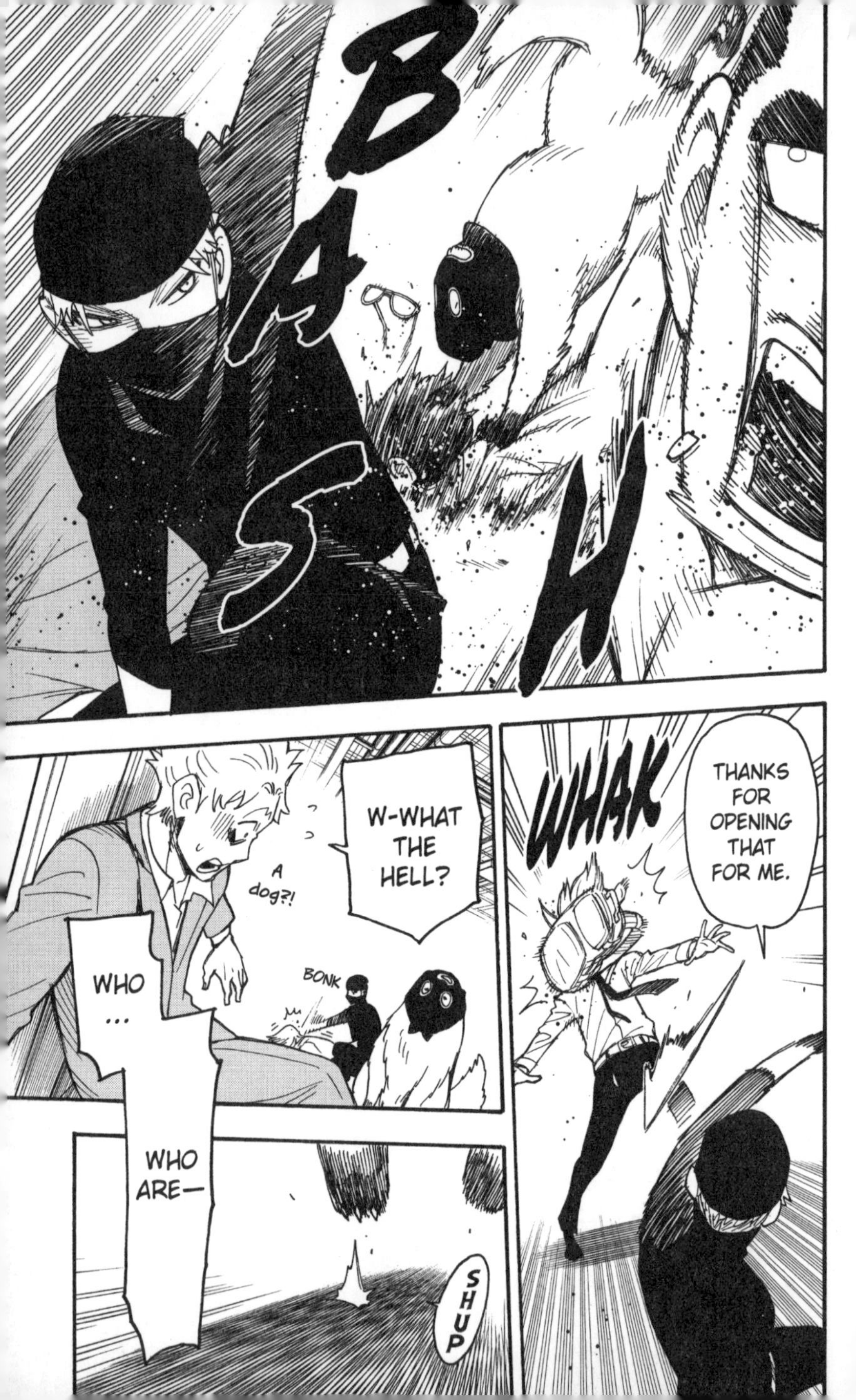
BASH
WHAK
THANKS FOR OPENING THAT FOR ME.
W-WHAT THE HELL?
A dog?!
BONK
WHO ...
WHO ARE—
SHUP

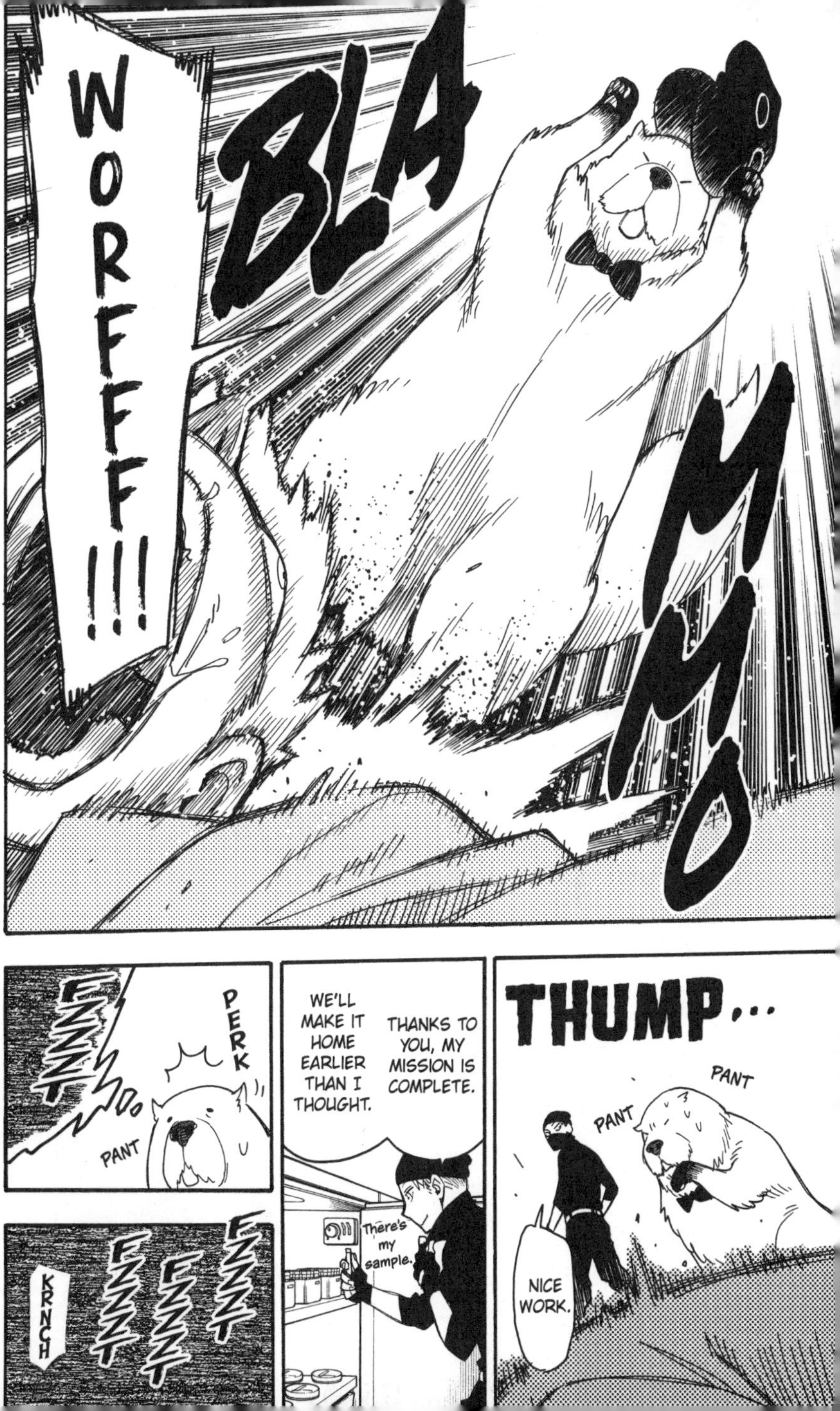
BLAMMO
WORFFF!!!
THUMP...
PANT
PANT
NICE WORK.
THANKS TO YOU, MY MISSION IS COMPLETE.
WE'LL MAKE IT HOME EARLIER THAN I THOUGHT.
There's my sample.
FZZZT
PERK
PANT
FZZZT
FZZZT
FZZZT
KRNCH

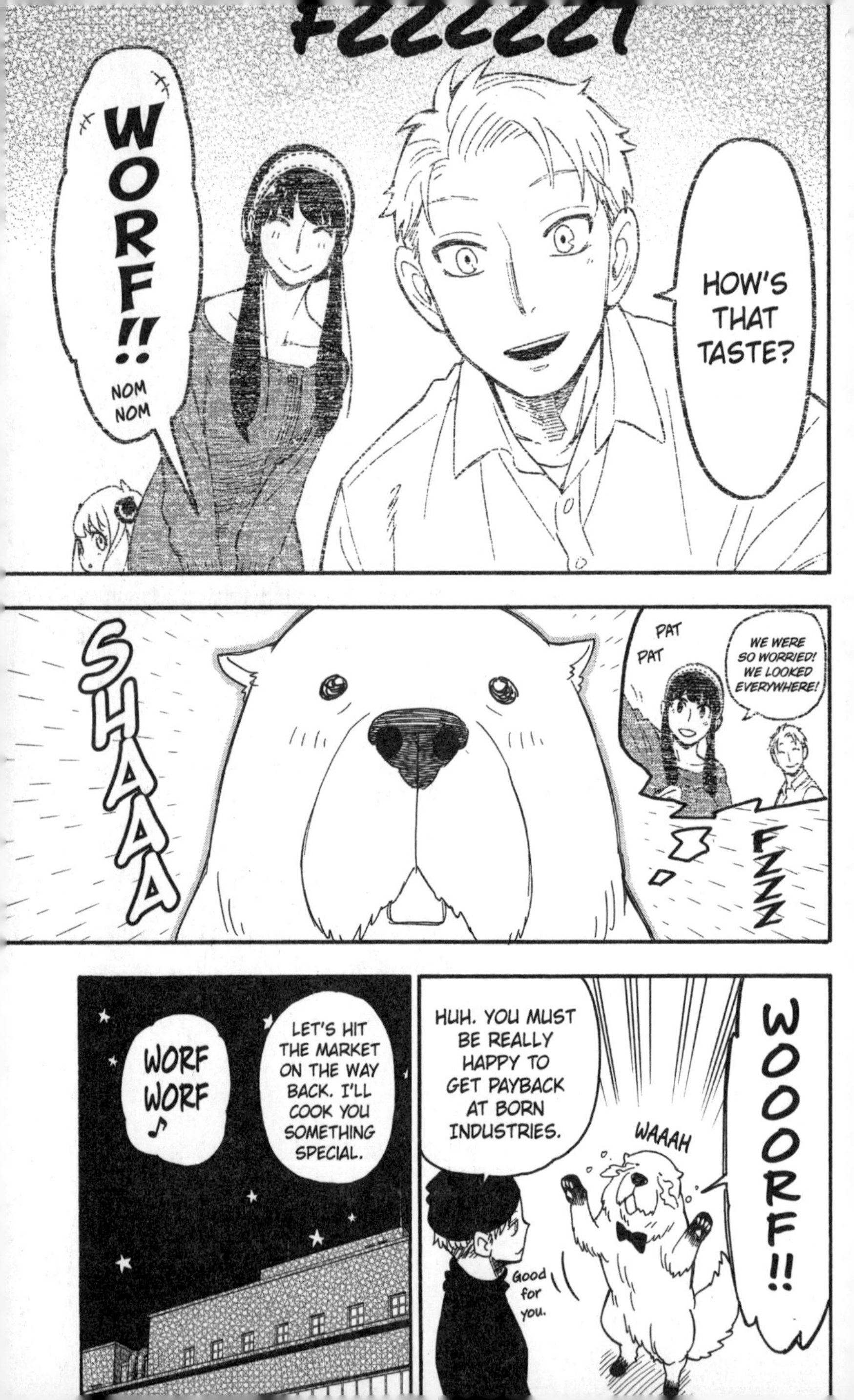
FZZZZZT
HOW'S THAT TASTE?
WORF!!
NOM NOM
PAT PAT
WE WERE SO WORRIED! WE LOOKED EVERYWHERE!
FZZZ
SHAAAA
WOOOORF!!
HUH. YOU MUST BE REALLY HAPPY TO GET PAYBACK AT BORN INDUSTRIES.
WAAAH
Good for you.
LET'S HIT THE MARKET ON THE WAY BACK. I'LL COOK YOU SOMETHING SPECIAL.
WORF WORF ♪

SPY×FAMILY

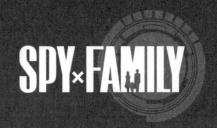

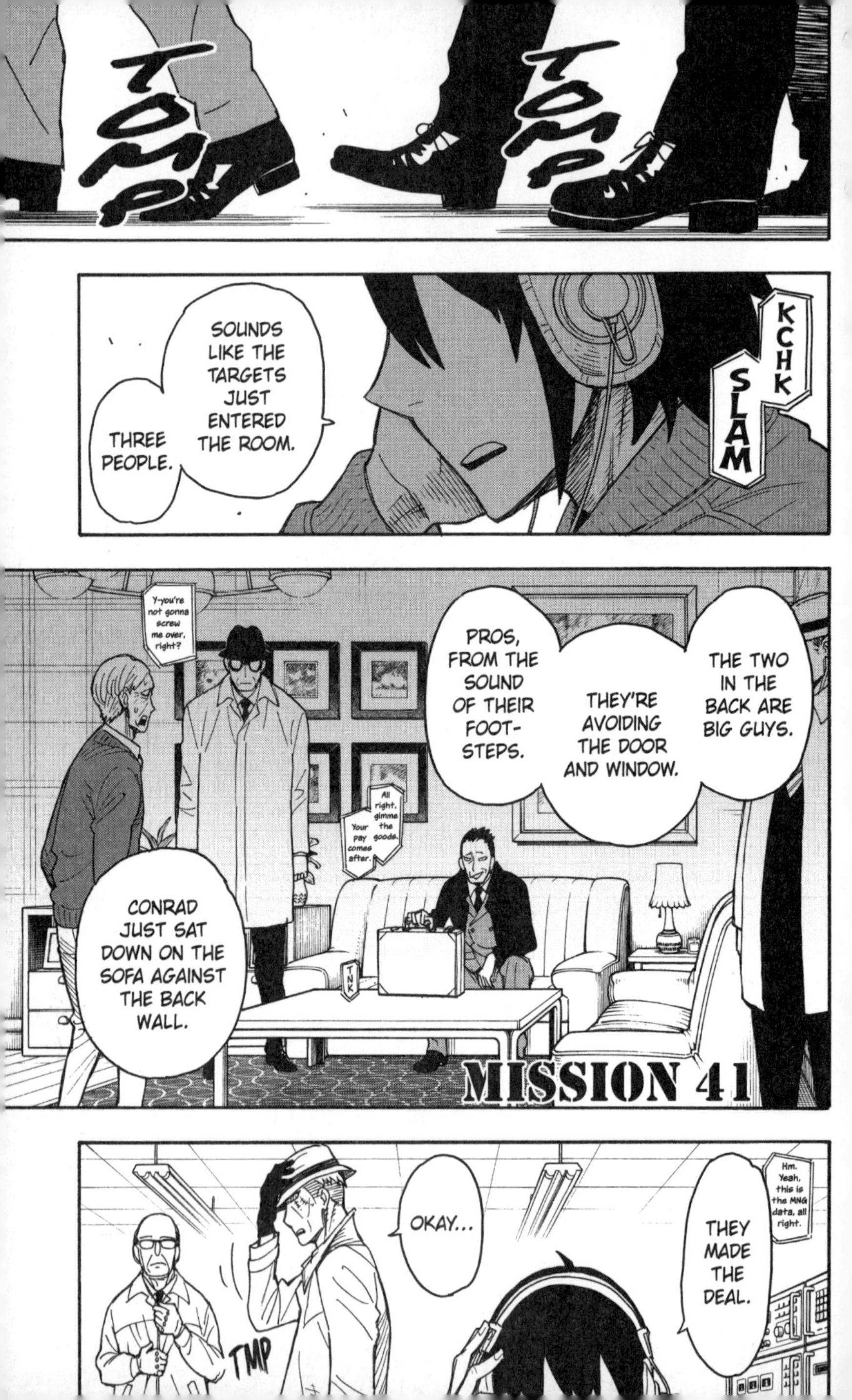
TOMP
TOMP
KCHK
SLAM
SOUNDS LIKE THE TARGETS JUST ENTERED THE ROOM.
THREE PEOPLE.
THE TWO IN THE BACK ARE BIG GUYS.
THEY'RE AVOIDING THE DOOR AND WINDOW.
PROS, FROM THE SOUND OF THEIR FOOT-STEPS.
All right, gimme the goods.
Your pay comes after.
Y-you're not gonna screw me over, right?
TNK
CONRAD JUST SAT DOWN ON THE SOFA AGAINST THE BACK WALL.
MISSION 41
Hm. Yeah, this is the MNG data, all right.
THEY MADE THE DEAL.
OKAY...
TMP

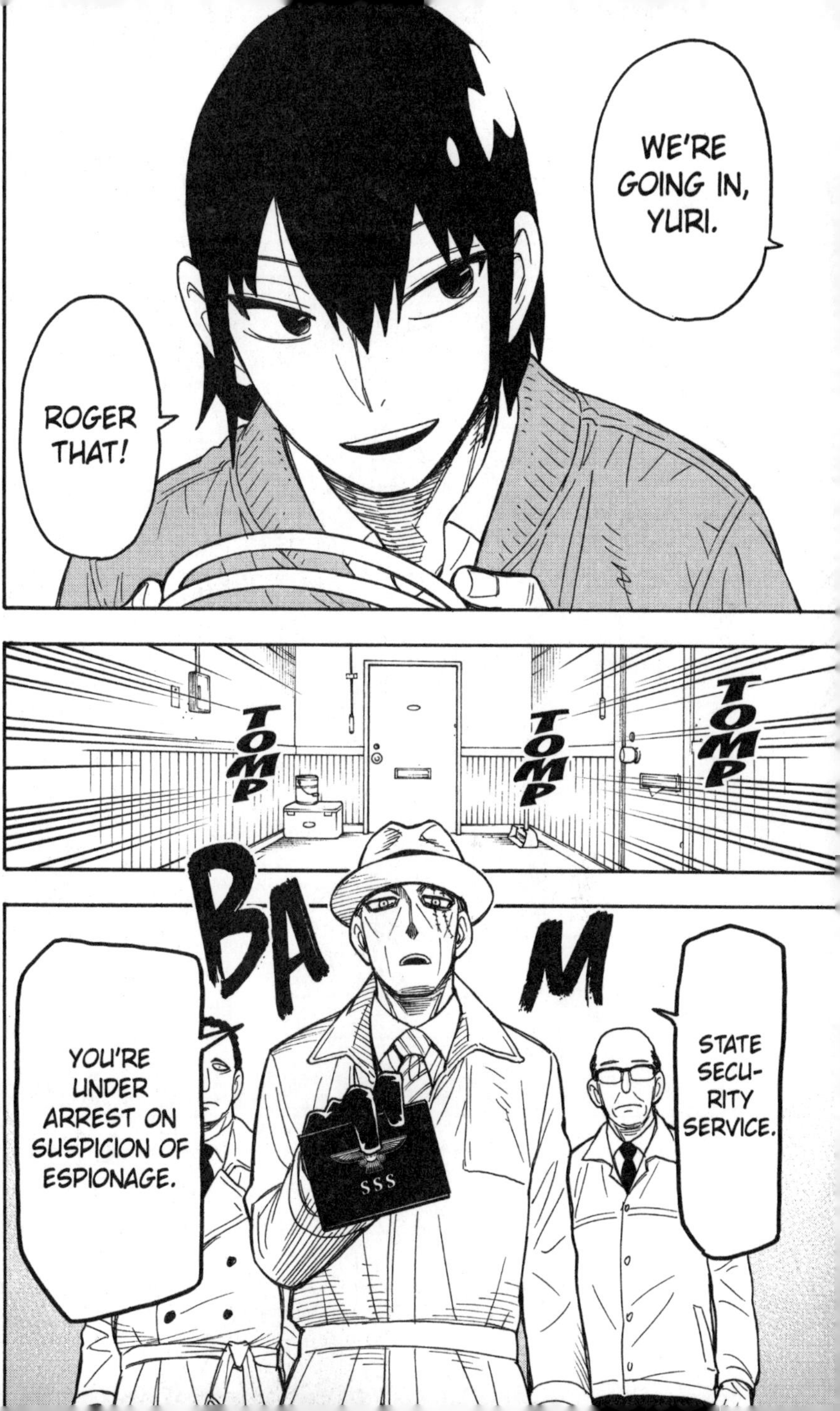
WE'RE GOING IN, YURI.
ROGER THAT!
TOMP
TOMP
TOMP
BAM
STATE SECU-RITY SERVICE.
YOU'RE UNDER ARREST ON SUSPICION OF ESPIONAGE.
SSS

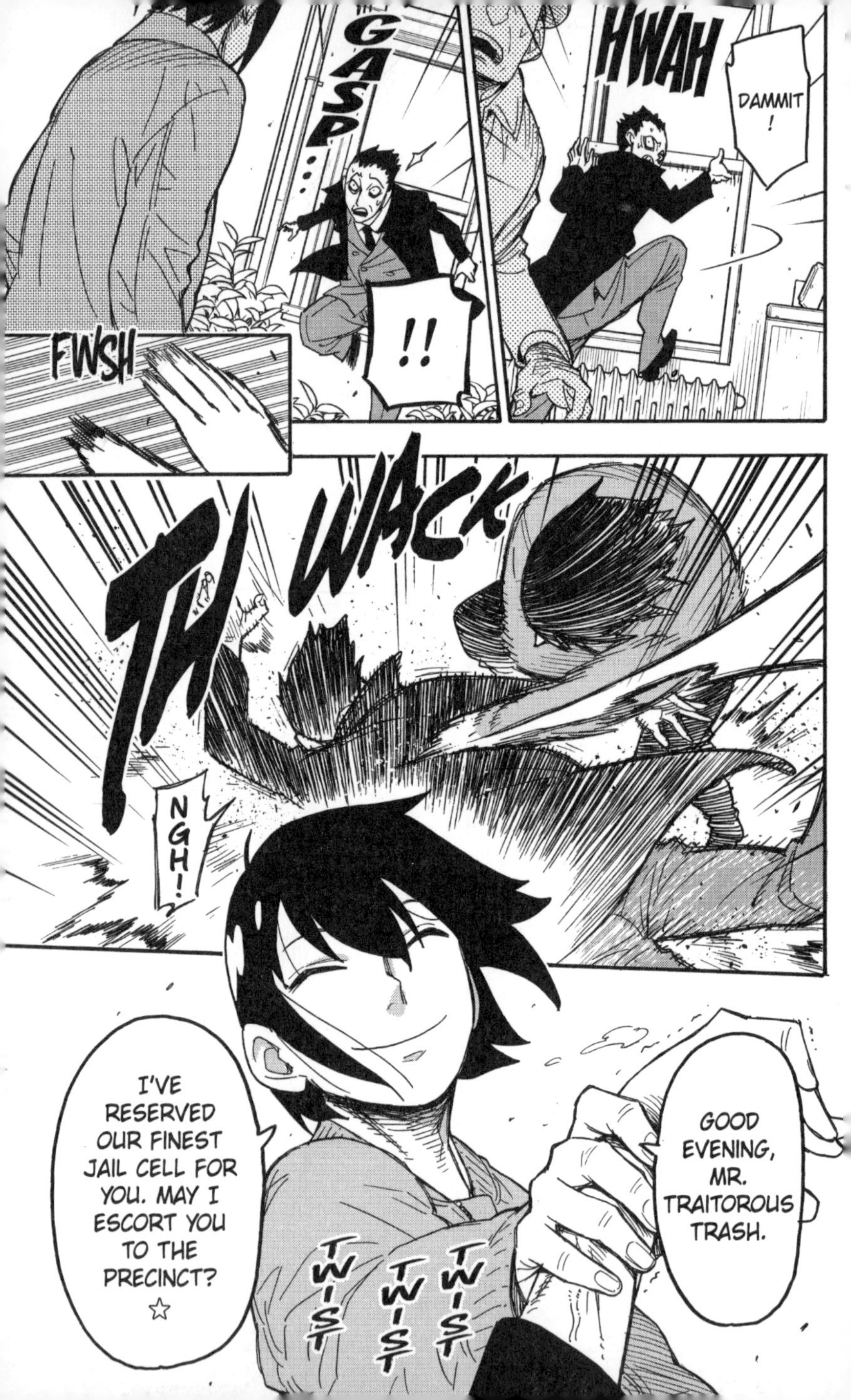
HWAH
DAMMIT!
GASP...
!!
FWSH
THWACK
NGH!
GOOD EVENING, MR. TRAITOROUS TRASH.
I'VE RESERVED OUR FINEST JAIL CELL FOR YOU. MAY I ESCORT YOU TO THE PRECINCT? ☆
TWIST TWIST TWIST

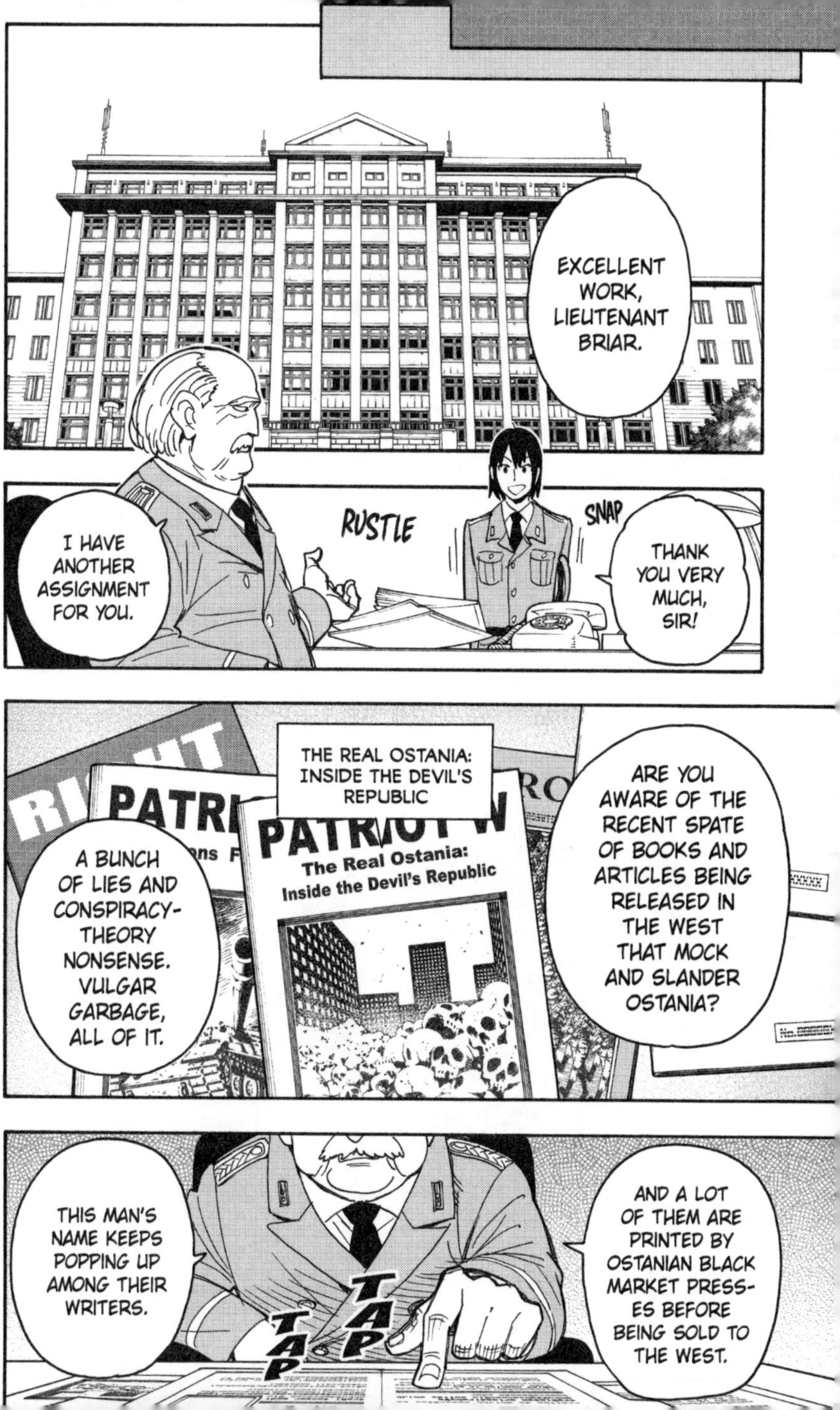
EXCELLENT WORK, LIEUTENANT BRIAR.
SNAP
THANK YOU VERY MUCH, SIR!
RUSTLE
I HAVE ANOTHER ASSIGNMENT FOR YOU.
ARE YOU AWARE OF THE RECENT SPATE OF BOOKS AND ARTICLES BEING RELEASED IN THE WEST THAT MOCK AND SLANDER OSTANIA?
THE REAL OSTANIA: INSIDE THE DEVIL'S REPUBLIC
PATRIOT W
The Real Ostania: Inside the Devil's Republic
A BUNCH OF LIES AND CONSPIRACY-THEORY NONSENSE. VULGAR GARBAGE, ALL OF IT.
AND A LOT OF THEM ARE PRINTED BY OSTANIAN BLACK MARKET PRESS-ES BEFORE BEING SOLD TO THE WEST.
TAP TAP
THIS MAN'S NAME KEEPS POPPING UP AMONG THEIR WRITERS.

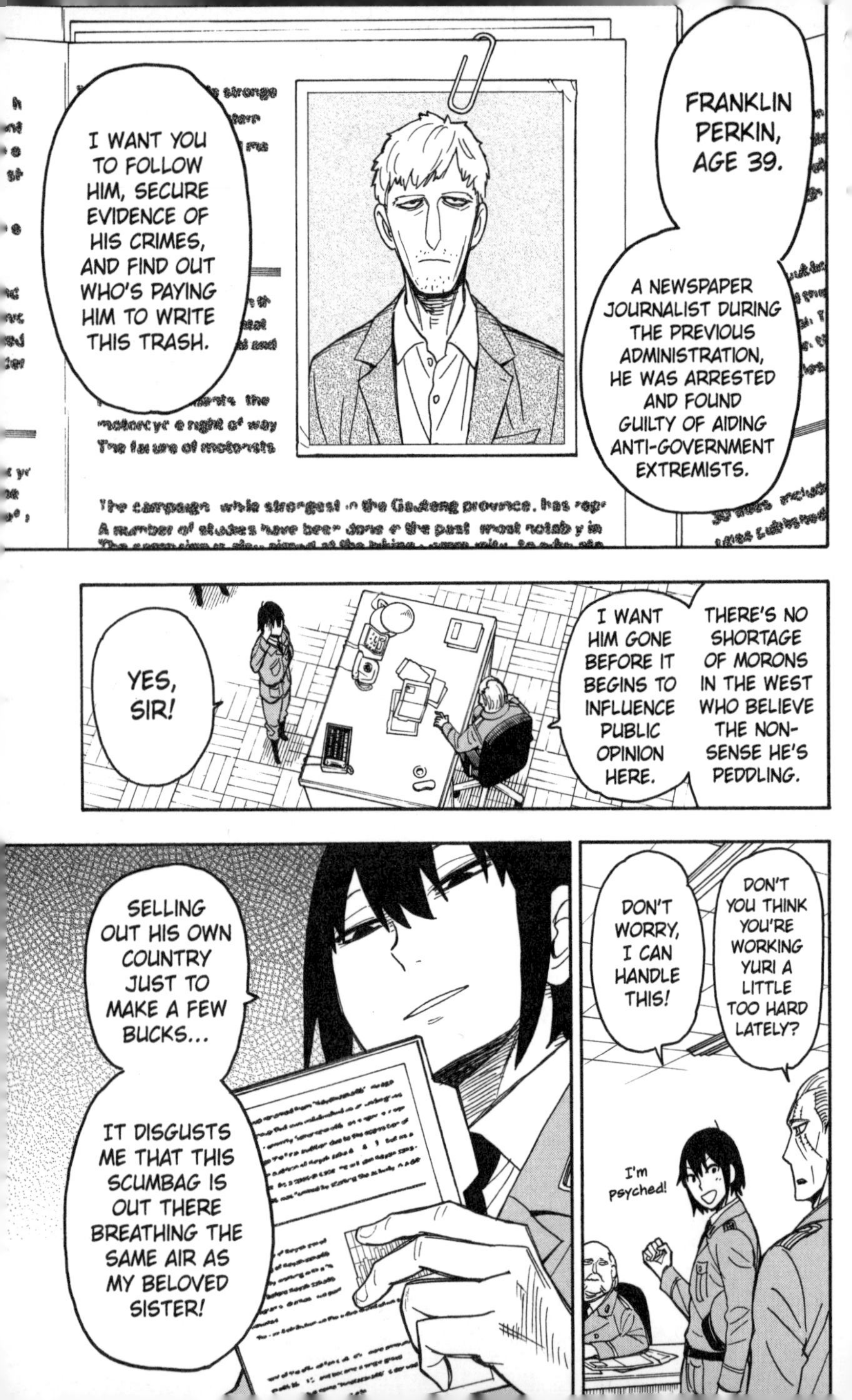
FRANKLIN PERKIN, AGE 39.
A NEWSPAPER JOURNALIST DURING THE PREVIOUS ADMINISTRATION, HE WAS ARRESTED AND FOUND GUILTY OF AIDING ANTI-GOVERNMENT EXTREMISTS.
I WANT YOU TO FOLLOW HIM, SECURE EVIDENCE OF HIS CRIMES, AND FIND OUT WHO'S PAYING HIM TO WRITE THIS TRASH.
THERE'S NO SHORTAGE OF MORONS IN THE WEST WHO BELIEVE THE NON-SENSE HE'S PEDDLING.
I WANT HIM GONE BEFORE IT BEGINS TO INFLUENCE PUBLIC OPINION HERE.
YES, SIR!
DON'T YOU THINK YOU'RE WORKING YURI A LITTLE TOO HARD LATELY?
DON'T WORRY, I CAN HANDLE THIS!
I'm psyched!
SELLING OUT HIS OWN COUNTRY JUST TO MAKE A FEW BUCKS...
IT DISGUSTS ME THAT THIS SCUMBAG IS OUT THERE BREATHING THE SAME AIR AS MY BELOVED SISTER!

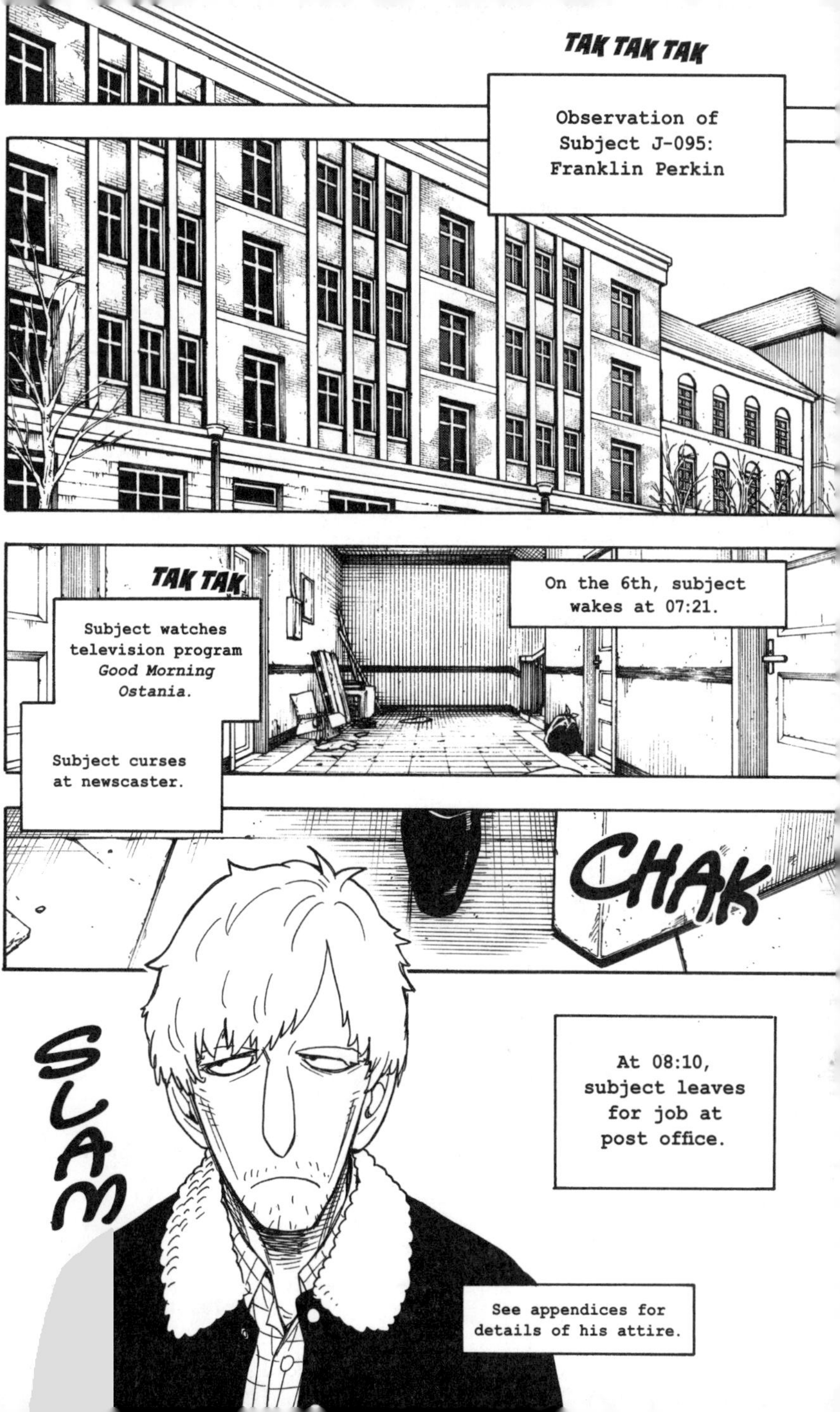
TAK TAK TAK
Observation of Subject J-095: Franklin Perkin
On the 6th, subject wakes at 07:21.
TAK TAK
Subject watches television program *Good Morning Ostania*.
Subject curses at newscaster.
CHAK
At 08:10, subject leaves for job at post office.
SLAM
See appendices for details of his attire.

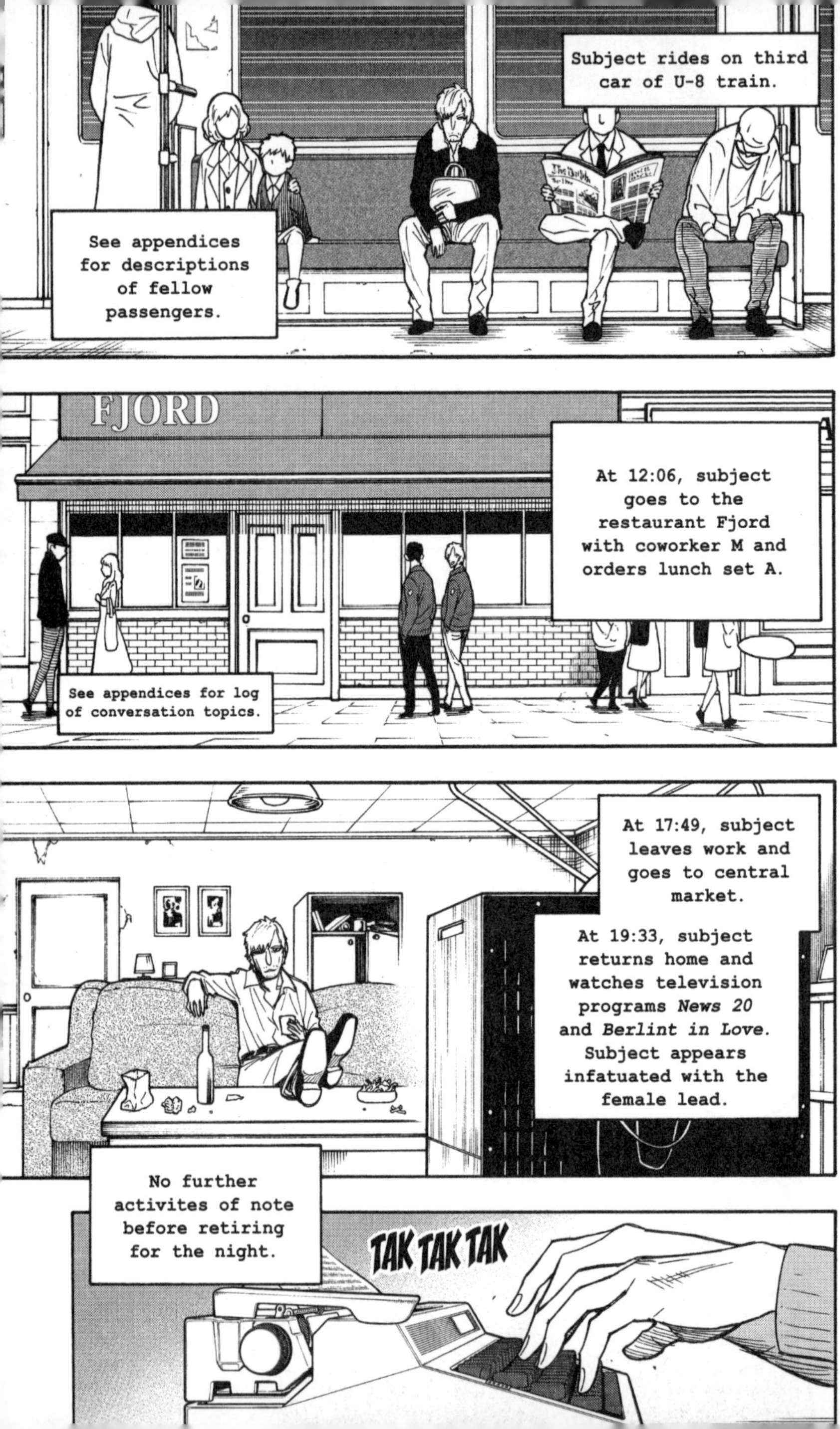
Subject rides on third car of U-8 train.
See appendices for descriptions of fellow passengers.
FJORD
At 12:06, subject goes to the restaurant Fjord with coworker M and orders lunch set A.
See appendices for log of conversation topics.
At 17:49, subject leaves work and goes to central market.
At 19:33, subject returns home and watches television programs *News 20* and *Berlint in Love*. Subject appears infatuated with the female lead.
No further activites of note before retiring for the night.
TAK TAK TAK

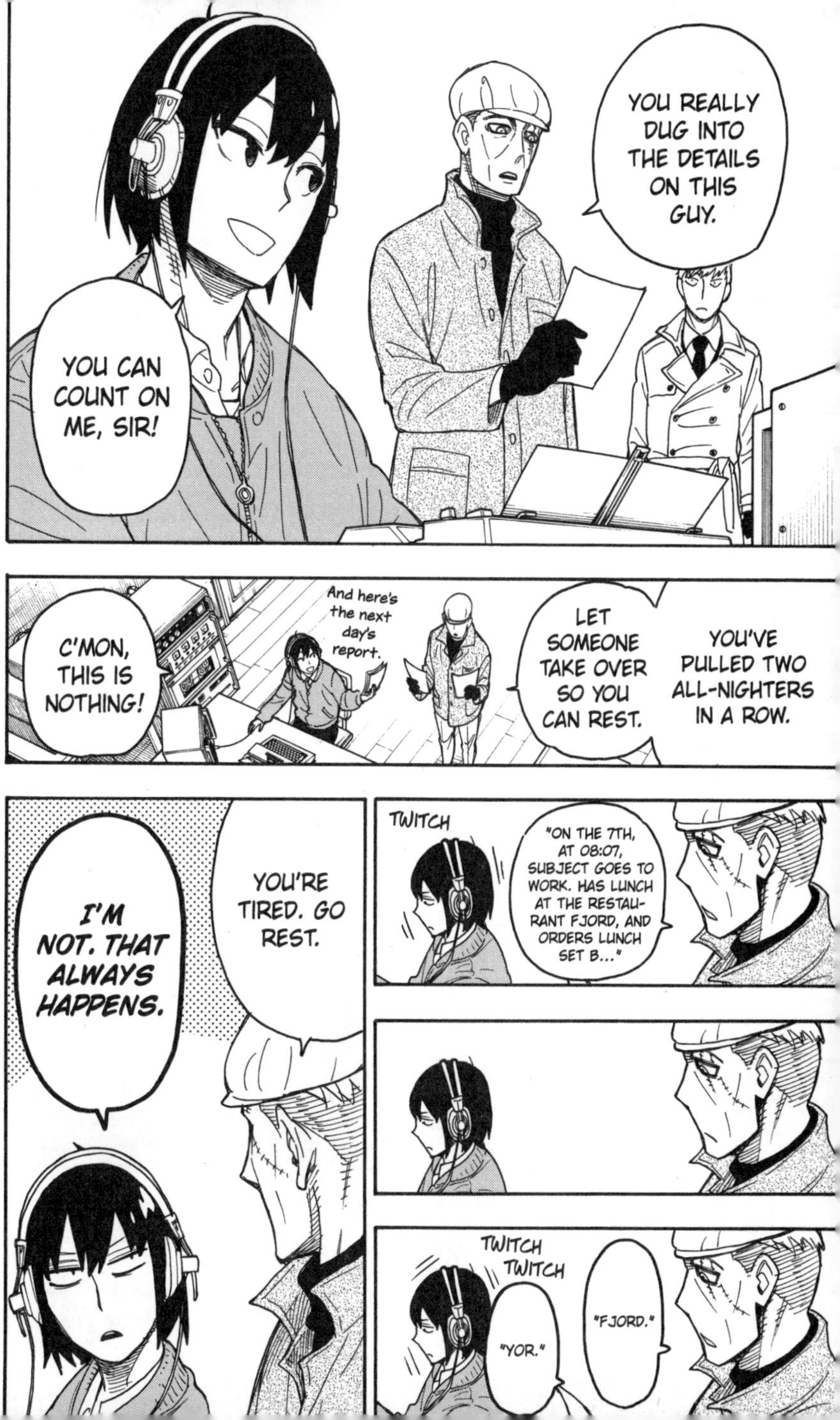
YOU REALLY DUG INTO THE DETAILS ON THIS GUY.
YOU CAN COUNT ON ME, SIR!
YOU'VE PULLED TWO ALL-NIGHTERS IN A ROW.
LET SOMEONE TAKE OVER SO YOU CAN REST.
And here's the next day's report.
C'MON, THIS IS NOTHING!
"ON THE 7TH, AT 08:07, SUBJECT GOES TO WORK. HAS LUNCH AT THE RESTAU-RANT FJORD, AND ORDERS LUNCH SET B..."
TWITCH
"FJORD."
TWITCH TWITCH
"YOR."
YOU'RE TIRED. GO REST.
I'M NOT. THAT ALWAYS HAPPENS.

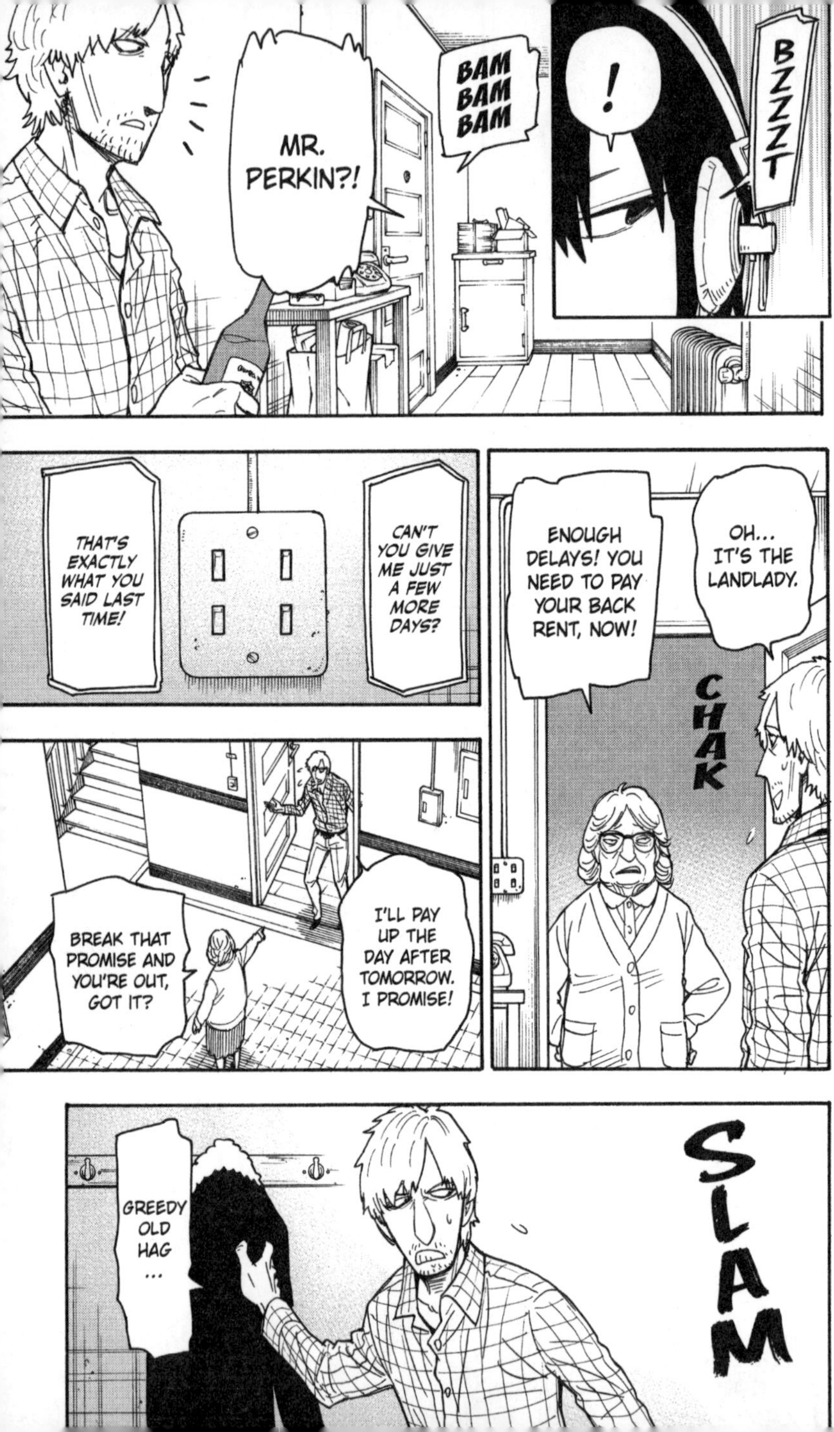
BZZZT
!
BAM BAM BAM
MR. PERKIN?!
OH... IT'S THE LANDLADY.
ENOUGH DELAYS! YOU NEED TO PAY YOUR BACK RENT, NOW!
CHAK
CAN'T YOU GIVE ME JUST A FEW MORE DAYS?
THAT'S EXACTLY WHAT YOU SAID LAST TIME!
I'LL PAY UP THE DAY AFTER TOMORROW. I PROMISE!
BREAK THAT PROMISE AND YOU'RE OUT, GOT IT?
SLAM
GREEDY OLD HAG ...

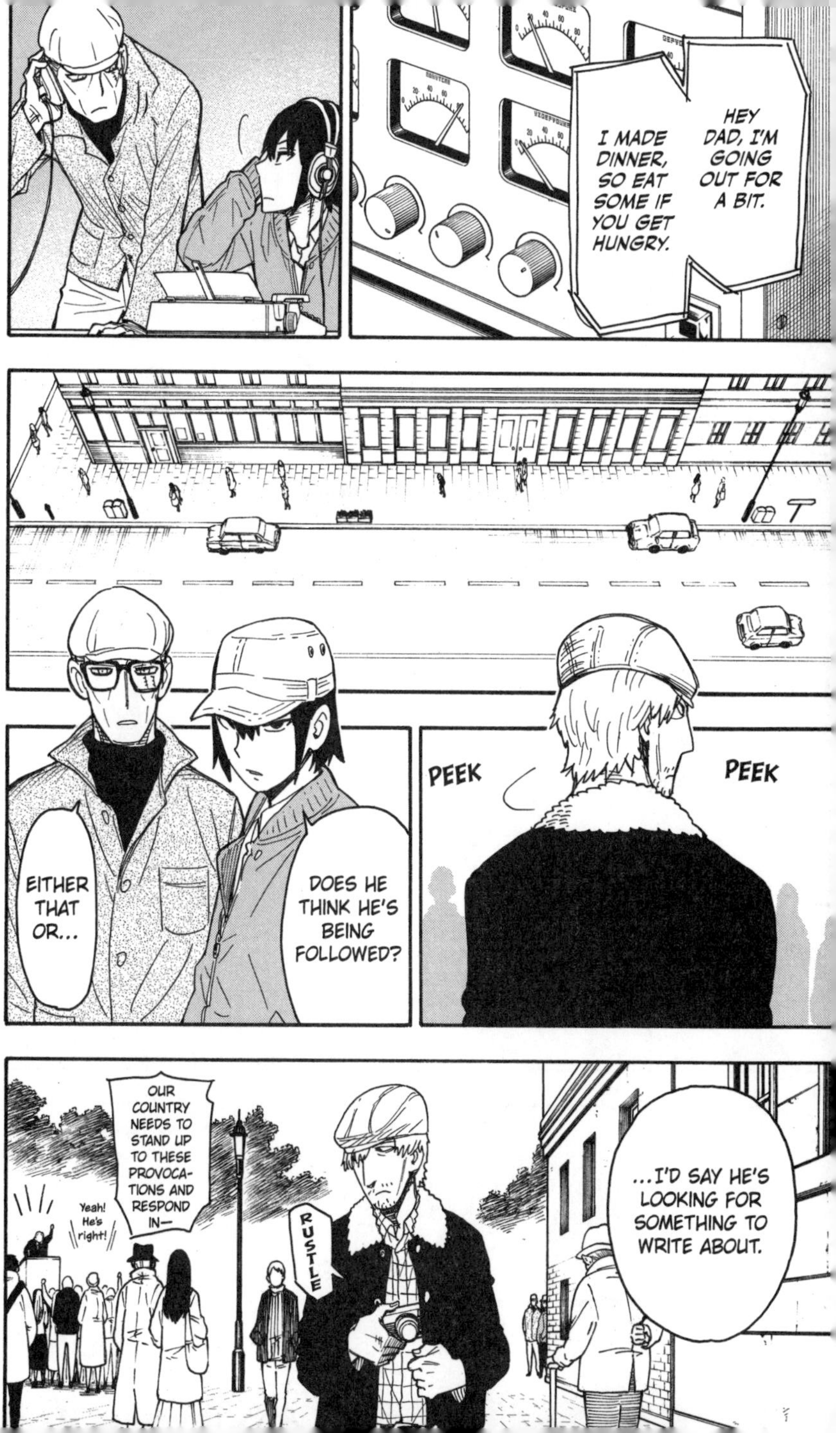
HEY DAD, I'M GOING OUT FOR A BIT.
I MADE DINNER, SO EAT SOME IF YOU GET HUNGRY.
PEEK
PEEK
DOES HE THINK HE'S BEING FOLLOWED?
EITHER THAT OR...
...I'D SAY HE'S LOOKING FOR SOMETHING TO WRITE ABOUT.
RUSTLE
OUR COUNTRY NEEDS TO STAND UP TO THESE PROVOCA-TIONS AND RESPOND IN—
Yeah! He's right!

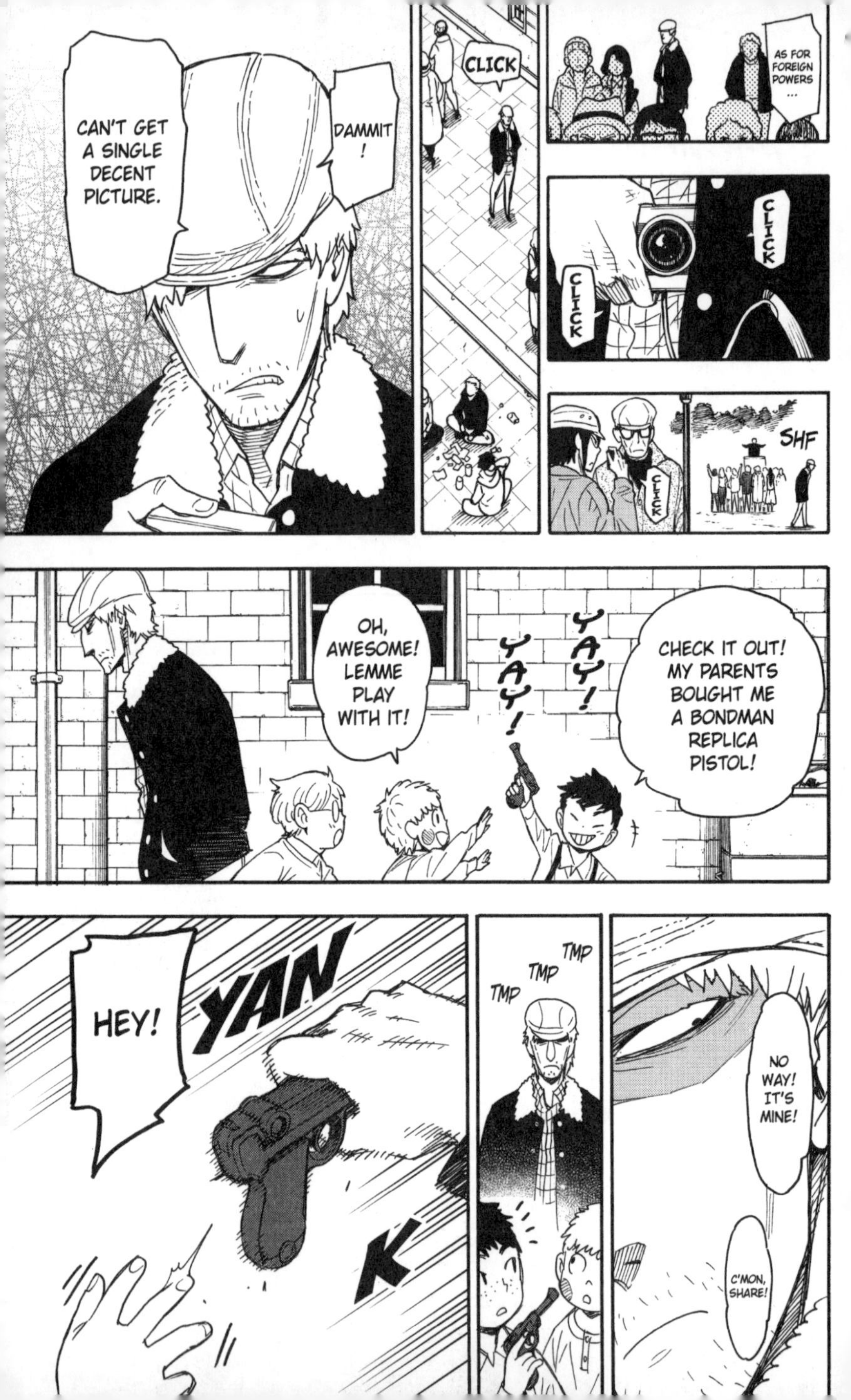
AS FOR FOREIGN POWERS ...
CLICK
CLICK
SHF
CLICK
CLICK
DAMMIT!
CAN'T GET A SINGLE DECENT PICTURE.
CHECK IT OUT! MY PARENTS BOUGHT ME A BONDMAN REPLICA PISTOL!
YAY!
YAY!
OH, AWESOME! LEMME PLAY WITH IT!
NO WAY! IT'S MINE!
C'MON, SHARE!
TMP
TMP
TMP
YANK
HEY!

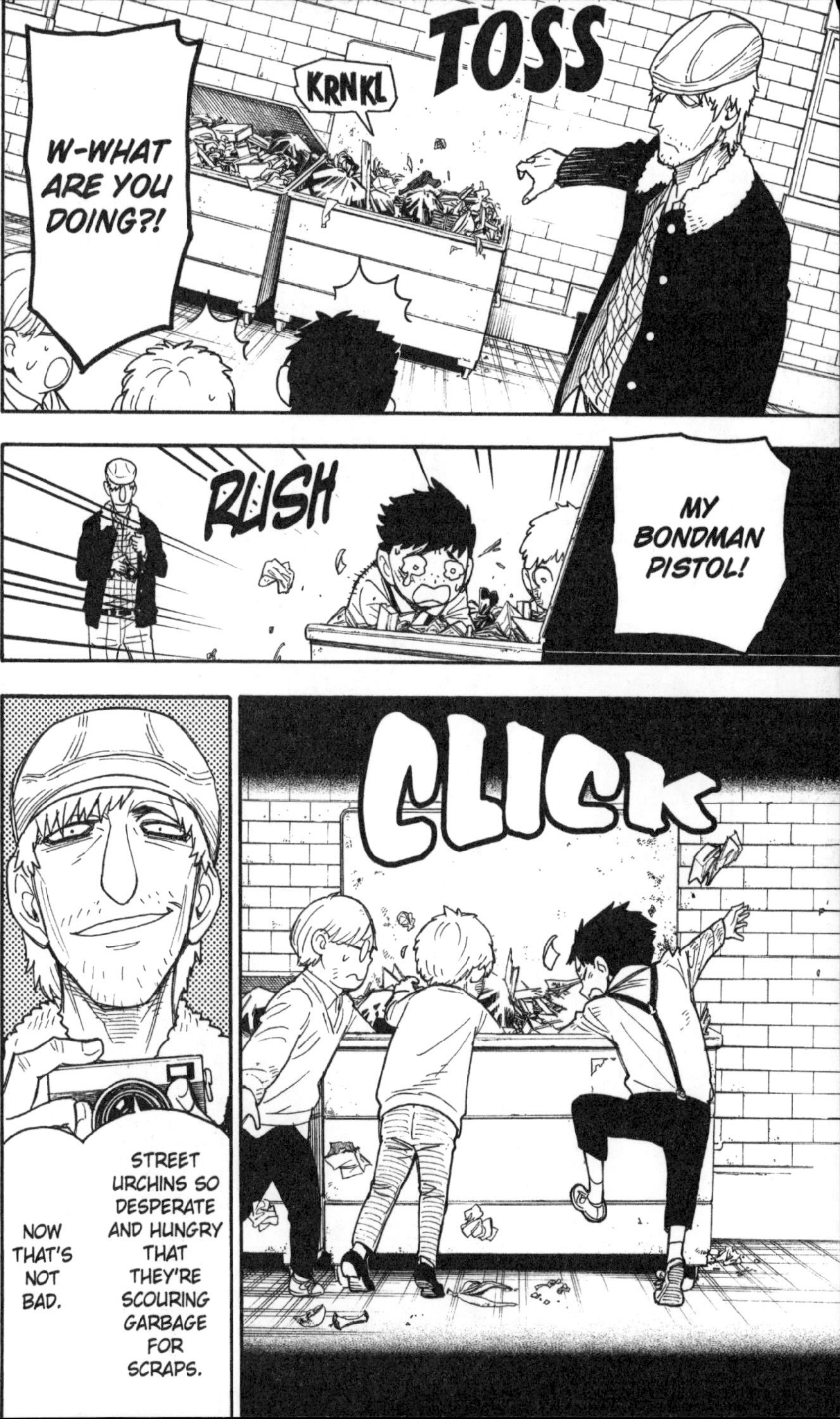
TOSS
KRNKL
W-WHAT ARE YOU DOING?!
MY BONDMAN PISTOL!
RUSH
CLICK
STREET URCHINS SO DESPERATE AND HUNGRY THAT THEY'RE SCOURING GARBAGE FOR SCRAPS.
NOW THAT'S NOT BAD.

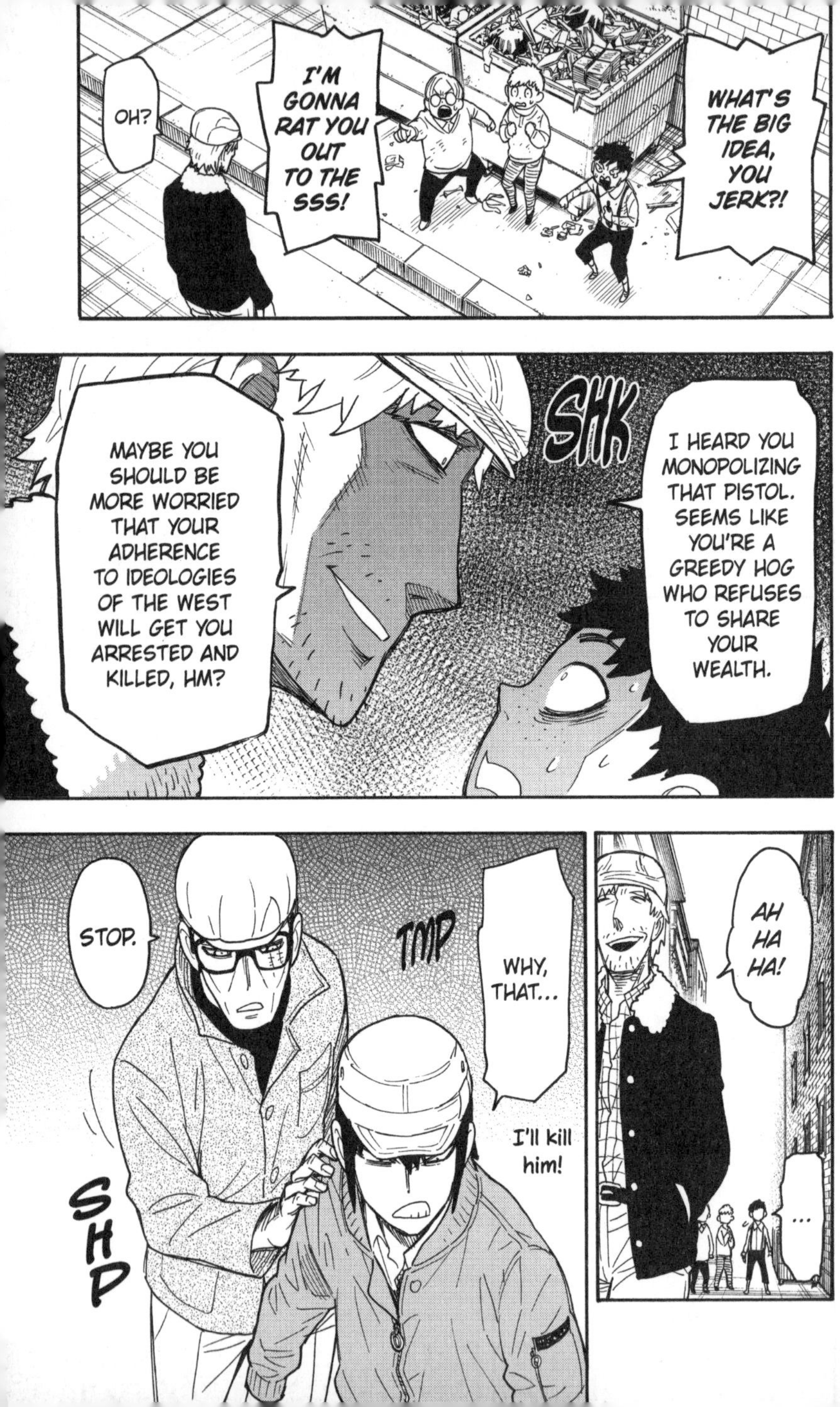
WHAT'S THE BIG IDEA, YOU JERK?!
I'M GONNA RAT YOU OUT TO THE SSS!
OH?
SHK
I HEARD YOU MONOPOLIZING THAT PISTOL. SEEMS LIKE YOU'RE A GREEDY HOG WHO REFUSES TO SHARE YOUR WEALTH.
MAYBE YOU SHOULD BE MORE WORRIED THAT YOUR ADHERENCE TO IDEOLOGIES OF THE WEST WILL GET YOU ARRESTED AND KILLED, HM?
AH HA HA!
...
WHY, THAT...
TMP
I'll kill him!
STOP.
SHP

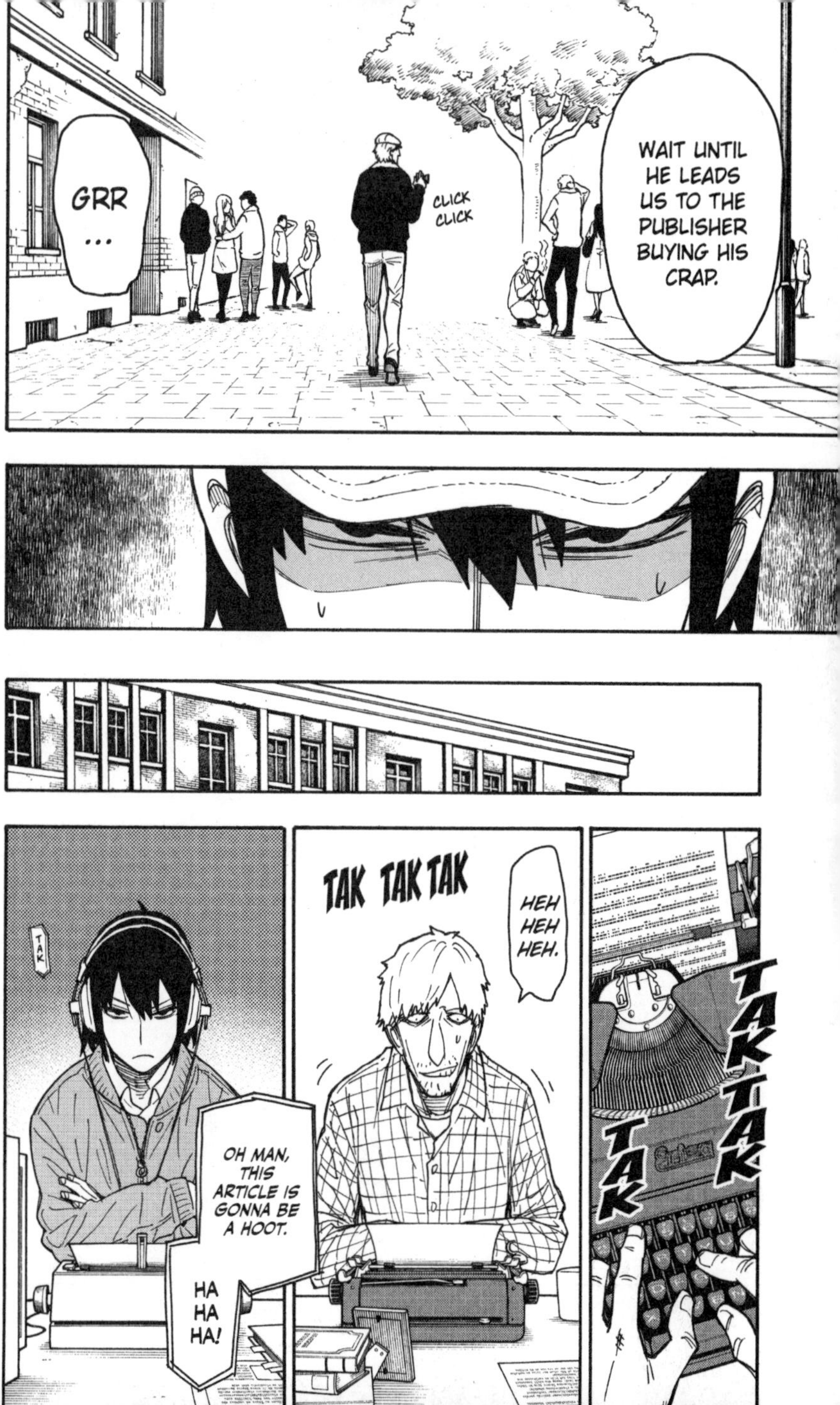
WAIT UNTIL HE LEADS US TO THE PUBLISHER BUYING HIS CRAP.
CLICK CLICK
GRR ...
TAK TAK
TAK
TAK TAK TAK
HEH HEH HEH.
OH MAN, THIS ARTICLE IS GONNA BE A HOOT.
TAK
HA HA HA!

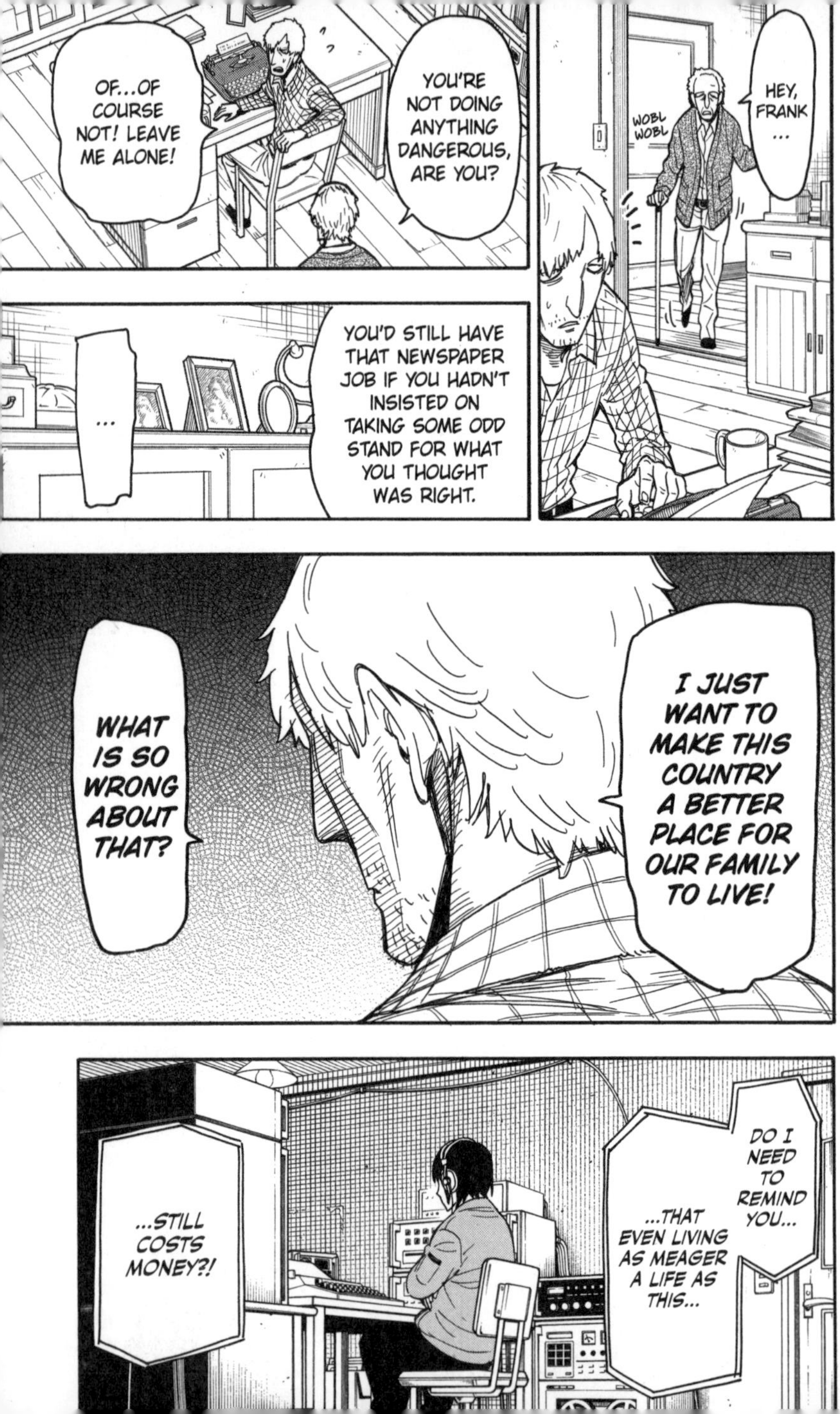
WOBL WOBL
HEY, FRANK ...
YOU'RE NOT DOING ANYTHING DANGEROUS, ARE YOU?
OF...OF COURSE NOT! LEAVE ME ALONE!
YOU'D STILL HAVE THAT NEWSPAPER JOB IF YOU HADN'T INSISTED ON TAKING SOME ODD STAND FOR WHAT YOU THOUGHT WAS RIGHT.
...
I JUST WANT TO MAKE THIS COUNTRY A BETTER PLACE FOR OUR FAMILY TO LIVE!
WHAT IS SO WRONG ABOUT THAT?
DO I NEED TO REMIND YOU...
...THAT EVEN LIVING AS MEAGER A LIFE AS THIS...
...STILL COSTS MONEY?!

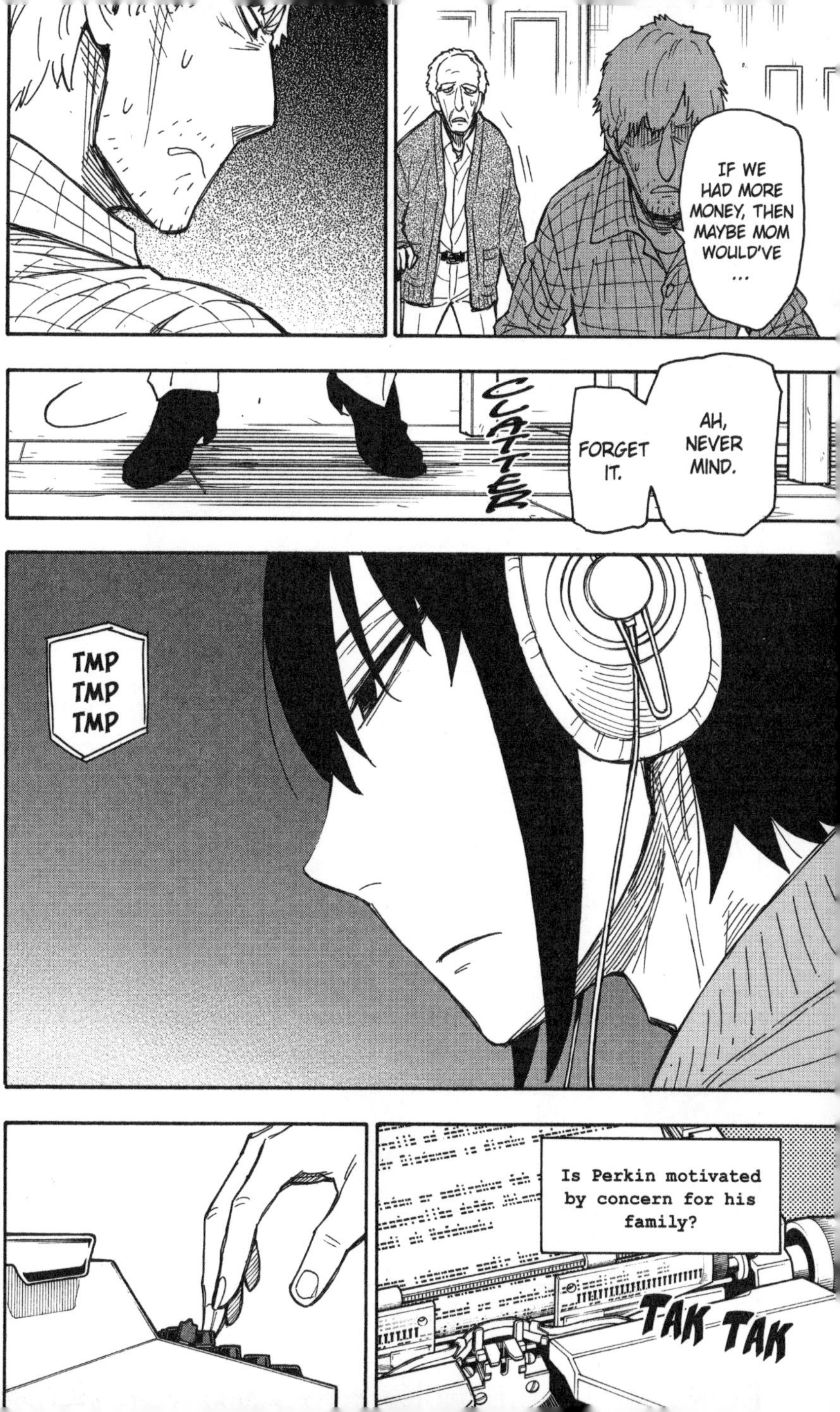
IF WE HAD MORE MONEY, THEN MAYBE MOM WOULD'VE ...
AH, NEVER MIND.
FORGET IT.
CLATTER
TMP TMP TMP
Is Perkin motivated by concern for his family?
TAK TAK

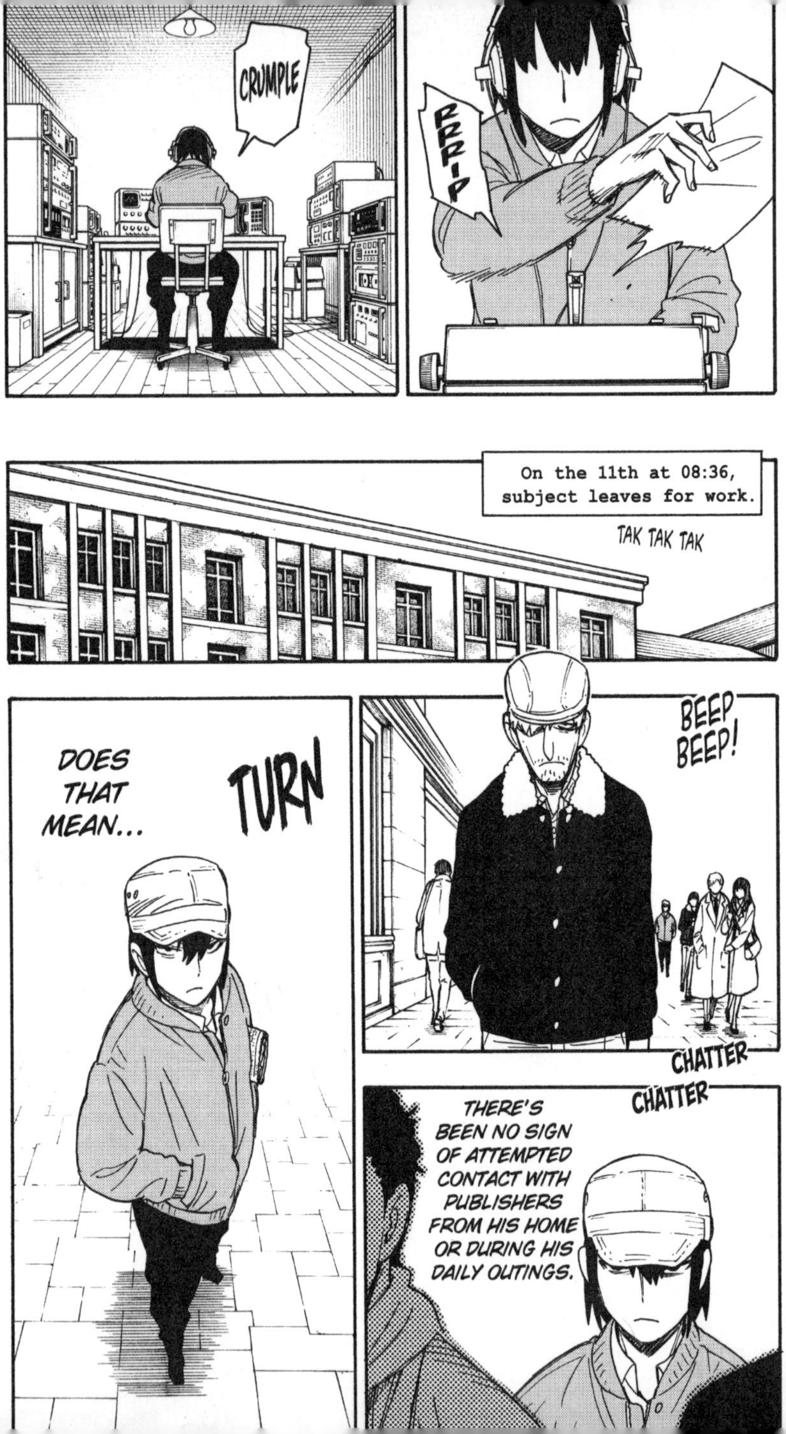
RRRIP
CRUMPLE
On the 11th at 08:36, subject leaves for work.
TAK TAK TAK
BEEP BEEP!
CHATTER
CHATTER
TURN
DOES THAT MEAN...
THERE'S BEEN NO SIGN OF ATTEMPTED CONTACT WITH PUBLISHERS FROM HIS HOME OR DURING HIS DAILY OUTINGS.

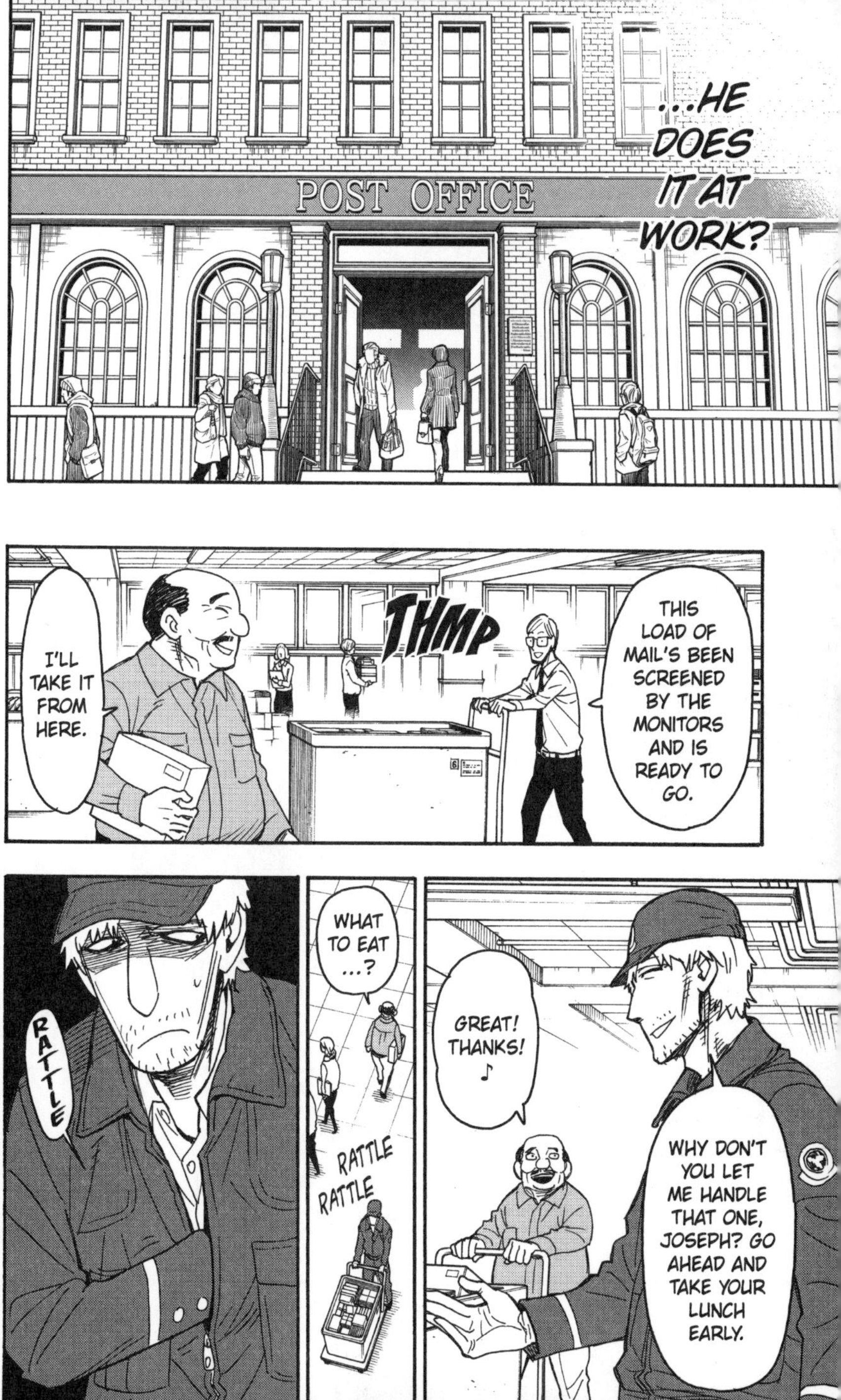
POST OFFICE
...HE DOES IT AT WORK?
THIS LOAD OF MAIL'S BEEN SCREENED BY THE MONITORS AND IS READY TO GO.
THMP
I'LL TAKE IT FROM HERE.
WHY DON'T YOU LET ME HANDLE THAT ONE, JOSEPH? GO AHEAD AND TAKE YOUR LUNCH EARLY.
GREAT! THANKS! ♪
WHAT TO EAT ...?
RATTLE RATTLE
RATTLE

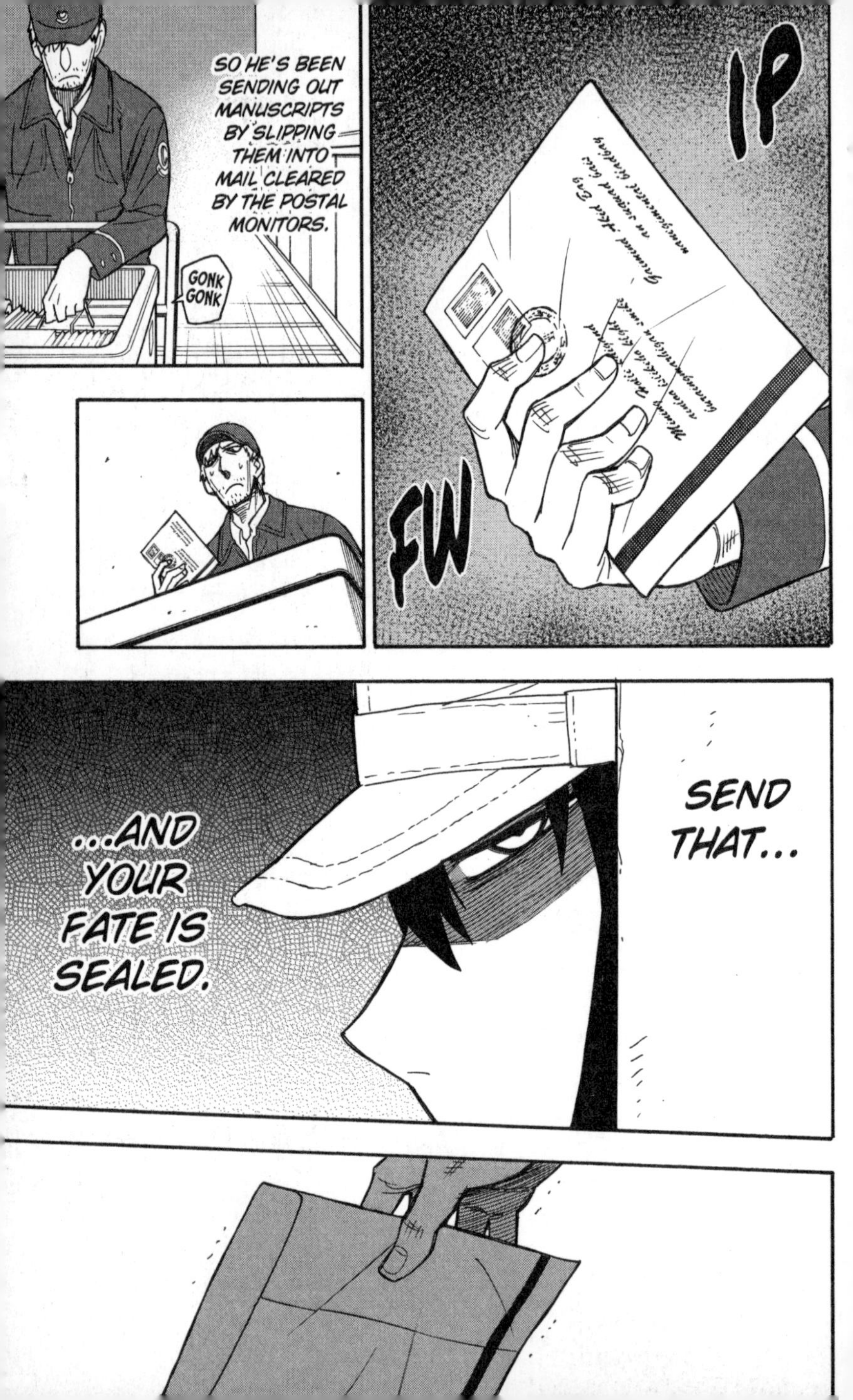
IP
FW
SO HE'S BEEN SENDING OUT MANUSCRIPTS BY SLIPPING THEM INTO MAIL CLEARED BY THE POSTAL MONITORS.
GONK GONK
SEND THAT...
...AND YOUR FATE IS SEALED.

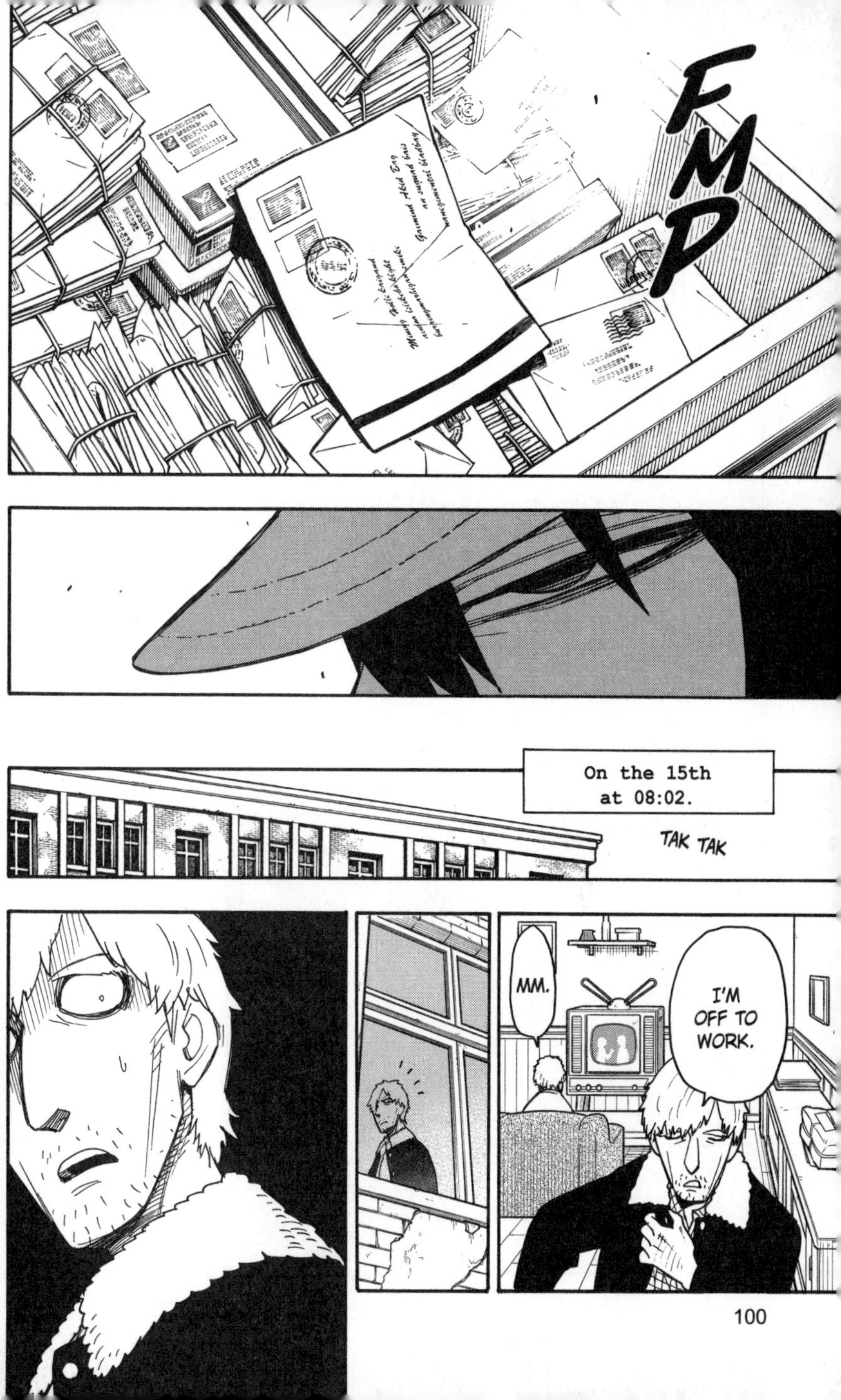
FMP
On the 15th at 08:02.
TAK TAK
I'M OFF TO WORK.
MM.

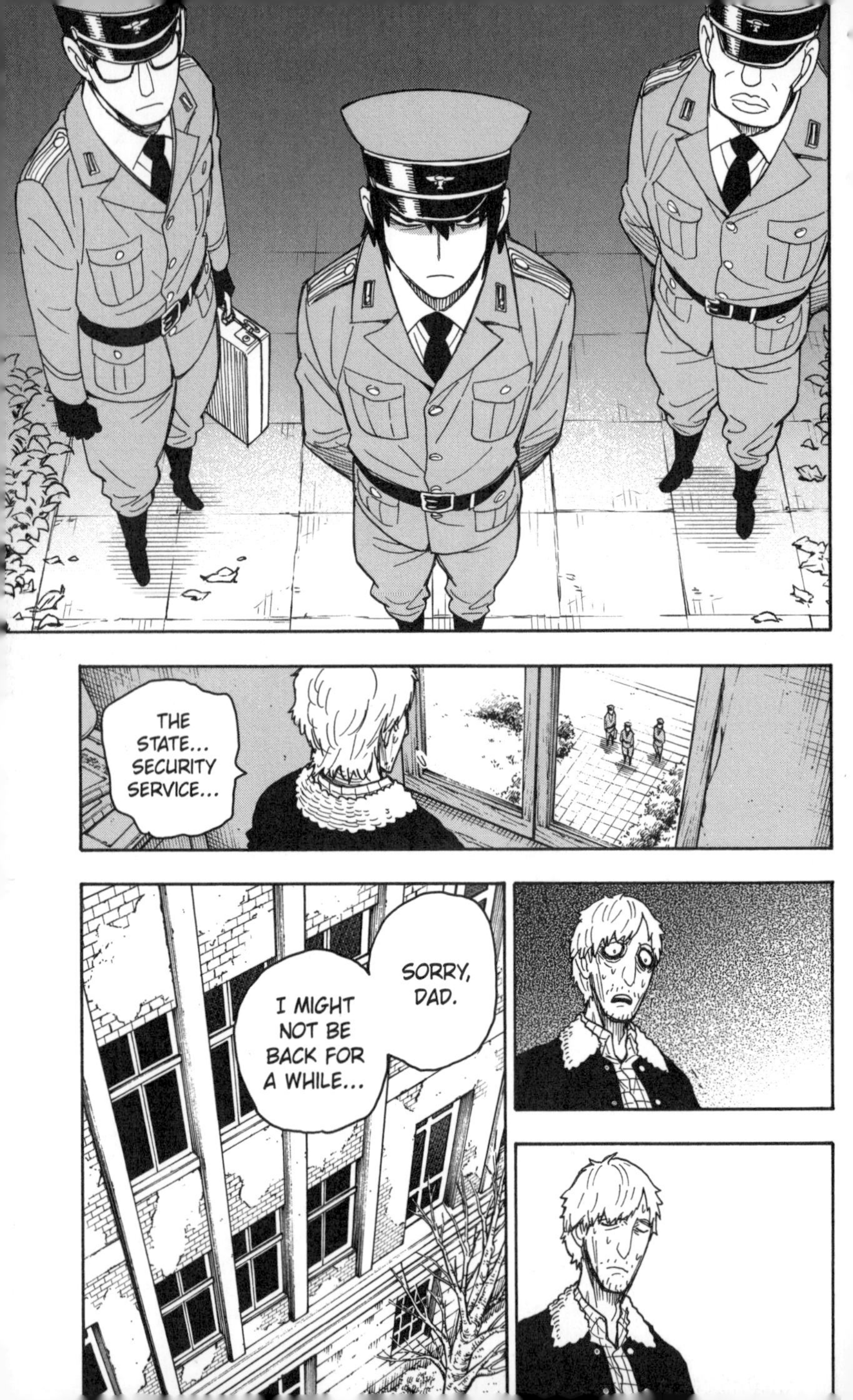
THE STATE... SECURITY SERVICE...
SORRY, DAD.
I MIGHT NOT BE BACK FOR A WHILE...

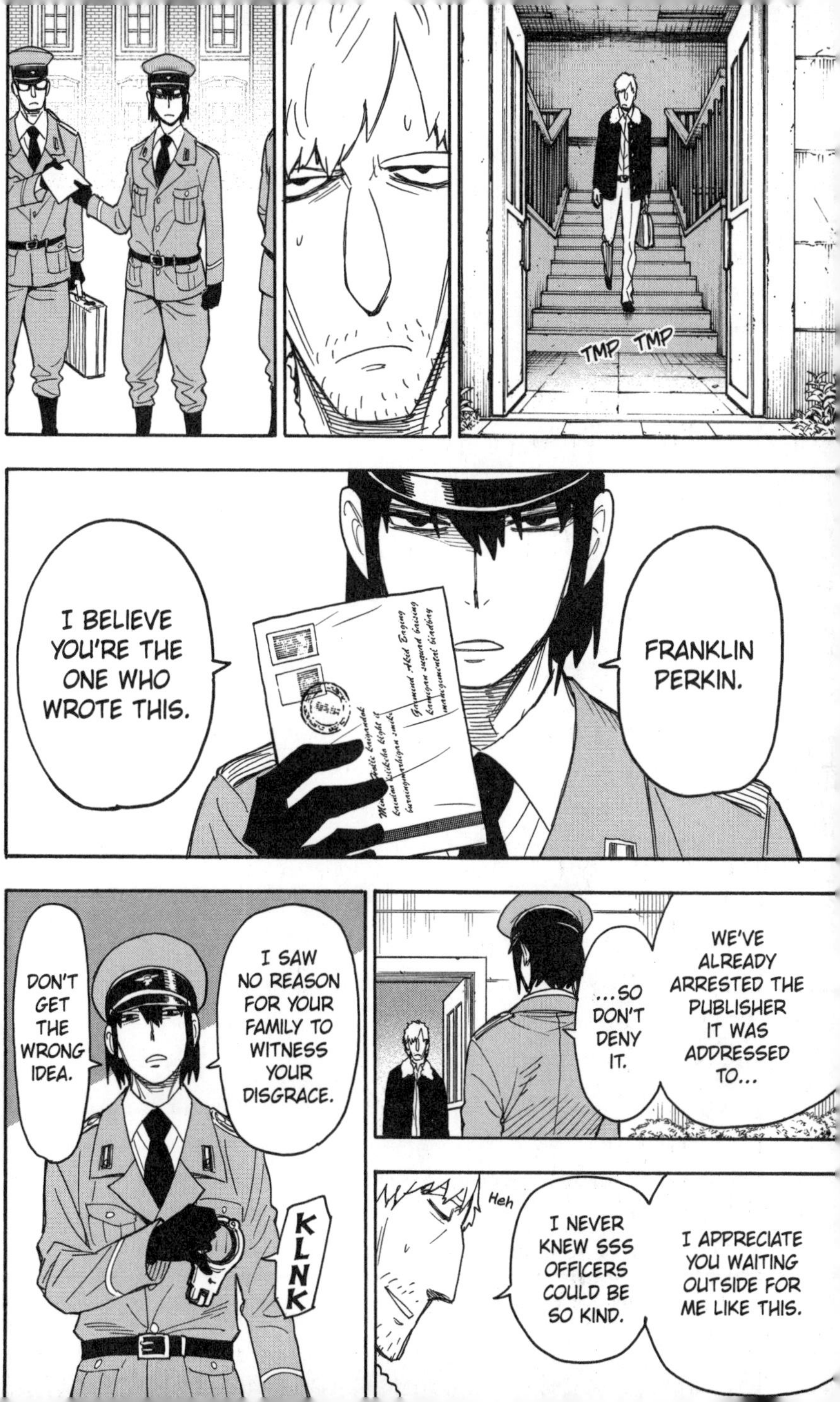
TMP TMP
FRANKLIN PERKIN.
I BELIEVE YOU'RE THE ONE WHO WROTE THIS.
WE'VE ALREADY ARRESTED THE PUBLISHER IT WAS ADDRESSED TO...
...SO DON'T DENY IT.
Heh
I APPRECIATE YOU WAITING OUTSIDE FOR ME LIKE THIS.
I NEVER KNEW SSS OFFICERS COULD BE SO KIND.
I SAW NO REASON FOR YOUR FAMILY TO WITNESS YOUR DISGRACE.
DON'T GET THE WRONG IDEA.
KLNK

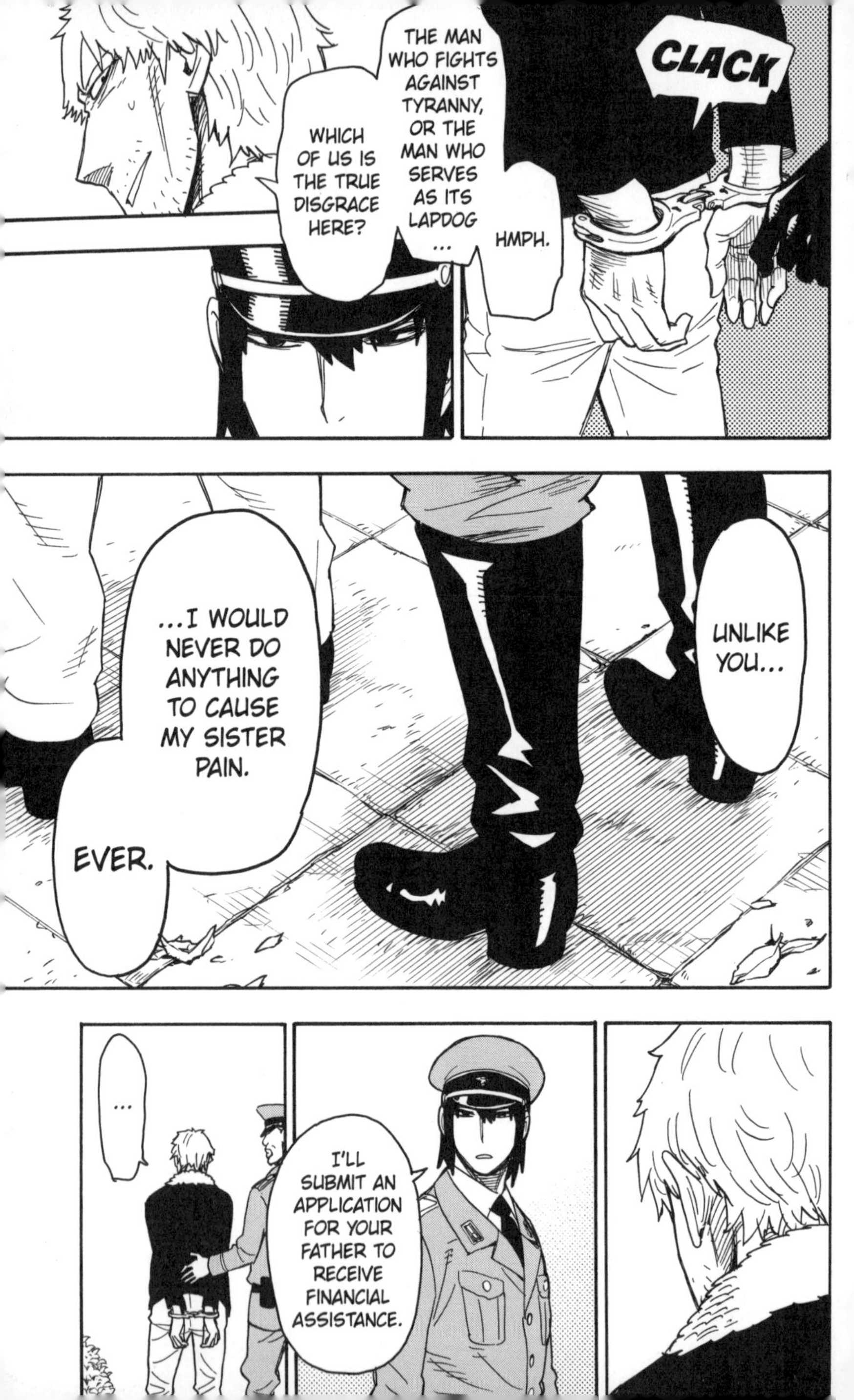
CLACK
HMPH.
THE MAN WHO FIGHTS AGAINST TYRANNY, OR THE MAN WHO SERVES AS ITS LAPDOG...
WHICH OF US IS THE TRUE DISGRACE HERE?
UNLIKE YOU...
...I WOULD NEVER DO ANYTHING TO CAUSE MY SISTER PAIN.
EVER.
I'LL SUBMIT AN APPLICATION FOR YOUR FATHER TO RECEIVE FINANCIAL ASSISTANCE.
...

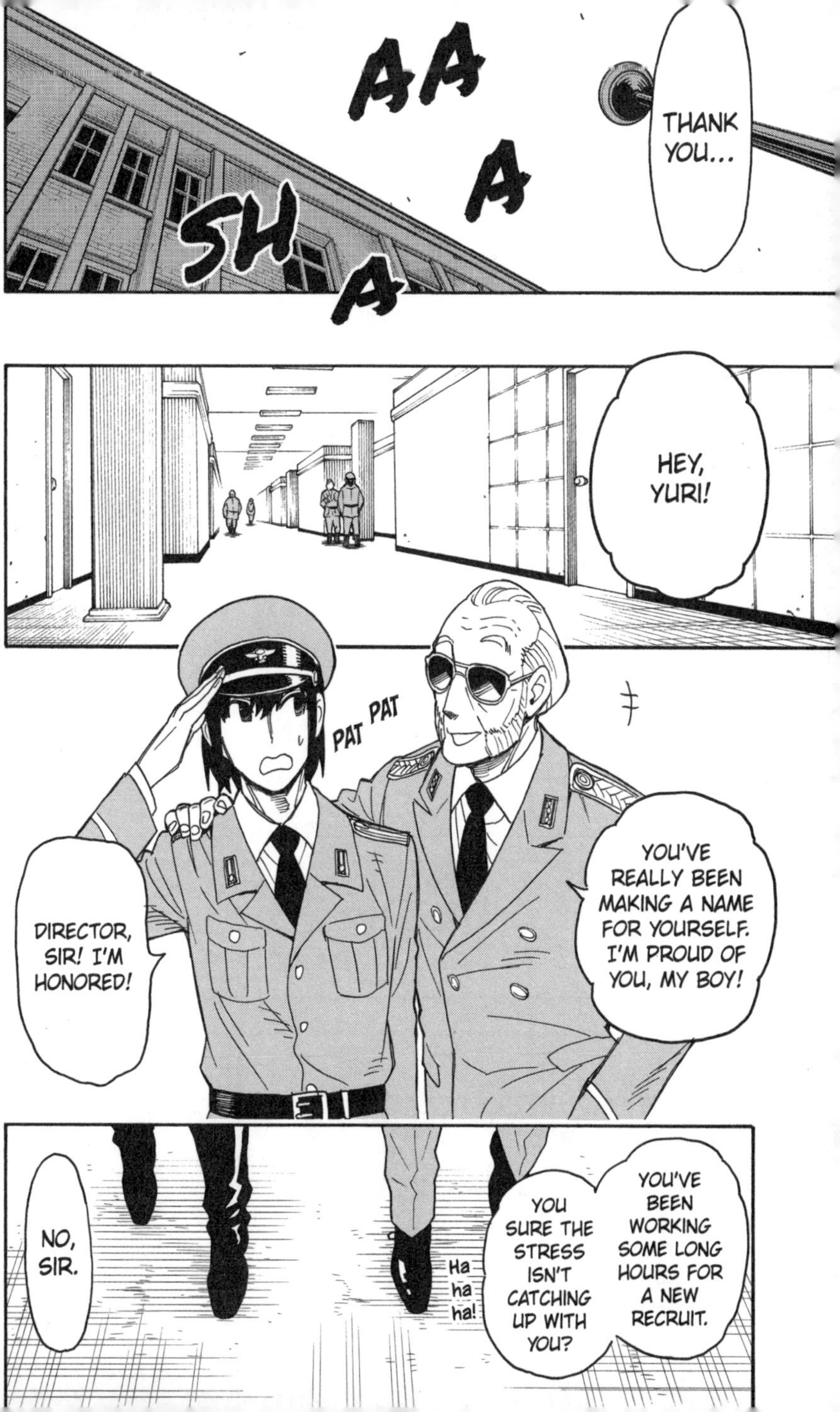
THANK YOU...
SHAAAA
HEY, YURI!
PAT PAT
YOU'VE REALLY BEEN MAKING A NAME FOR YOURSELF. I'M PROUD OF YOU, MY BOY!
DIRECTOR, SIR! I'M HONORED!
YOU'VE BEEN WORKING SOME LONG HOURS FOR A NEW RECRUIT.
YOU SURE THE STRESS ISN'T CATCHING UP WITH YOU?
Ha ha ha!
NO, SIR.

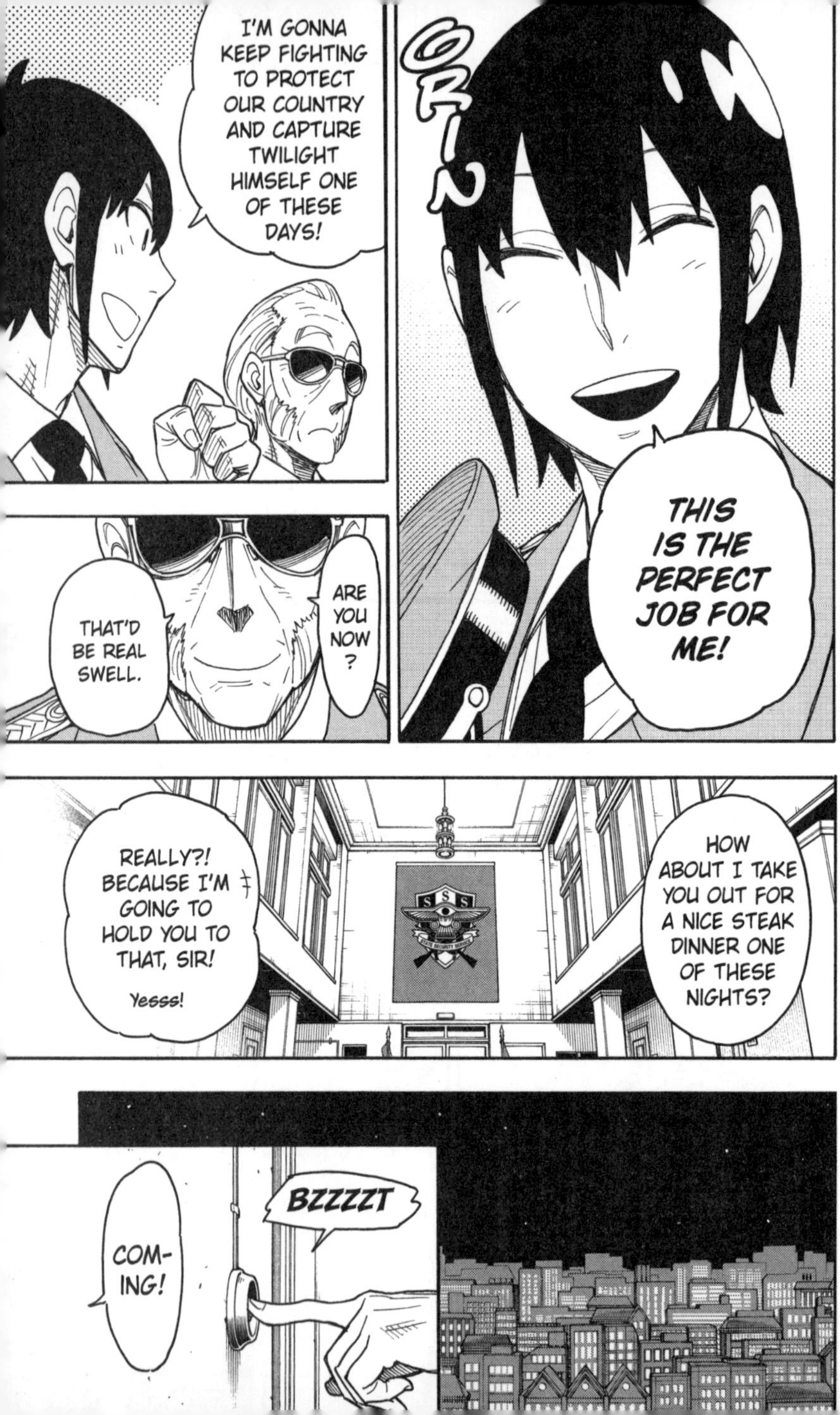
GRIN
THIS IS THE PERFECT JOB FOR ME!
I'M GONNA KEEP FIGHTING TO PROTECT OUR COUNTRY AND CAPTURE TWILIGHT HIMSELF ONE OF THESE DAYS!
ARE YOU NOW?
THAT'D BE REAL SWELL.
HOW ABOUT I TAKE YOU OUT FOR A NICE STEAK DINNER ONE OF THESE NIGHTS?
REALLY?! BECAUSE I'M GOING TO HOLD YOU TO THAT, SIR!
Yesss!
BZZZZT
COM-ING!

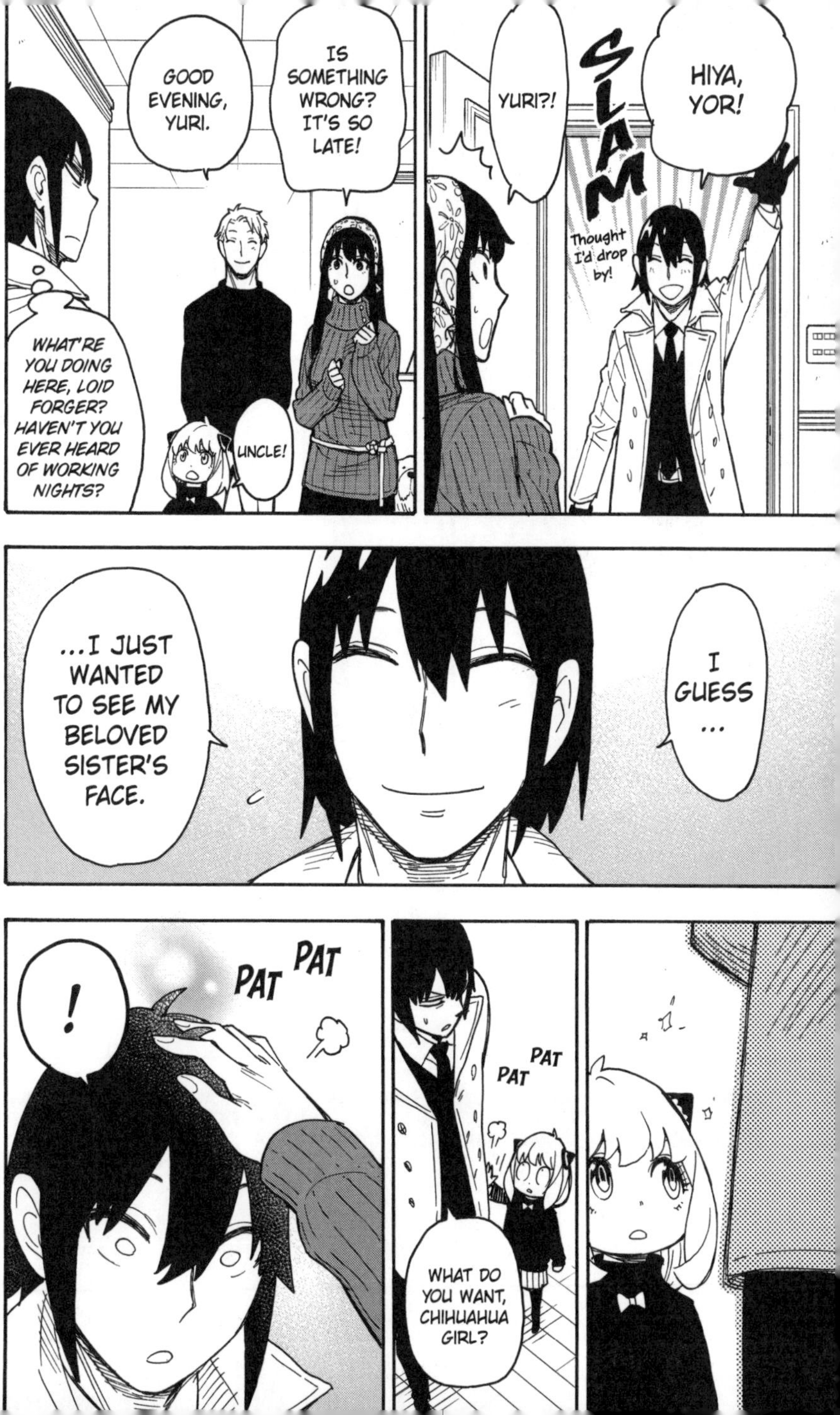
HIYA, YOR!
SLAM
Thought I'd drop by!
YURI?!
IS SOMETHING WRONG? IT'S SO LATE!
GOOD EVENING, YURI.
UNCLE!
WHAT'RE YOU DOING HERE, LOID FORGER? HAVEN'T YOU EVER HEARD OF WORKING NIGHTS?
I GUESS...
...I JUST WANTED TO SEE MY BELOVED SISTER'S FACE.
PAT PAT
WHAT DO YOU WANT, CHIHUAHUA GIRL?
PAT PAT
!

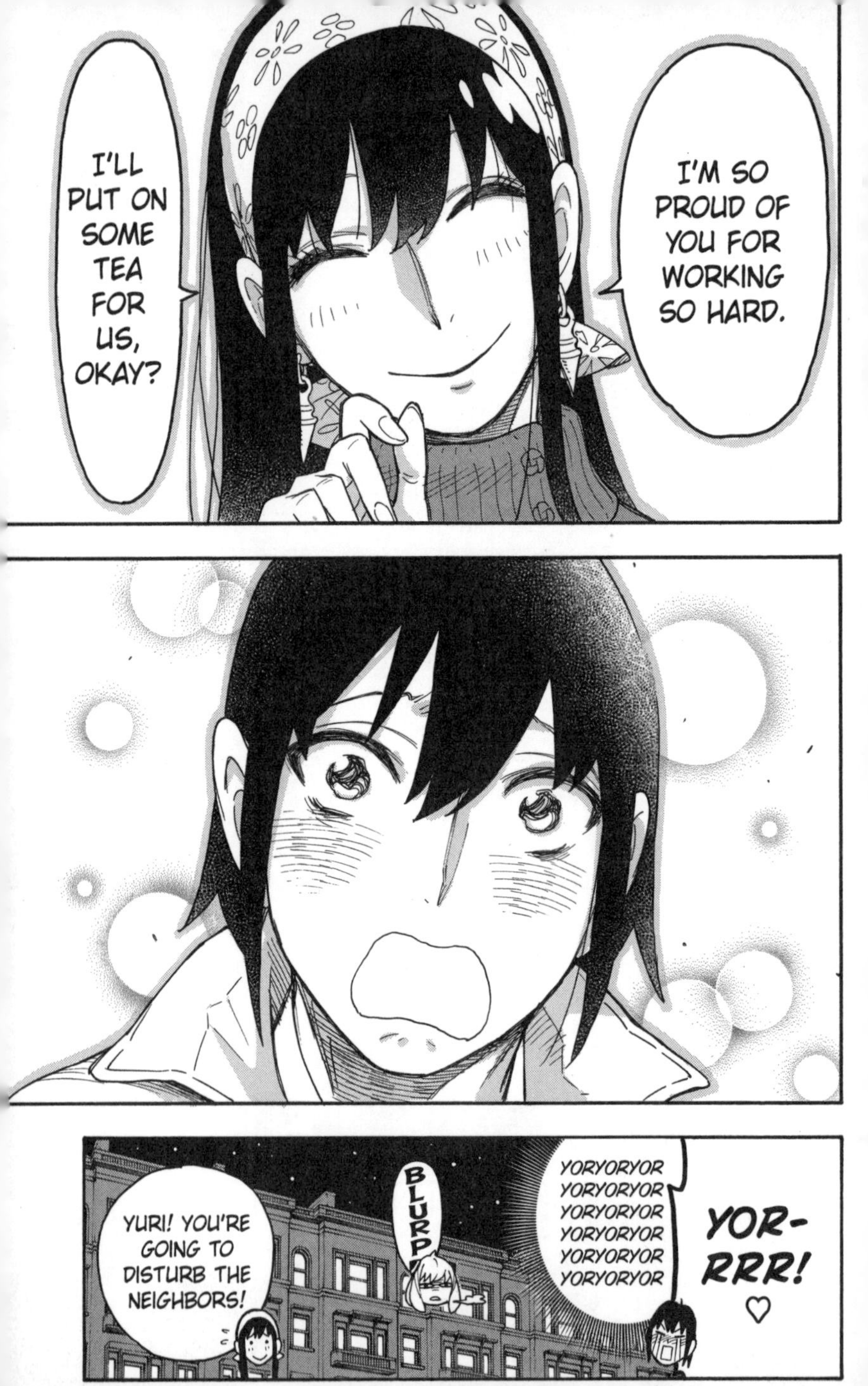
I'M SO PROUD OF YOU FOR WORKING SO HARD.
I'LL PUT ON SOME TEA FOR US, OKAY?
YOR-RRR! ♡
YORYORYOR YORYORYOR YORYORYOR YORYORYOR YORYORYOR YORYORYOR
BLURP
YURI! YOU'RE GOING TO DISTURB THE NEIGHBORS!

SPY×FAMILY

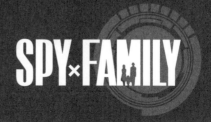

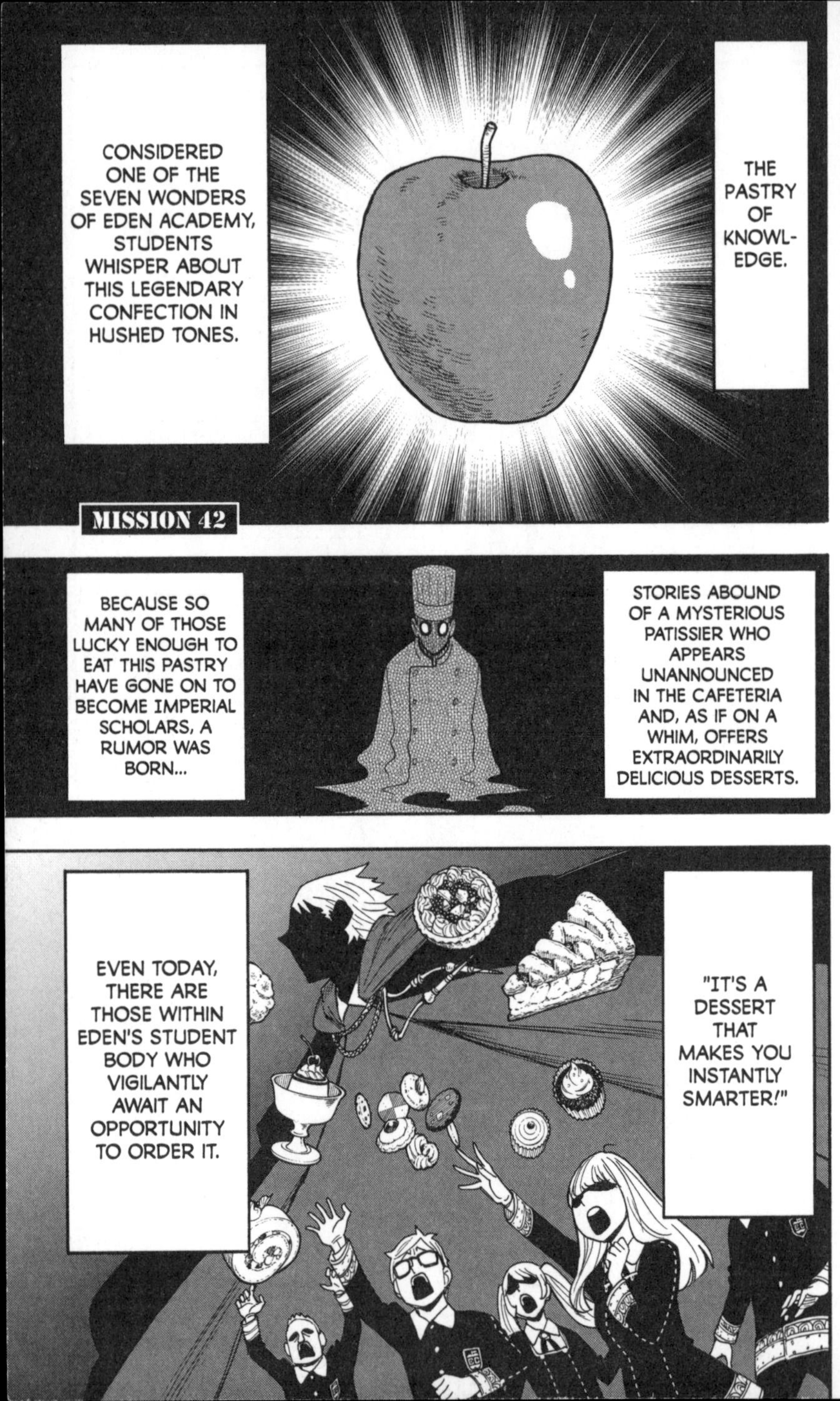
THE PASTRY OF KNOWL-EDGE.
CONSIDERED ONE OF THE SEVEN WONDERS OF EDEN ACADEMY, STUDENTS WHISPER ABOUT THIS LEGENDARY CONFECTION IN HUSHED TONES.
MISSION 42
STORIES ABOUND OF A MYSTERIOUS PATISSIER WHO APPEARS UNANNOUNCED IN THE CAFETERIA AND, AS IF ON A WHIM, OFFERS EXTRAORDINARILY DELICIOUS DESSERTS.
BECAUSE SO MANY OF THOSE LUCKY ENOUGH TO EAT THIS PASTRY HAVE GONE ON TO BECOME IMPERIAL SCHOLARS, A RUMOR WAS BORN...
"IT'S A DESSERT THAT MAKES YOU INSTANTLY SMARTER!"
EVEN TODAY, THERE ARE THOSE WITHIN EDEN'S STUDENT BODY WHO VIGILANTLY AWAIT AN OPPORTUNITY TO ORDER IT.

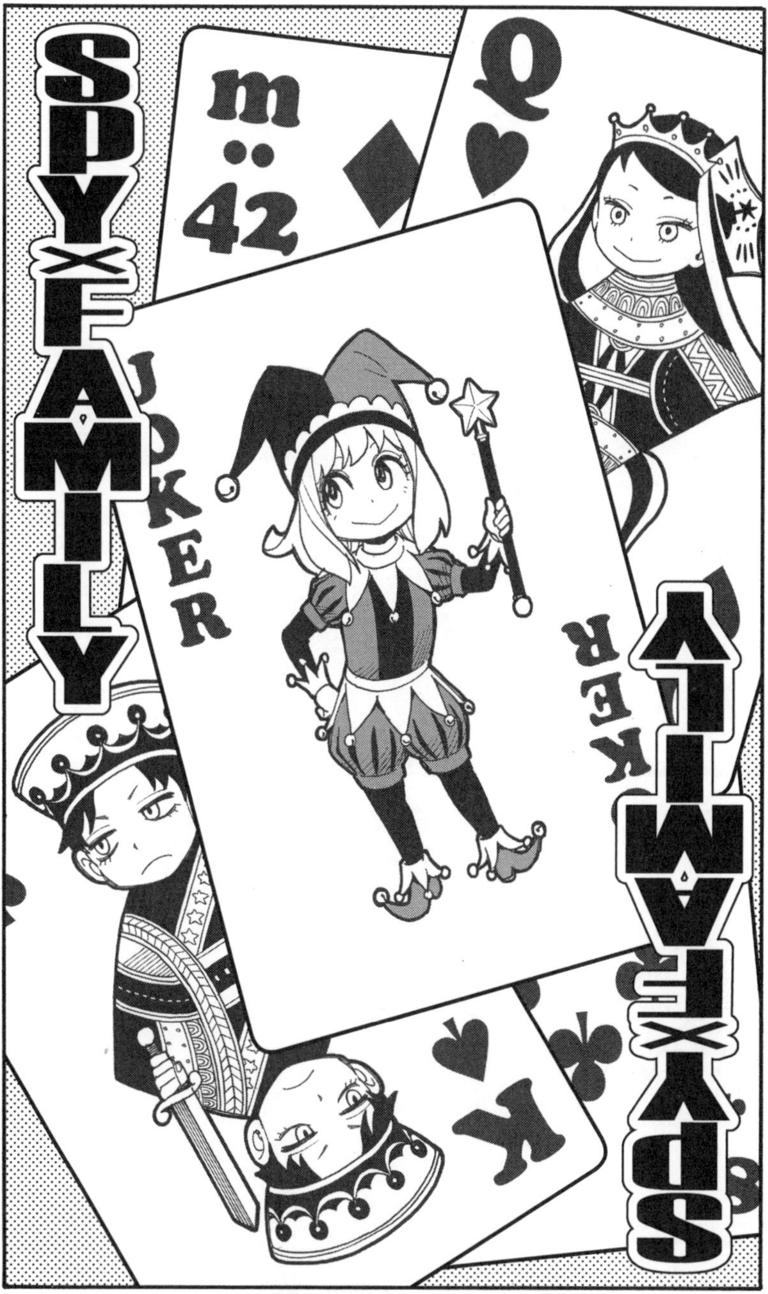
SPY×FAMILY
m
42
Q
JOKER
K

MISSION 42

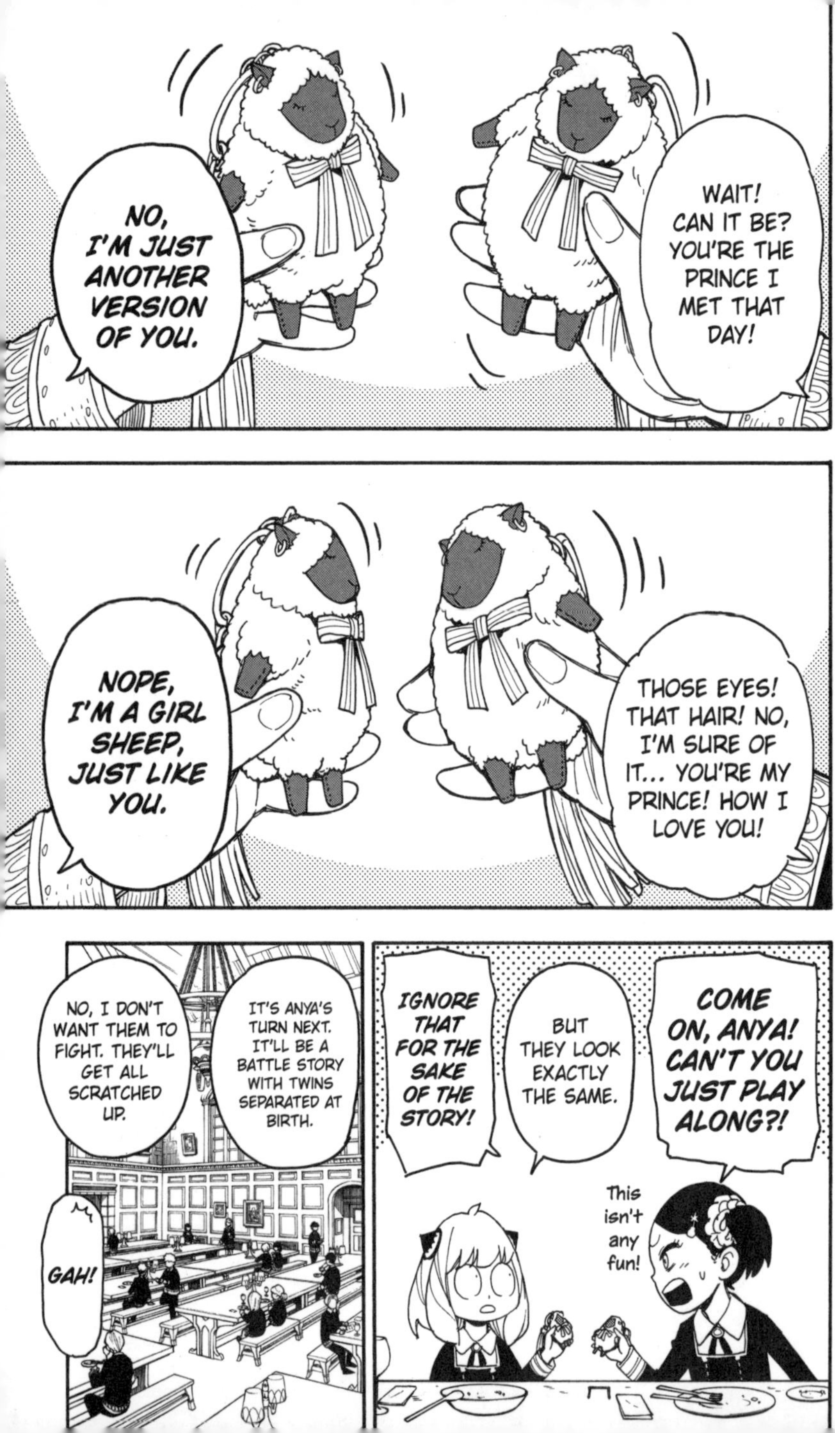
WAIT! CAN IT BE? YOU'RE THE PRINCE I MET THAT DAY!
NO, I'M JUST ANOTHER VERSION OF YOU.
THOSE EYES! THAT HAIR! NO, I'M SURE OF IT... YOU'RE MY PRINCE! HOW I LOVE YOU!
NOPE, I'M A GIRL SHEEP, JUST LIKE YOU.
COME ON, ANYA! CAN'T YOU JUST PLAY ALONG?!
This isn't any fun!
BUT THEY LOOK EXACTLY THE SAME.
IGNORE THAT FOR THE SAKE OF THE STORY!
IT'S ANYA'S TURN NEXT. IT'LL BE A BATTLE STORY WITH TWINS SEPARATED AT BIRTH.
NO, I DON'T WANT THEM TO FIGHT. THEY'LL GET ALL SCRATCHED UP.
GAH!

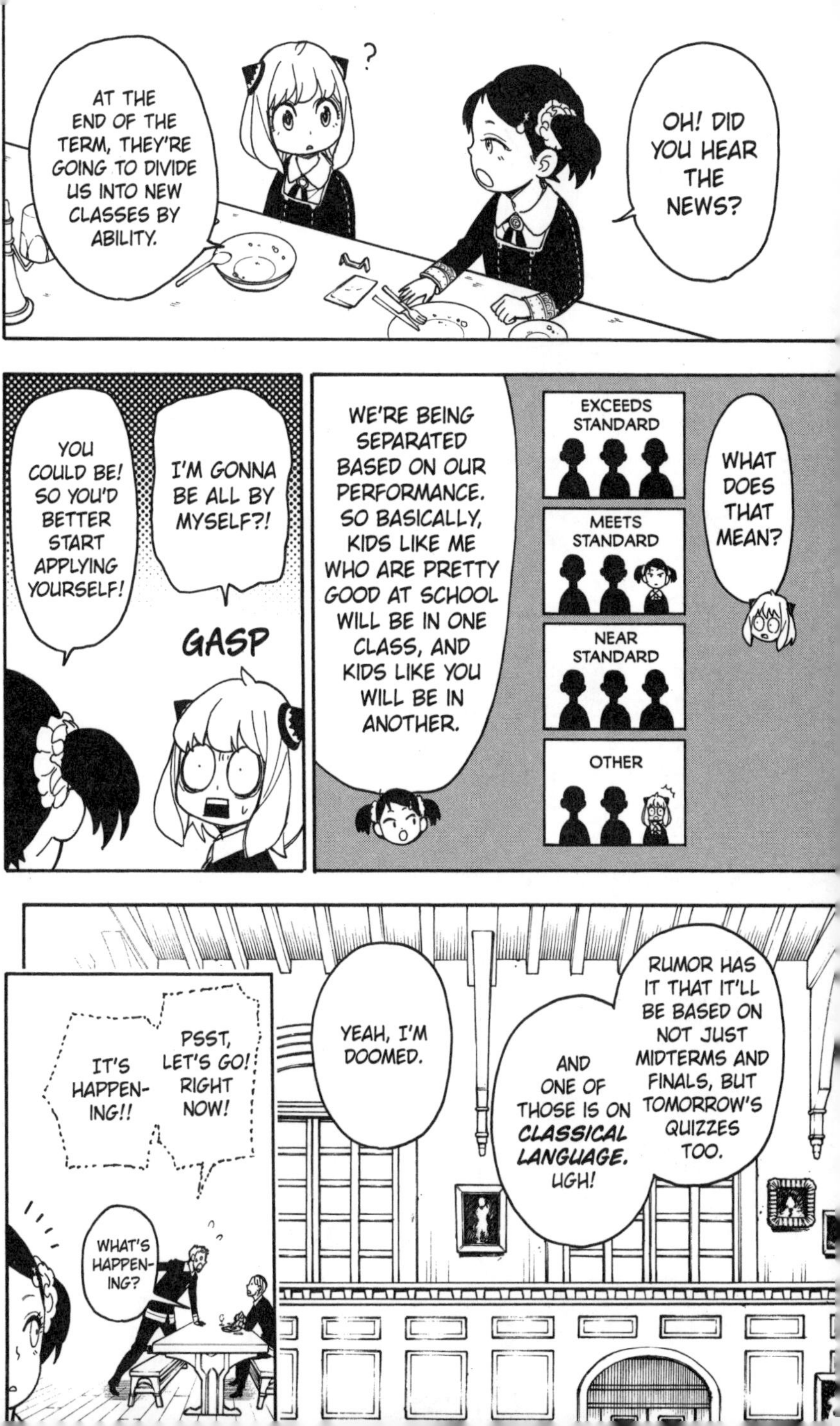
OH! DID YOU HEAR THE NEWS?
AT THE END OF THE TERM, THEY'RE GOING TO DIVIDE US INTO NEW CLASSES BY ABILITY.
WHAT DOES THAT MEAN?
WE'RE BEING SEPARATED BASED ON OUR PERFORMANCE. SO BASICALLY, KIDS LIKE ME WHO ARE PRETTY GOOD AT SCHOOL WILL BE IN ONE CLASS, AND KIDS LIKE YOU WILL BE IN ANOTHER.
EXCEEDS STANDARD
MEETS STANDARD
NEAR STANDARD
OTHER
GASP
I'M GONNA BE ALL BY MYSELF?!
YOU COULD BE! SO YOU'D BETTER START APPLYING YOURSELF!
RUMOR HAS IT THAT IT'LL BE BASED ON NOT JUST MIDTERMS AND FINALS, BUT TOMORROW'S QUIZZES TOO.
AND ONE OF THOSE IS ON *CLASSICAL LANGUAGE.* UGH!
YEAH, I'M DOOMED.
PSST, LET'S GO! RIGHT NOW!
IT'S HAPPEN-ING!!
WHAT'S HAPPEN-ING?

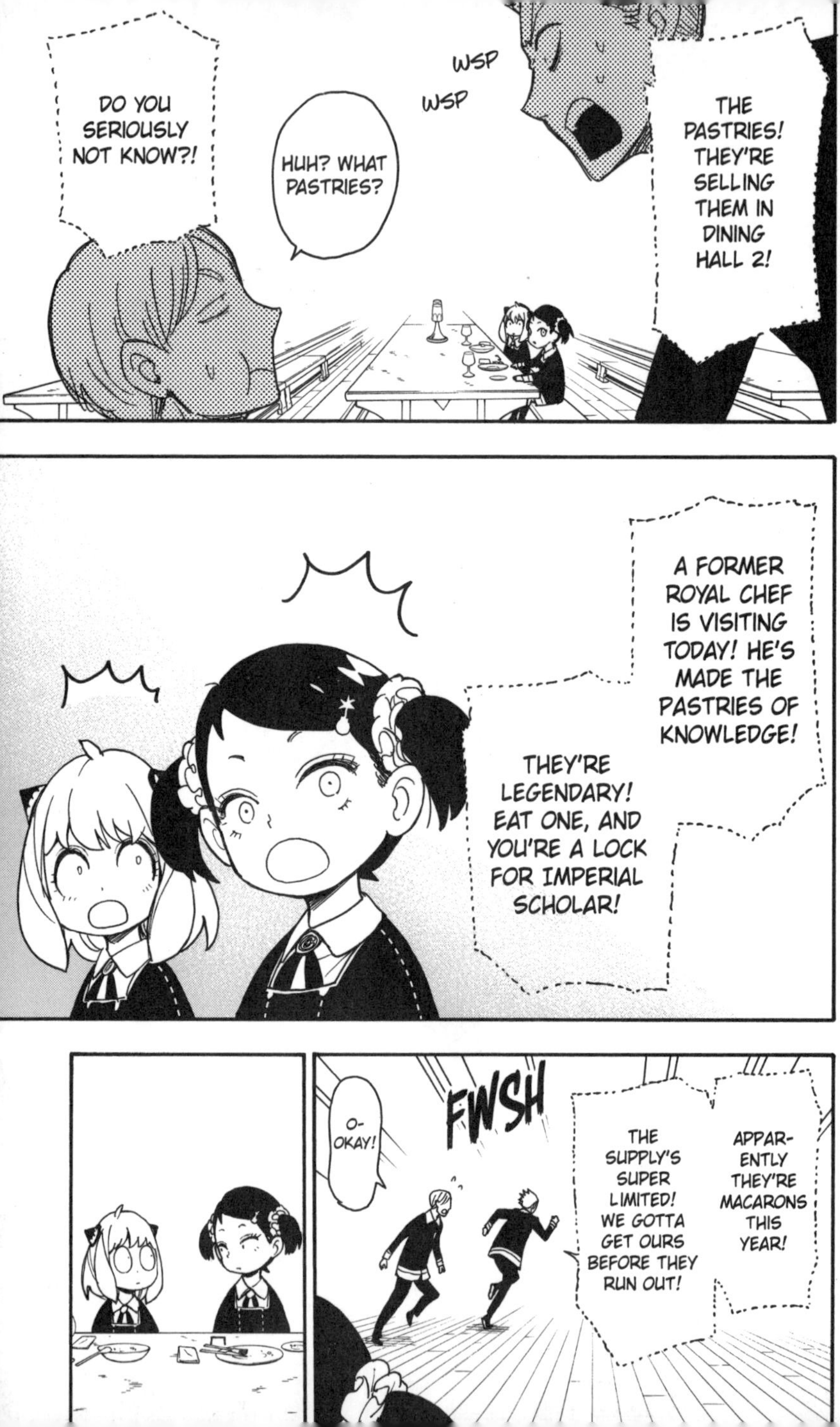
THE PASTRIES! THEY'RE SELLING THEM IN DINING HALL 2!
WSP
WSP
HUH? WHAT PASTRIES?
DO YOU SERIOUSLY NOT KNOW?!
A FORMER ROYAL CHEF IS VISITING TODAY! HE'S MADE THE PASTRIES OF KNOWLEDGE!
THEY'RE LEGENDARY! EAT ONE, AND YOU'RE A LOCK FOR IMPERIAL SCHOLAR!
APPAR-ENTLY THEY'RE MACARONS THIS YEAR!
THE SUPPLY'S SUPER LIMITED! WE GOTTA GET OURS BEFORE THEY RUN OUT!
FWSH
O-OKAY!

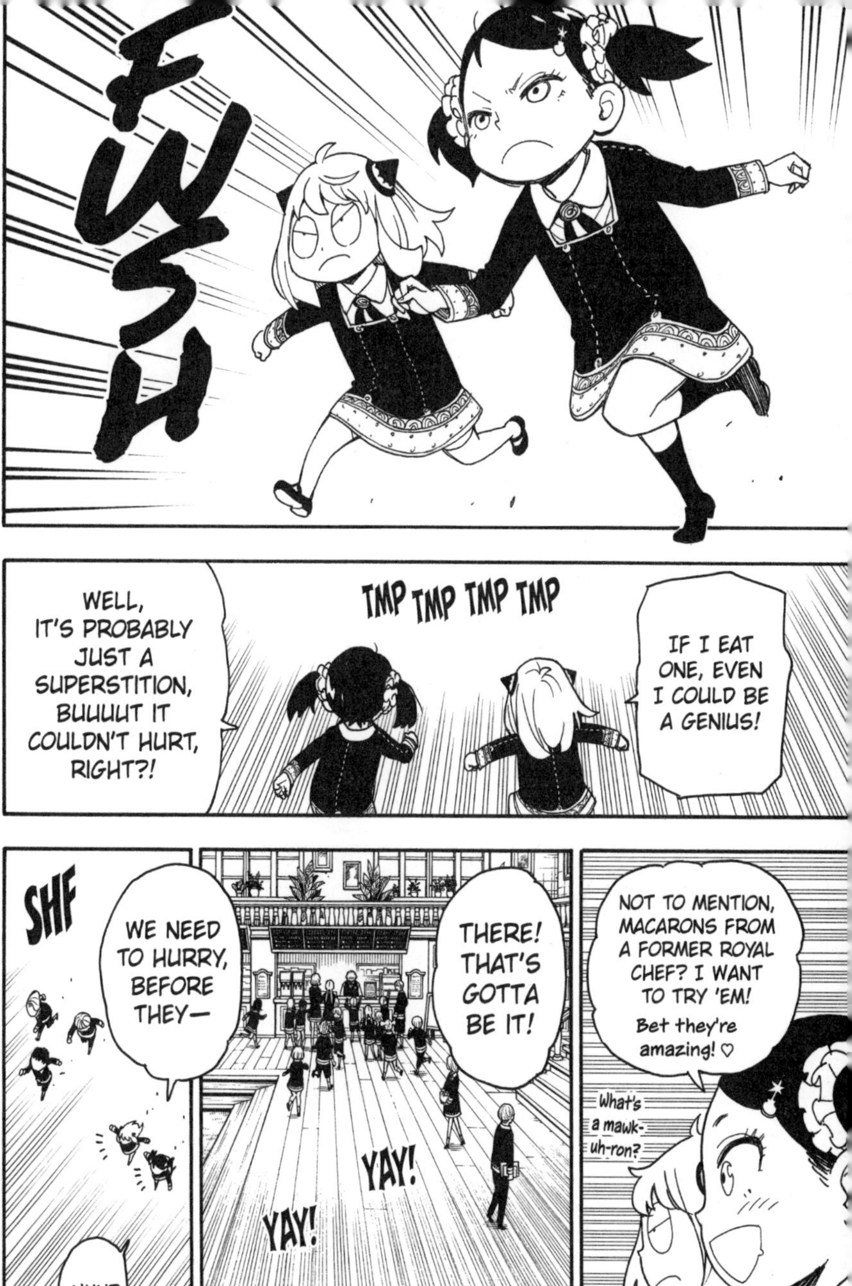
IF I EAT ONE, EVEN I COULD BE A GENIUS!
TMP TMP TMP TMP
WELL, IT'S PROBABLY JUST A SUPERSTITION, BUUUUT IT COULDN'T HURT, RIGHT?!
NOT TO MENTION, MACARONS FROM A FORMER ROYAL CHEF? I WANT TO TRY 'EM!
Bet they're amazing! ♡
What's a mawk-uh-ron?
THERE! THAT'S GOTTA BE IT!
YAY!
YAY!
SHF
WE NEED TO HURRY, BEFORE THEY—
HUH?

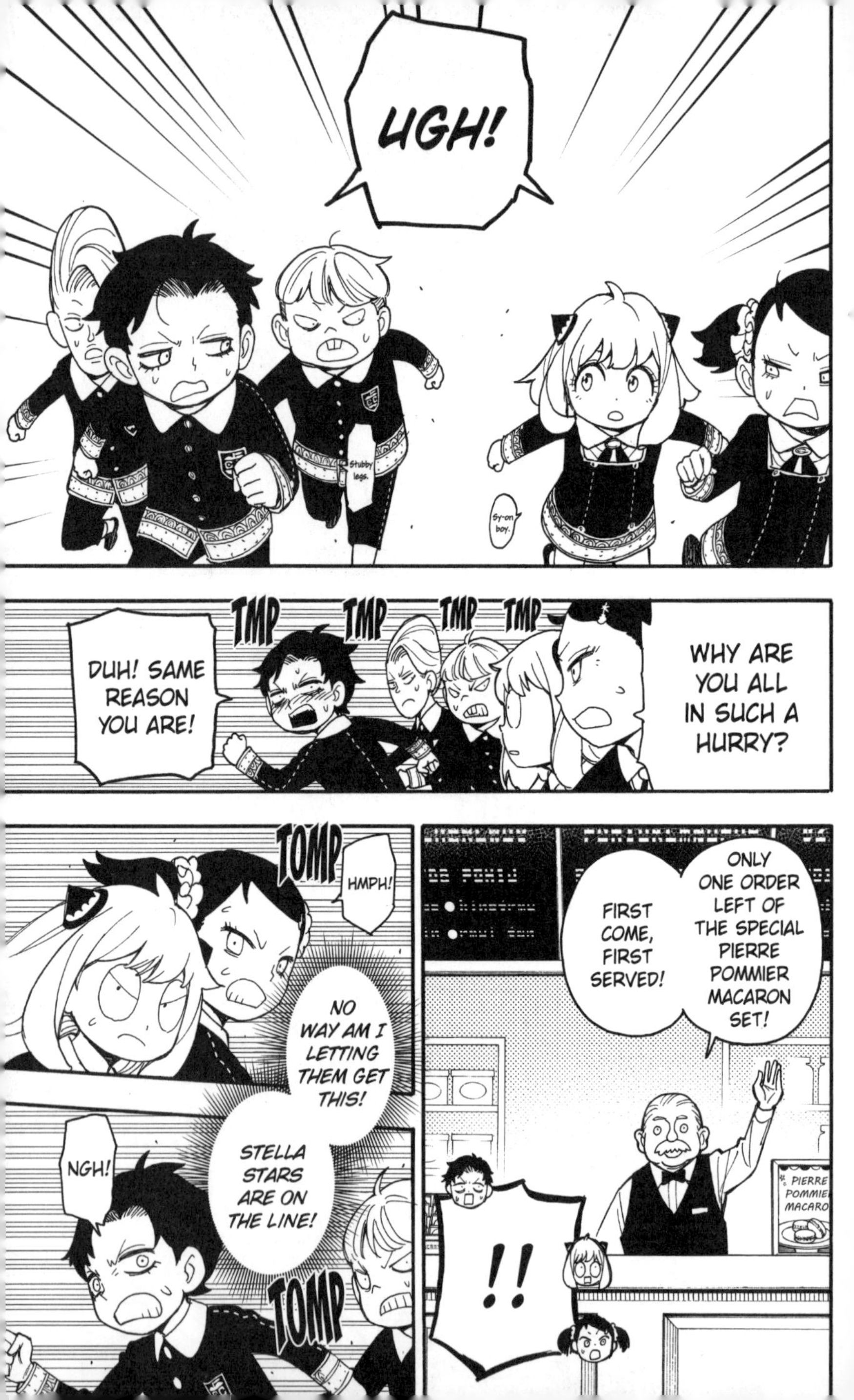
UGH!
Sy-on boy.
Stubby legs.
WHY ARE YOU ALL IN SUCH A HURRY?
TMP TMP TMP TMP
DUH! SAME REASON YOU ARE!
ONLY ONE ORDER LEFT OF THE SPECIAL PIERRE POMMIER MACARON SET!
FIRST COME, FIRST SERVED!
!!
TOMP
HMPH!
NO WAY AM I LETTING THEM GET THIS!
STELLA STARS ARE ON THE LINE!
NGH!
TOMP

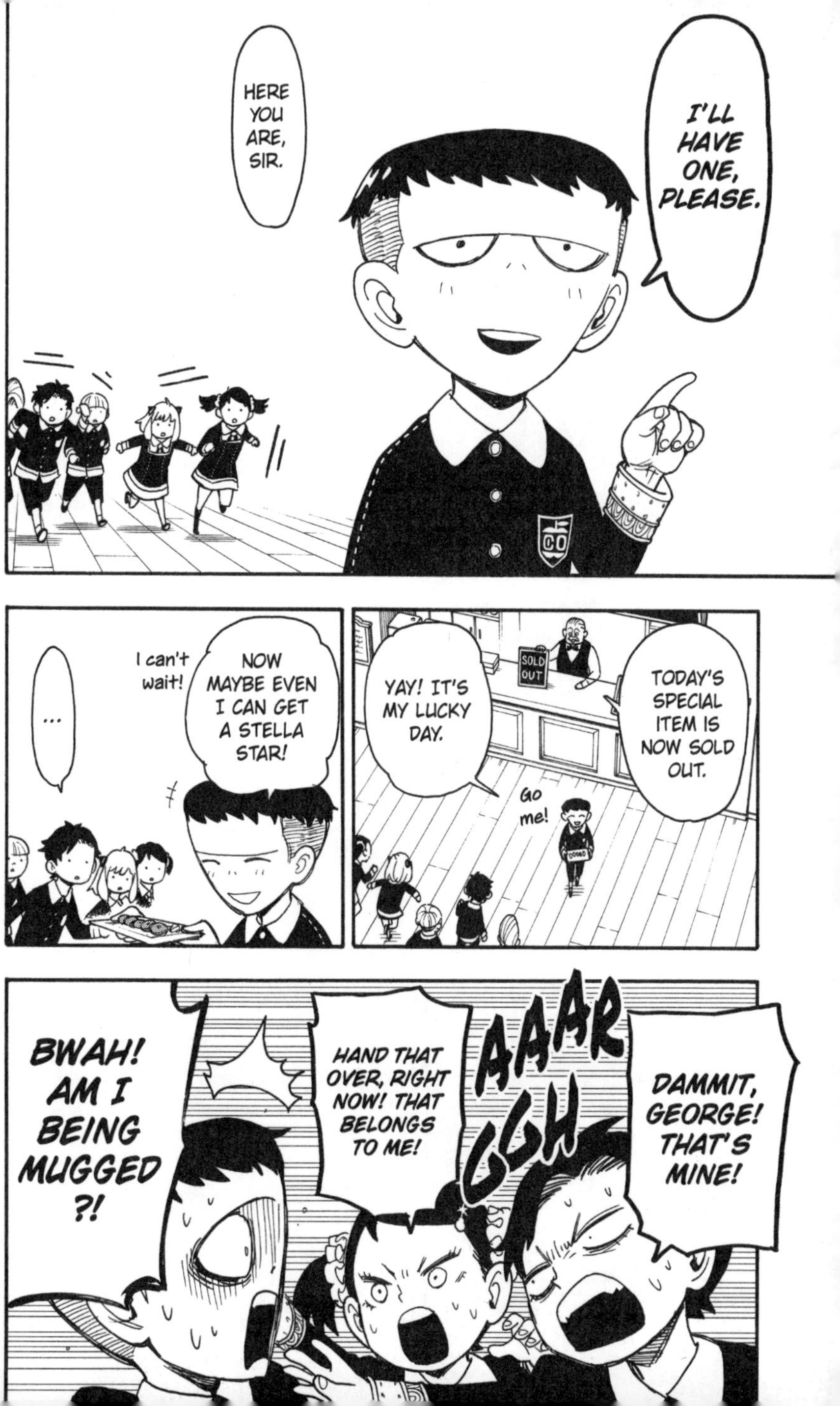
I'LL HAVE ONE, PLEASE.
HERE YOU ARE, SIR.
TODAY'S SPECIAL ITEM IS NOW SOLD OUT.
SOLD OUT
YAY! IT'S MY LUCKY DAY.
Go me!
NOW MAYBE EVEN I CAN GET A STELLA STAR!
I can't wait!
...
DAMMIT, GEORGE! THAT'S MINE!
AAARGGH
HAND THAT OVER, RIGHT NOW! THAT BELONGS TO ME!
BWAH! AM I BEING MUGGED?!

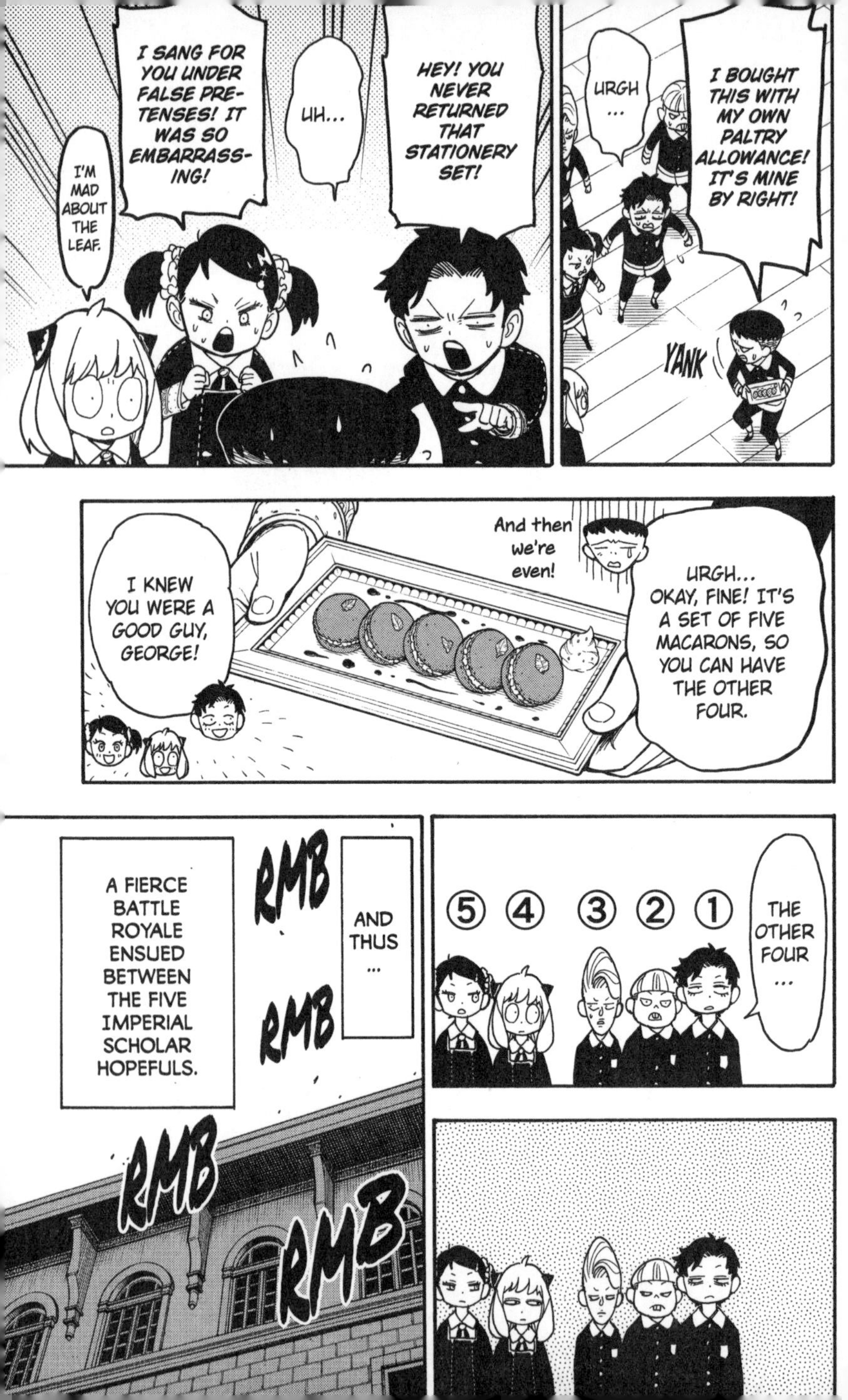

I BOUGHT THIS WITH MY OWN PALTRY ALLOWANCE! IT'S MINE BY RIGHT!
URGH...
YANK
HEY! YOU NEVER RETURNED THAT STATIONERY SET!
UH...
I SANG FOR YOU UNDER FALSE PRETENSES! IT WAS SO EMBARRASSING!
I'M MAD ABOUT THE LEAF.
URGH... OKAY, FINE! IT'S A SET OF FIVE MACARONS, SO YOU CAN HAVE THE OTHER FOUR.
And then we're even!
I KNEW YOU WERE A GOOD GUY, GEORGE!
THE OTHER FOUR...
① ② ③ ④ ⑤
AND THUS...
RMB
RMB
A FIERCE BATTLE ROYALE ENSUED BETWEEN THE FIVE IMPERIAL SCHOLAR HOPEFULS.
RMB
RMB

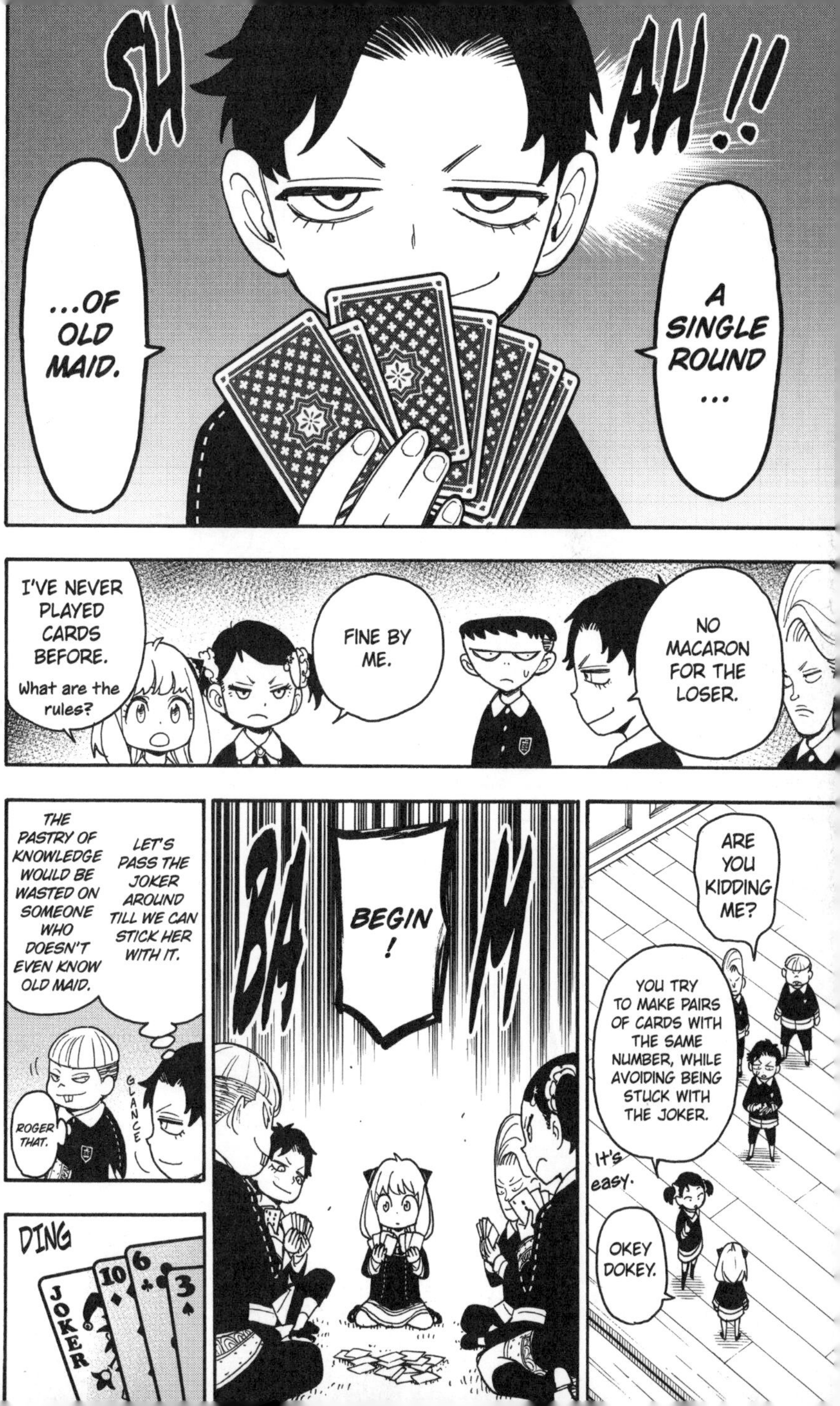
SH
AH!!
A SINGLE ROUND...
...OF OLD MAID.
NO MACARON FOR THE LOSER.
FINE BY ME.
I'VE NEVER PLAYED CARDS BEFORE.
What are the rules?
ARE YOU KIDDING ME?
YOU TRY TO MAKE PAIRS OF CARDS WITH THE SAME NUMBER, WHILE AVOIDING BEING STUCK WITH THE JOKER.
It's easy.
OKEY DOKEY.
BAM
BEGIN!
THE PASTRY OF KNOWLEDGE WOULD BE WASTED ON SOMEONE WHO DOESN'T EVEN KNOW OLD MAID.
LET'S PASS THE JOKER AROUND TILL WE CAN STICK HER WITH IT.
GLANCE
ROGER THAT.
DING
JOKER
10
6
3

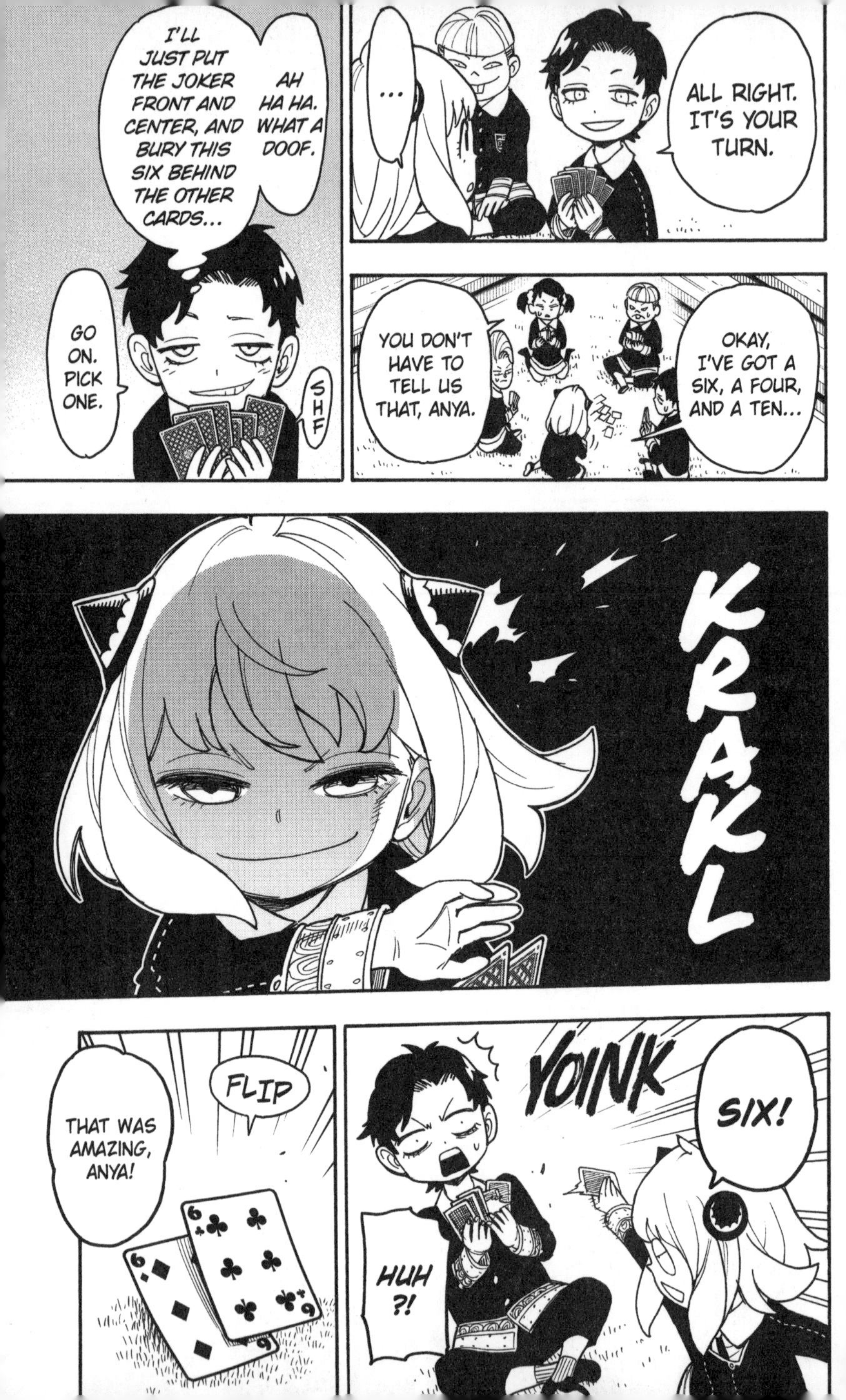
ALL RIGHT. IT'S YOUR TURN.
...
OKAY, I'VE GOT A SIX, A FOUR, AND A TEN...
YOU DON'T HAVE TO TELL US THAT, ANYA.
AH HA HA. WHAT A DOOF.
I'LL JUST PUT THE JOKER FRONT AND CENTER, AND BURY THIS SIX BEHIND THE OTHER CARDS...
SHF
GO ON. PICK ONE.
KRAKL
YOINK
SIX!
HUH ?!
FLIP
THAT WAS AMAZING, ANYA!

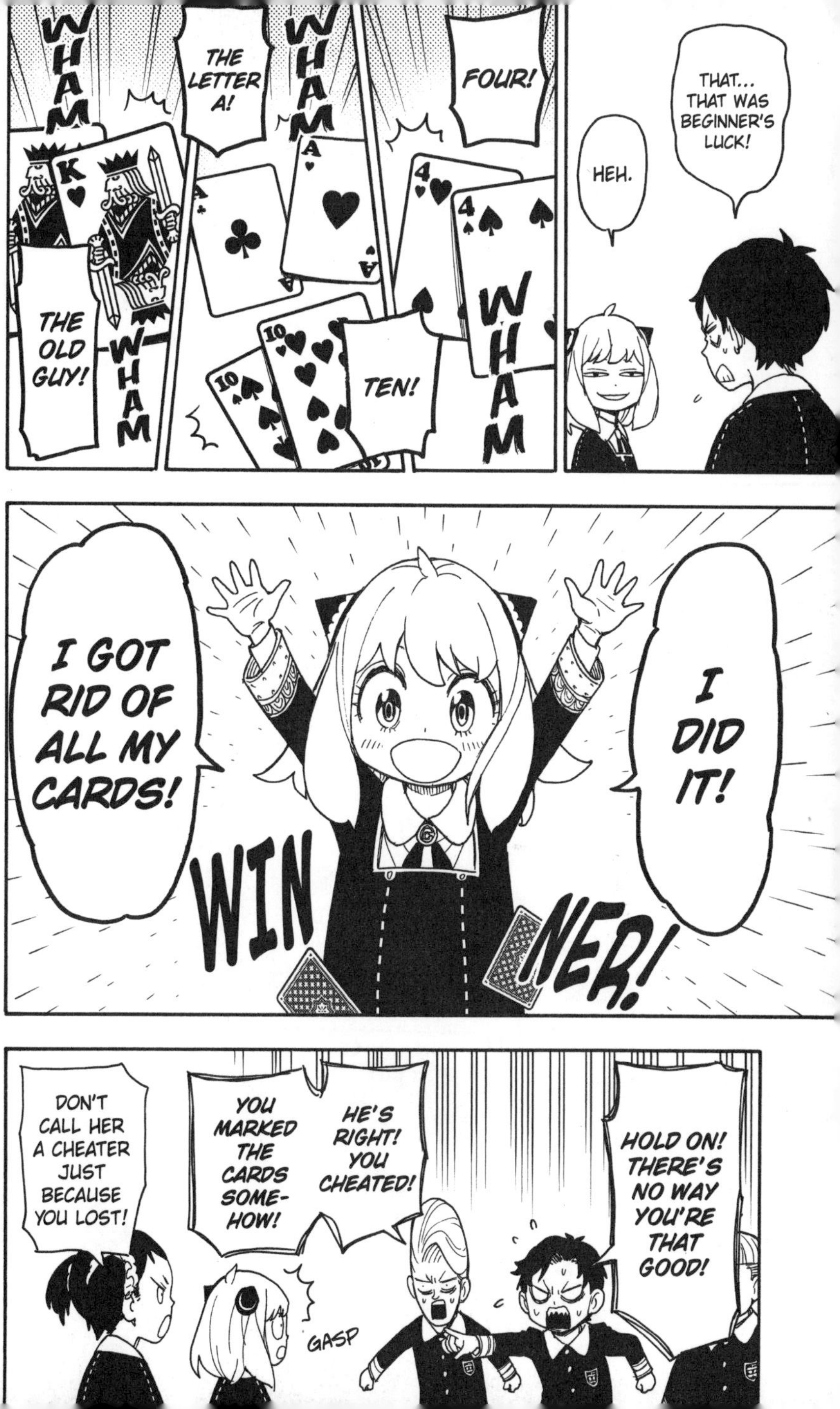
THAT... THAT WAS BEGINNER'S LUCK!
HEH.
FOUR!
WHAM
THE LETTER A!
WHAM
TEN!
THE OLD GUY!
WHAM
WHAM
I DID IT!
I GOT RID OF ALL MY CARDS!
WINNER!
HOLD ON! THERE'S NO WAY YOU'RE THAT GOOD!
HE'S RIGHT! YOU CHEATED!
YOU MARKED THE CARDS SOMEHOW!
GASP
DON'T CALL HER A CHEATER JUST BECAUSE YOU LOST!

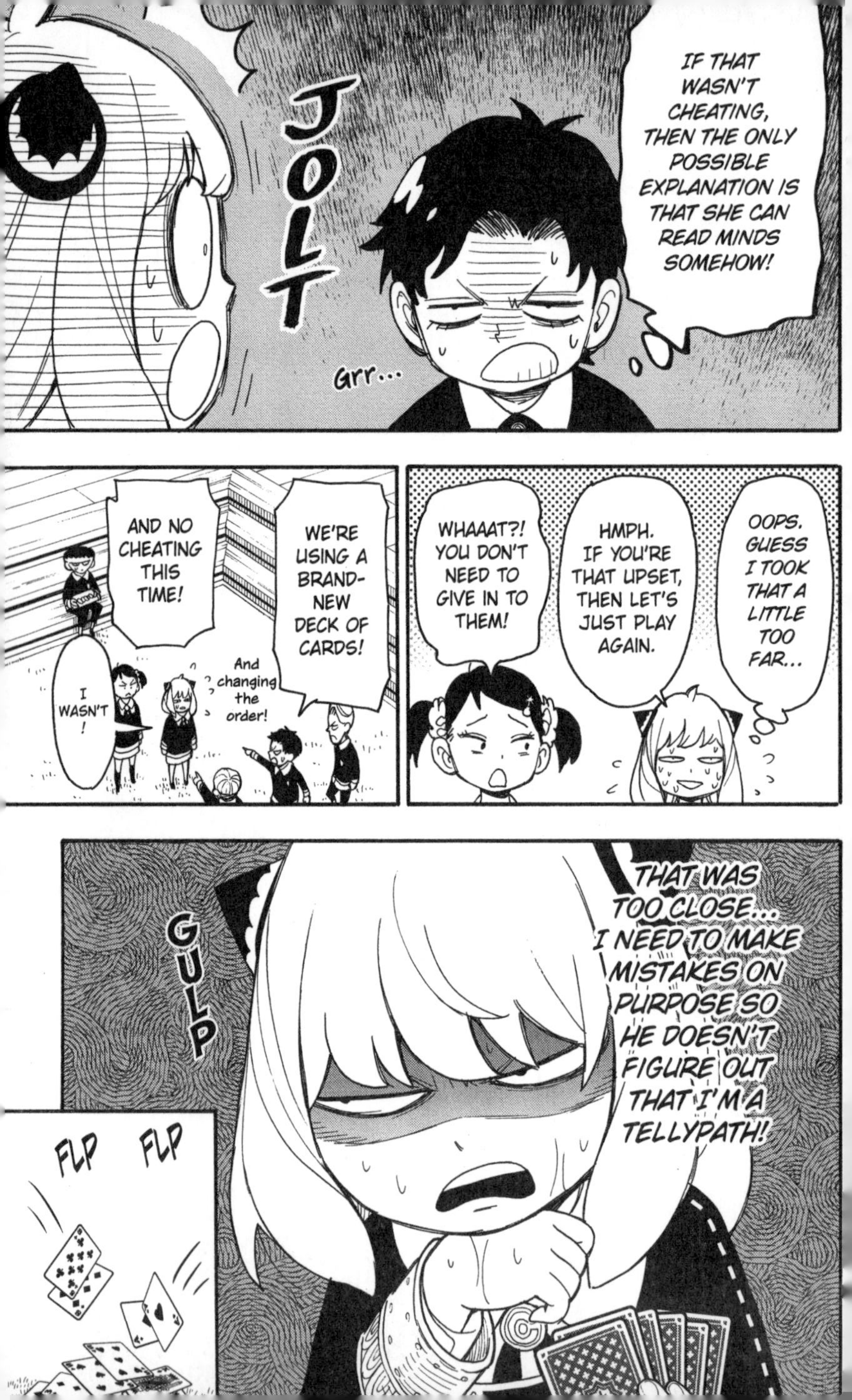
IF THAT WASN'T CHEATING, THEN THE ONLY POSSIBLE EXPLANATION IS THAT SHE CAN READ MINDS SOMEHOW!
JOLT
Grr...
OOPS. GUESS I TOOK THAT A LITTLE TOO FAR...
HMPH. IF YOU'RE THAT UPSET, THEN LET'S JUST PLAY AGAIN.
WHAAAT?! YOU DON'T NEED TO GIVE IN TO THEM!
WE'RE USING A BRAND-NEW DECK OF CARDS!
AND NO CHEATING THIS TIME!
And changing the order!
I WASN'T!
THAT WAS TOO CLOSE... I NEED TO MAKE MISTAKES ON PURPOSE SO HE DOESN'T FIGURE OUT THAT I'M A TELLYPATH!
GULP
FLP FLP

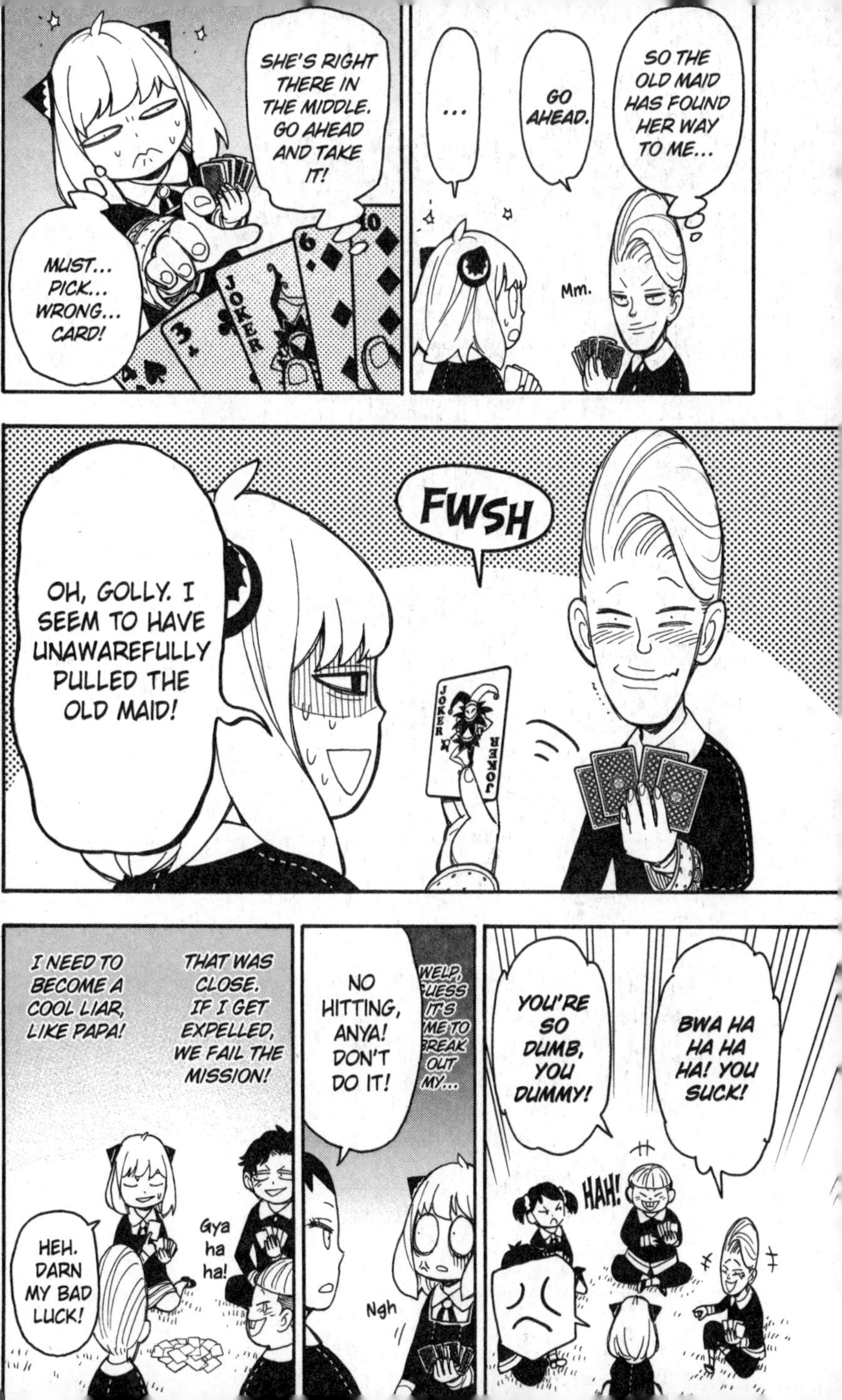
SO THE OLD MAID HAS FOUND HER WAY TO ME...
GO AHEAD.
...
Mm.
SHE'S RIGHT THERE IN THE MIDDLE. GO AHEAD AND TAKE IT!
MUST... PICK... WRONG... CARD!
JOKER
FWSH
OH, GOLLY. I SEEM TO HAVE UNAWAREFULLY PULLED THE OLD MAID!
JOKER
BWA HA HA HA HA! YOU SUCK!
YOU'RE SO DUMB, YOU DUMMY!
HAH!
WELP, GUESS IT'S TIME TO BREAK OUT MY...
NO HITTING, ANYA! DON'T DO IT!
Ngh
THAT WAS CLOSE. IF I GET EXPELLED, WE FAIL THE MISSION!
I NEED TO BECOME A COOL LIAR, LIKE PAPA!
Gya ha ha!
HEH. DARN MY BAD LUCK!

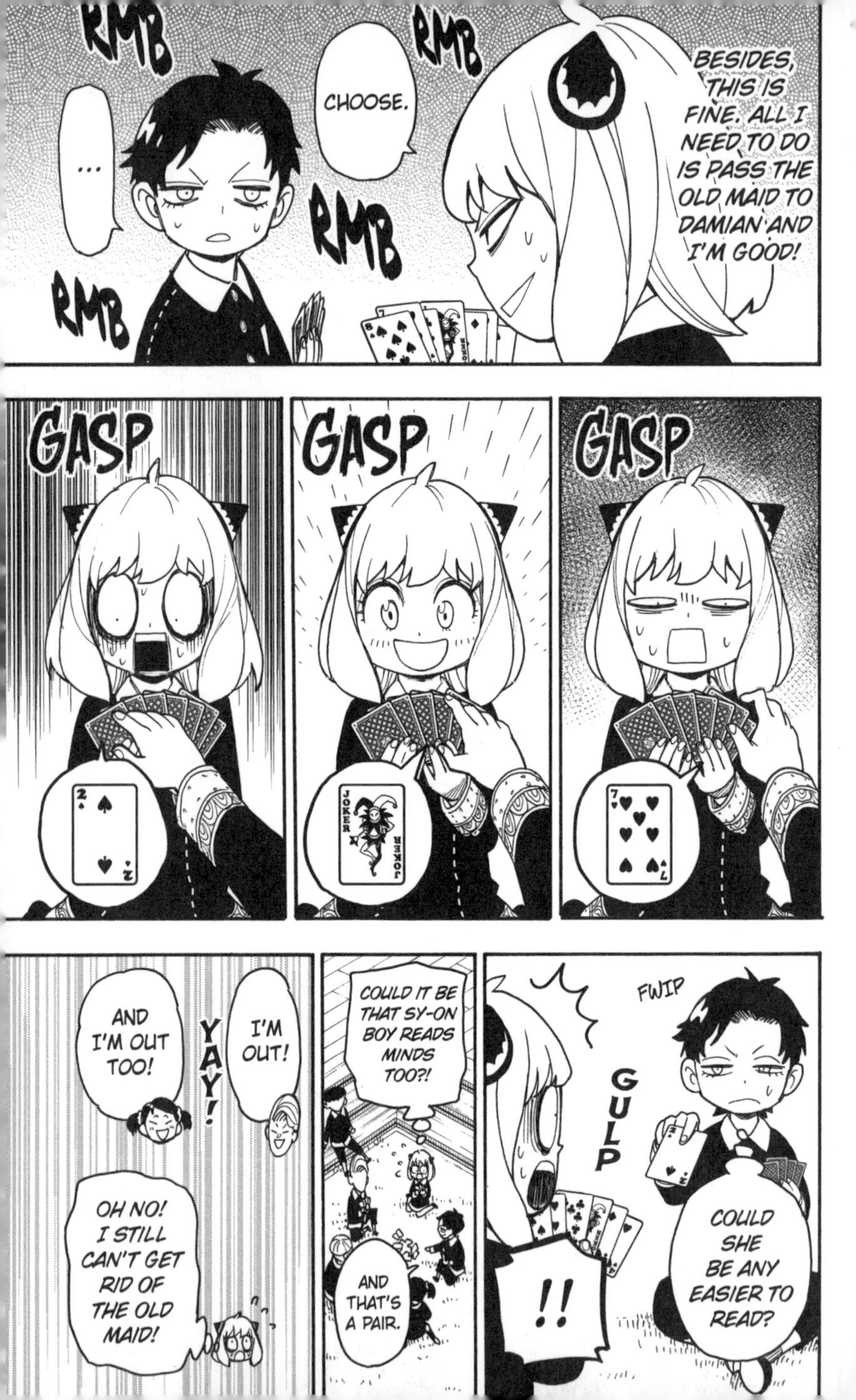
BESIDES, THIS IS FINE. ALL I NEED TO DO IS PASS THE OLD MAID TO DAMIAN AND I'M GOOD!
RMB
CHOOSE.
RMB
...
RMB
RMB
GASP
GASP
GASP
FWIP
GULP
COULD SHE BE ANY EASIER TO READ?
!!
COULD IT BE THAT SY-ON BOY READS MINDS TOO?!
AND THAT'S A PAIR.
I'M OUT!
YAY!
AND I'M OUT TOO!
OH NO! I STILL CAN'T GET RID OF THE OLD MAID!

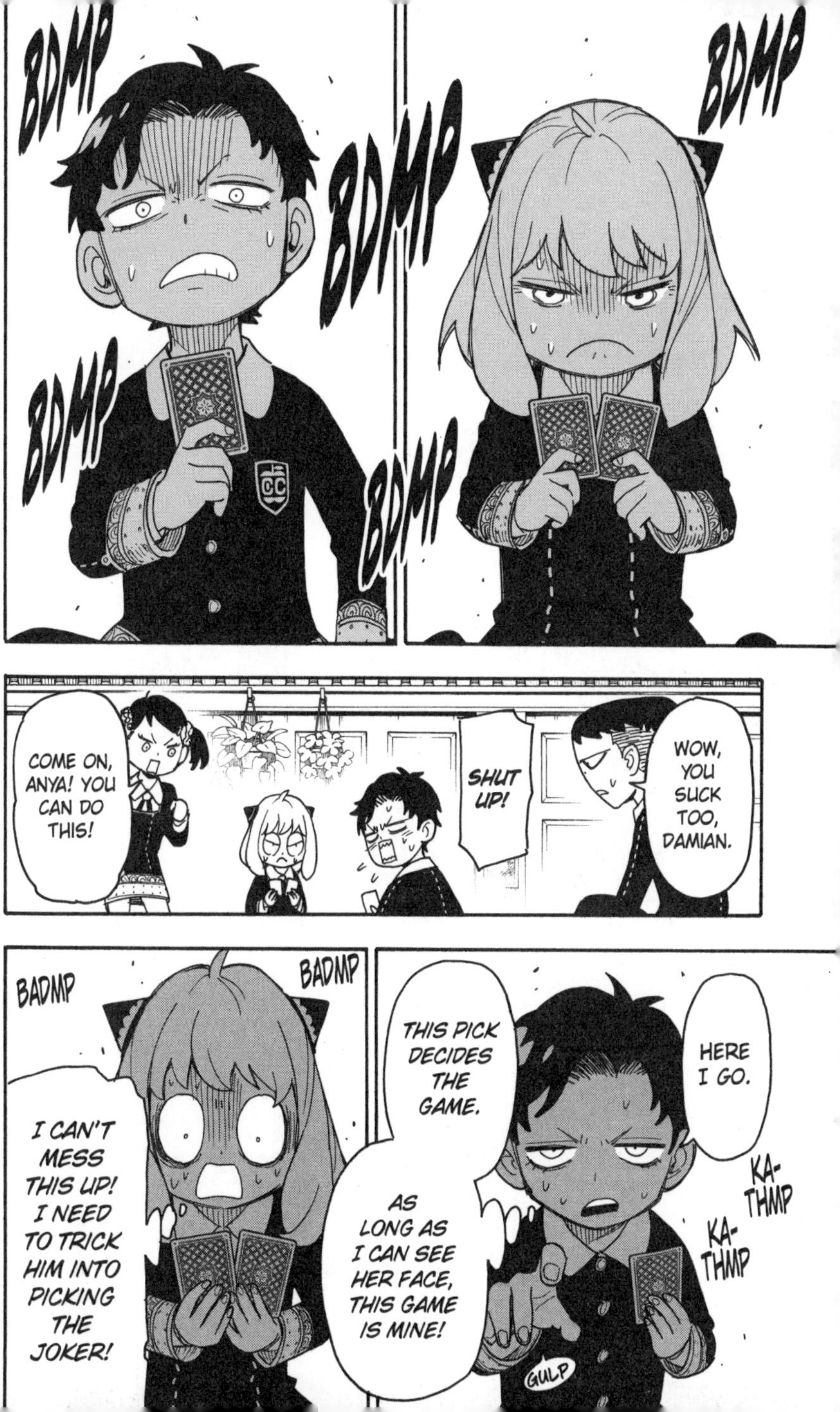
BDMP
BDMP
BDMP
BDMP
BDMP
WOW, YOU SUCK TOO, DAMIAN.
SHUT UP!
COME ON, ANYA! YOU CAN DO THIS!
HERE I GO.
THIS PICK DECIDES THE GAME.
KA-THMP
KA-THMP
AS LONG AS I CAN SEE HER FACE, THIS GAME IS MINE!
GULP
BADMP
BADMP
I CAN'T MESS THIS UP! I NEED TO TRICK HIM INTO PICKING THE JOKER!

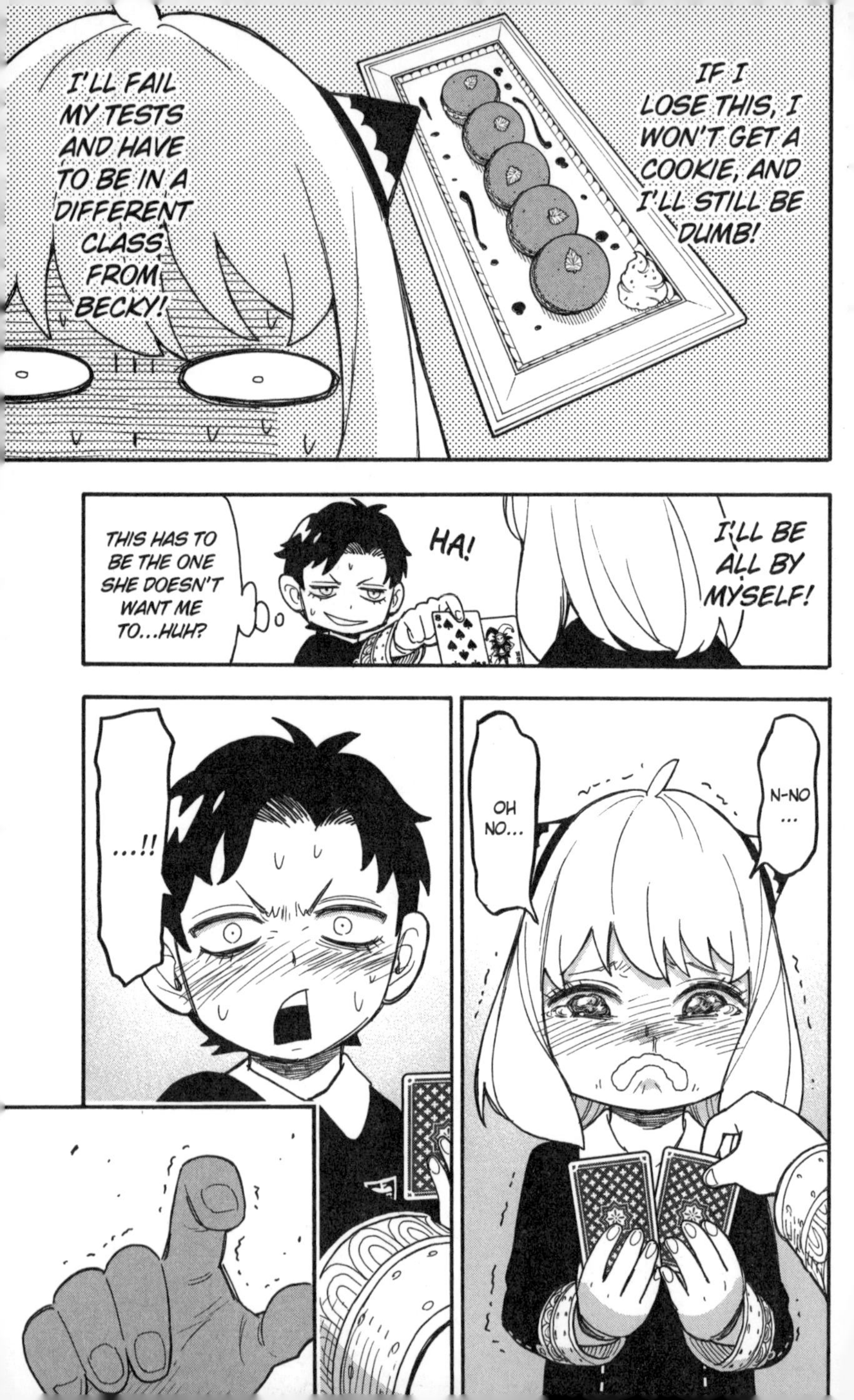
IF I LOSE THIS, I WON'T GET A COOKIE, AND I'LL STILL BE DUMB!
I'LL FAIL MY TESTS AND HAVE TO BE IN A DIFFERENT CLASS FROM BECKY!
I'LL BE ALL BY MYSELF!
HA!
THIS HAS TO BE THE ONE SHE DOESN'T WANT ME TO...HUH?
N-NO ...
OH NO...
...!!

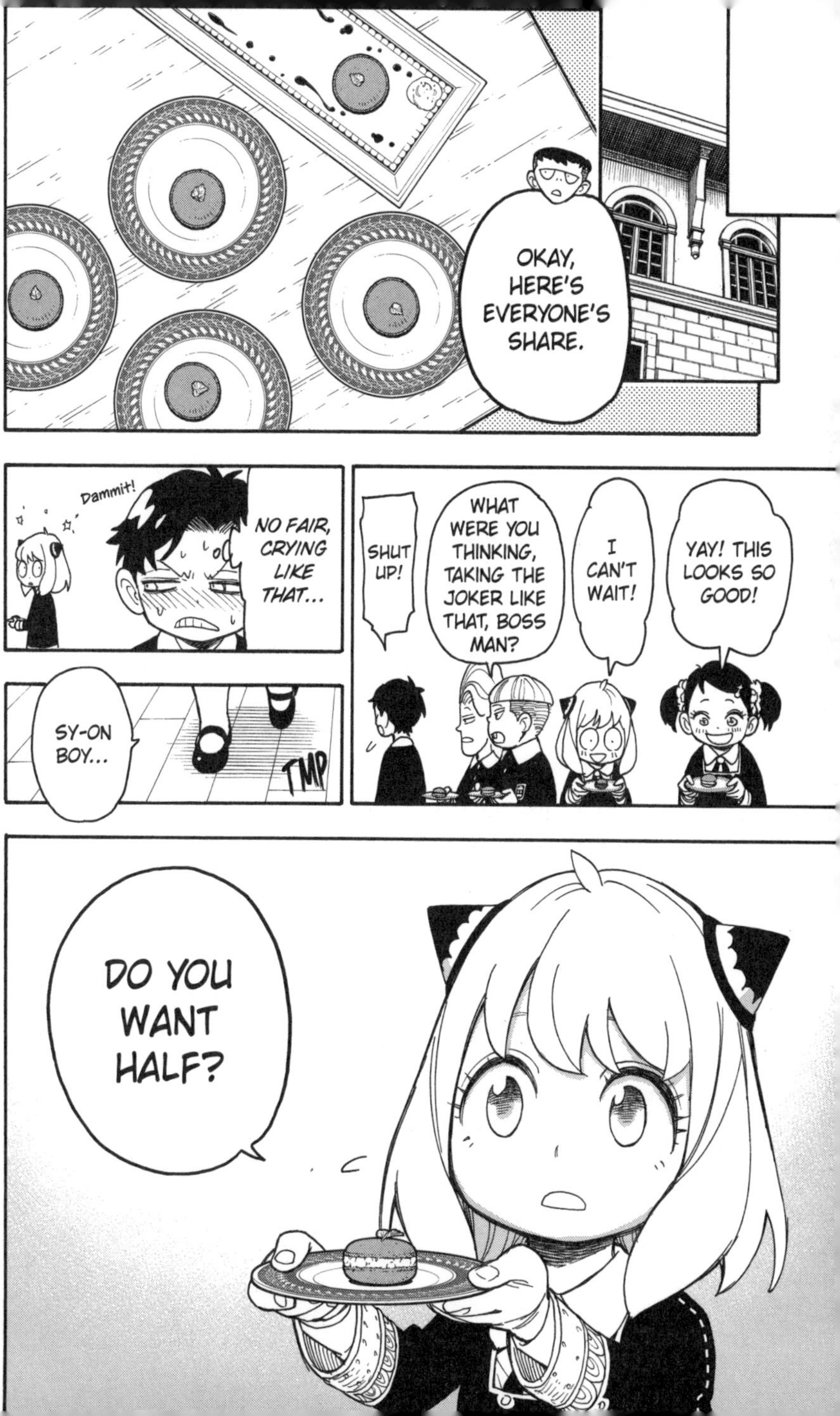
OKAY, HERE'S EVERYONE'S SHARE.
YAY! THIS LOOKS SO GOOD!
I CAN'T WAIT!
WHAT WERE YOU THINKING, TAKING THE JOKER LIKE THAT, BOSS MAN?
SHUT UP!
NO FAIR, CRYING LIKE THAT...
Dammit!
TMP
SY-ON BOY...
DO YOU WANT HALF?

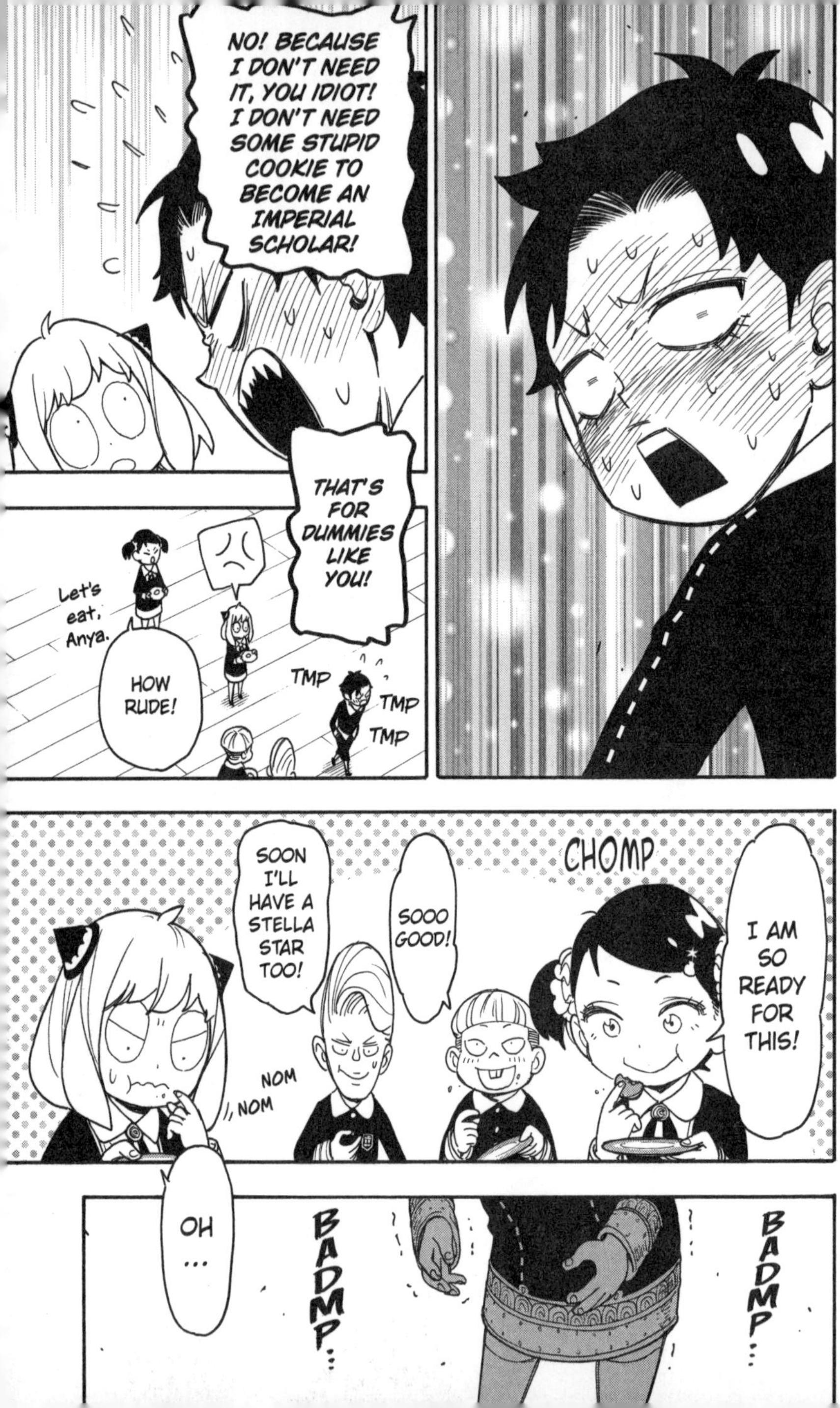
NO! BECAUSE I DON'T NEED IT, YOU IDIOT! I DON'T NEED SOME STUPID COOKIE TO BECOME AN IMPERIAL SCHOLAR!
THAT'S FOR DUMMIES LIKE YOU!
TMP
TMP
TMP
Let's eat, Anya.
HOW RUDE!
CHOMP
I AM SO READY FOR THIS!
SOOO GOOD!
SOON I'LL HAVE A STELLA STAR TOO!
NOM
NOM
BADMP...
OH...
BADMP...

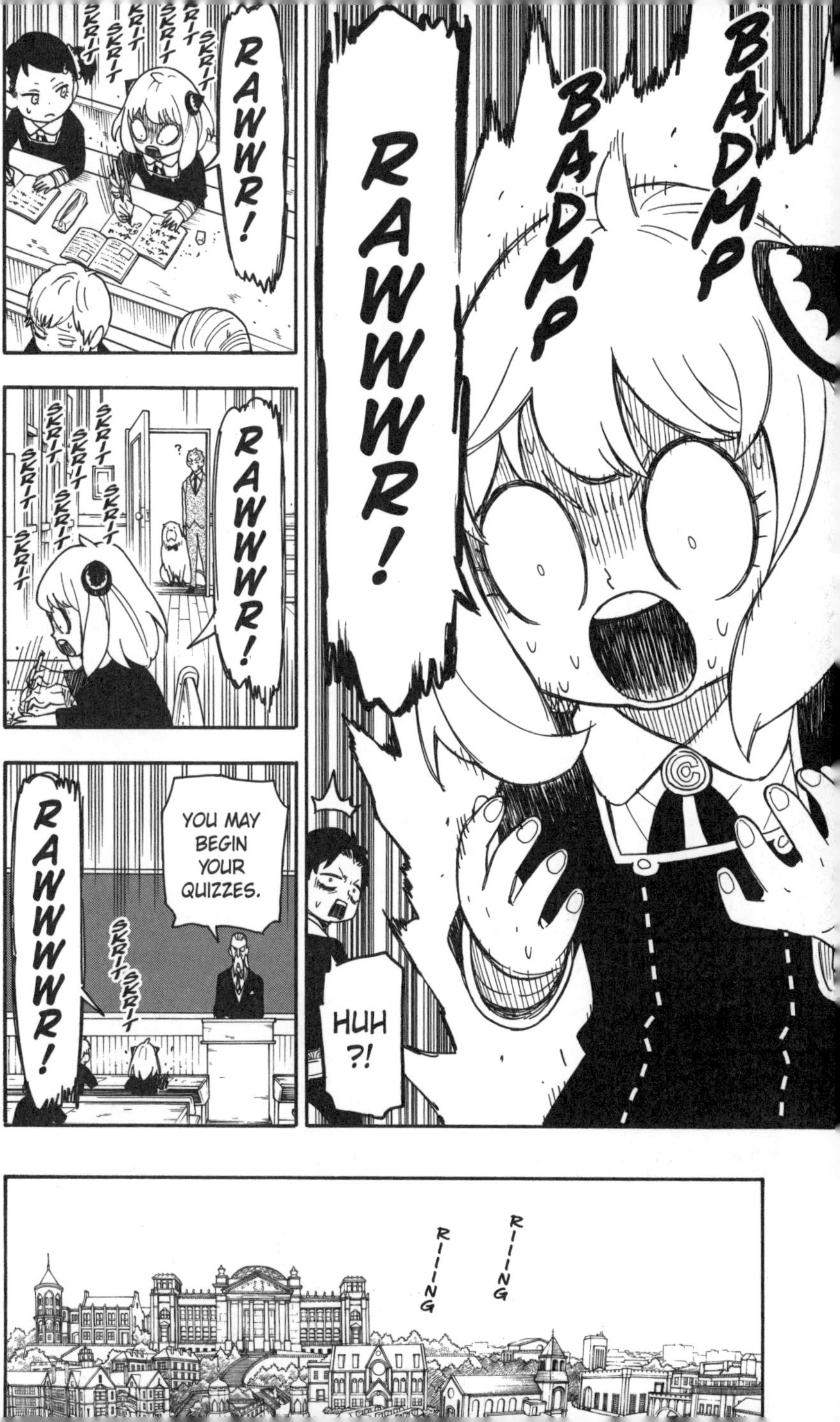
BADMP
BADMP
RAWWWWR!
HUH ?!
RAWWWR!
SKRIT SKRIT SKRIT SKRIT
RAWWWWR!
?
SKRIT SKRIT SKRIT SKRIT SKRIT SKRIT
RAWWWWWR!
YOU MAY BEGIN YOUR QUIZZES.
SKRIT SKRIT
RIIING
RIIING

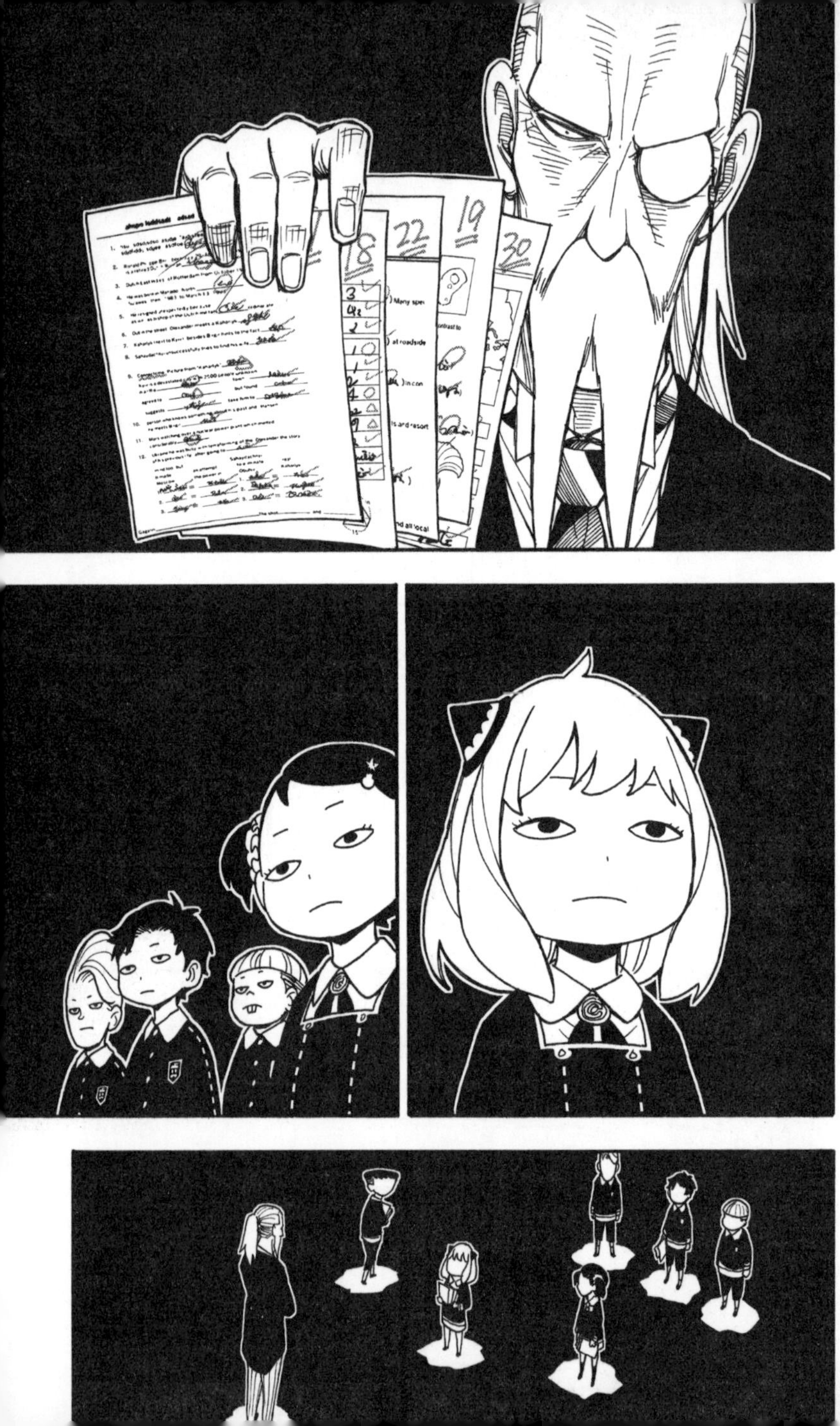
30
19
22
18

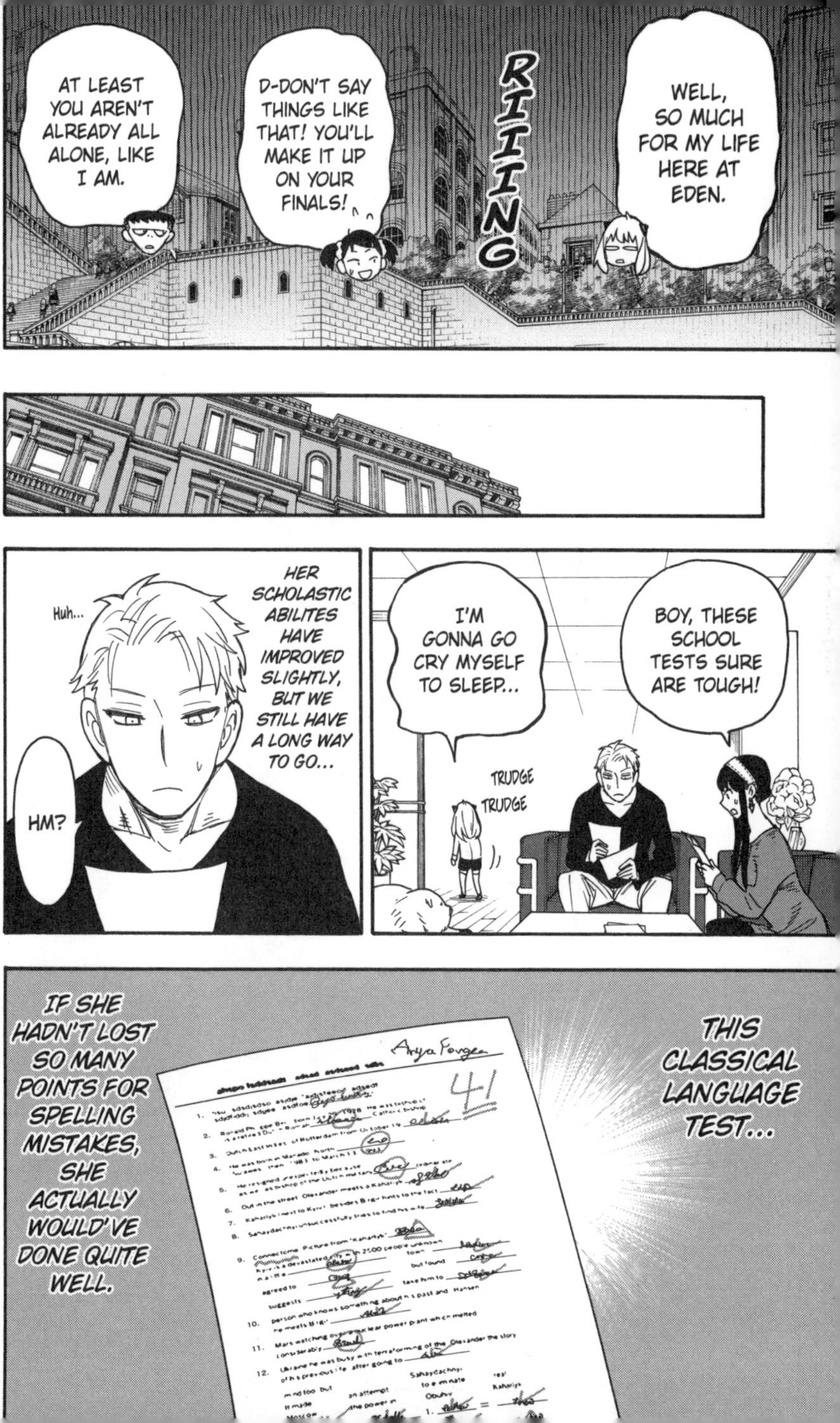
WELL, SO MUCH FOR MY LIFE HERE AT EDEN.
RIIIING
D-DON'T SAY THINGS LIKE THAT! YOU'LL MAKE IT UP ON YOUR FINALS!
AT LEAST YOU AREN'T ALREADY ALL ALONE, LIKE I AM.
BOY, THESE SCHOOL TESTS SURE ARE TOUGH!
I'M GONNA GO CRY MYSELF TO SLEEP...
TRUDGE
TRUDGE
HER SCHOLASTIC ABILITES HAVE IMPROVED SLIGHTLY, BUT WE STILL HAVE A LONG WAY TO GO...
Huh...
HM?
THIS CLASSICAL LANGUAGE TEST...
Anya Forger
41
IF SHE HADN'T LOST SO MANY POINTS FOR SPELLING MISTAKES, SHE ACTUALLY WOULD'VE DONE QUITE WELL.

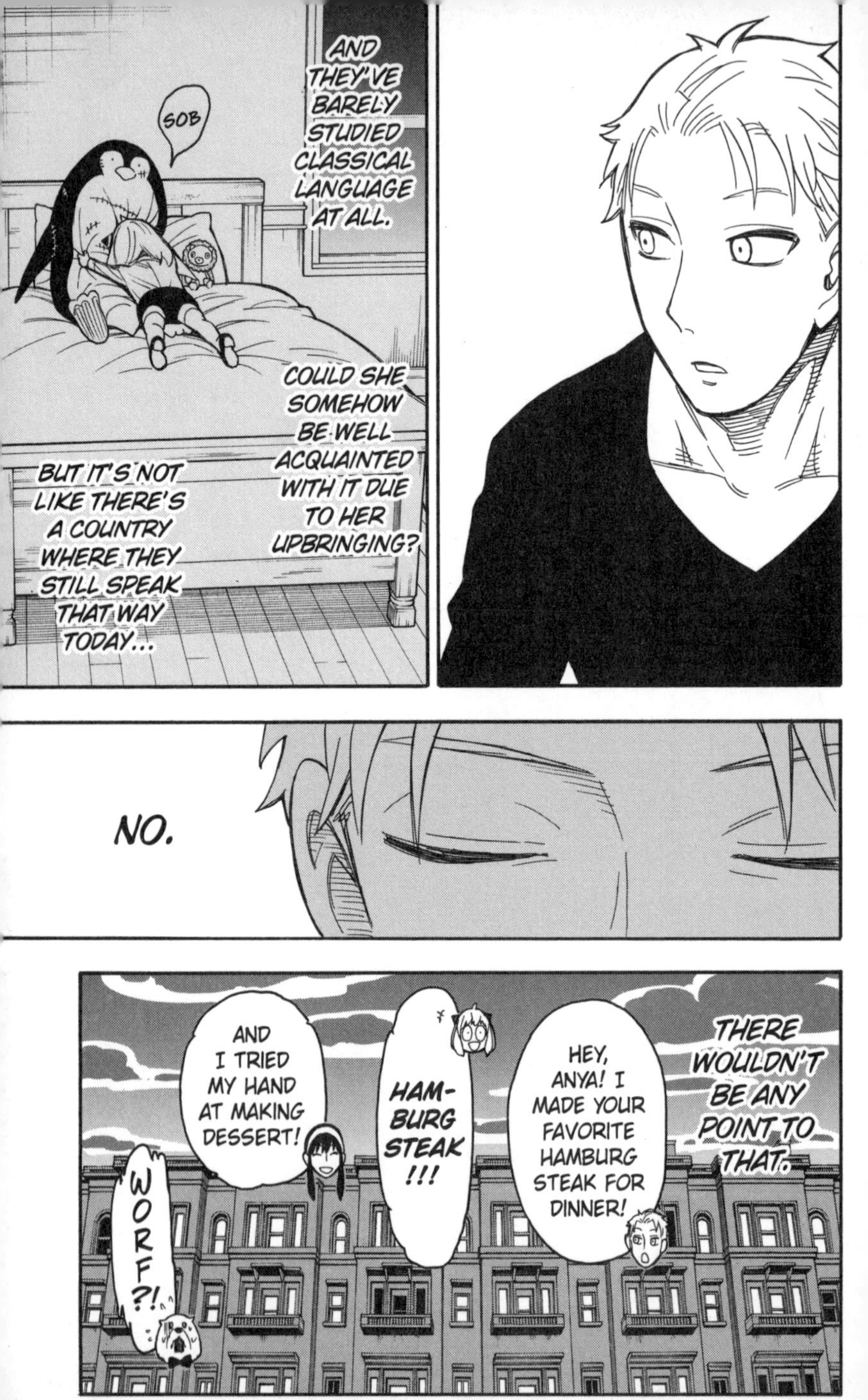
AND THEY'VE BARELY STUDIED CLASSICAL LANGUAGE AT ALL.
SOB
COULD SHE SOMEHOW BE WELL ACQUAINTED WITH IT DUE TO HER UPBRINGING?
BUT IT'S NOT LIKE THERE'S A COUNTRY WHERE THEY STILL SPEAK THAT WAY TODAY...
NO.
THERE WOULDN'T BE ANY POINT TO THAT.
HEY, ANYA! I MADE YOUR FAVORITE HAMBURG STEAK FOR DINNER!
HAM-BURG STEAK !!!
AND I TRIED MY HAND AT MAKING DESSERT!
WORF?!

SPY×FAMILY

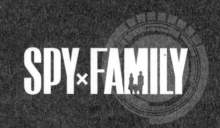

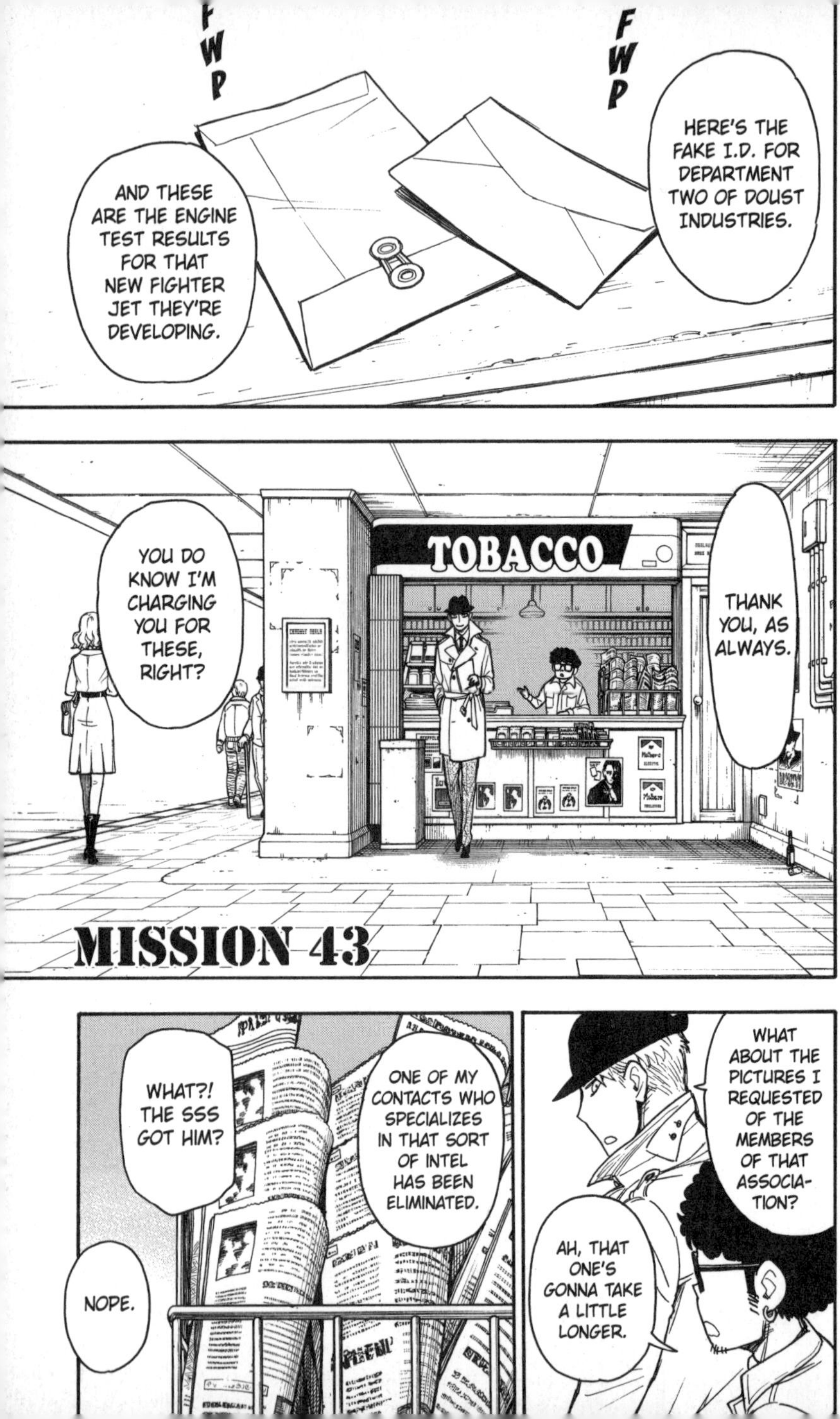
FWP
FWP
HERE'S THE FAKE I.D. FOR DEPARTMENT TWO OF DOUST INDUSTRIES.
AND THESE ARE THE ENGINE TEST RESULTS FOR THAT NEW FIGHTER JET THEY'RE DEVELOPING.
TOBACCO
THANK YOU, AS ALWAYS.
YOU DO KNOW I'M CHARGING YOU FOR THESE, RIGHT?
MISSION 43
WHAT ABOUT THE PICTURES I REQUESTED OF THE MEMBERS OF THAT ASSOCIA-TION?
AH, THAT ONE'S GONNA TAKE A LITTLE LONGER.
ONE OF MY CONTACTS WHO SPECIALIZES IN THAT SORT OF INTEL HAS BEEN ELIMINATED.
WHAT?! THE SSS GOT HIM?
NOPE.

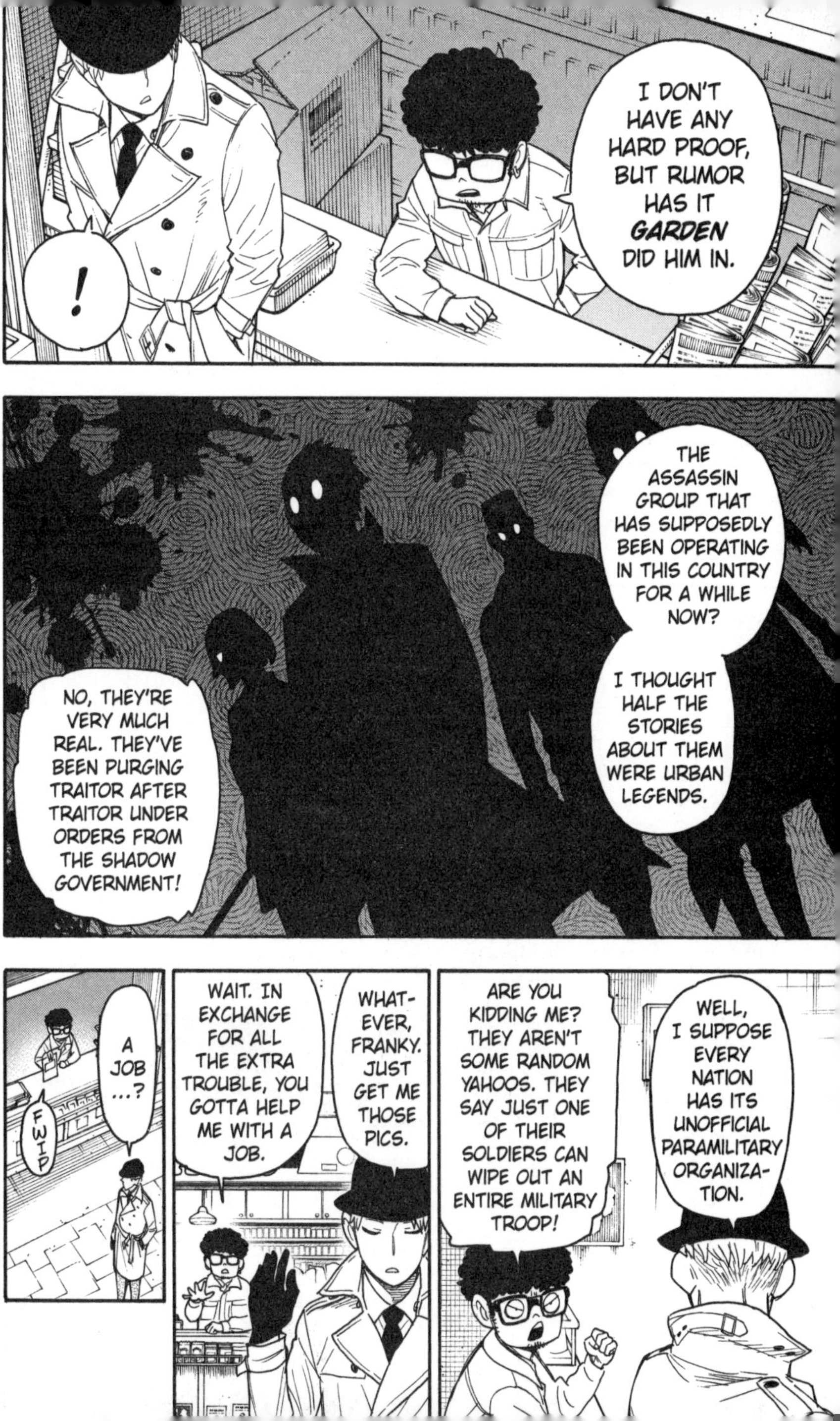
I DON'T HAVE ANY HARD PROOF, BUT RUMOR HAS IT **GARDEN** DID HIM IN.
!
THE ASSASSIN GROUP THAT HAS SUPPOSEDLY BEEN OPERATING IN THIS COUNTRY FOR A WHILE NOW?
I THOUGHT HALF THE STORIES ABOUT THEM WERE URBAN LEGENDS.
NO, THEY'RE VERY MUCH REAL. THEY'VE BEEN PURGING TRAITOR AFTER TRAITOR UNDER ORDERS FROM THE SHADOW GOVERNMENT!
WELL, I SUPPOSE EVERY NATION HAS ITS UNOFFICIAL PARAMILITARY ORGANIZATION.
ARE YOU KIDDING ME? THEY AREN'T SOME RANDOM YAHOOS. THEY SAY JUST ONE OF THEIR SOLDIERS CAN WIPE OUT AN ENTIRE MILITARY TROOP!
WHATEVER, FRANKY. JUST GET ME THOSE PICS.
WAIT. IN EXCHANGE FOR ALL THE EXTRA TROUBLE, YOU GOTTA HELP ME WITH A JOB.
A JOB ...?
FWIP

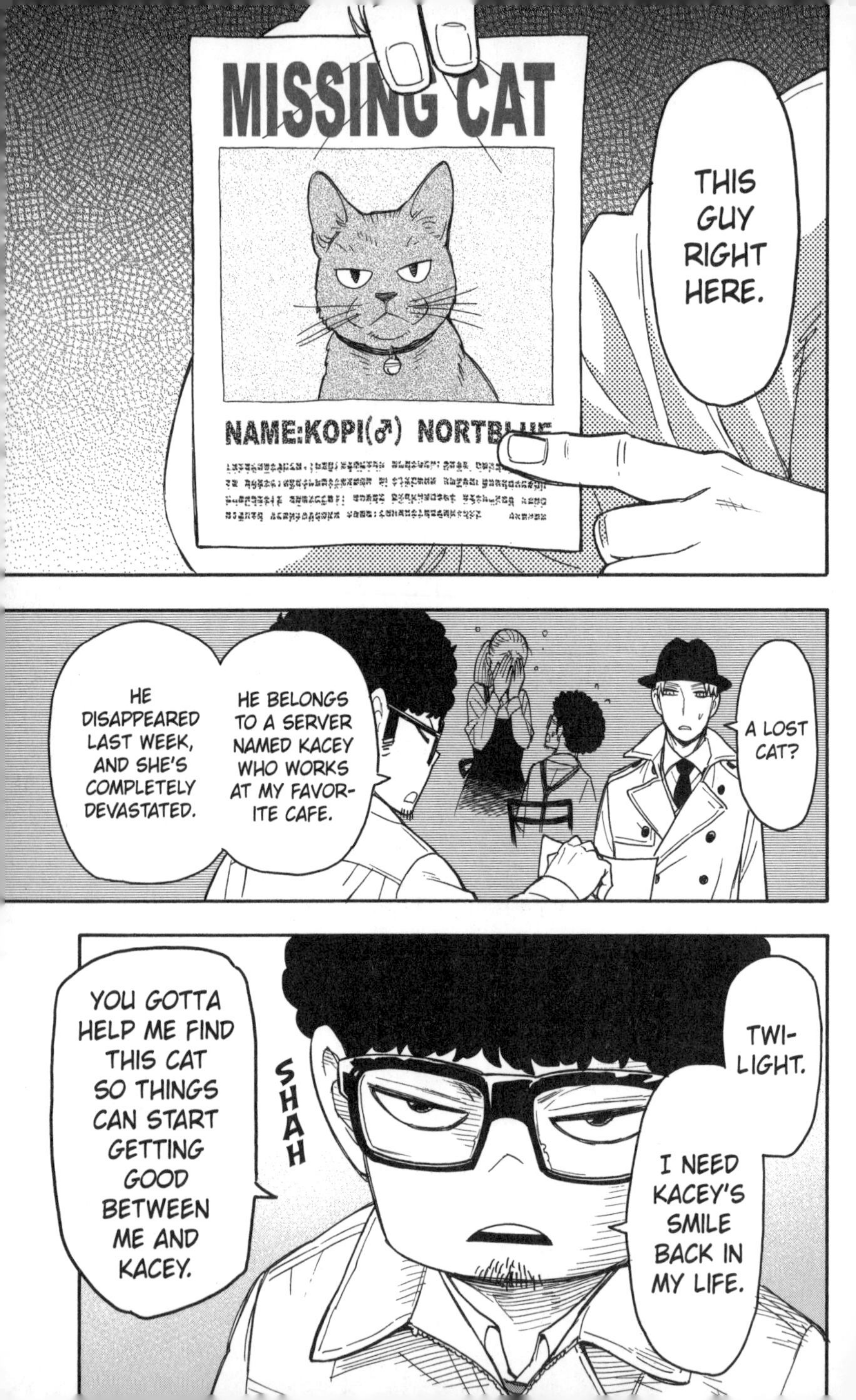
MISSING CAT
NAME:KOPI(♂) NORTB
THIS GUY RIGHT HERE.
A LOST CAT?
HE BELONGS TO A SERVER NAMED KACEY WHO WORKS AT MY FAVOR-ITE CAFE.
HE DISAPPEARED LAST WEEK, AND SHE'S COMPLETELY DEVASTATED.
TWI-LIGHT.
I NEED KACEY'S SMILE BACK IN MY LIFE.
SHAH
YOU GOTTA HELP ME FIND THIS CAT SO THINGS CAN START GETTING GOOD BETWEEN ME AND KACEY.

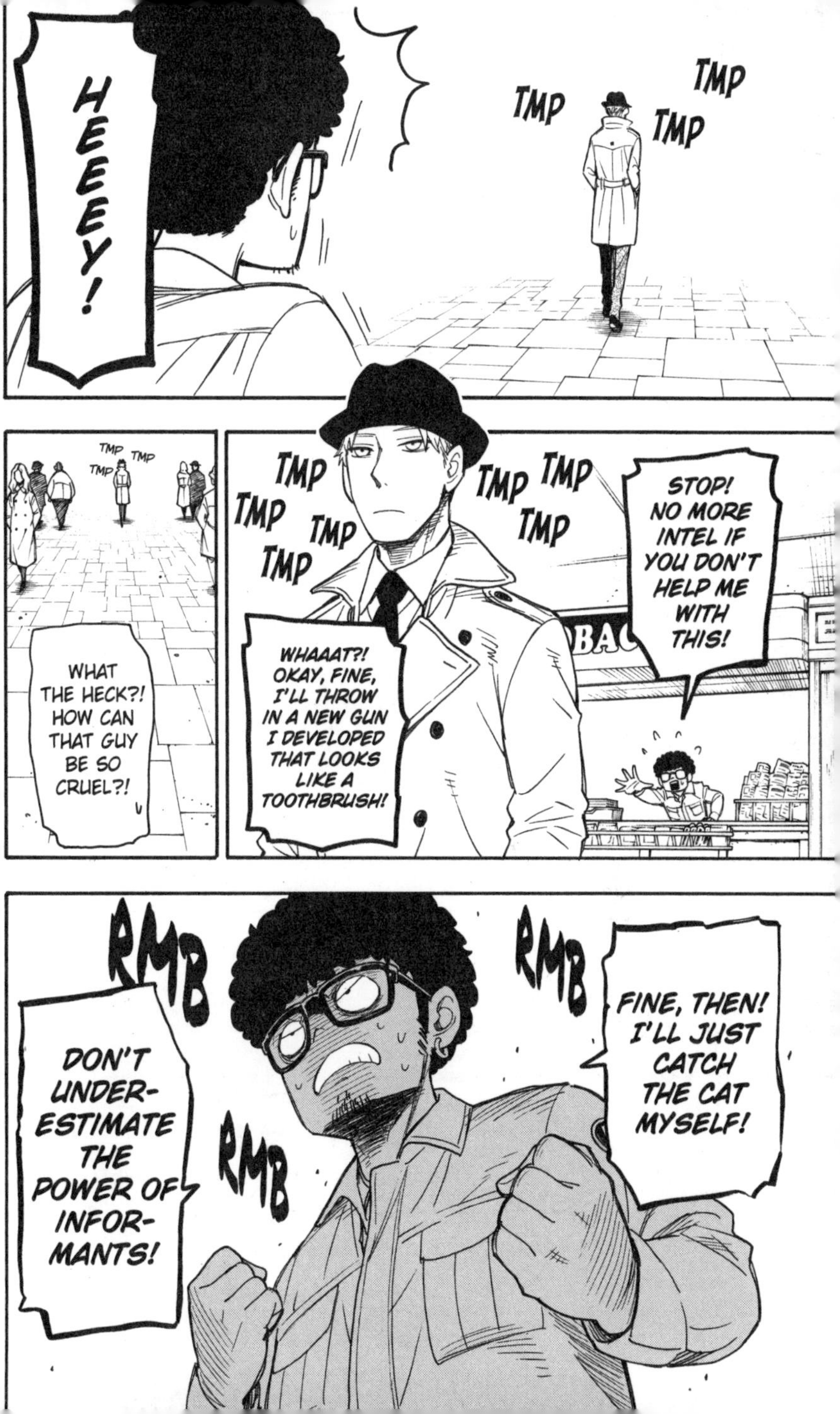
TMP
TMP
TMP
HEEEEY!
STOP! NO MORE INTEL IF YOU DON'T HELP ME WITH THIS!
TMP
TMP
TMP
TMP
TMP
TMP
WHAAAT?! OKAY, FINE, I'LL THROW IN A NEW GUN I DEVELOPED THAT LOOKS LIKE A TOOTHBRUSH!
TMP
TMP
TMP
WHAT THE HECK?! HOW CAN THAT GUY BE SO CRUEL?!
FINE, THEN! I'LL JUST CATCH THE CAT MYSELF!
RMB
RMB
RMB
DON'T UNDER-ESTIMATE THE POWER OF INFOR-MANTS!

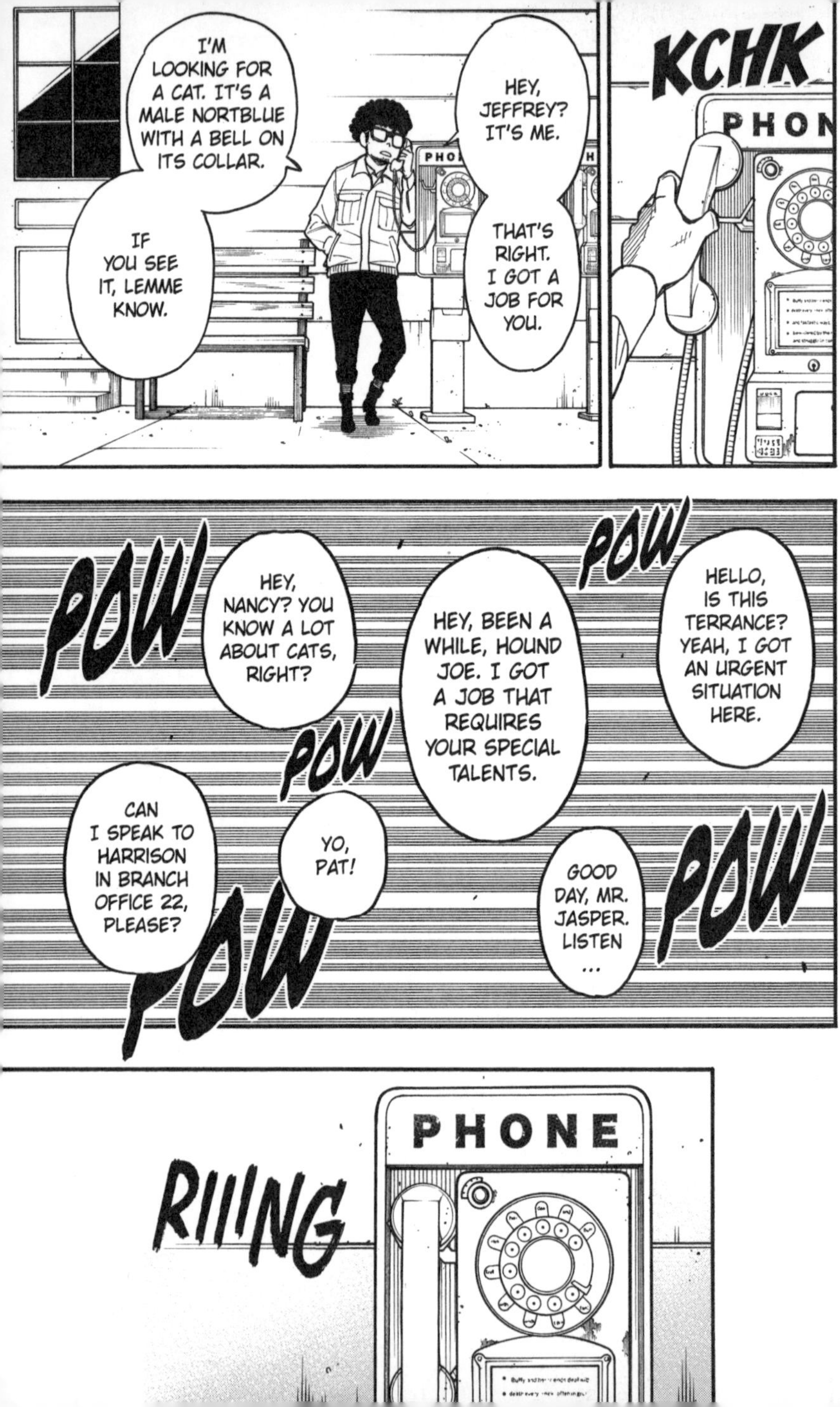
KCHK
PHON
HEY, JEFFREY? IT'S ME.
THAT'S RIGHT. I GOT A JOB FOR YOU.
I'M LOOKING FOR A CAT. IT'S A MALE NORTBLUE WITH A BELL ON ITS COLLAR.
IF YOU SEE IT, LEMME KNOW.
HELLO, IS THIS TERRANCE? YEAH, I GOT AN URGENT SITUATION HERE.
POW
HEY, BEEN A WHILE, HOUND JOE. I GOT A JOB THAT REQUIRES YOUR SPECIAL TALENTS.
HEY, NANCY? YOU KNOW A LOT ABOUT CATS, RIGHT?
POW
POW
POW
GOOD DAY, MR. JASPER. LISTEN ...
YO, PAT!
CAN I SPEAK TO HARRISON IN BRANCH OFFICE 22, PLEASE?
POW
PHONE
RIIING

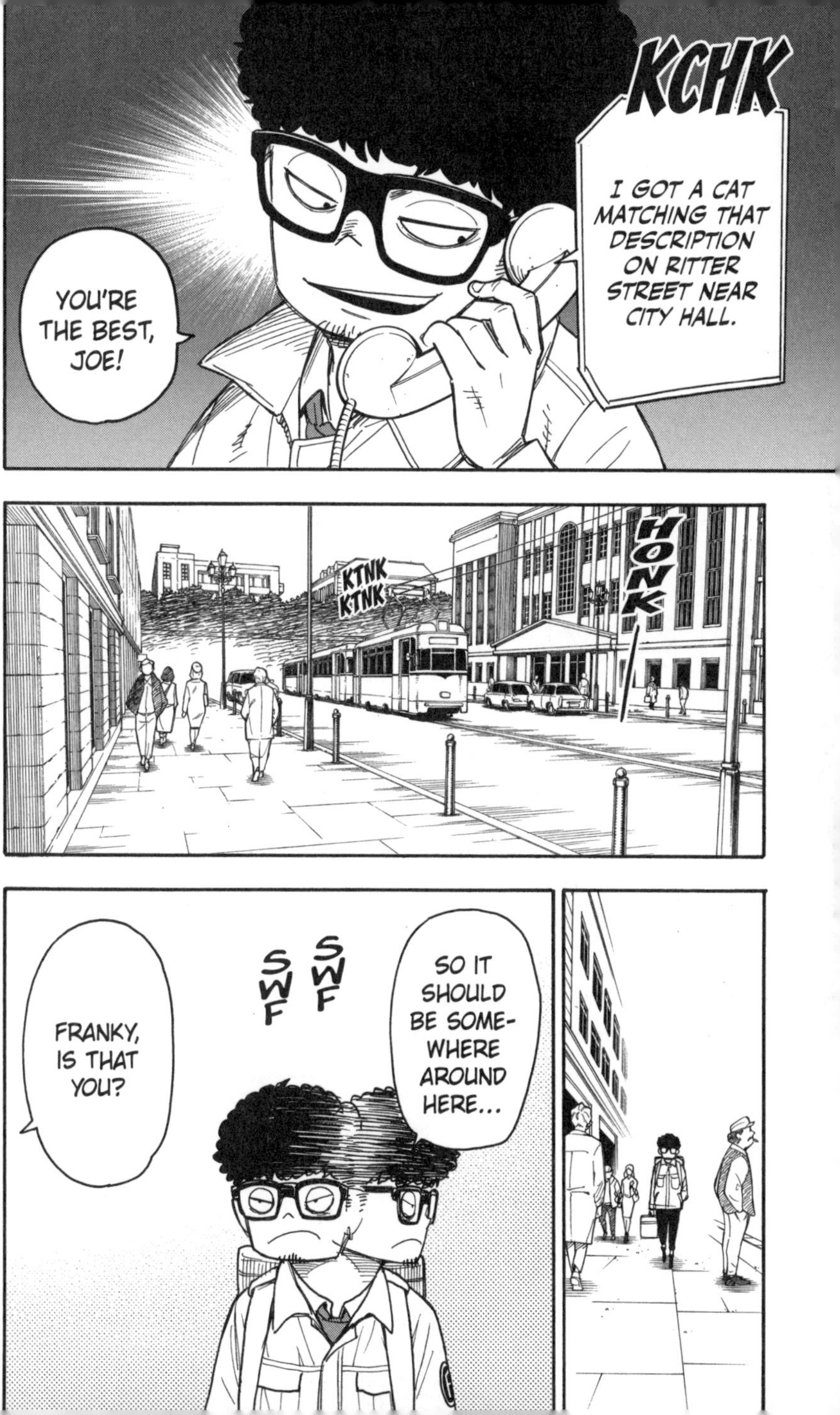
KCHK
I GOT A CAT MATCHING THAT DESCRIPTION ON RITTER STREET NEAR CITY HALL.
YOU'RE THE BEST, JOE!
HONK
KTNK KTNK
SWF SWF
SO IT SHOULD BE SOME-WHERE AROUND HERE...
FRANKY, IS THAT YOU?

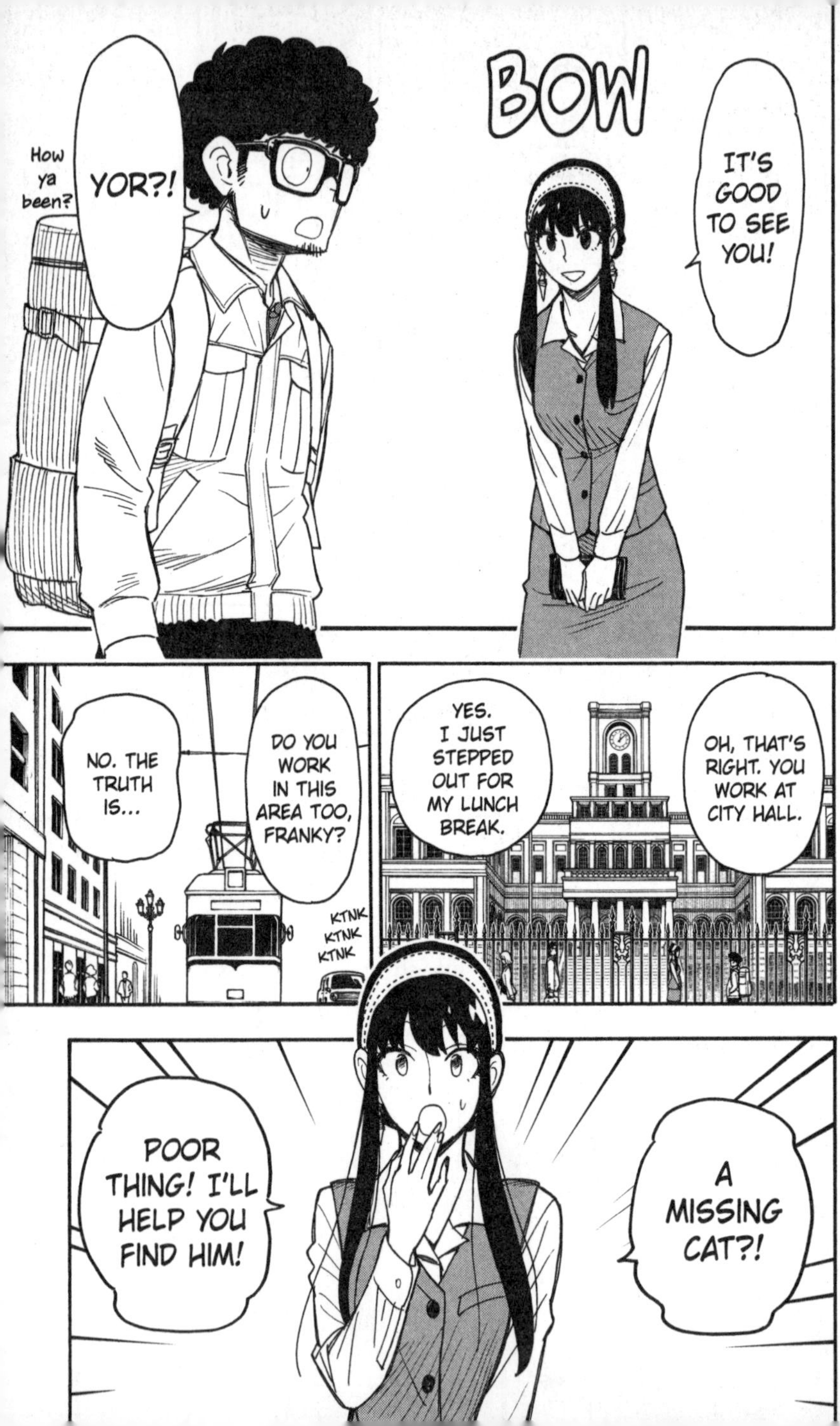
IT'S GOOD TO SEE YOU!
BOW
YOR?!
How ya been?
OH, THAT'S RIGHT. YOU WORK AT CITY HALL.
YES. I JUST STEPPED OUT FOR MY LUNCH BREAK.
DO YOU WORK IN THIS AREA TOO, FRANKY?
NO. THE TRUTH IS...
KTNK KTNK KTNK
A MISSING CAT?!
POOR THING! I'LL HELP YOU FIND HIM!

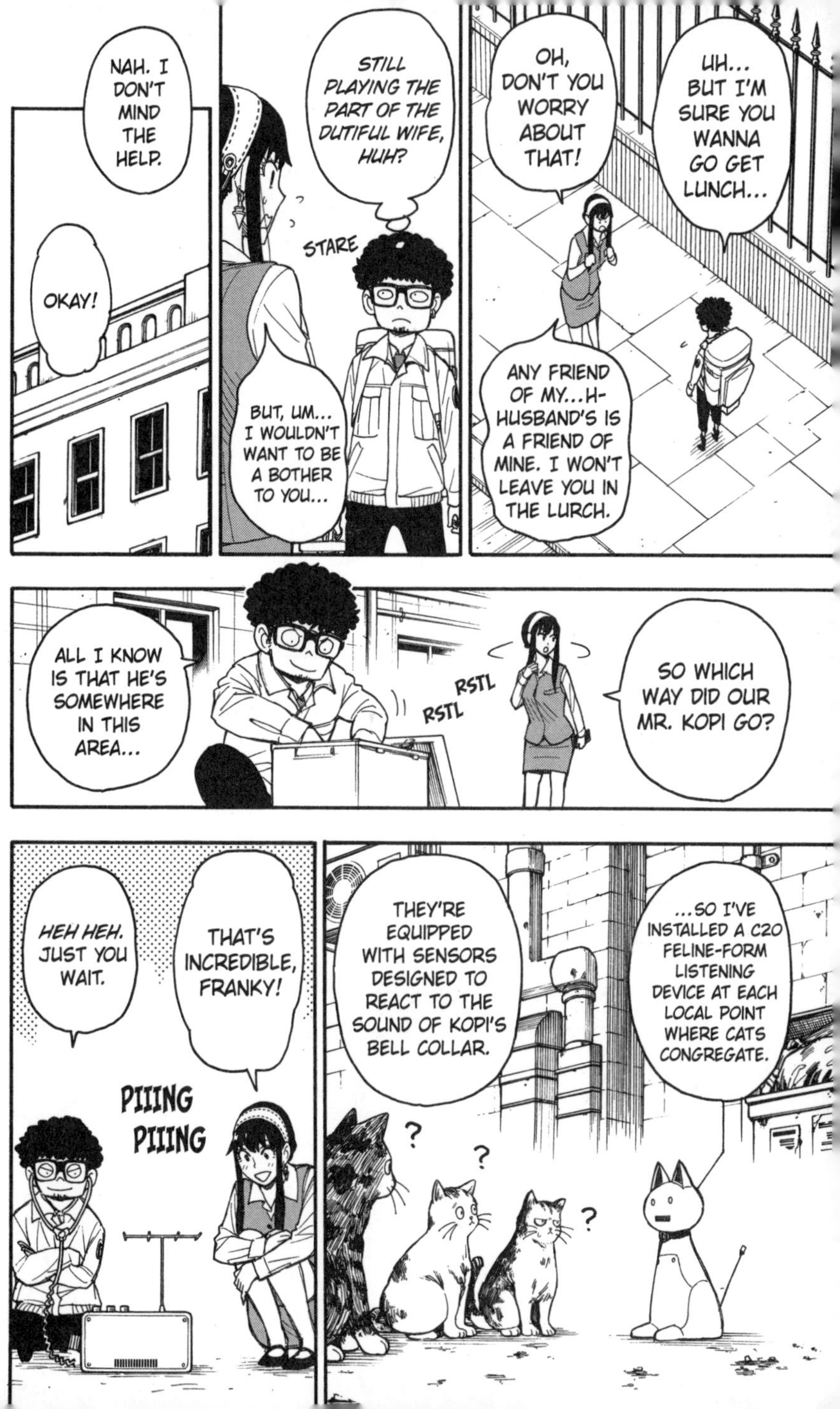
UH... BUT I'M SURE YOU WANNA GO GET LUNCH...
OH, DON'T YOU WORRY ABOUT THAT!
ANY FRIEND OF MY...H-HUSBAND'S IS A FRIEND OF MINE. I WON'T LEAVE YOU IN THE LURCH.
STILL PLAYING THE PART OF THE DUTIFUL WIFE, HUH?
STARE
BUT, UM... I WOULDN'T WANT TO BE A BOTHER TO YOU...
NAH. I DON'T MIND THE HELP.
OKAY!
SO WHICH WAY DID OUR MR. KOPI GO?
RSTL
RSTL
ALL I KNOW IS THAT HE'S SOMEWHERE IN THIS AREA...
...SO I'VE INSTALLED A C20 FELINE-FORM LISTENING DEVICE AT EACH LOCAL POINT WHERE CATS CONGREGATE.
THEY'RE EQUIPPED WITH SENSORS DESIGNED TO REACT TO THE SOUND OF KOPI'S BELL COLLAR.
?
?
?
THAT'S INCREDIBLE, FRANKY!
HEH HEH. JUST YOU WAIT.
PIIING
PIIING

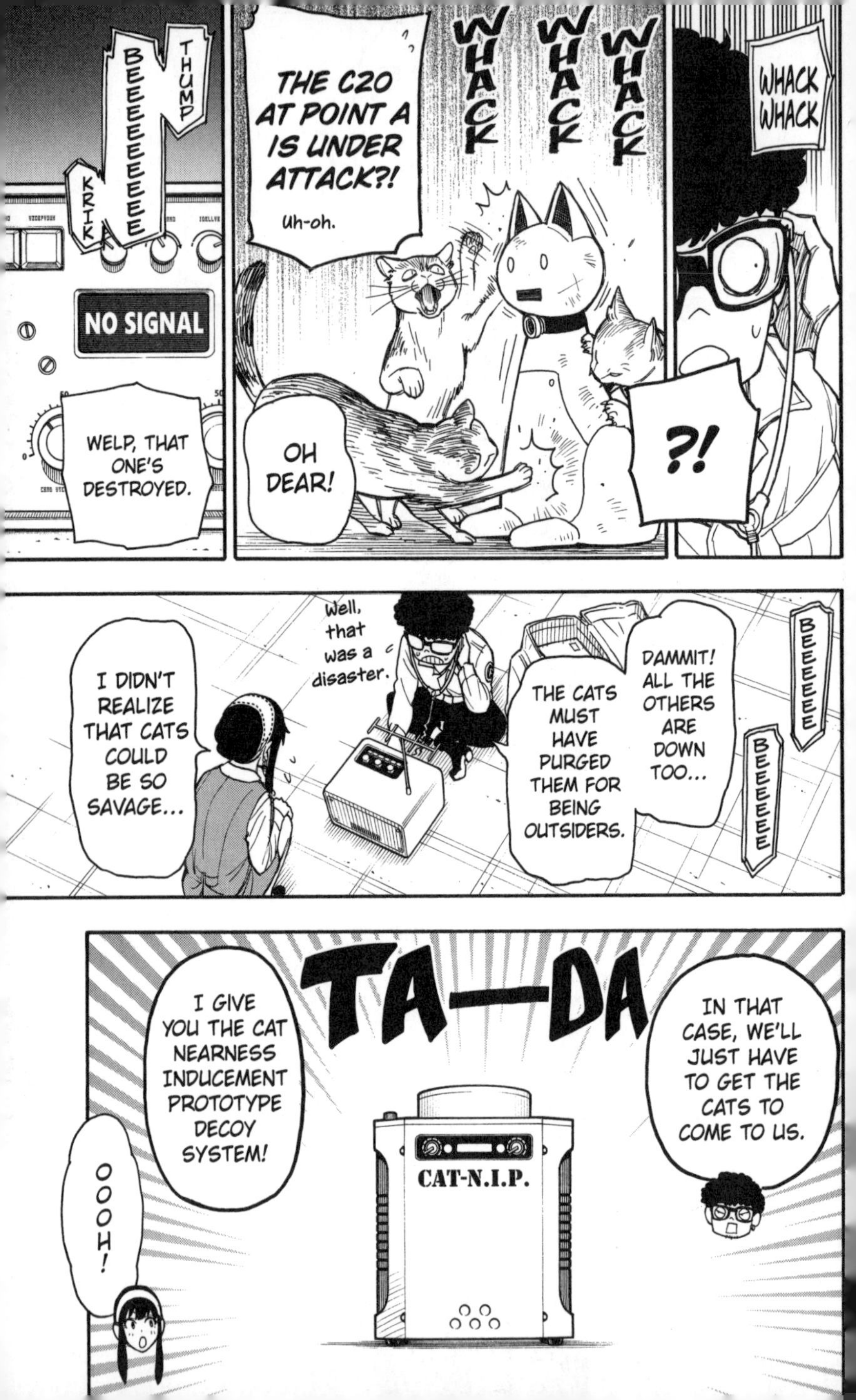
WHACK WHACK
?!
WHACK WHACK WHACK
THE C20 AT POINT A IS UNDER ATTACK?!
Uh-oh.
OH DEAR!
THUMP
BEEEEEEEEEE
KRIK
NO SIGNAL
WELP, THAT ONE'S DESTROYED.
BEEEEEEE
BEEEEEEE
DAMMIT! ALL THE OTHERS ARE DOWN TOO...
THE CATS MUST HAVE PURGED THEM FOR BEING OUTSIDERS.
Well, that was a disaster.
I DIDN'T REALIZE THAT CATS COULD BE SO SAVAGE...
IN THAT CASE, WE'LL JUST HAVE TO GET THE CATS TO COME TO US.
TA—DA
I GIVE YOU THE CAT NEARNESS INDUCEMENT PROTOTYPE DECOY SYSTEM!
CAT-N.I.P.
OOOOH!

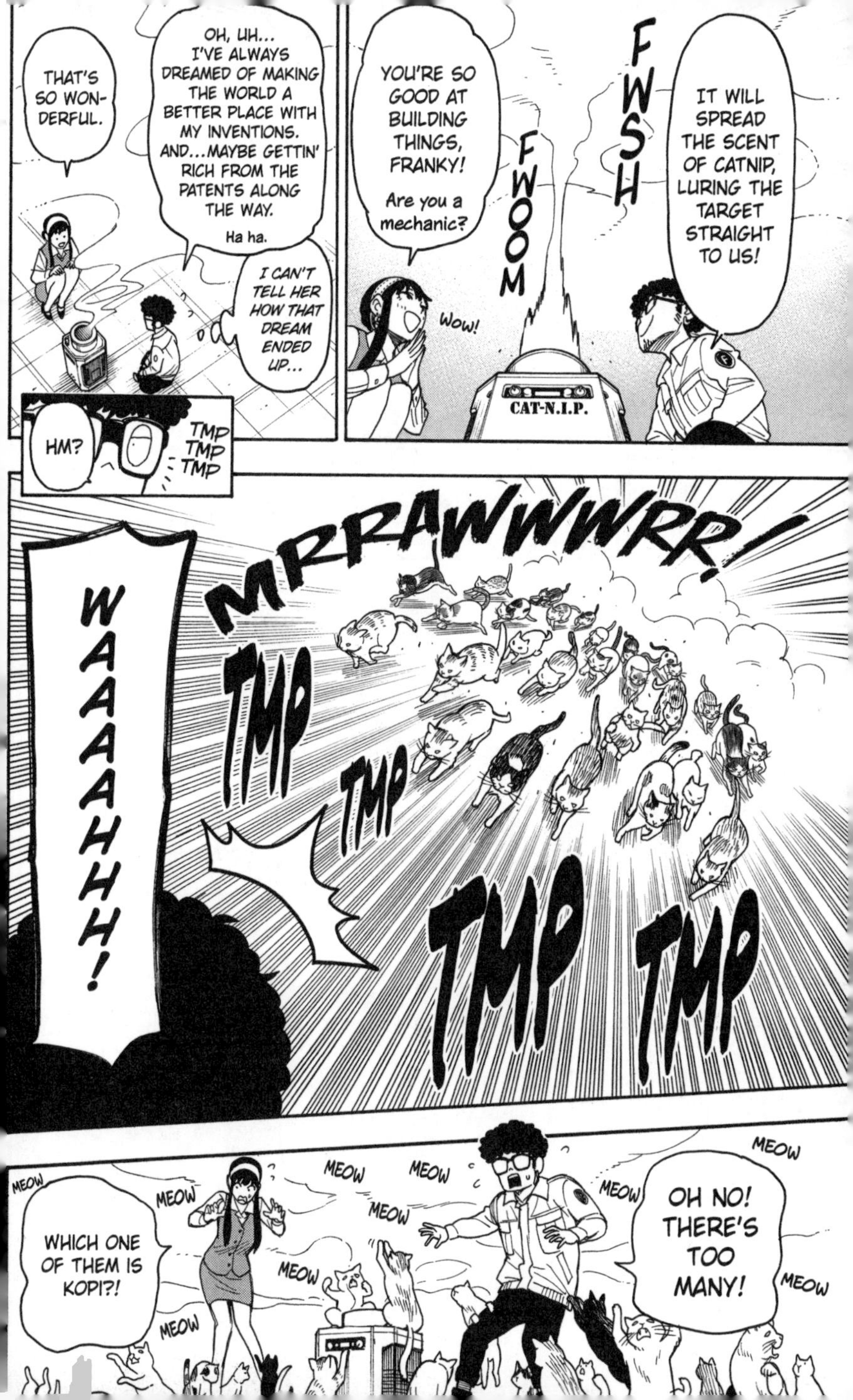
IT WILL SPREAD THE SCENT OF CATNIP, LURING THE TARGET STRAIGHT TO US!
FWSH
FWOOM
YOU'RE SO GOOD AT BUILDING THINGS, FRANKY!
Are you a mechanic?
Wow!
CAT-N.I.P.
OH, UH... I'VE ALWAYS DREAMED OF MAKING THE WORLD A BETTER PLACE WITH MY INVENTIONS. AND...MAYBE GETTIN' RICH FROM THE PATENTS ALONG THE WAY.
Ha ha.
THAT'S SO WON-DERFUL.
I CAN'T TELL HER HOW THAT DREAM ENDED UP...
TMP TMP TMP
HM?
MRRAWWWRR!
TMP
TMP
TMP
TMP
WAAAAAHHH!
MEOW
OH NO! THERE'S TOO MANY!
MEOW
MEOW
MEOW
MEOW
MEOW
MEOW
MEOW
MEOW
MEOW
WHICH ONE OF THEM IS KOPI?!
MEOW

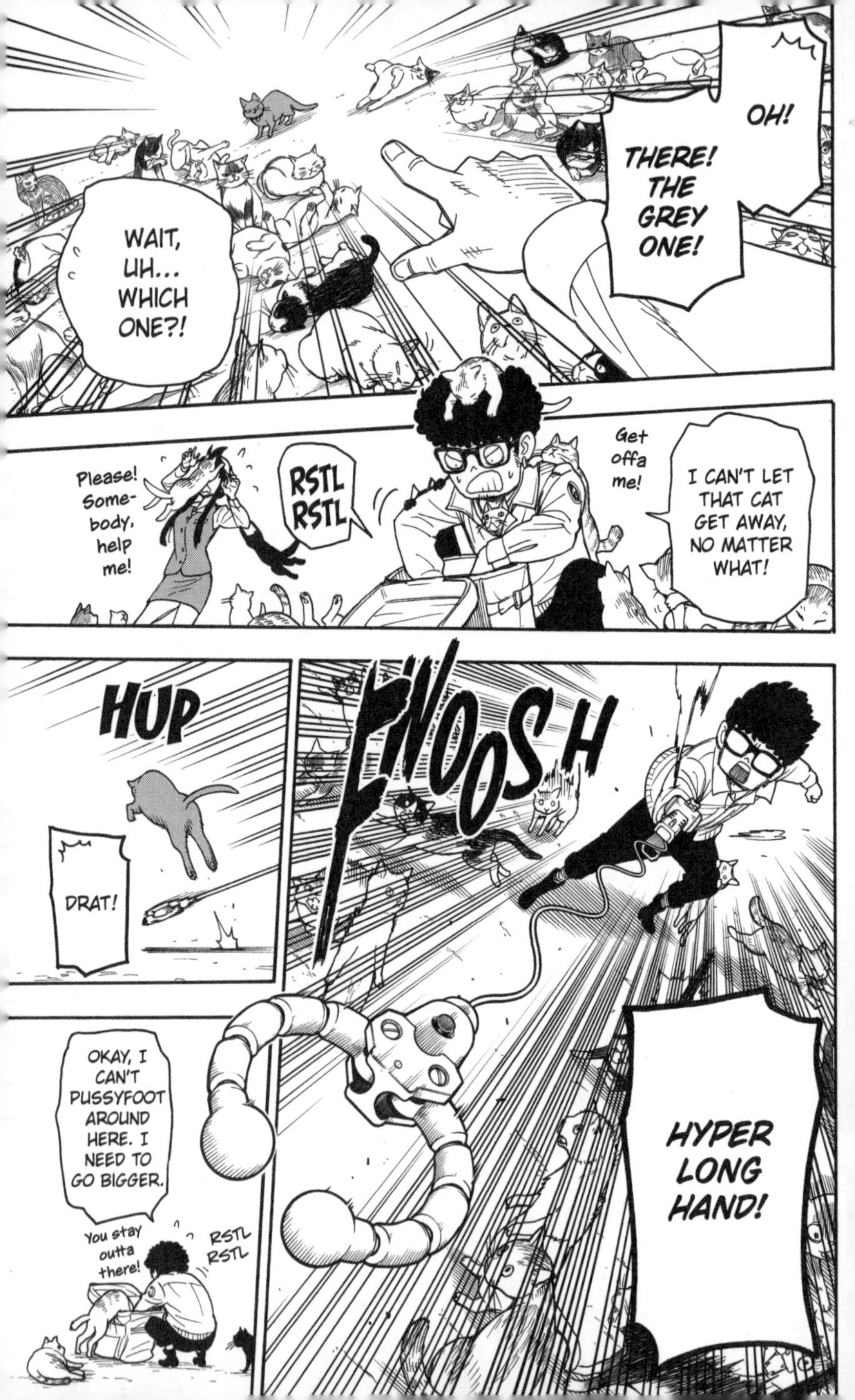
OH!
THERE! THE GREY ONE!
WAIT, UH... WHICH ONE?!
I CAN'T LET THAT CAT GET AWAY, NO MATTER WHAT!
Get offa me!
RSTL RSTL
Please! Some-body, help me!
FWOOSH
HYPER LONG HAND!
HUP
DRAT!
OKAY, I CAN'T PUSSYFOOT AROUND HERE. I NEED TO GO BIGGER.
You stay outta there!
RSTL RSTL

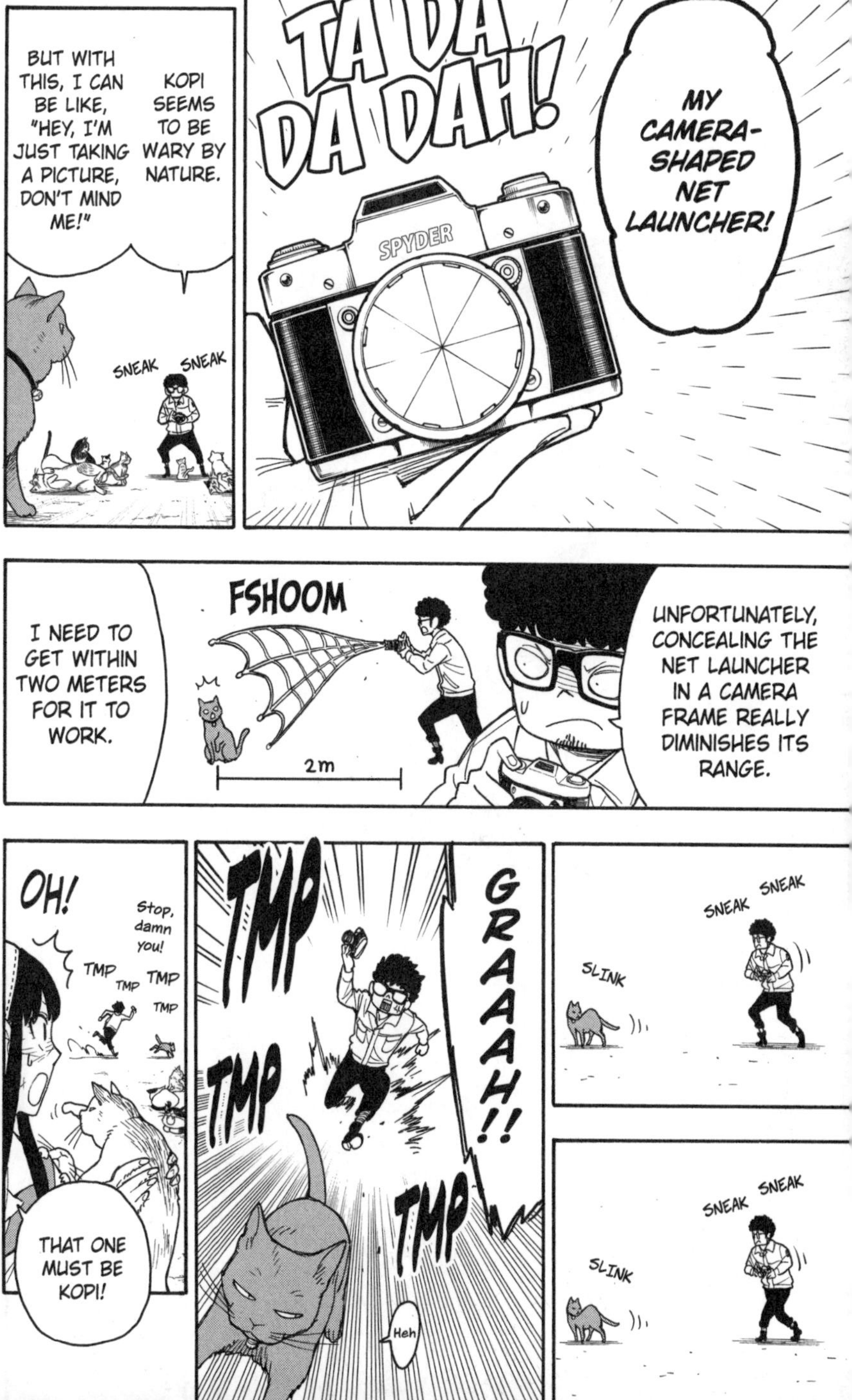
TA DA DA DAH!
MY CAMERA-SHAPED NET LAUNCHER!
SPYDER
KOPI SEEMS TO BE WARY BY NATURE.
BUT WITH THIS, I CAN BE LIKE, "HEY, I'M JUST TAKING A PICTURE, DON'T MIND ME!"
SNEAK SNEAK
UNFORTUNATELY, CONCEALING THE NET LAUNCHER IN A CAMERA FRAME REALLY DIMINISHES ITS RANGE.
FSHOOM
2m
I NEED TO GET WITHIN TWO METERS FOR IT TO WORK.
SNEAK SNEAK
SLINK
SNEAK SNEAK
SLINK
TMP
GRAAAAH!!
TMP
TMP
Heh
OH!
Stop, damn you!
TMP TMP TMP TMP
THAT ONE MUST BE KOPI!

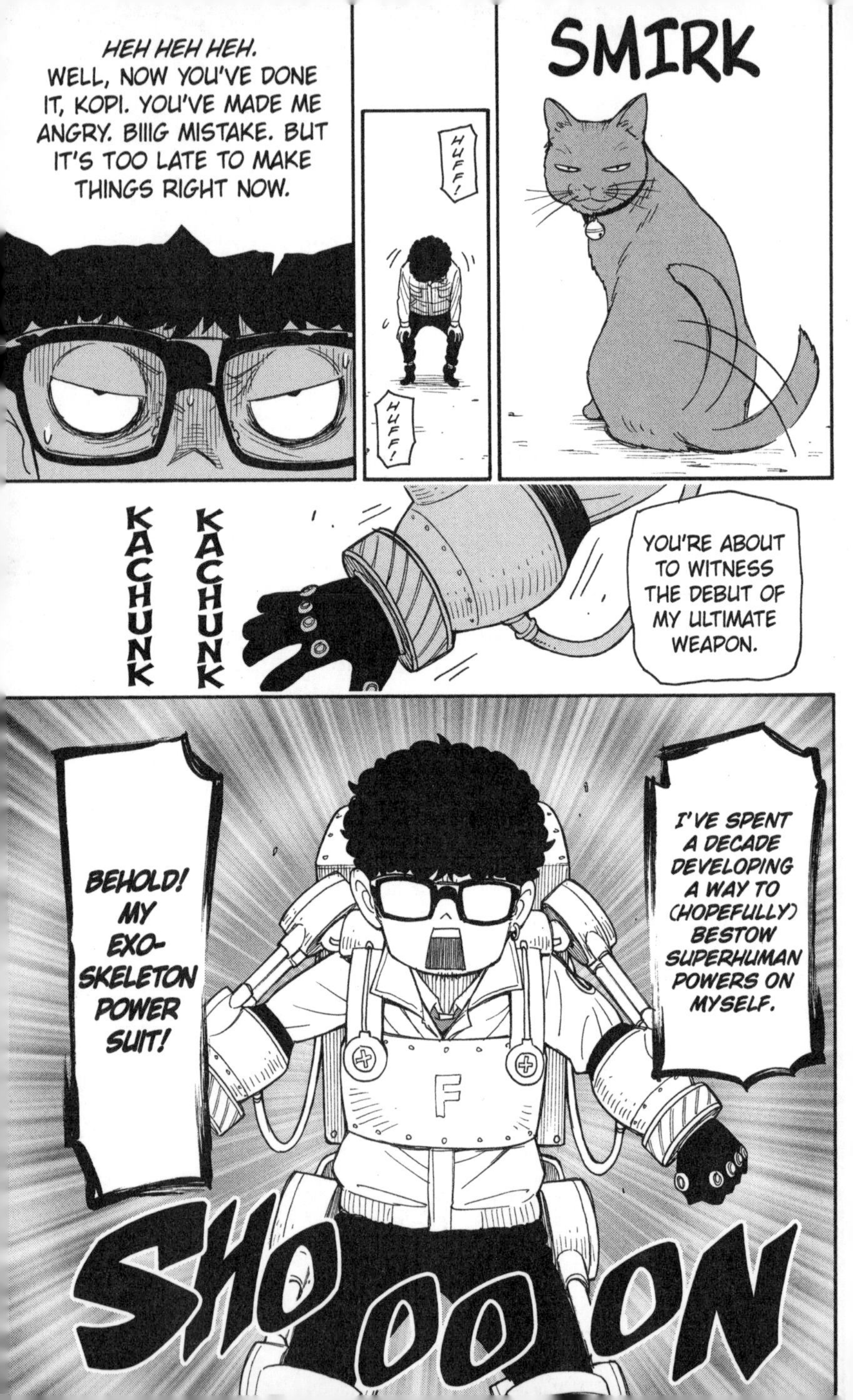
SMIRK
HUFF!
HUFF!
HEH HEH HEH.
WELL, NOW YOU'VE DONE IT, KOPI. YOU'VE MADE ME ANGRY. BIIIG MISTAKE. BUT IT'S TOO LATE TO MAKE THINGS RIGHT NOW.
YOU'RE ABOUT TO WITNESS THE DEBUT OF MY ULTIMATE WEAPON.
KACHUNK
KACHUNK
I'VE SPENT A DECADE DEVELOPING A WAY TO (HOPEFULLY) BESTOW SUPERHUMAN POWERS ON MYSELF.
BEHOLD! MY EXO-SKELETON POWER SUIT!
SHOOOOON

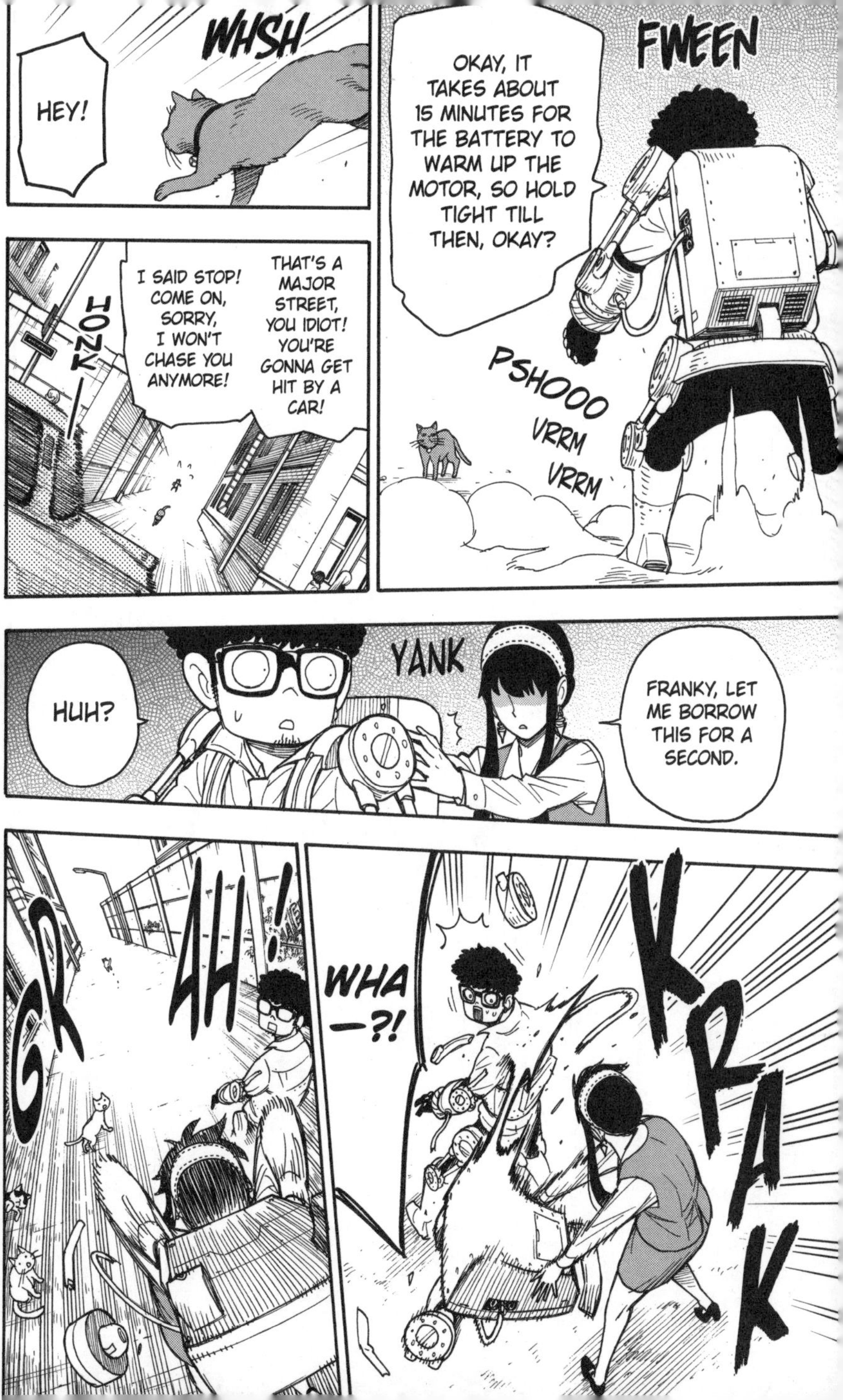
FWEEN
OKAY, IT TAKES ABOUT 15 MINUTES FOR THE BATTERY TO WARM UP THE MOTOR, SO HOLD TIGHT TILL THEN, OKAY?
PSHOOO
VRRM
VRRM
WHSH
HEY!
THAT'S A MAJOR STREET, YOU IDIOT! YOU'RE GONNA GET HIT BY A CAR!
I SAID STOP! COME ON, SORRY, I WON'T CHASE YOU ANYMORE!
HONK
FRANKY, LET ME BORROW THIS FOR A SECOND.
YANK
HUH?
KRAK
WHA—?!
AH!
GR

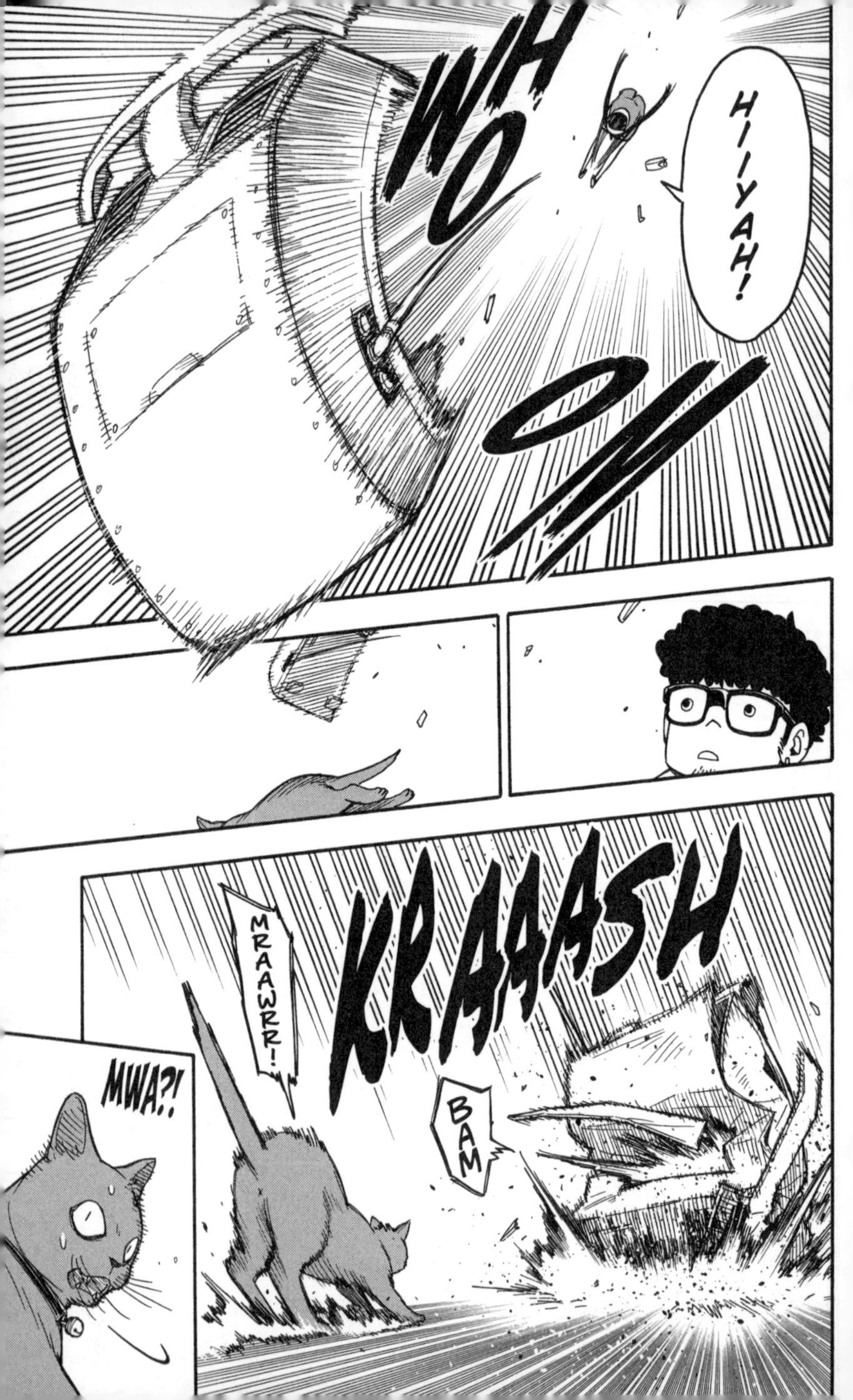
HIIYAH!
WHOOM
KRAAASH
BAM
MRAAWRR!
MWA?!

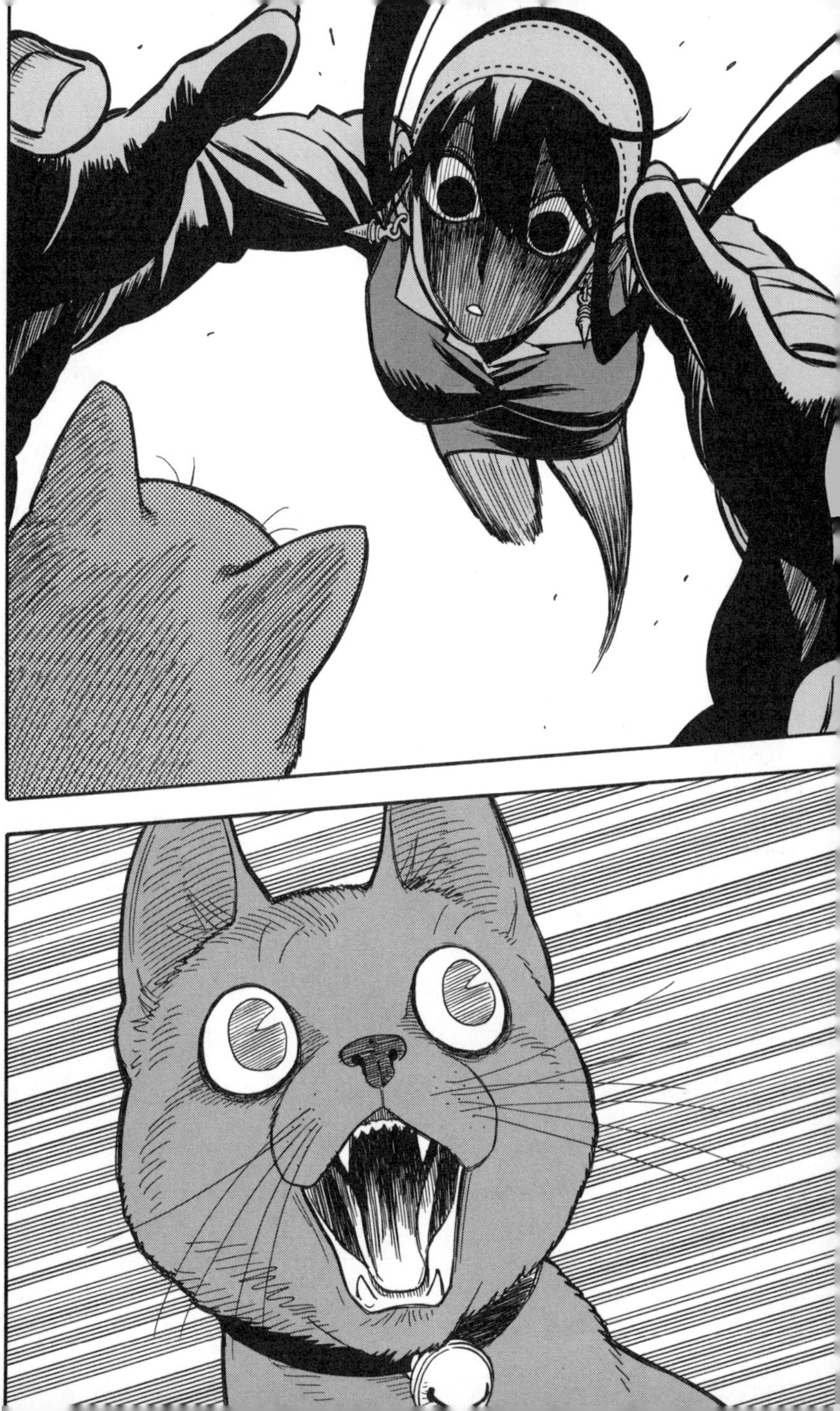

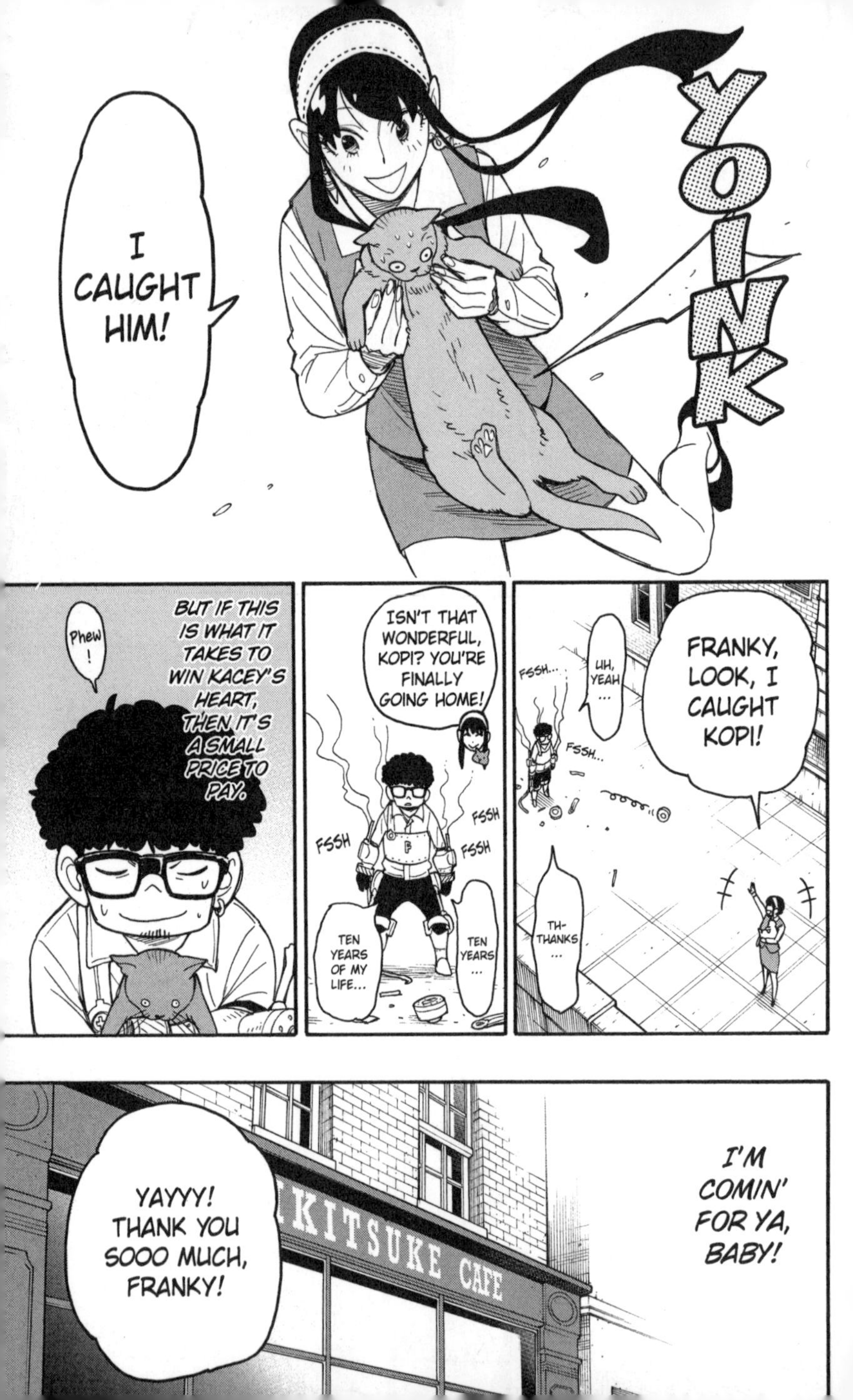
YOINK
I CAUGHT HIM!
FRANKY, LOOK, I CAUGHT KOPI!
UH, YEAH ...
FSSH...
FSSH...
TH-THANKS ...
ISN'T THAT WONDERFUL, KOPI? YOU'RE FINALLY GOING HOME!
FSSH
FSSH
FSSH
TEN YEARS ...
TEN YEARS OF MY LIFE...
BUT IF THIS IS WHAT IT TAKES TO WIN KACEY'S HEART, THEN IT'S A SMALL PRICE TO PAY.
Phew !
I'M COMIN' FOR YA, BABY!
KITSUKE CAFE
YAYYY! THANK YOU SOOO MUCH, FRANKY!

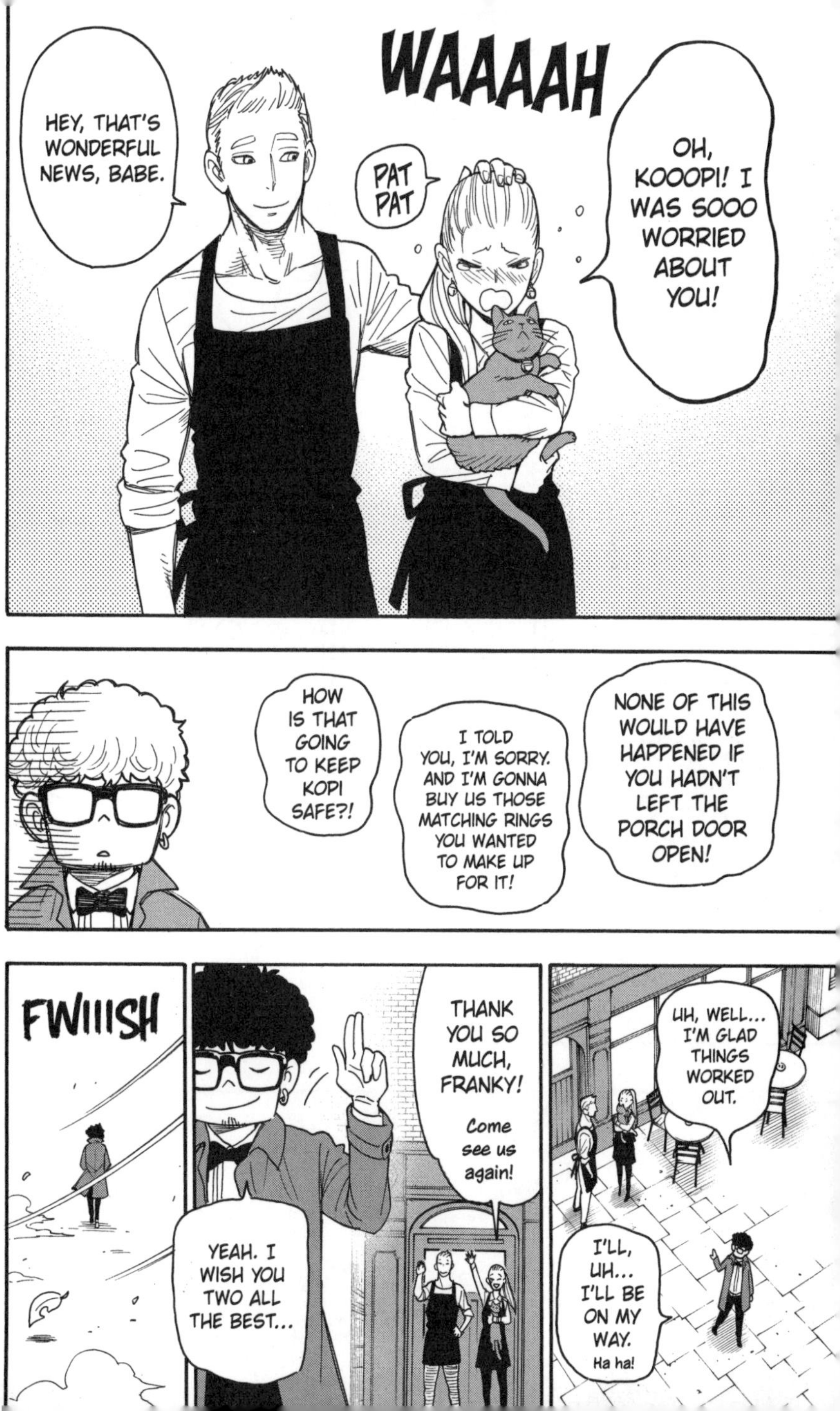
WAAAAH
OH, KOOOPI! I WAS SOOO WORRIED ABOUT YOU!
PAT PAT
HEY, THAT'S WONDERFUL NEWS, BABE.
NONE OF THIS WOULD HAVE HAPPENED IF YOU HADN'T LEFT THE PORCH DOOR OPEN!
I TOLD YOU, I'M SORRY. AND I'M GONNA BUY US THOSE MATCHING RINGS YOU WANTED TO MAKE UP FOR IT!
HOW IS THAT GOING TO KEEP KOPI SAFE?!
UH, WELL... I'M GLAD THINGS WORKED OUT.
I'LL, UH... I'LL BE ON MY WAY.
Ha ha!
THANK YOU SO MUCH, FRANKY!
Come see us again!
YEAH. I WISH YOU TWO ALL THE BEST...
FWIIISH

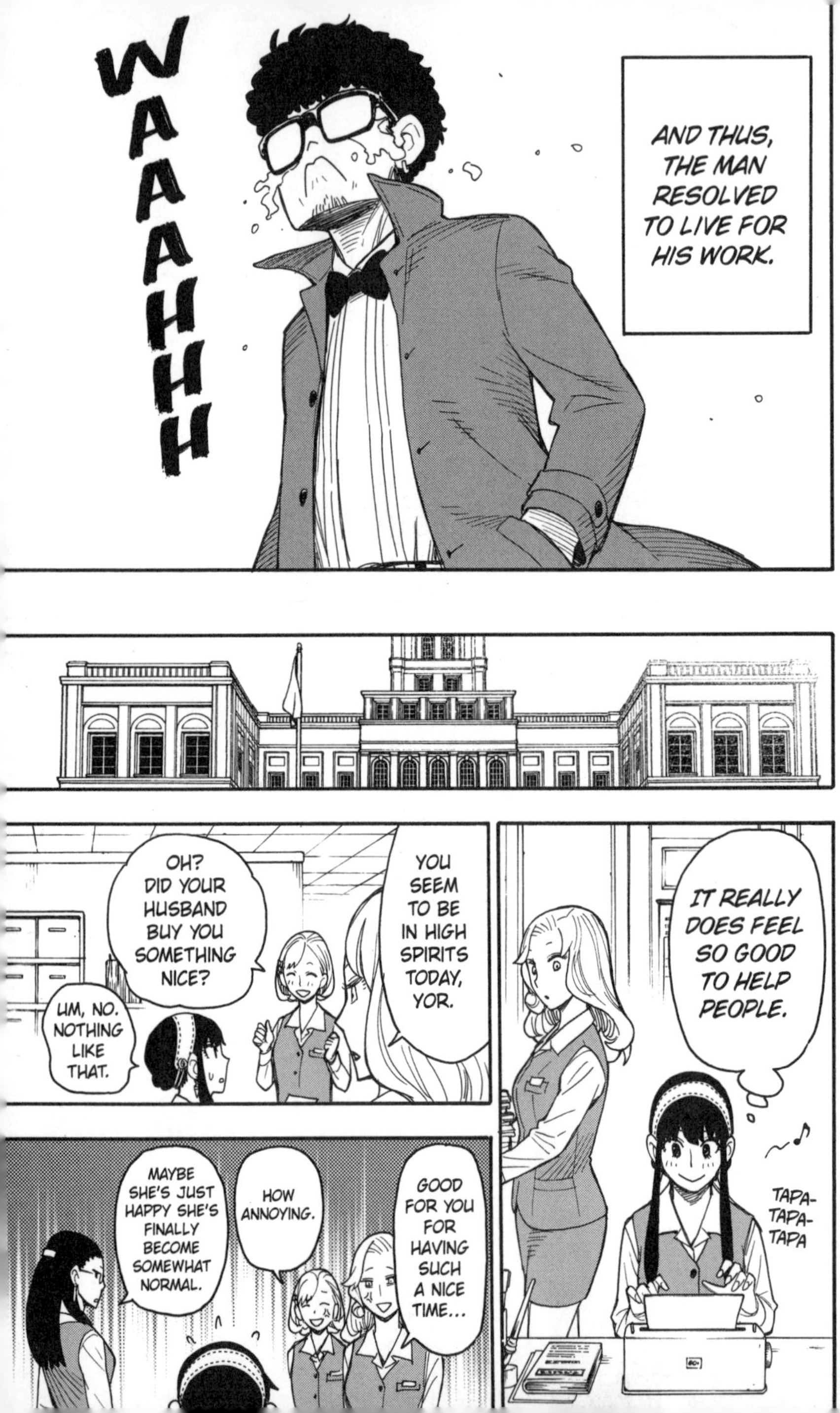
AND THUS, THE MAN RESOLVED TO LIVE FOR HIS WORK.
WAAAHHH
IT REALLY DOES FEEL SO GOOD TO HELP PEOPLE.
TAPA-TAPA-TAPA
YOU SEEM TO BE IN HIGH SPIRITS TODAY, YOR.
OH? DID YOUR HUSBAND BUY YOU SOMETHING NICE?
UM, NO. NOTHING LIKE THAT.
GOOD FOR YOU FOR HAVING SUCH A NICE TIME...
HOW ANNOYING.
MAYBE SHE'S JUST HAPPY SHE'S FINALLY BECOME SOMEWHAT NORMAL.

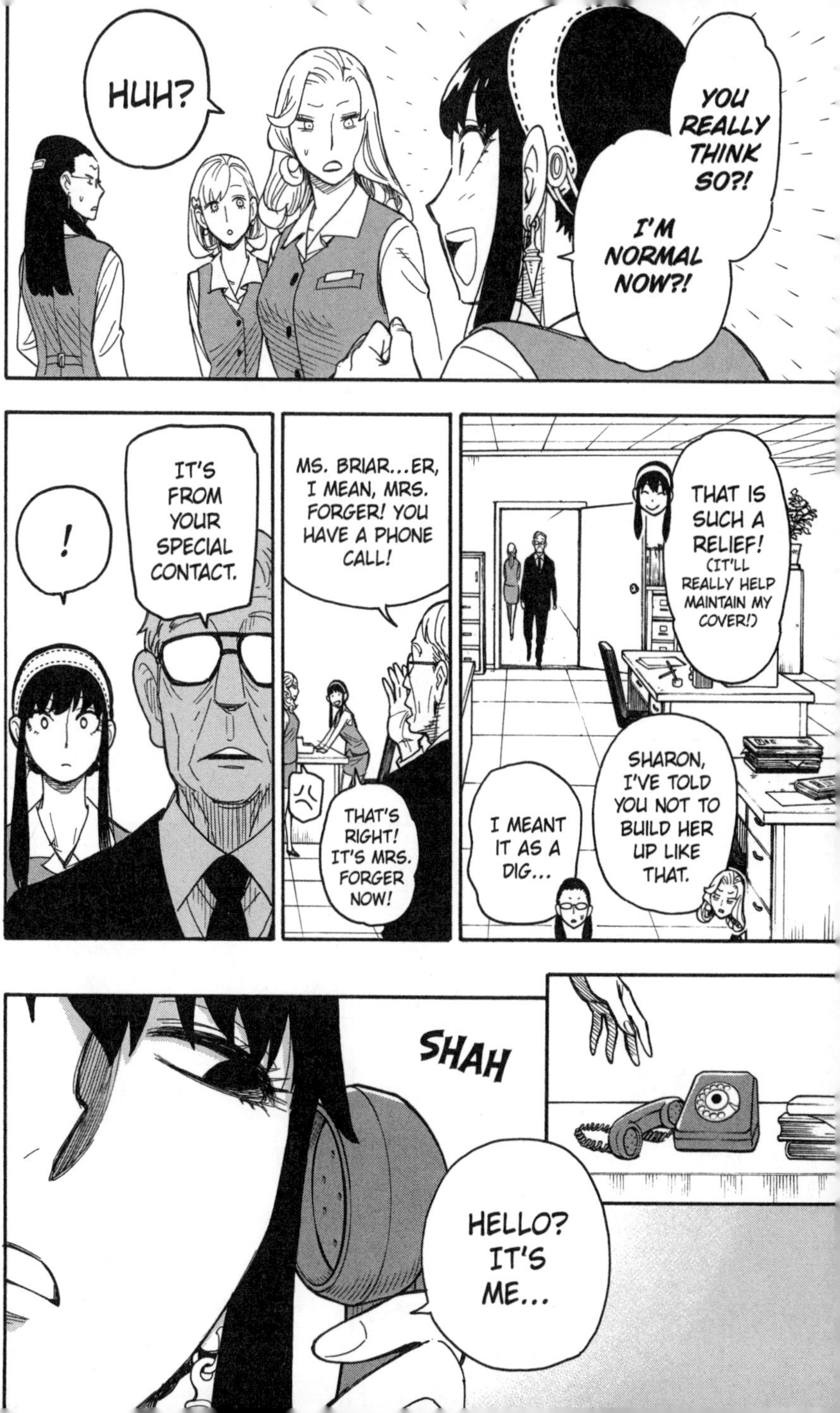
YOU REALLY THINK SO?!
I'M NORMAL NOW?!
HUH?
THAT IS SUCH A RELIEF! (IT'LL REALLY HELP MAINTAIN MY COVER!)
SHARON, I'VE TOLD YOU NOT TO BUILD HER UP LIKE THAT.
I MEANT IT AS A DIG...
MS. BRIAR...ER, I MEAN, MRS. FORGER! YOU HAVE A PHONE CALL!
THAT'S RIGHT! IT'S MRS. FORGER NOW!
IT'S FROM YOUR SPECIAL CONTACT.
!
SHAH
HELLO? IT'S ME...

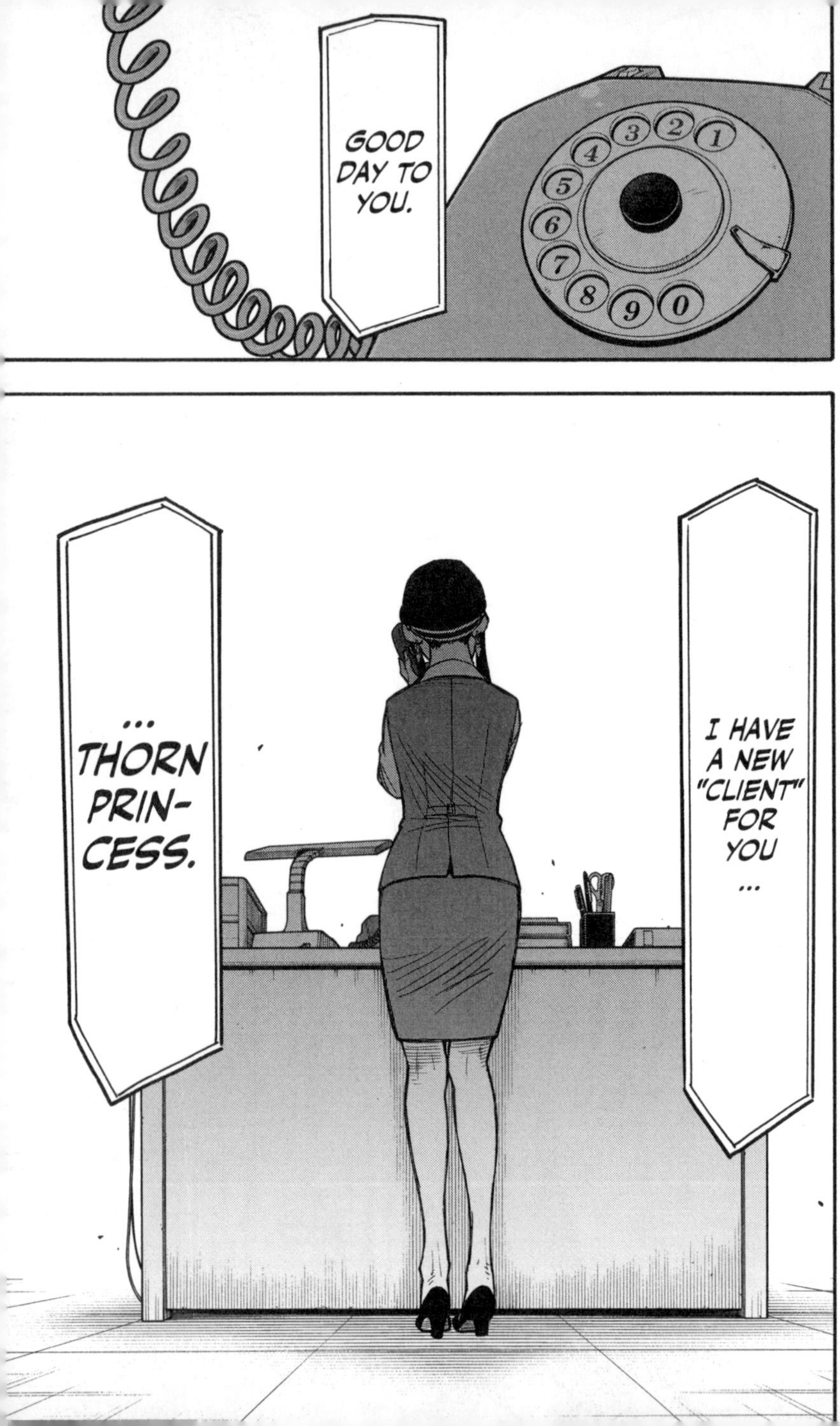
GOOD DAY TO YOU.
I HAVE A NEW "CLIENT" FOR YOU ...
... THORN PRIN-CESS.

SPY×FAMILY

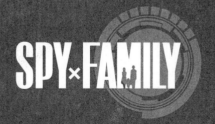

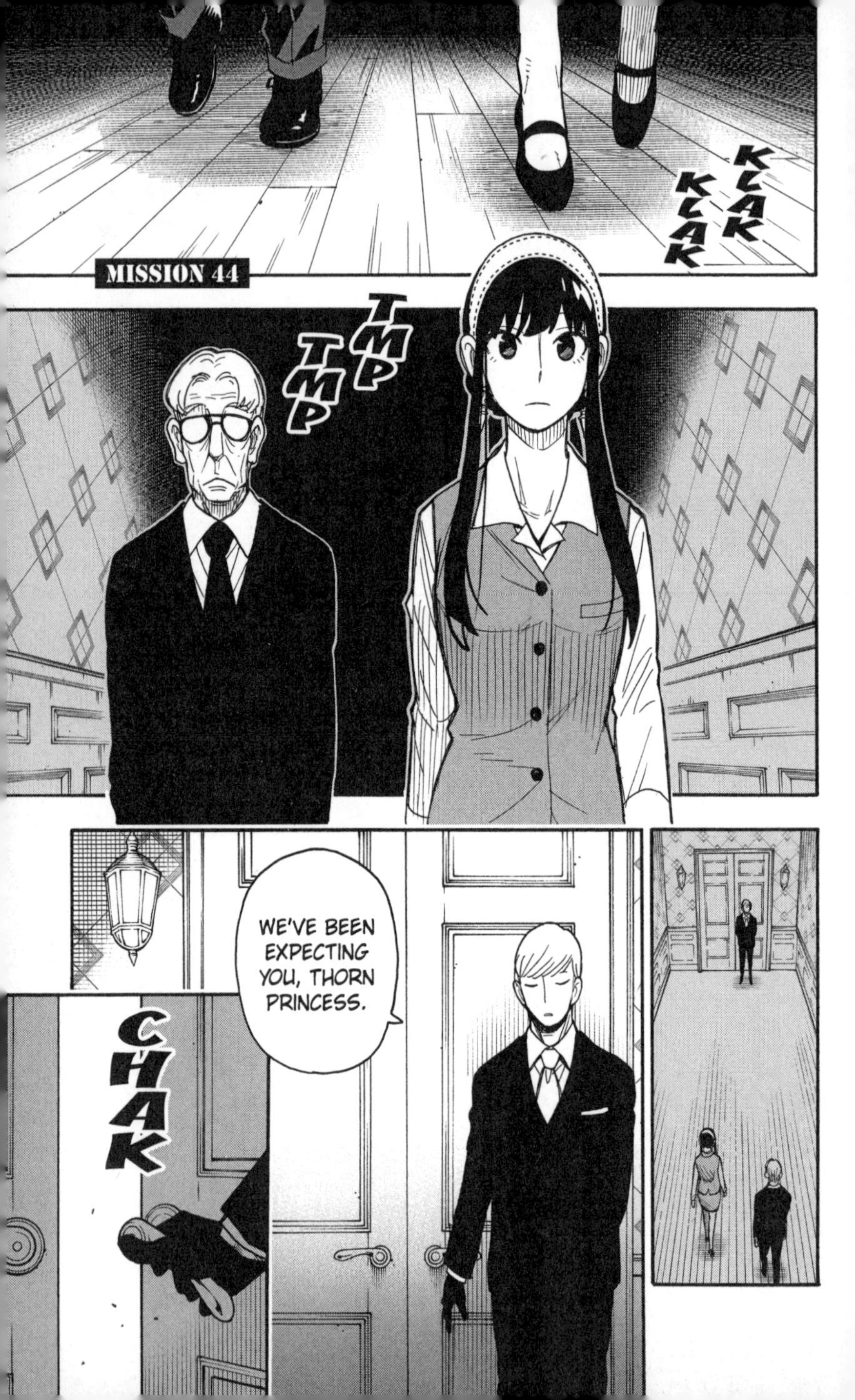
KLAK KLAK
MISSION 44
TMP TMP
WE'VE BEEN EXPECTING YOU, THORN PRINCESS.
CHAK

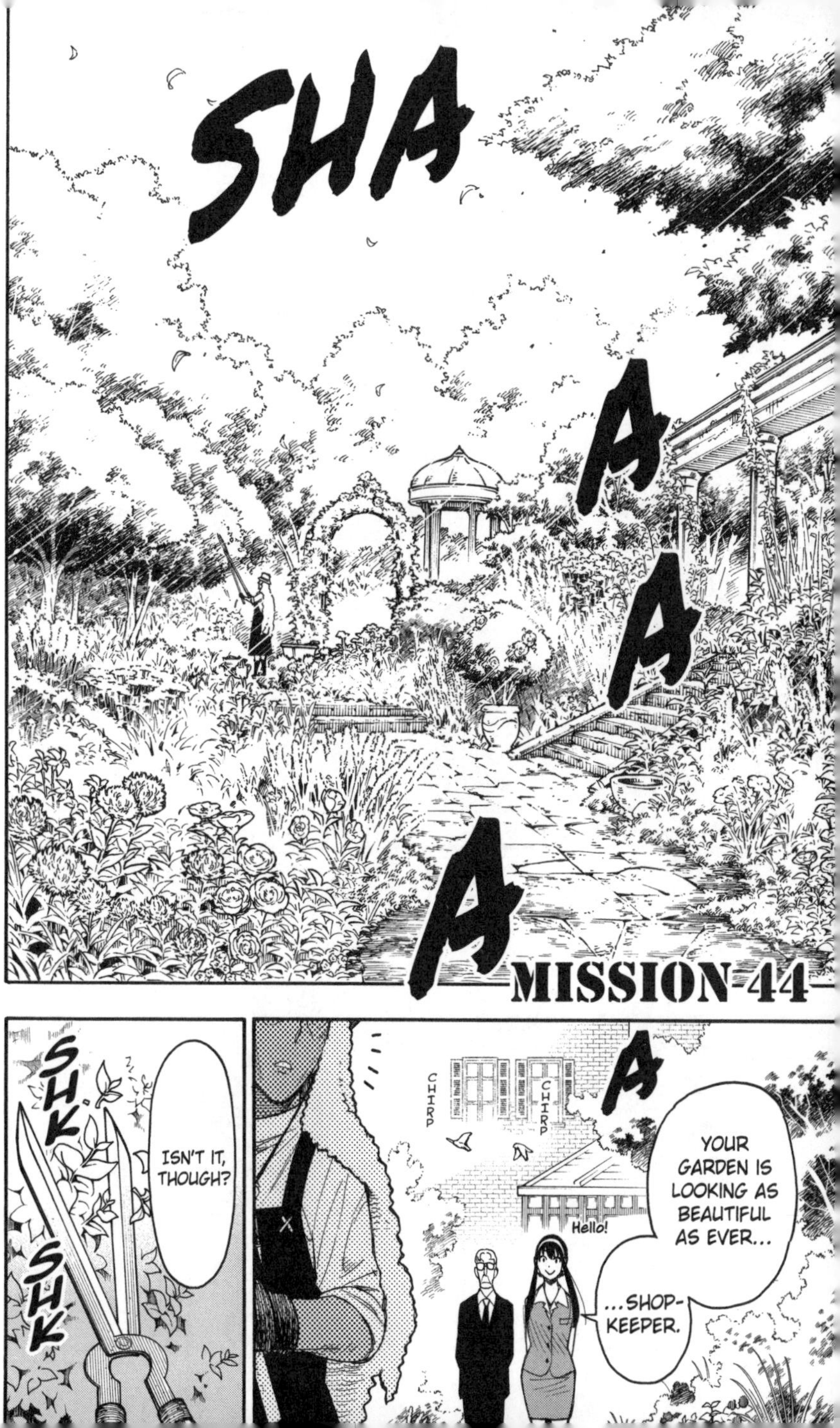
SHAAAAA
MISSION 44
CHIRP CHIRP
YOUR GARDEN IS LOOKING AS BEAUTIFUL AS EVER...
...SHOP-KEEPER.
Hello!
SHK SHK
ISN'T IT, THOUGH?

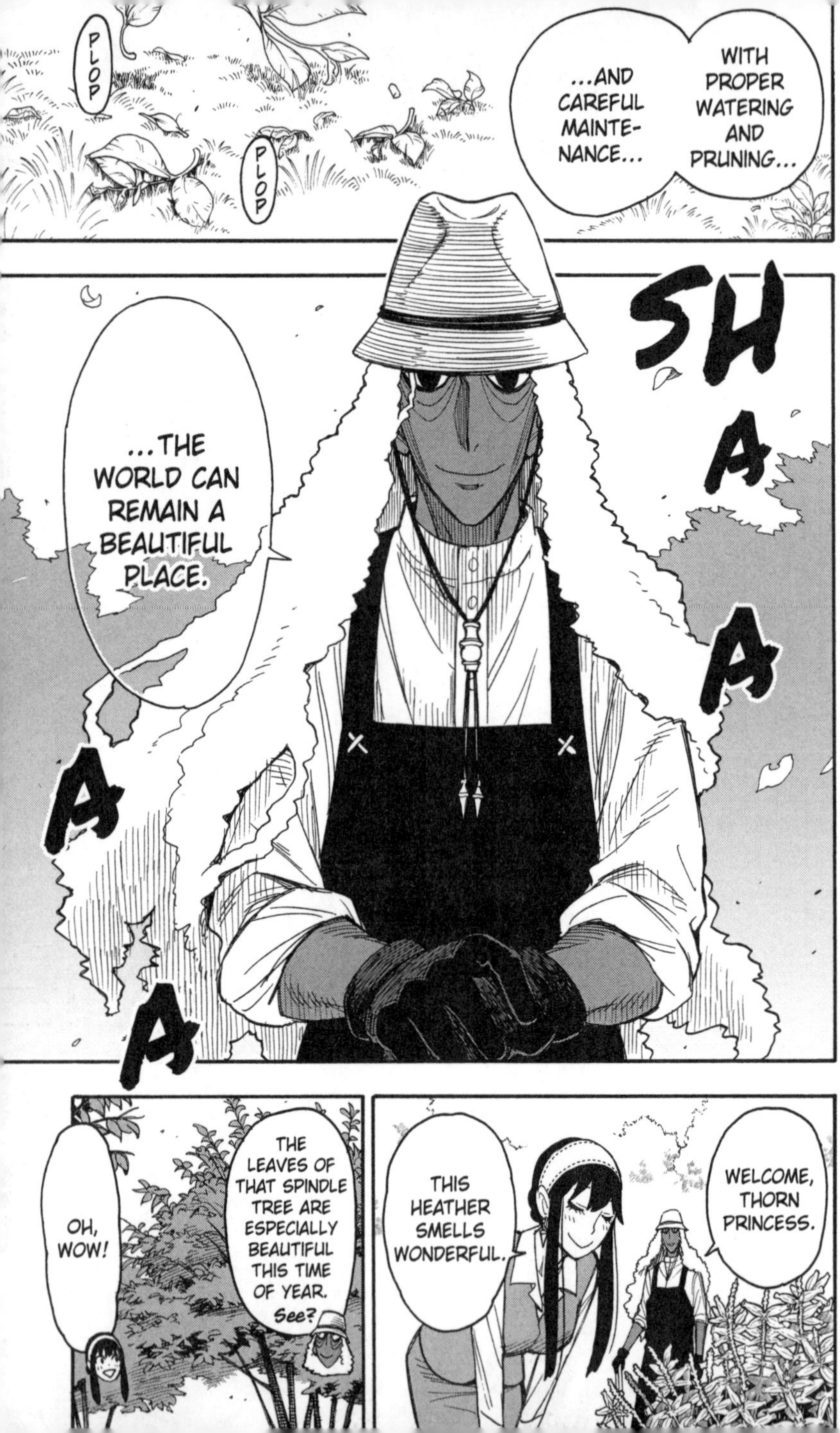
WITH PROPER WATERING AND PRUNING...
...AND CAREFUL MAINTE-NANCE...
PLOP
PLOP
SHAAAA
...THE WORLD CAN REMAIN A BEAUTIFUL PLACE.
WELCOME, THORN PRINCESS.
THIS HEATHER SMELLS WONDERFUL.
THE LEAVES OF THAT SPINDLE TREE ARE ESPECIALLY BEAUTIFUL THIS TIME OF YEAR.
See?
OH, WOW!

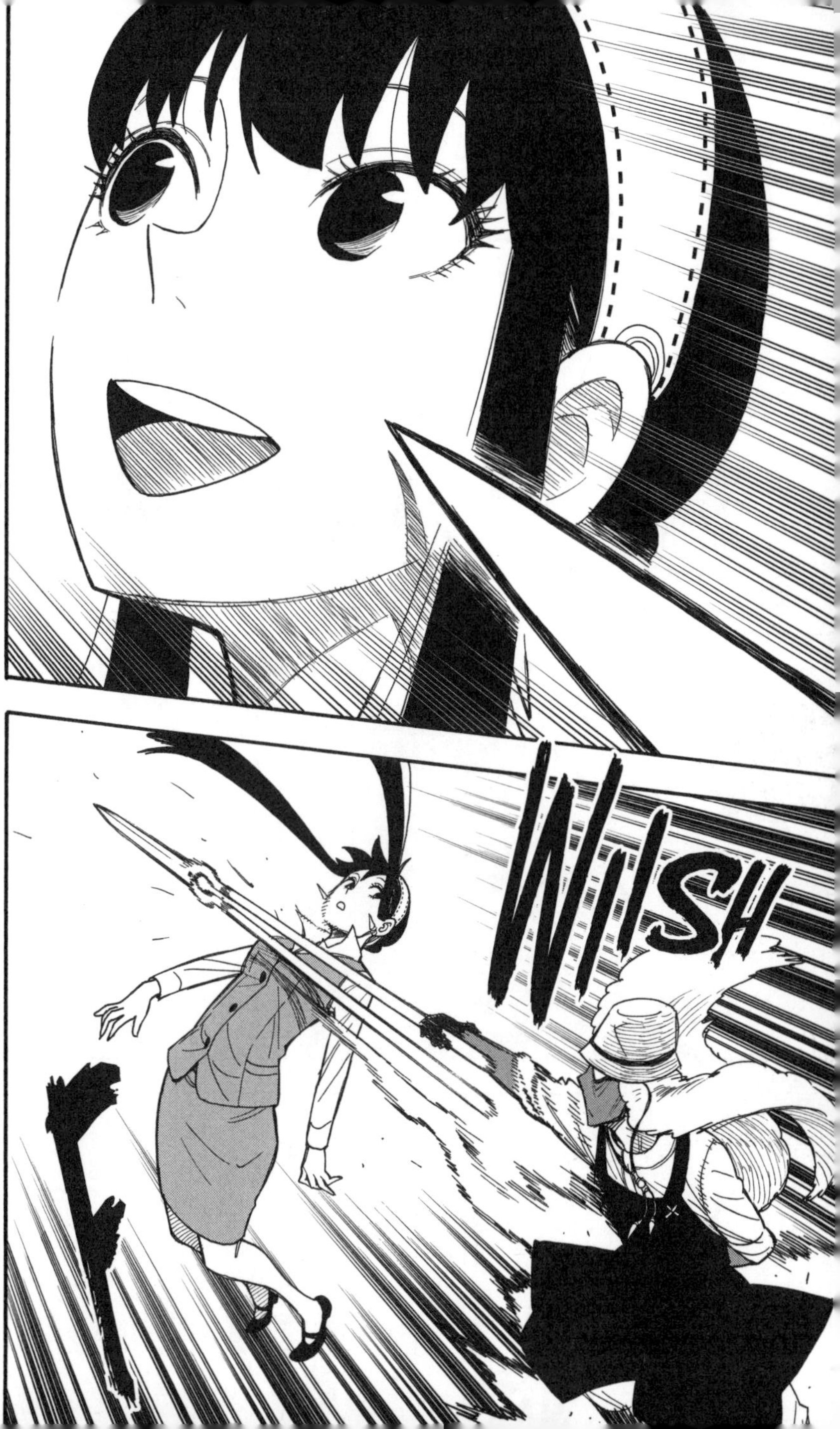
WHISH

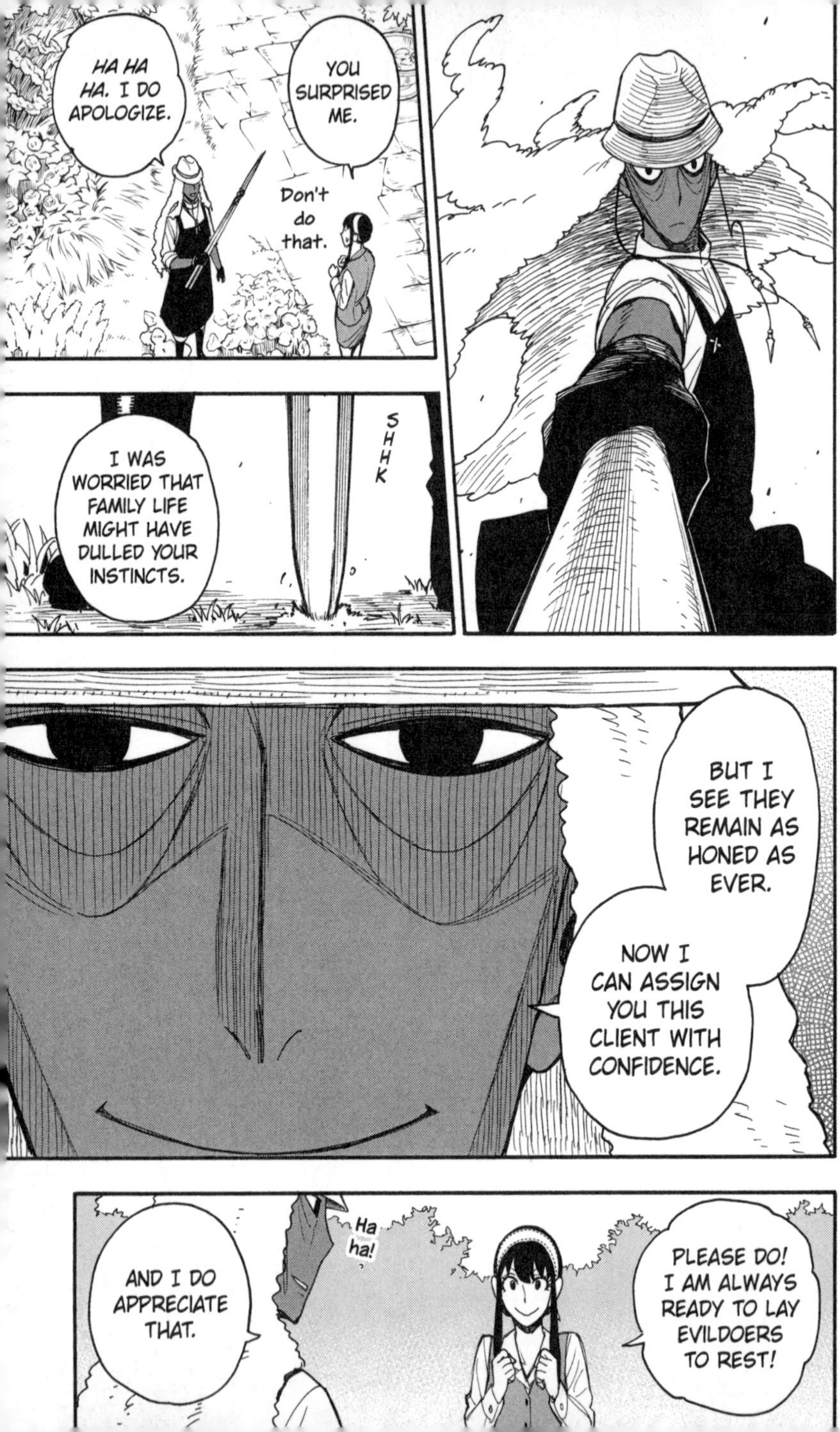
YOU SURPRISED ME.
Don't do that.
HA HA HA. I DO APOLOGIZE.
SHHK
I WAS WORRIED THAT FAMILY LIFE MIGHT HAVE DULLED YOUR INSTINCTS.
BUT I SEE THEY REMAIN AS HONED AS EVER.
NOW I CAN ASSIGN YOU THIS CLIENT WITH CONFIDENCE.
PLEASE DO! I AM ALWAYS READY TO LAY EVILDOERS TO REST!
Ha ha!
AND I DO APPRECIATE THAT.

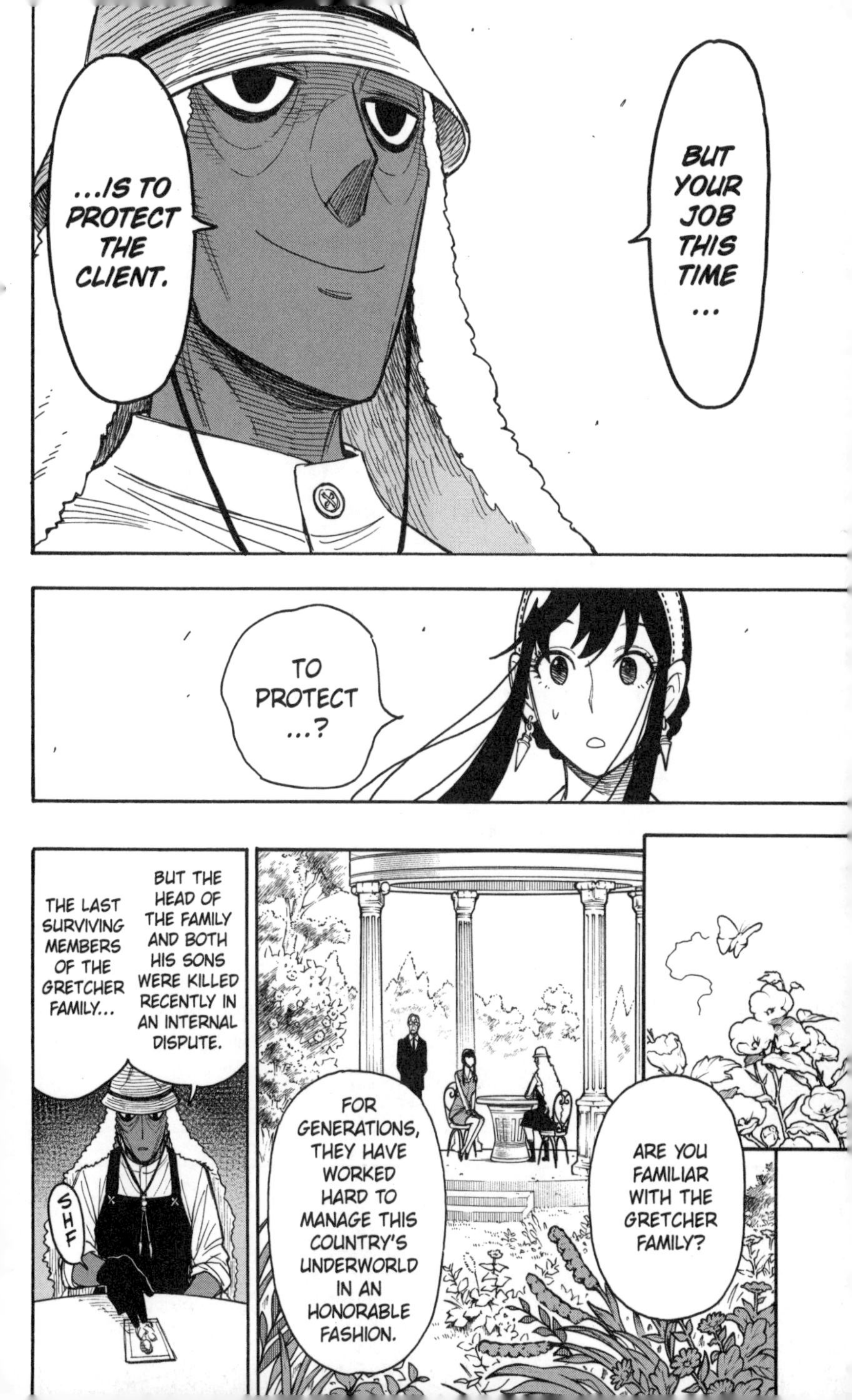
BUT YOUR JOB THIS TIME...
...IS TO PROTECT THE CLIENT.
TO PROTECT...?
ARE YOU FAMILIAR WITH THE GRETCHER FAMILY?
FOR GENERATIONS, THEY HAVE WORKED HARD TO MANAGE THIS COUNTRY'S UNDERWORLD IN AN HONORABLE FASHION.
BUT THE HEAD OF THE FAMILY AND BOTH HIS SONS WERE KILLED RECENTLY IN AN INTERNAL DISPUTE.
THE LAST SURVIVING MEMBERS OF THE GRETCHER FAMILY...
SHF

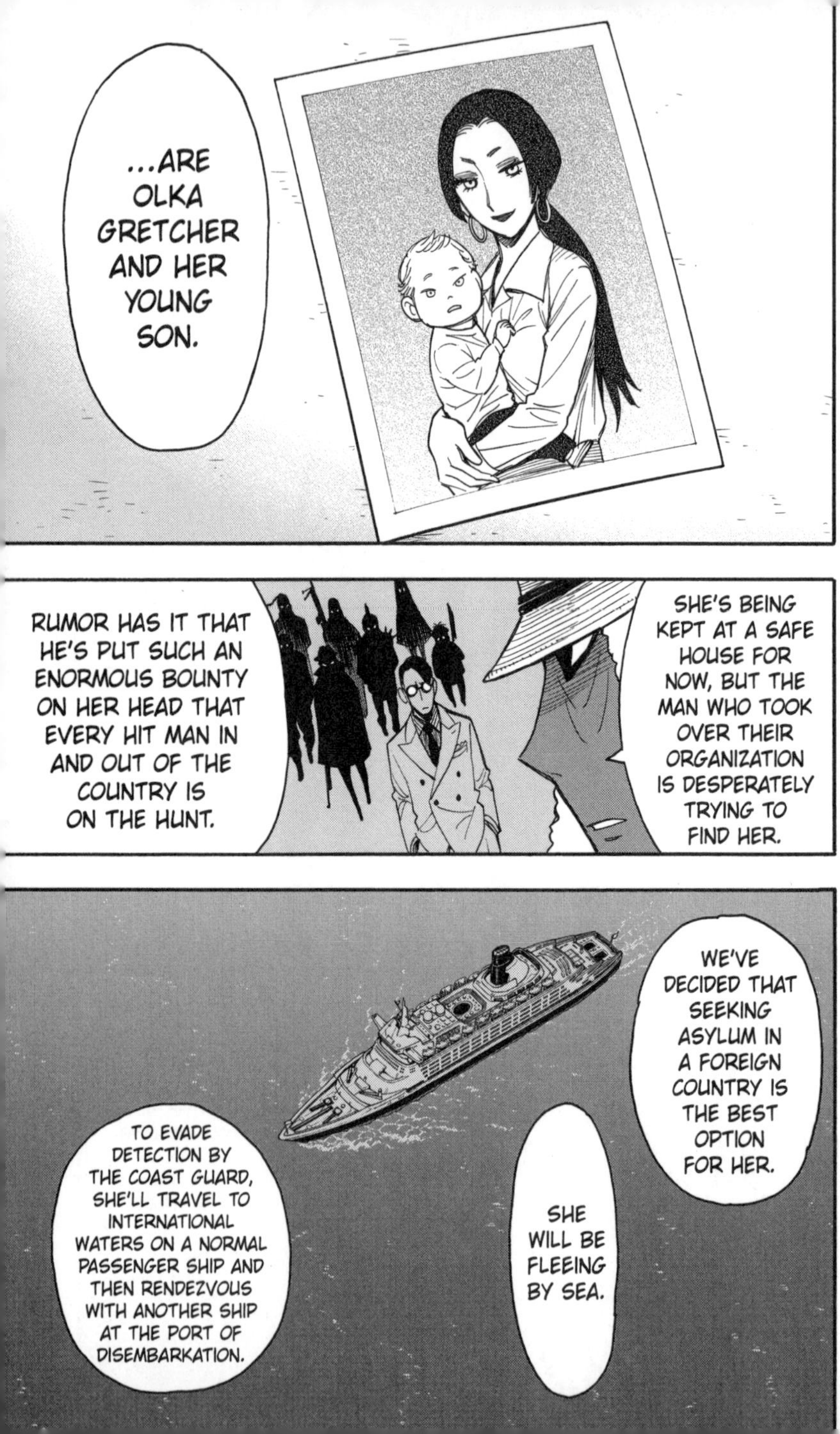
...ARE OLKA GRETCHER AND HER YOUNG SON.
SHE'S BEING KEPT AT A SAFE HOUSE FOR NOW, BUT THE MAN WHO TOOK OVER THEIR ORGANIZATION IS DESPERATELY TRYING TO FIND HER.
RUMOR HAS IT THAT HE'S PUT SUCH AN ENORMOUS BOUNTY ON HER HEAD THAT EVERY HIT MAN IN AND OUT OF THE COUNTRY IS ON THE HUNT.
WE'VE DECIDED THAT SEEKING ASYLUM IN A FOREIGN COUNTRY IS THE BEST OPTION FOR HER.
SHE WILL BE FLEEING BY SEA.
TO EVADE DETECTION BY THE COAST GUARD, SHE'LL TRAVEL TO INTERNATIONAL WATERS ON A NORMAL PASSENGER SHIP AND THEN RENDEZVOUS WITH ANOTHER SHIP AT THE PORT OF DISEMBARKATION.

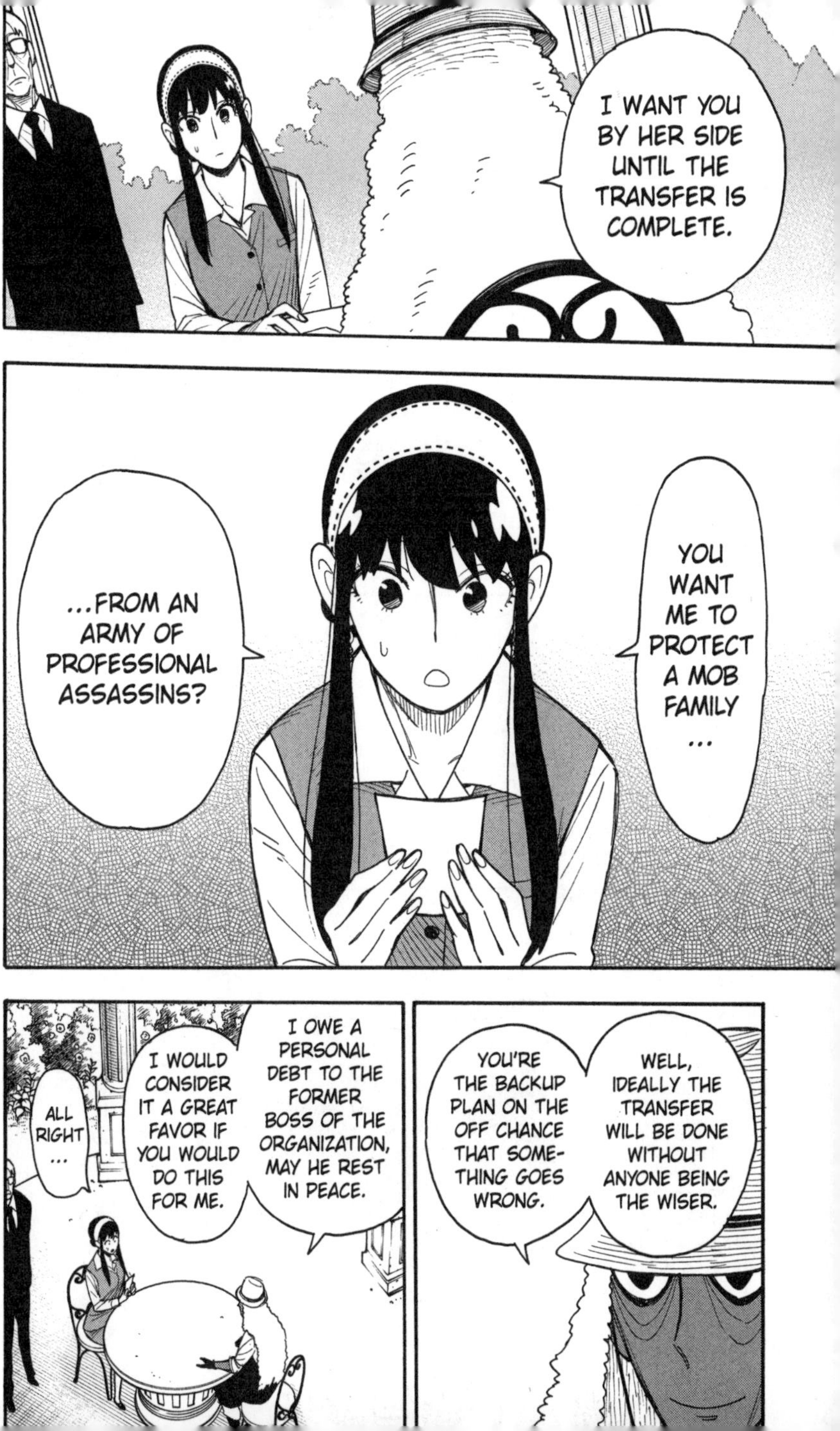
I WANT YOU BY HER SIDE UNTIL THE TRANSFER IS COMPLETE.
YOU WANT ME TO PROTECT A MOB FAMILY ...
...FROM AN ARMY OF PROFESSIONAL ASSASSINS?
WELL, IDEALLY THE TRANSFER WILL BE DONE WITHOUT ANYONE BEING THE WISER.
YOU'RE THE BACKUP PLAN ON THE OFF CHANCE THAT SOME-THING GOES WRONG.
I OWE A PERSONAL DEBT TO THE FORMER BOSS OF THE ORGANIZATION, MAY HE REST IN PEACE.
I WOULD CONSIDER IT A GREAT FAVOR IF YOU WOULD DO THIS FOR ME.
ALL RIGHT ...

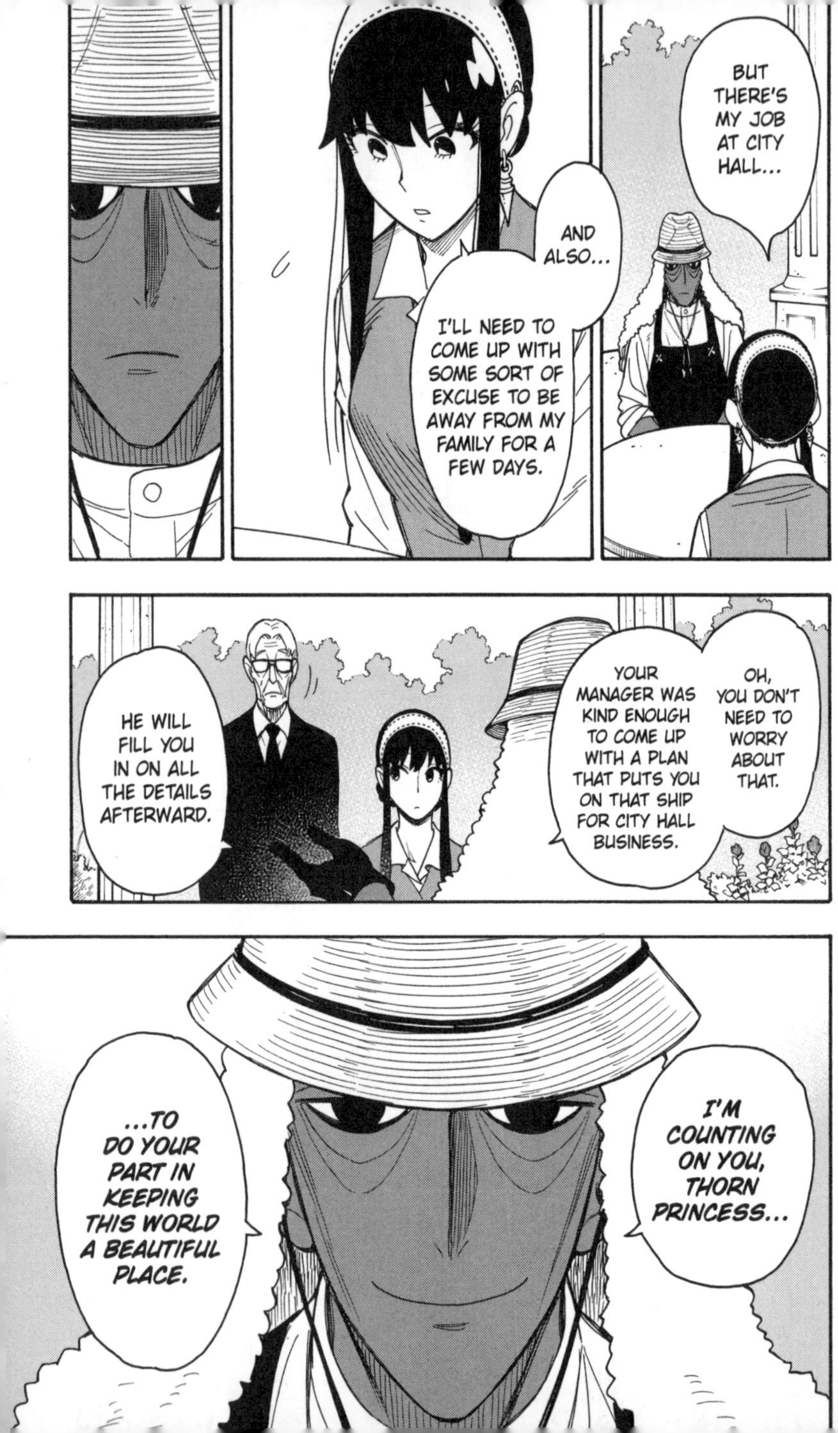
BUT THERE'S MY JOB AT CITY HALL...
AND ALSO...
I'LL NEED TO COME UP WITH SOME SORT OF EXCUSE TO BE AWAY FROM MY FAMILY FOR A FEW DAYS.
OH, YOU DON'T NEED TO WORRY ABOUT THAT.
YOUR MANAGER WAS KIND ENOUGH TO COME UP WITH A PLAN THAT PUTS YOU ON THAT SHIP FOR CITY HALL BUSINESS.
HE WILL FILL YOU IN ON ALL THE DETAILS AFTERWARD.
I'M COUNTING ON YOU, THORN PRINCESS...
...TO DO YOUR PART IN KEEPING THIS WORLD A BEAUTIFUL PLACE.

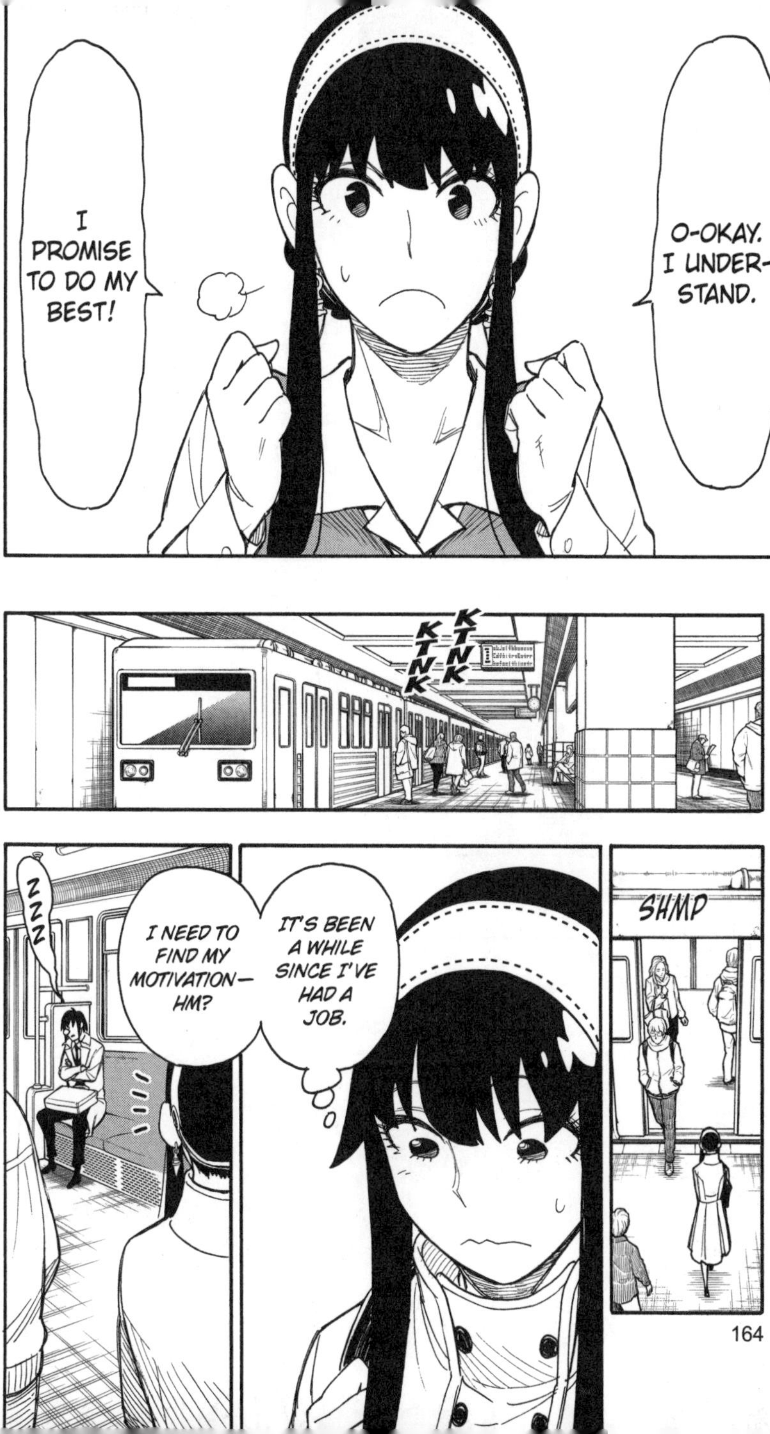
O-OKAY. I UNDER-STAND.
I PROMISE TO DO MY BEST!
KTNK KTNK
SHMP
IT'S BEEN A WHILE SINCE I'VE HAD A JOB.
I NEED TO FIND MY MOTIVATION— HM?
ZZZ

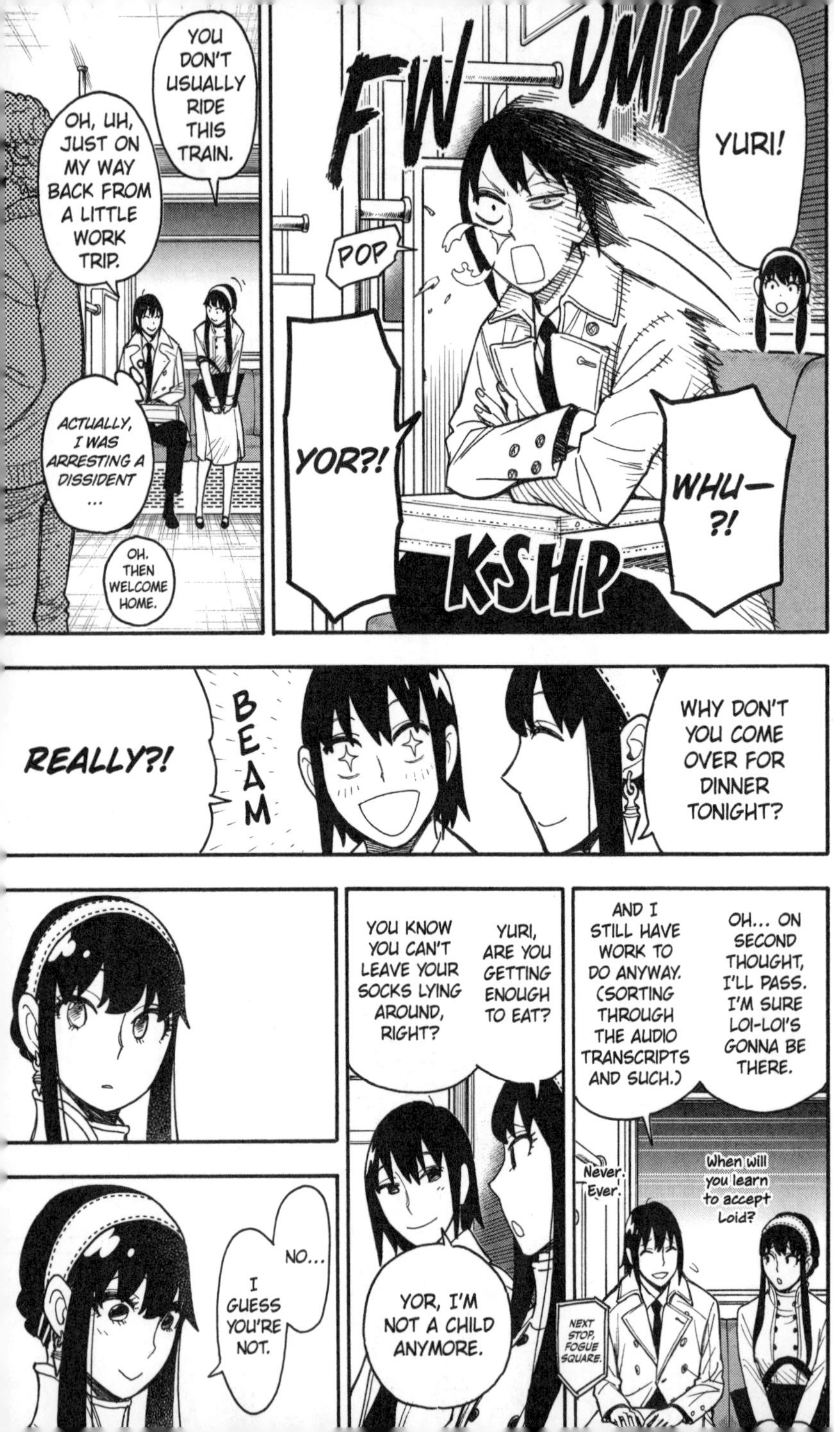
FWUMP
YURI!
POP
WHU— ?!
YOR?!
KSHP
YOU DON'T USUALLY RIDE THIS TRAIN.
OH, UH, JUST ON MY WAY BACK FROM A LITTLE WORK TRIP.
ACTUALLY, I WAS ARRESTING A DISSIDENT ...
OH. THEN WELCOME HOME.
WHY DON'T YOU COME OVER FOR DINNER TONIGHT?
BEAM
REALLY?!
OH... ON SECOND THOUGHT, I'LL PASS. I'M SURE LOI-LOI'S GONNA BE THERE.
AND I STILL HAVE WORK TO DO ANYWAY. (SORTING THROUGH THE AUDIO TRANSCRIPTS AND SUCH.)
When will you learn to accept Loid?
Never. Ever.
NEXT STOP, FOGUE SQUARE.
YURI, ARE YOU GETTING ENOUGH TO EAT?
YOU KNOW YOU CAN'T LEAVE YOUR SOCKS LYING AROUND, RIGHT?
YOR, I'M NOT A CHILD ANYMORE.
NO...
I GUESS YOU'RE NOT.

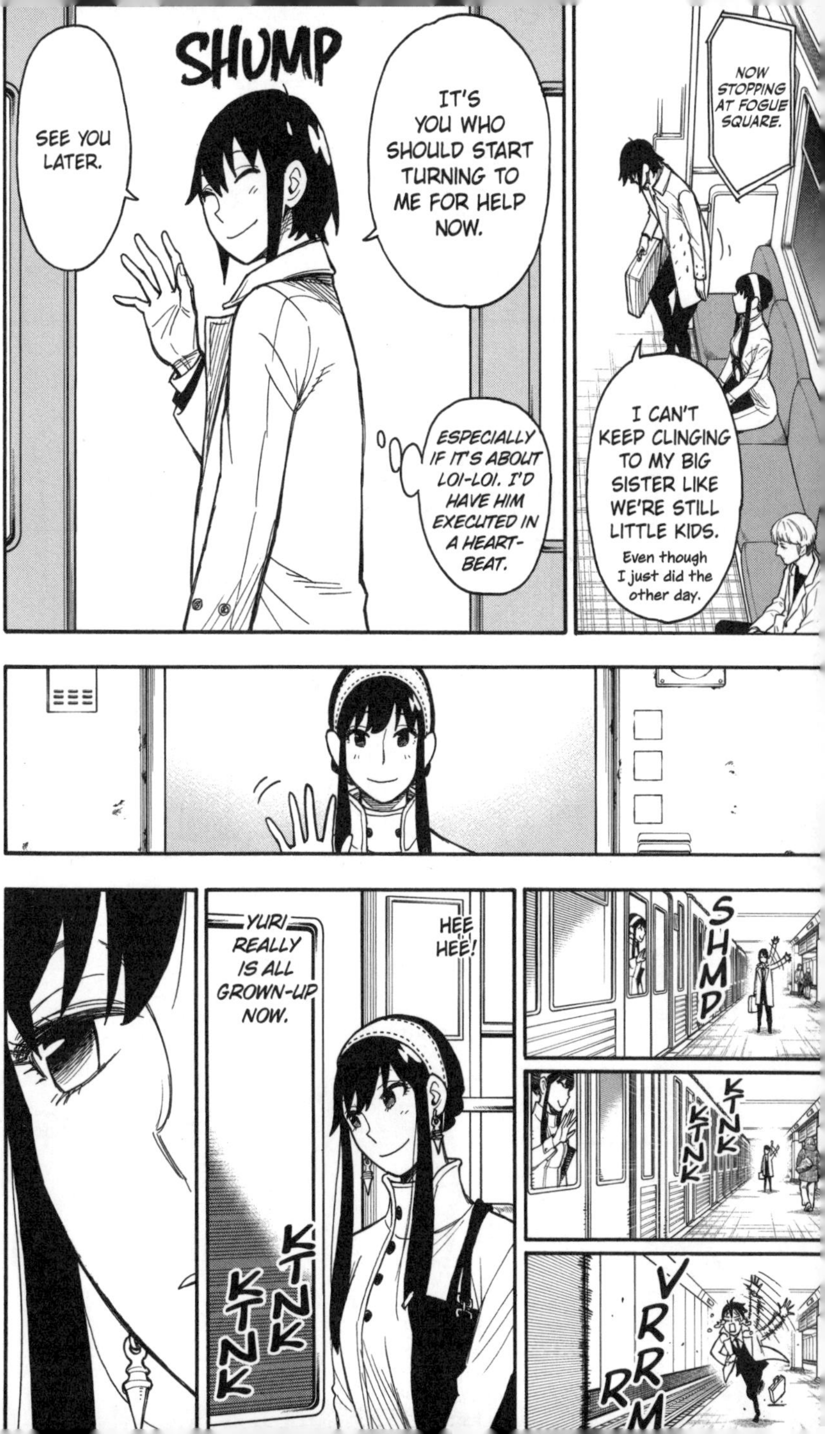
NOW STOPPING AT FOGUE SQUARE.
I CAN'T KEEP CLINGING TO MY BIG SISTER LIKE WE'RE STILL LITTLE KIDS.
Even though I just did the other day.
SHUMP
IT'S YOU WHO SHOULD START TURNING TO ME FOR HELP NOW.
SEE YOU LATER.
ESPECIALLY IF IT'S ABOUT LOI-LOI. I'D HAVE HIM EXECUTED IN A HEART-BEAT.
SHMP
KTNK
KTNK
VRRRM
HEE HEE!
YURI REALLY IS ALL GROWN-UP NOW.
KTNK
KTNK

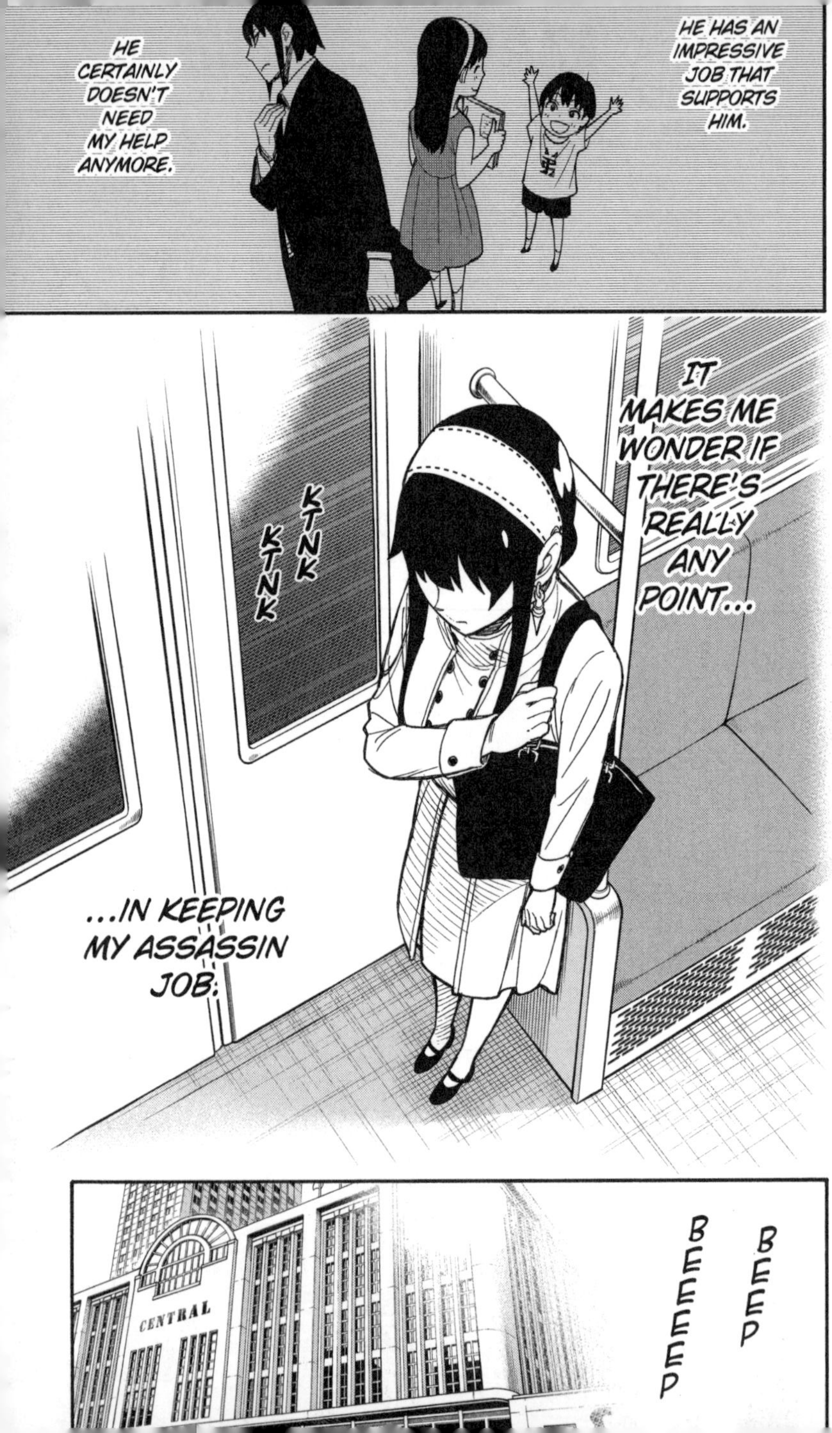
HE HAS AN IMPRESSIVE JOB THAT SUPPORTS HIM.
HE CERTAINLY DOESN'T NEED MY HELP ANYMORE.
IT MAKES ME WONDER IF THERE'S REALLY ANY POINT...
KTNK
KTNK
...IN KEEPING MY ASSASSIN JOB.
BEEP
BEEEEEP
CENTRAL

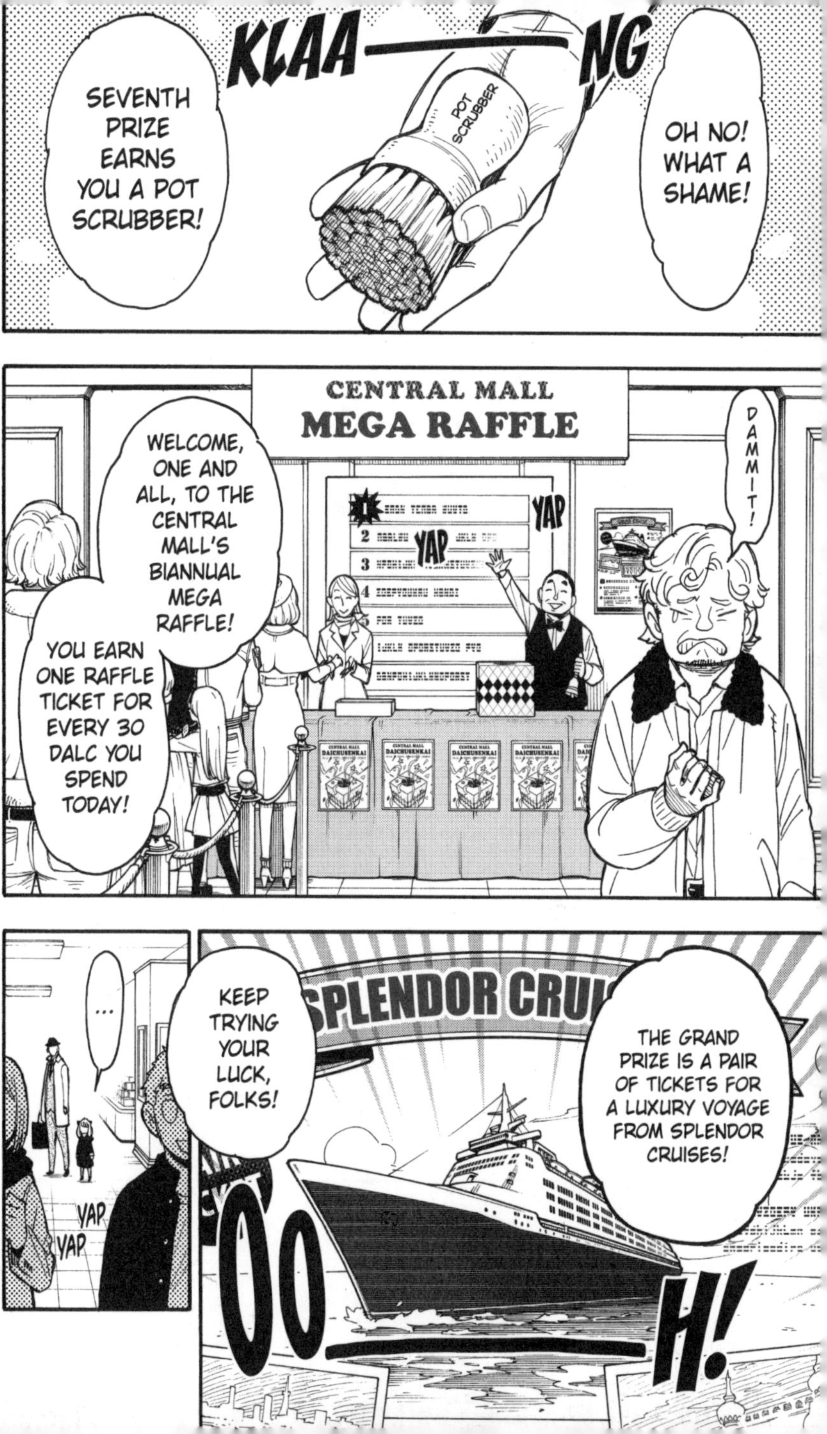
KLAA—NG
OH NO! WHAT A SHAME!
POT SCRUBBER
SEVENTH PRIZE EARNS YOU A POT SCRUBBER!
CENTRAL MALL
MEGA RAFFLE
DAMMIT!
YAP
YAP
WELCOME, ONE AND ALL, TO THE CENTRAL MALL'S BIANNUAL MEGA RAFFLE!
YOU EARN ONE RAFFLE TICKET FOR EVERY 30 DALC YOU SPEND TODAY!
CENTRAL MALL DAICHUSENKAI
THE GRAND PRIZE IS A PAIR OF TICKETS FOR A LUXURY VOYAGE FROM SPLENDOR CRUISES!
SPLENDOR CRUI
KEEP TRYING YOUR LUCK, FOLKS!
OOO—H!
...
YAP
YAP

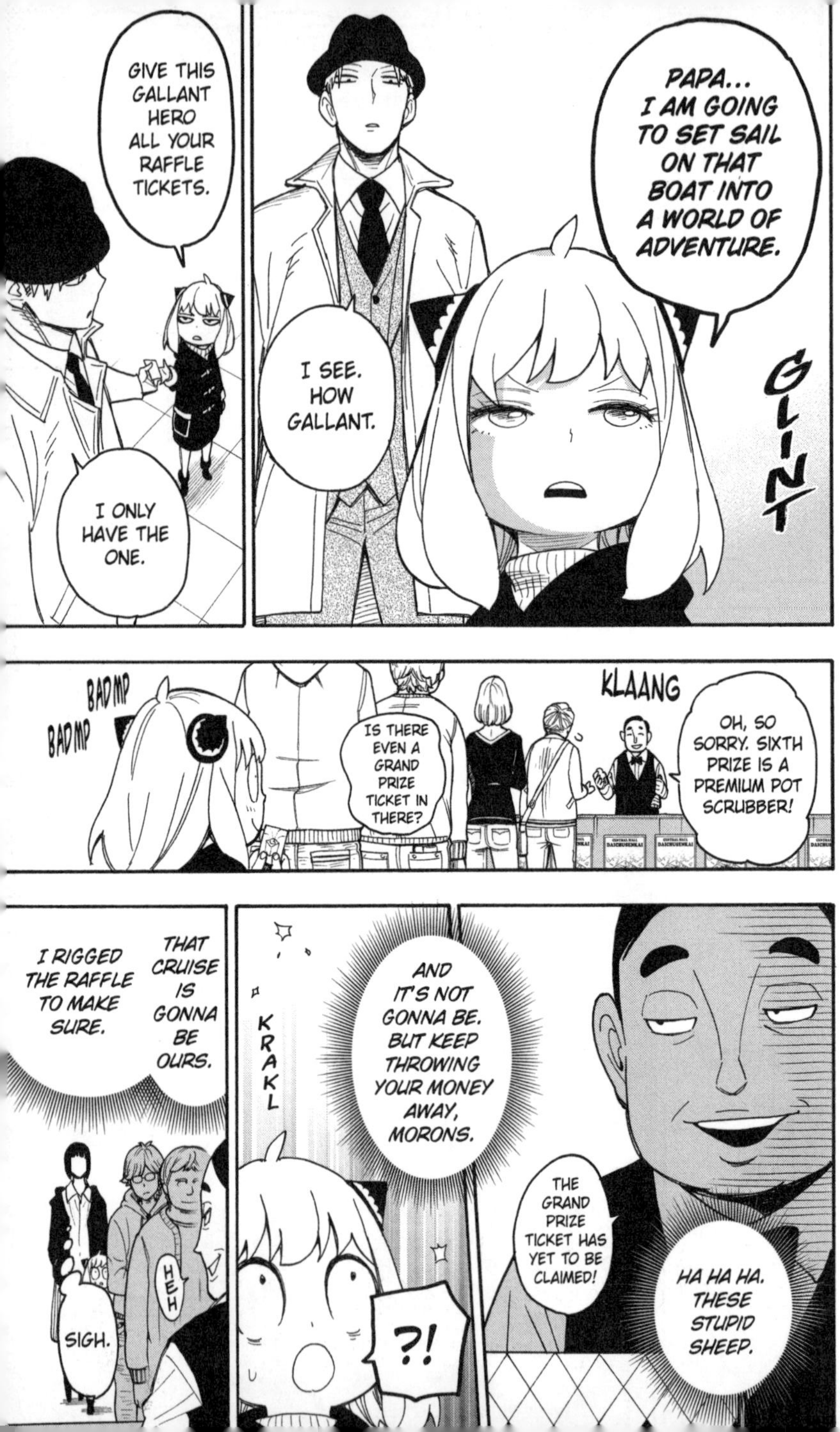
PAPA... I AM GOING TO SET SAIL ON THAT BOAT INTO A WORLD OF ADVENTURE.
GLINT
I SEE. HOW GALLANT.
GIVE THIS GALLANT HERO ALL YOUR RAFFLE TICKETS.
I ONLY HAVE THE ONE.
OH, SO SORRY. SIXTH PRIZE IS A PREMIUM POT SCRUBBER!
KLAANG
IS THERE EVEN A GRAND PRIZE TICKET IN THERE?
BADMP
BADMP
HA HA HA. THESE STUPID SHEEP.
THE GRAND PRIZE TICKET HAS YET TO BE CLAIMED!
AND IT'S NOT GONNA BE. BUT KEEP THROWING YOUR MONEY AWAY, MORONS.
KRAKL
?!
THAT CRUISE IS GONNA BE OURS.
I RIGGED THE RAFFLE TO MAKE SURE.
HEH
SIGH.

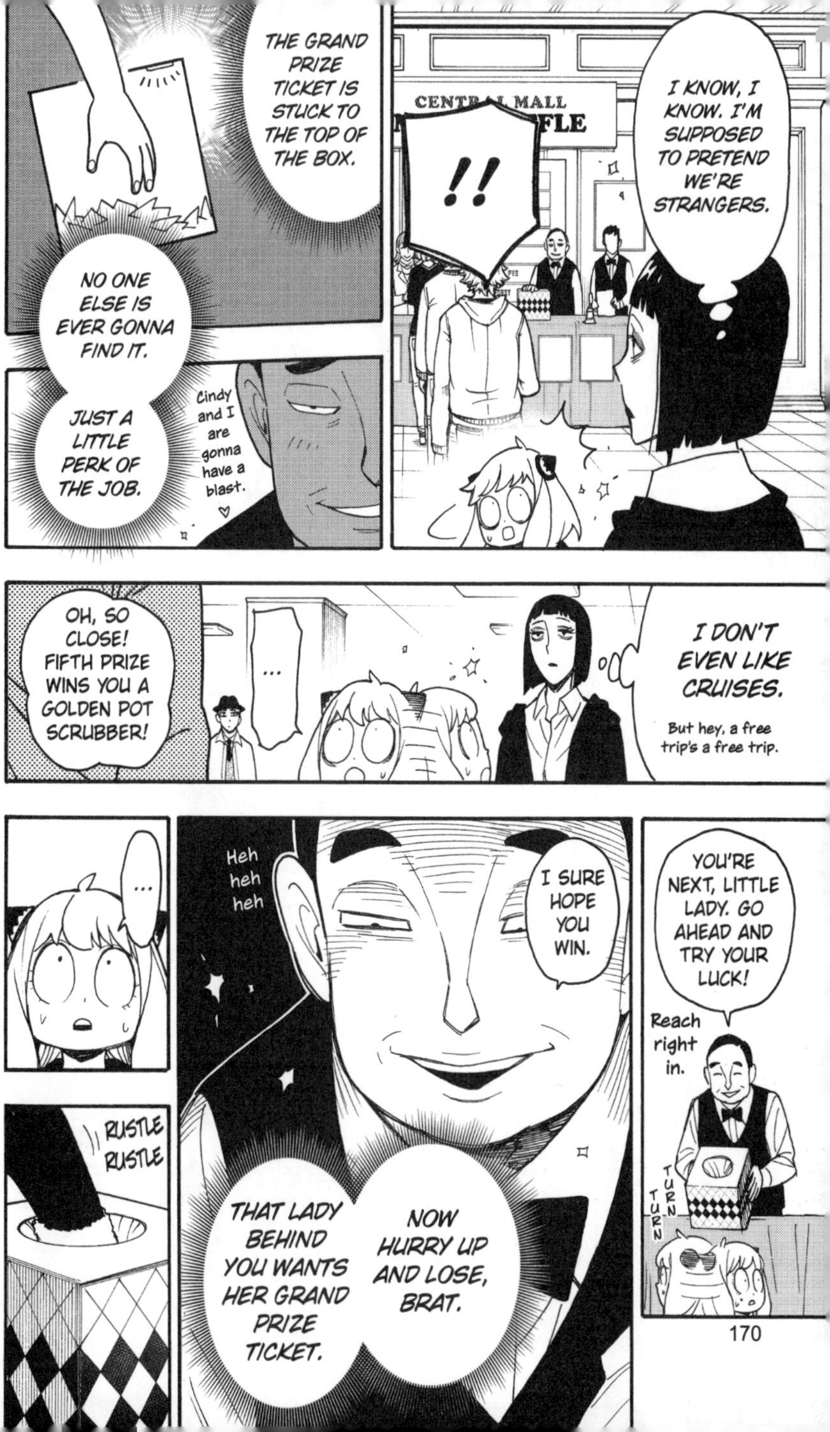
CENTRAL MALL
FLE
!!
I KNOW, I KNOW. I'M SUPPOSED TO PRETEND WE'RE STRANGERS.
THE GRAND PRIZE TICKET IS STUCK TO THE TOP OF THE BOX.
NO ONE ELSE IS EVER GONNA FIND IT.
JUST A LITTLE PERK OF THE JOB.
Cindy and I are gonna have a blast. ♡
I DON'T EVEN LIKE CRUISES.
But hey, a free trip's a free trip.
...
OH, SO CLOSE! FIFTH PRIZE WINS YOU A GOLDEN POT SCRUBBER!
YOU'RE NEXT, LITTLE LADY. GO AHEAD AND TRY YOUR LUCK!
Reach right in.
TURN TURN
I SURE HOPE YOU WIN.
Heh heh heh
NOW HURRY UP AND LOSE, BRAT.
THAT LADY BEHIND YOU WANTS HER GRAND PRIZE TICKET.
...
RUSTLE RUSTLE

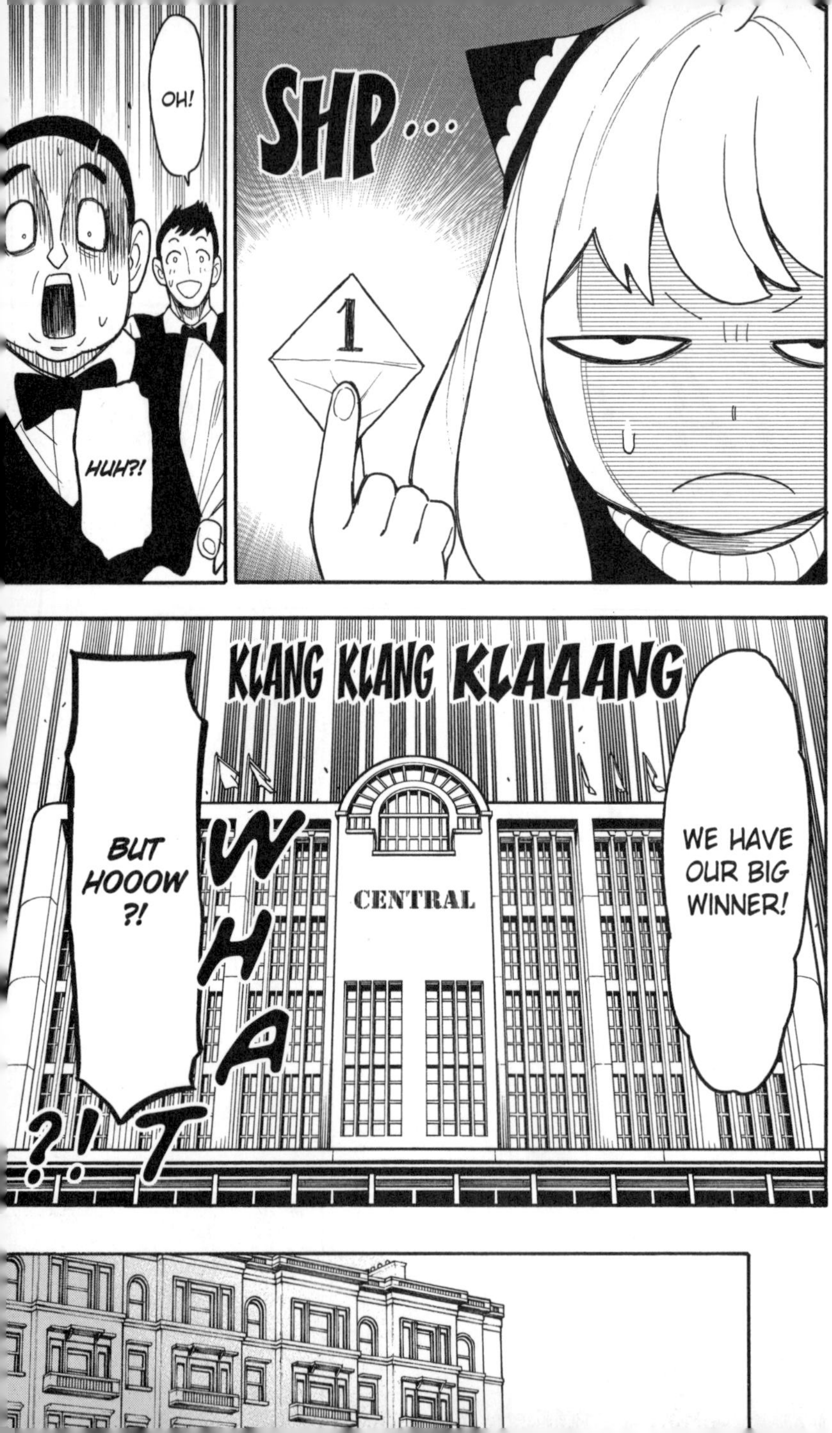
SHP...
1
OH!
HUH?!
WE HAVE OUR BIG WINNER!
KLANG KLANG KLAAANG
CENTRAL
BUT HOOOW?!
WHAT?!

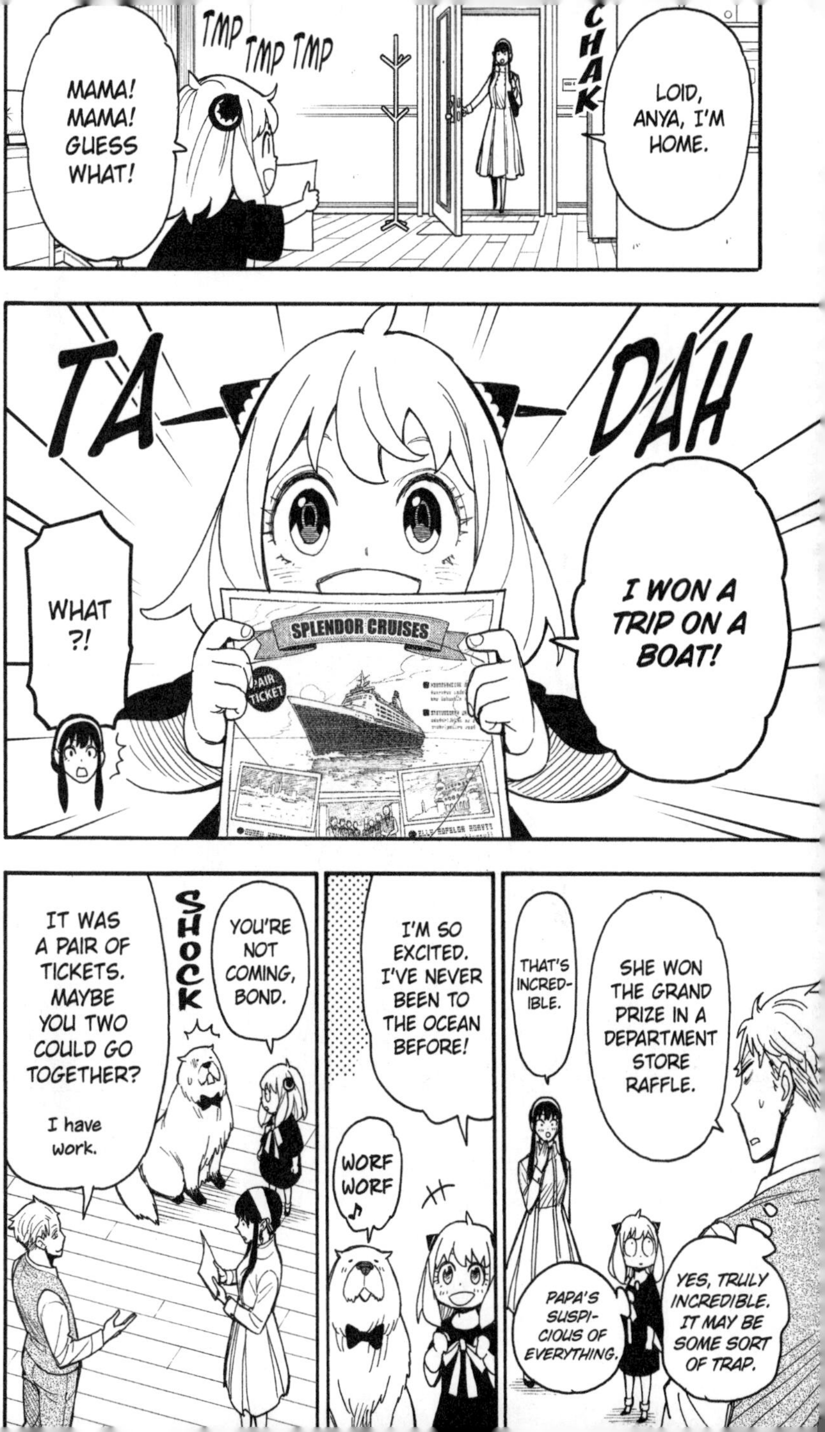
CHAK
LOID, ANYA, I'M HOME.
TMP TMP TMP
MAMA! MAMA! GUESS WHAT!
TA-DAH
I WON A TRIP ON A BOAT!
SPLENDOR CRUISES
PAIR TICKET
WHAT ?!
SHE WON THE GRAND PRIZE IN A DEPARTMENT STORE RAFFLE.
THAT'S INCRED-IBLE.
YES, TRULY INCREDIBLE. IT MAY BE SOME SORT OF TRAP.
PAPA'S SUSPI-CIOUS OF EVERYTHING.
I'M SO EXCITED. I'VE NEVER BEEN TO THE OCEAN BEFORE!
WORF WORF ♪
YOU'RE NOT COMING, BOND.
SHOCK
IT WAS A PAIR OF TICKETS. MAYBE YOU TWO COULD GO TOGETHER?
I have work.

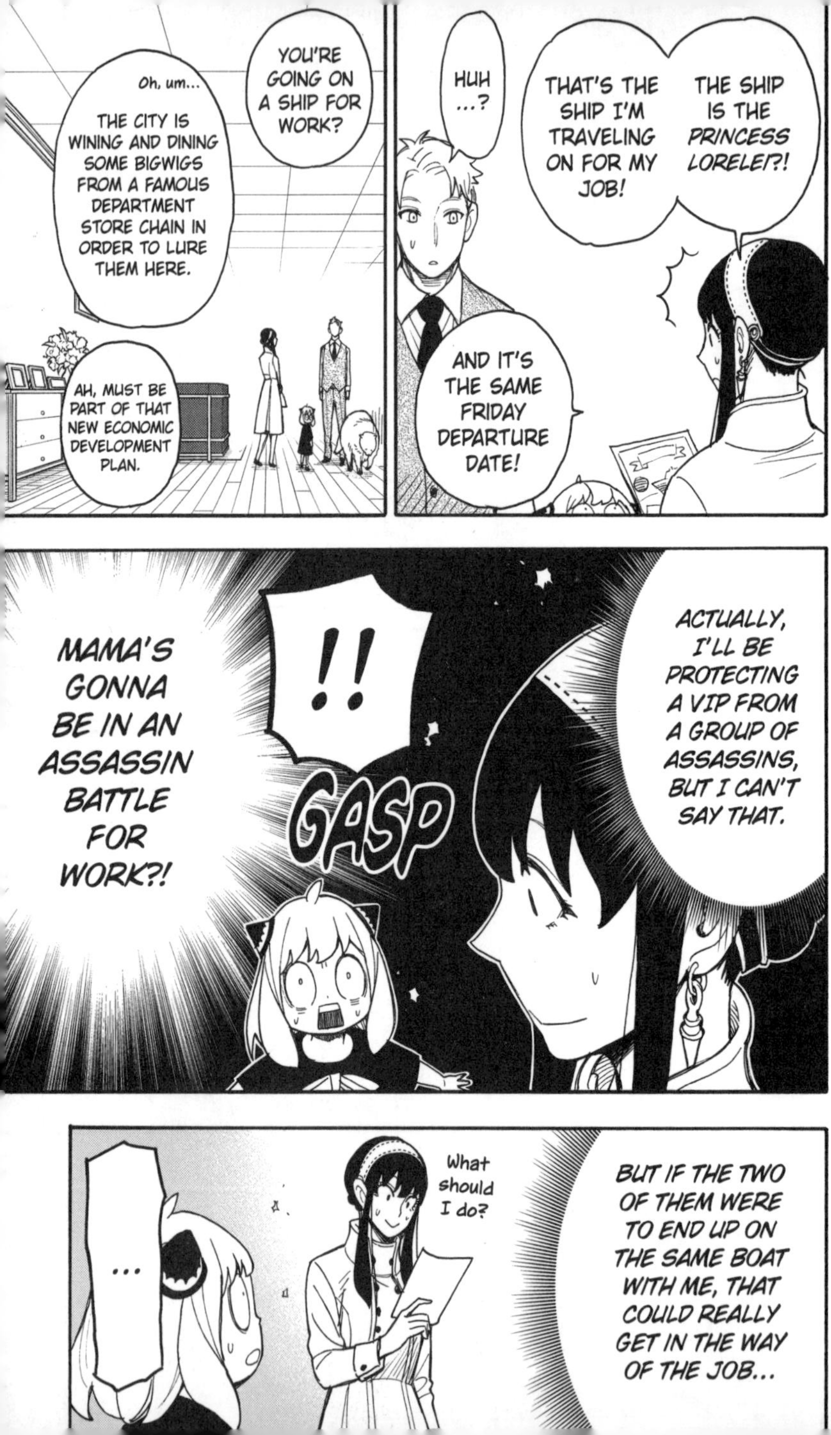
THE SHIP IS THE PRINCESS LORELEI?!
THAT'S THE SHIP I'M TRAVELING ON FOR MY JOB!
HUH ...?
AND IT'S THE SAME FRIDAY DEPARTURE DATE!
YOU'RE GOING ON A SHIP FOR WORK?
Oh, um...
THE CITY IS WINING AND DINING SOME BIGWIGS FROM A FAMOUS DEPARTMENT STORE CHAIN IN ORDER TO LURE THEM HERE.
AH, MUST BE PART OF THAT NEW ECONOMIC DEVELOPMENT PLAN.
ACTUALLY, I'LL BE PROTECTING A VIP FROM A GROUP OF ASSASSINS, BUT I CAN'T SAY THAT.
!!
GASP
MAMA'S GONNA BE IN AN ASSASSIN BATTLE FOR WORK?!
BUT IF THE TWO OF THEM WERE TO END UP ON THE SAME BOAT WITH ME, THAT COULD REALLY GET IN THE WAY OF THE JOB...
What should I do?
...

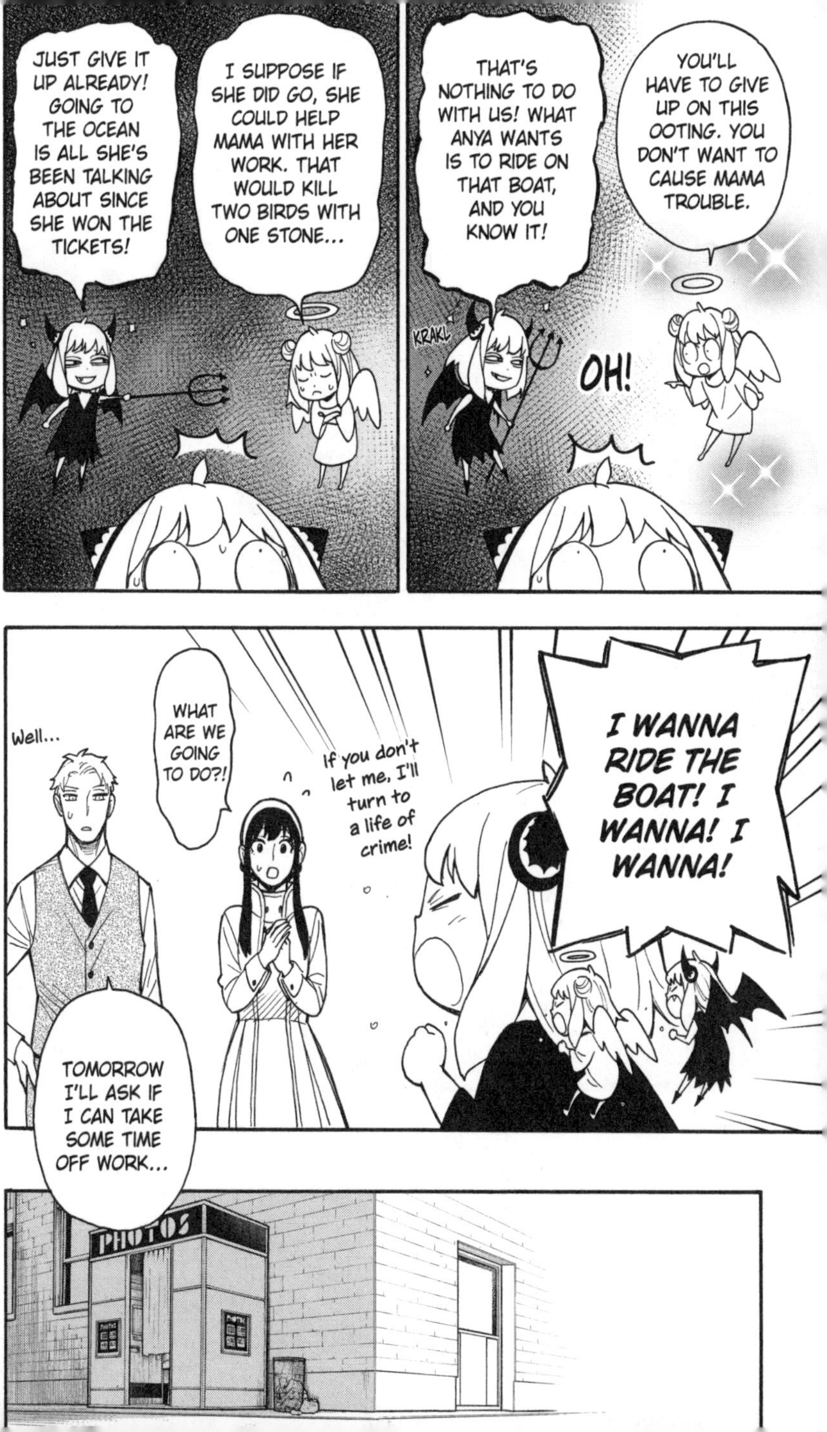
YOU'LL HAVE TO GIVE UP ON THIS OOTING. YOU DON'T WANT TO CAUSE MAMA TROUBLE.
THAT'S NOTHING TO DO WITH US! WHAT ANYA WANTS IS TO RIDE ON THAT BOAT, AND YOU KNOW IT!
KRAKL
OH!
I SUPPOSE IF SHE DID GO, SHE COULD HELP MAMA WITH HER WORK. THAT WOULD KILL TWO BIRDS WITH ONE STONE...
JUST GIVE IT UP ALREADY! GOING TO THE OCEAN IS ALL SHE'S BEEN TALKING ABOUT SINCE SHE WON THE TICKETS!
I WANNA RIDE THE BOAT! I WANNA! I WANNA!
If you don't let me, I'll turn to a life of crime!
WHAT ARE WE GOING TO DO?!
Well...
TOMORROW I'LL ASK IF I CAN TAKE SOME TIME OFF WORK...
PHOTOS

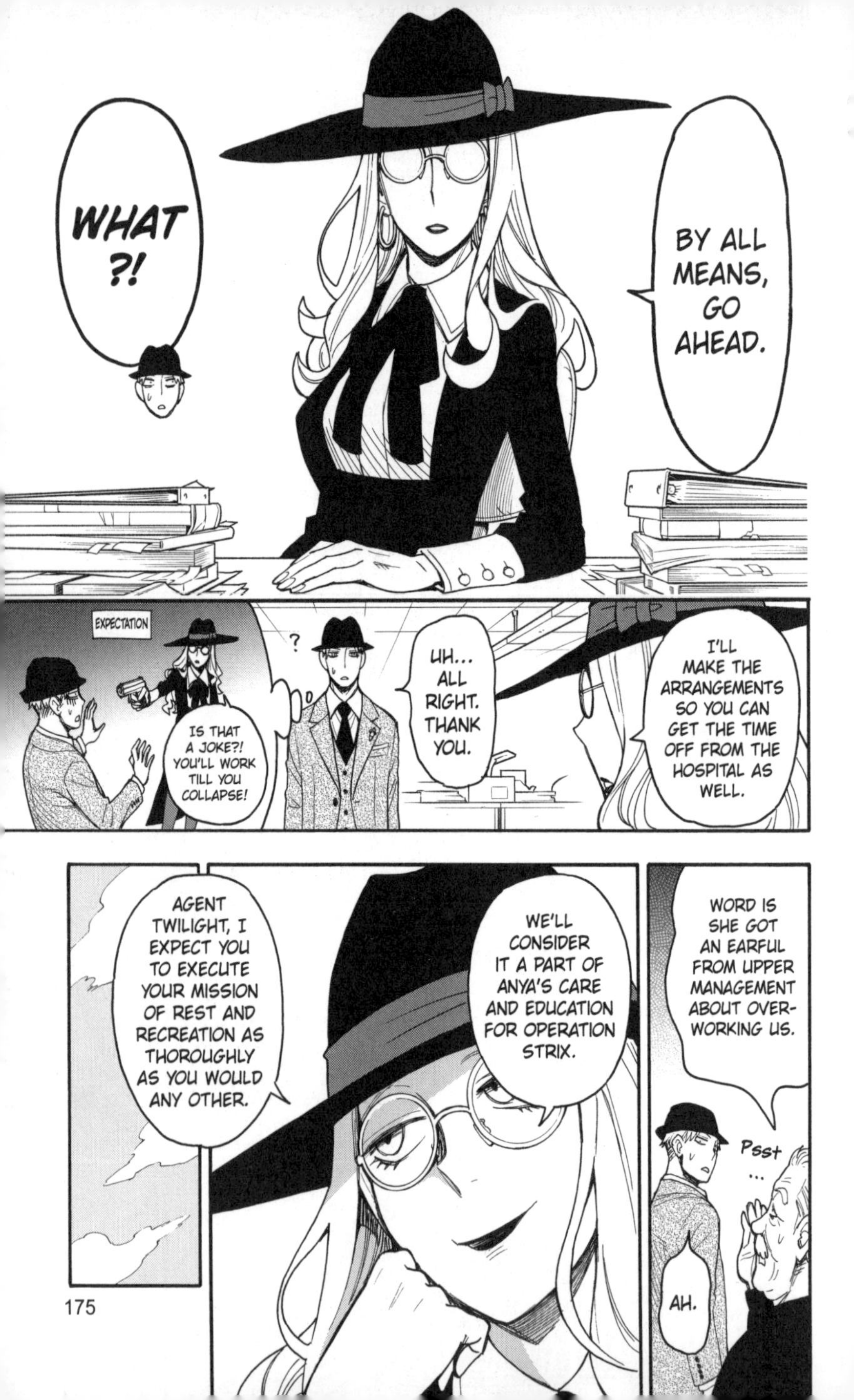
BY ALL MEANS, GO AHEAD.
WHAT?!
I'LL MAKE THE ARRANGEMENTS SO YOU CAN GET THE TIME OFF FROM THE HOSPITAL AS WELL.
UH... ALL RIGHT. THANK YOU.
?
EXPECTATION
IS THAT A JOKE?! YOU'LL WORK TILL YOU COLLAPSE!
WORD IS SHE GOT AN EARFUL FROM UPPER MANAGEMENT ABOUT OVER-WORKING US.
Psst...
AH.
WE'LL CONSIDER IT A PART OF ANYA'S CARE AND EDUCATION FOR OPERATION STRIX.
AGENT TWILIGHT, I EXPECT YOU TO EXECUTE YOUR MISSION OF REST AND RECREATION AS THOROUGHLY AS YOU WOULD ANY OTHER.

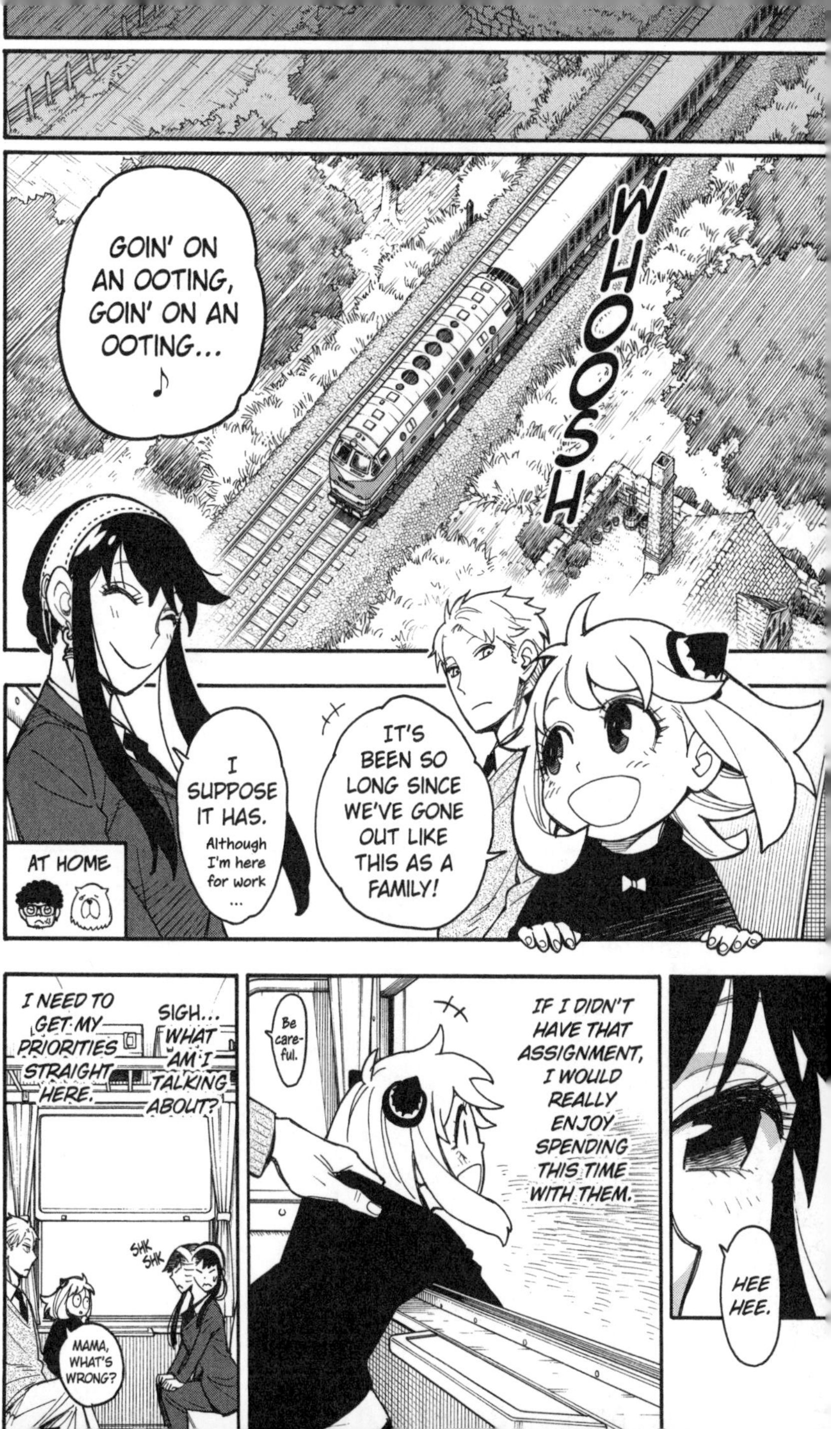
WHOOSH
GOIN' ON AN OOTING, GOIN' ON AN OOTING... ♪
IT'S BEEN SO LONG SINCE WE'VE GONE OUT LIKE THIS AS A FAMILY!
I SUPPOSE IT HAS.
Although I'm here for work ...
AT HOME
HEE HEE.
IF I DIDN'T HAVE THAT ASSIGNMENT, I WOULD REALLY ENJOY SPENDING THIS TIME WITH THEM.
Be careful.
SIGH... WHAT AM I TALKING ABOUT?
I NEED TO GET MY PRIORITIES STRAIGHT HERE.
SHK SHK
MAMA, WHAT'S WRONG?

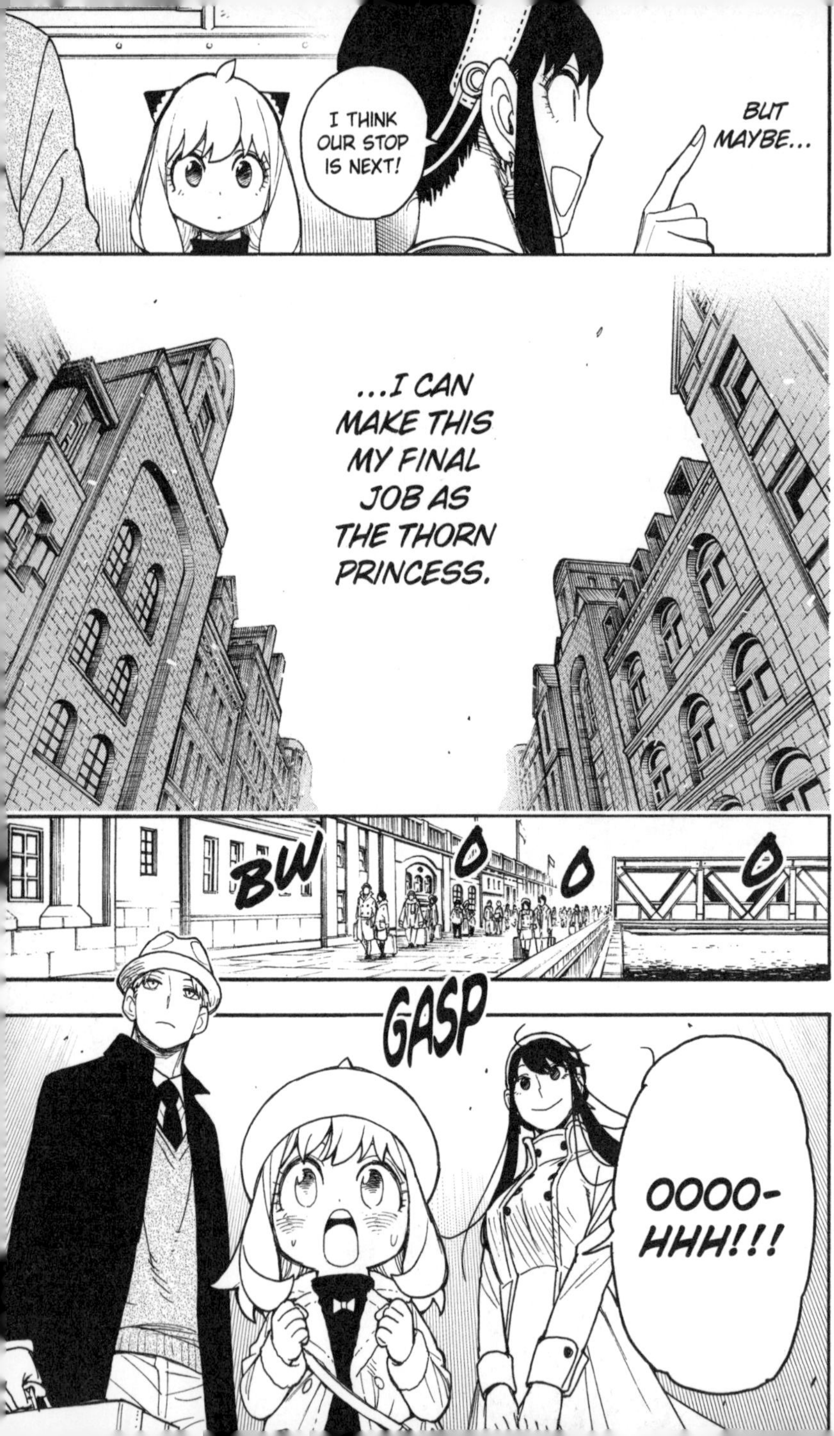
BUT MAYBE...
I THINK OUR STOP IS NEXT!
...I CAN MAKE THIS MY FINAL JOB AS THE THORN PRINCESS.
BWOOO
GASP
OOOO-HHH!!!

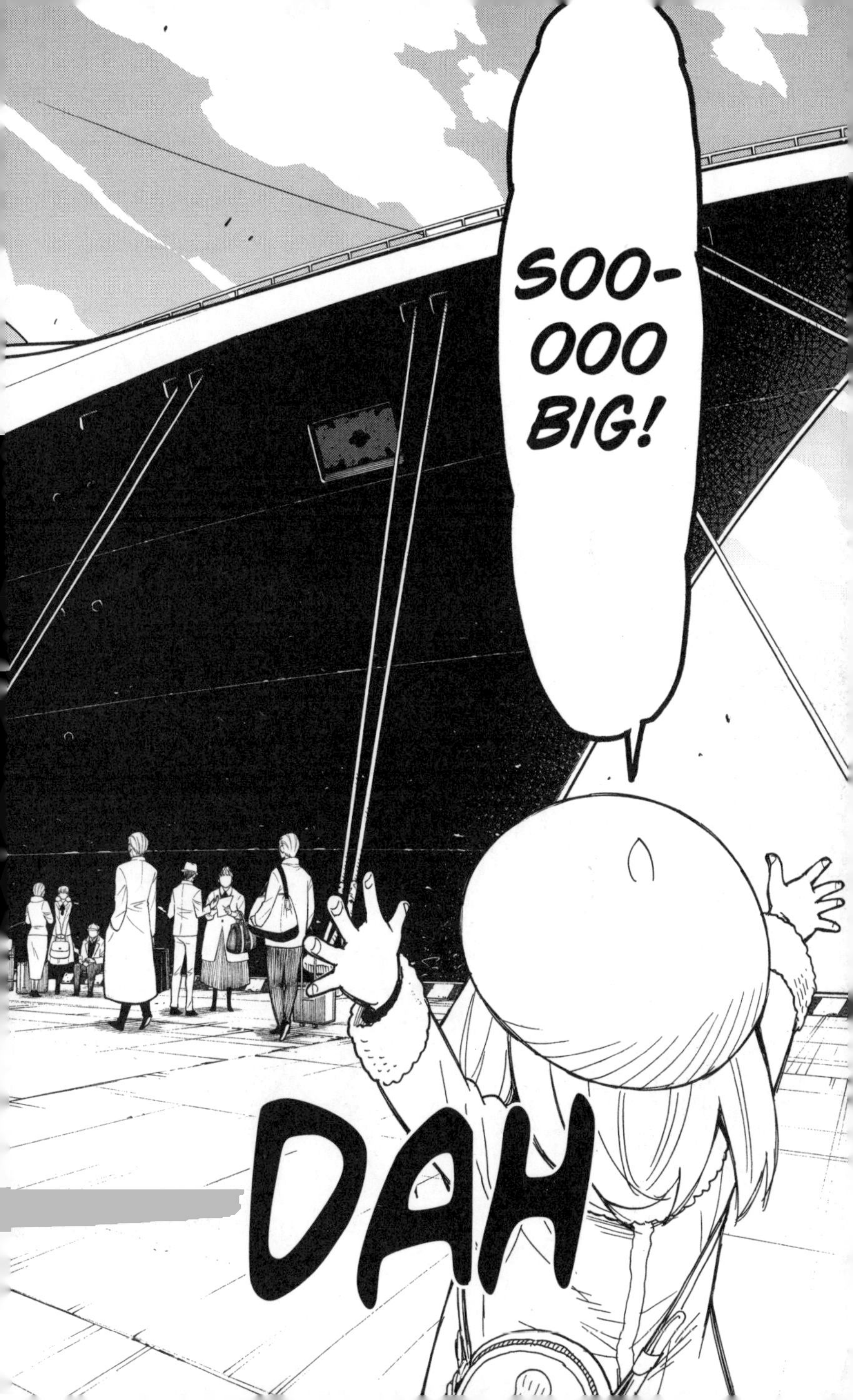
SOO-OOO BIG!
DAH

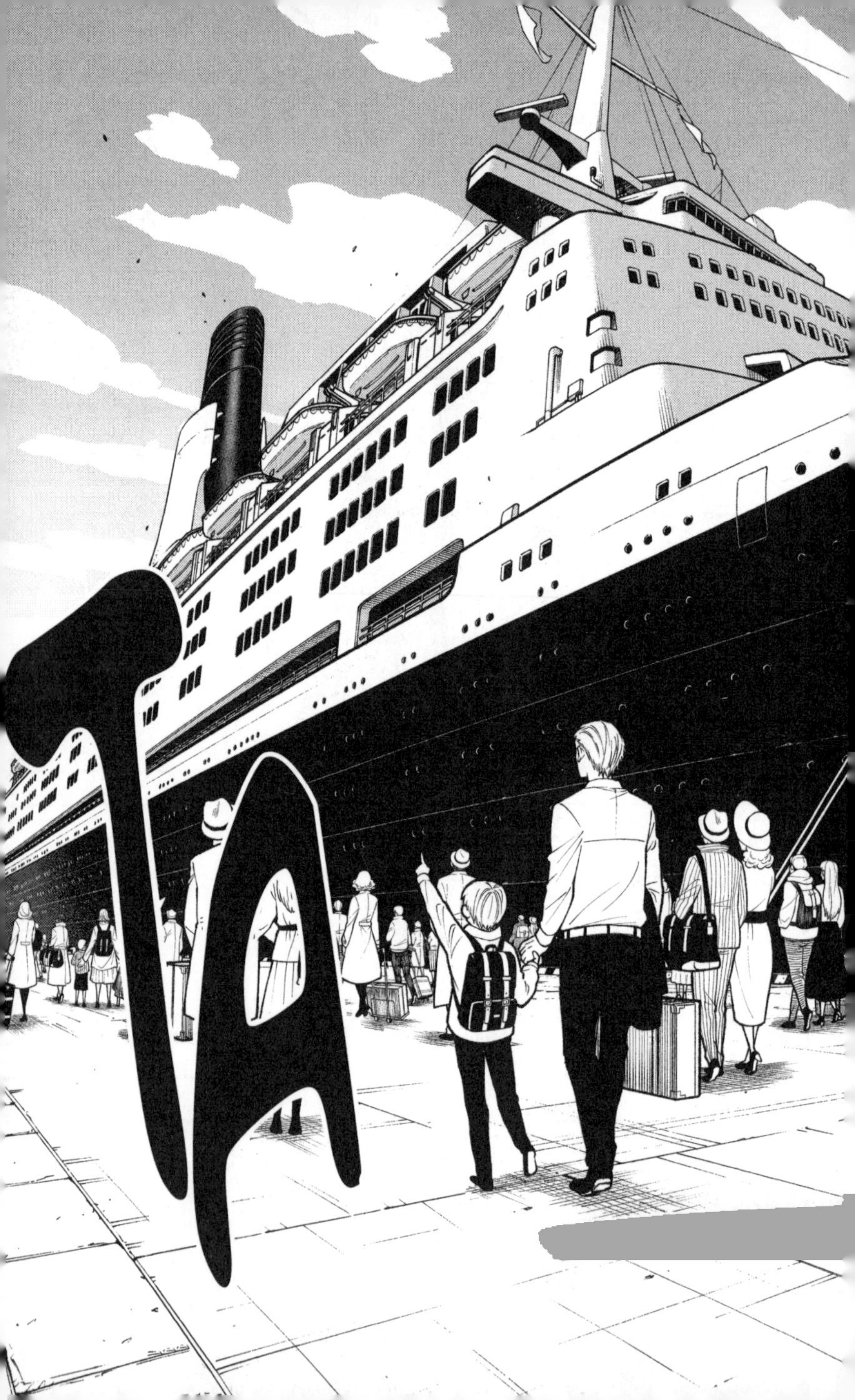
TA

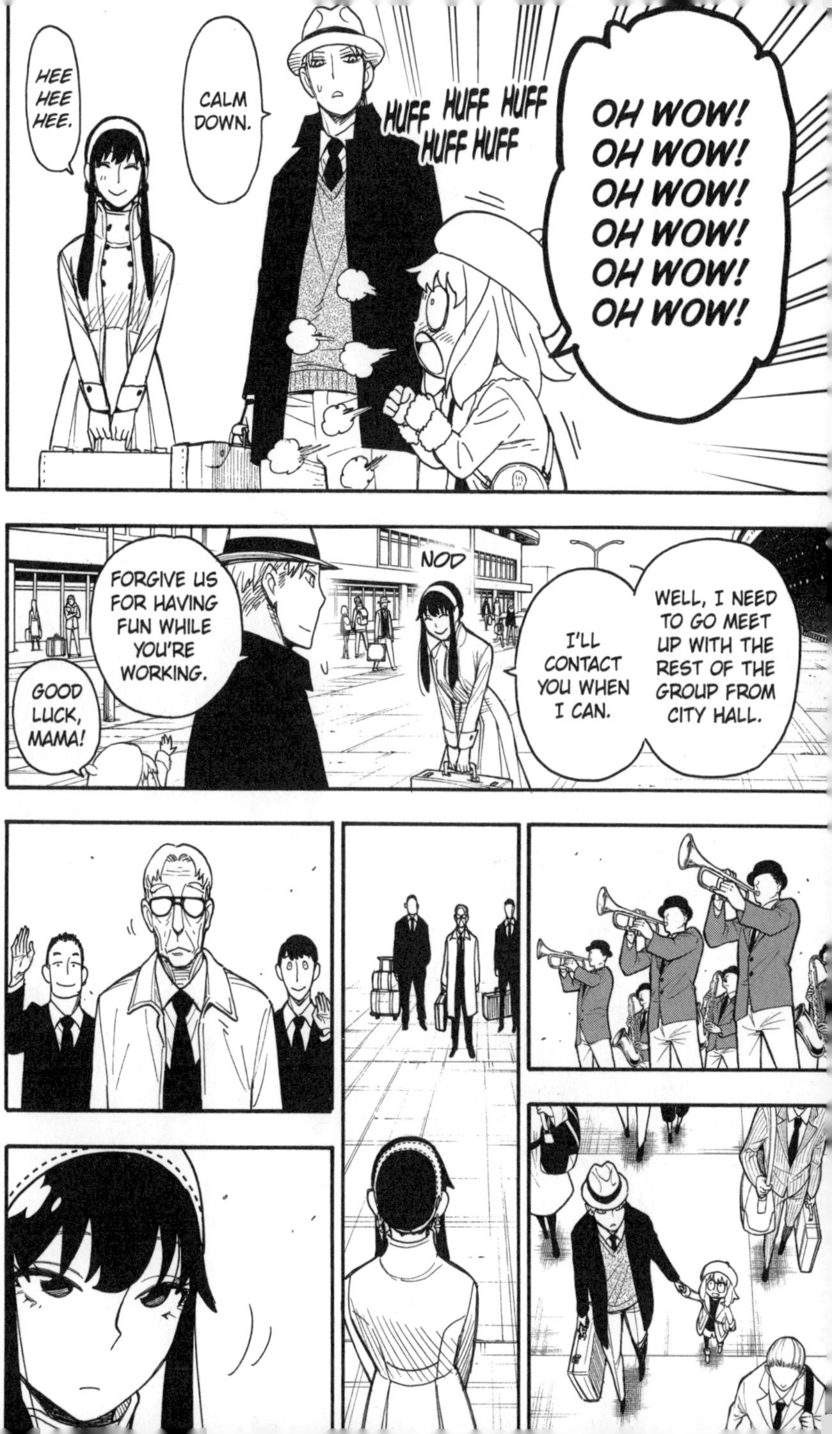
OH WOW! OH WOW! OH WOW! OH WOW! OH WOW! OH WOW!
HUFF HUFF HUFF HUFF HUFF
CALM DOWN.
HEE HEE HEE.
WELL, I NEED TO GO MEET UP WITH THE REST OF THE GROUP FROM CITY HALL.
I'LL CONTACT YOU WHEN I CAN.
NOD
FORGIVE US FOR HAVING FUN WHILE YOU'RE WORKING.
GOOD LUCK, MAMA!

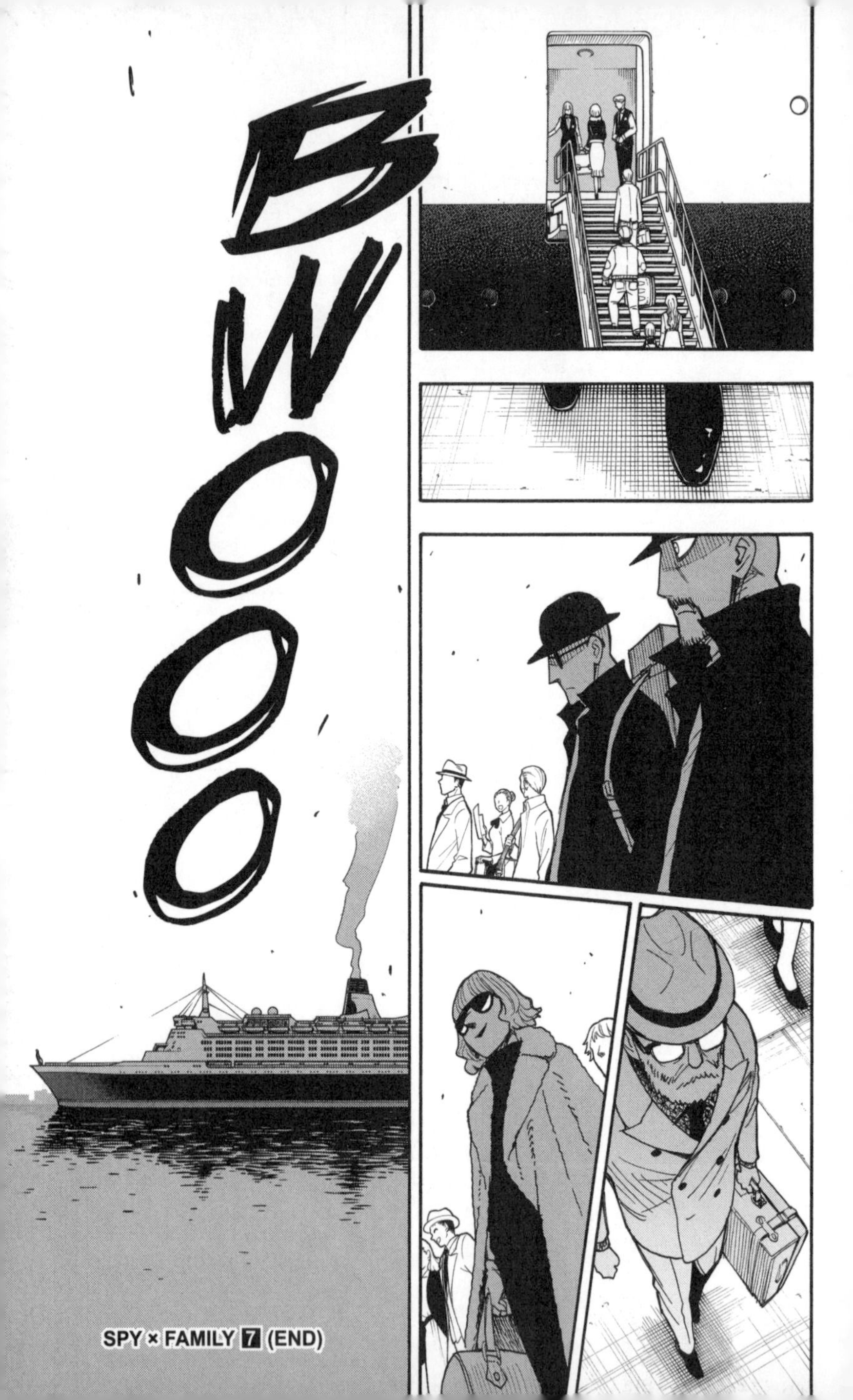
BWOOOO

SPY × FAMILY 7 (END)

SPY×FAMILY

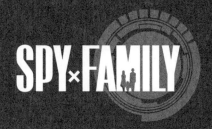

SHORT MISSION 5

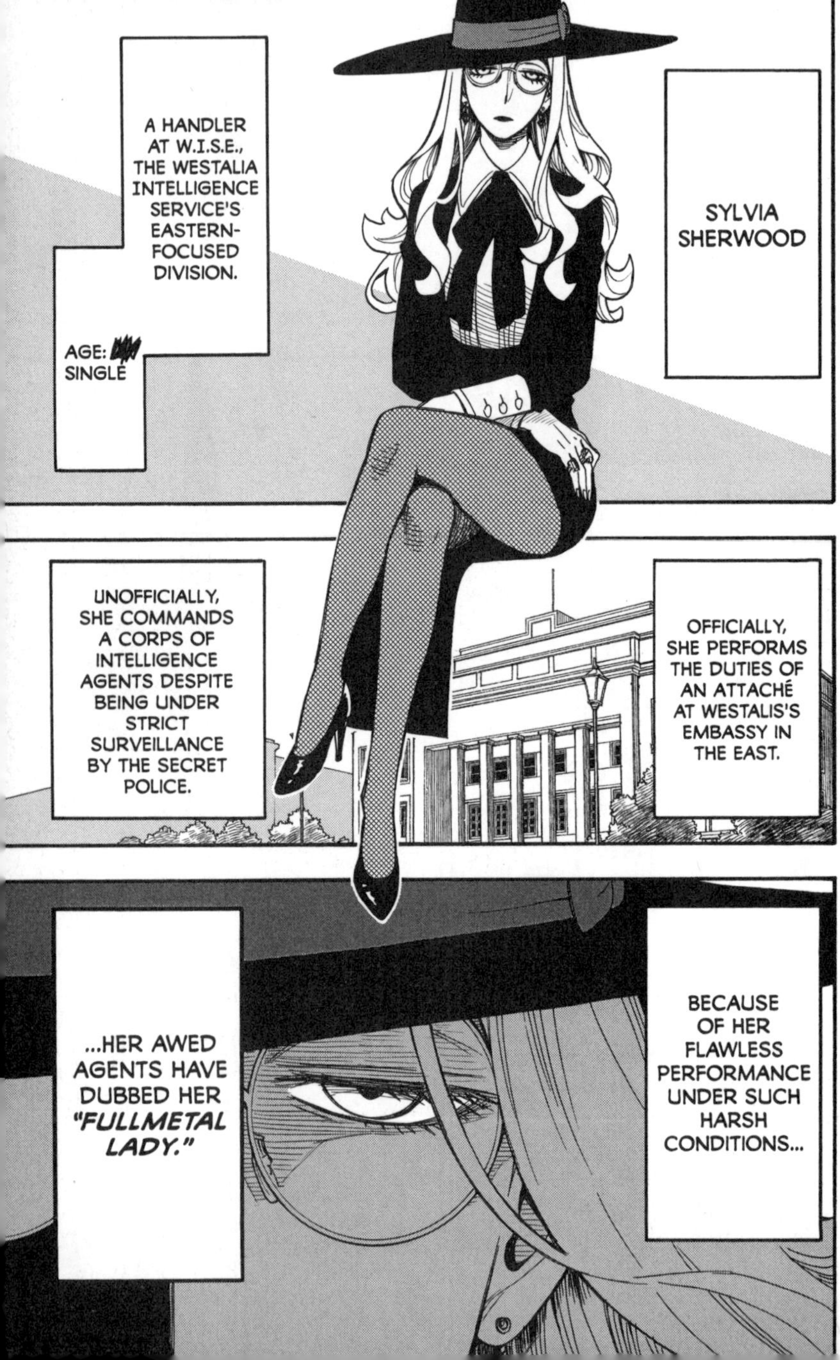
SYLVIA SHERWOOD
A HANDLER AT W.I.S.E., THE WESTALIA INTELLIGENCE SERVICE'S EASTERN-FOCUSED DIVISION.
AGE: [redacted] SINGLE
OFFICIALLY, SHE PERFORMS THE DUTIES OF AN ATTACHÉ AT WESTALIS'S EMBASSY IN THE EAST.
UNOFFICIALLY, SHE COMMANDS A CORPS OF INTELLIGENCE AGENTS DESPITE BEING UNDER STRICT SURVEILLANCE BY THE SECRET POLICE.
BECAUSE OF HER FLAWLESS PERFORMANCE UNDER SUCH HARSH CONDITIONS...
...HER AWED AGENTS HAVE DUBBED HER *"FULLMETAL LADY."*

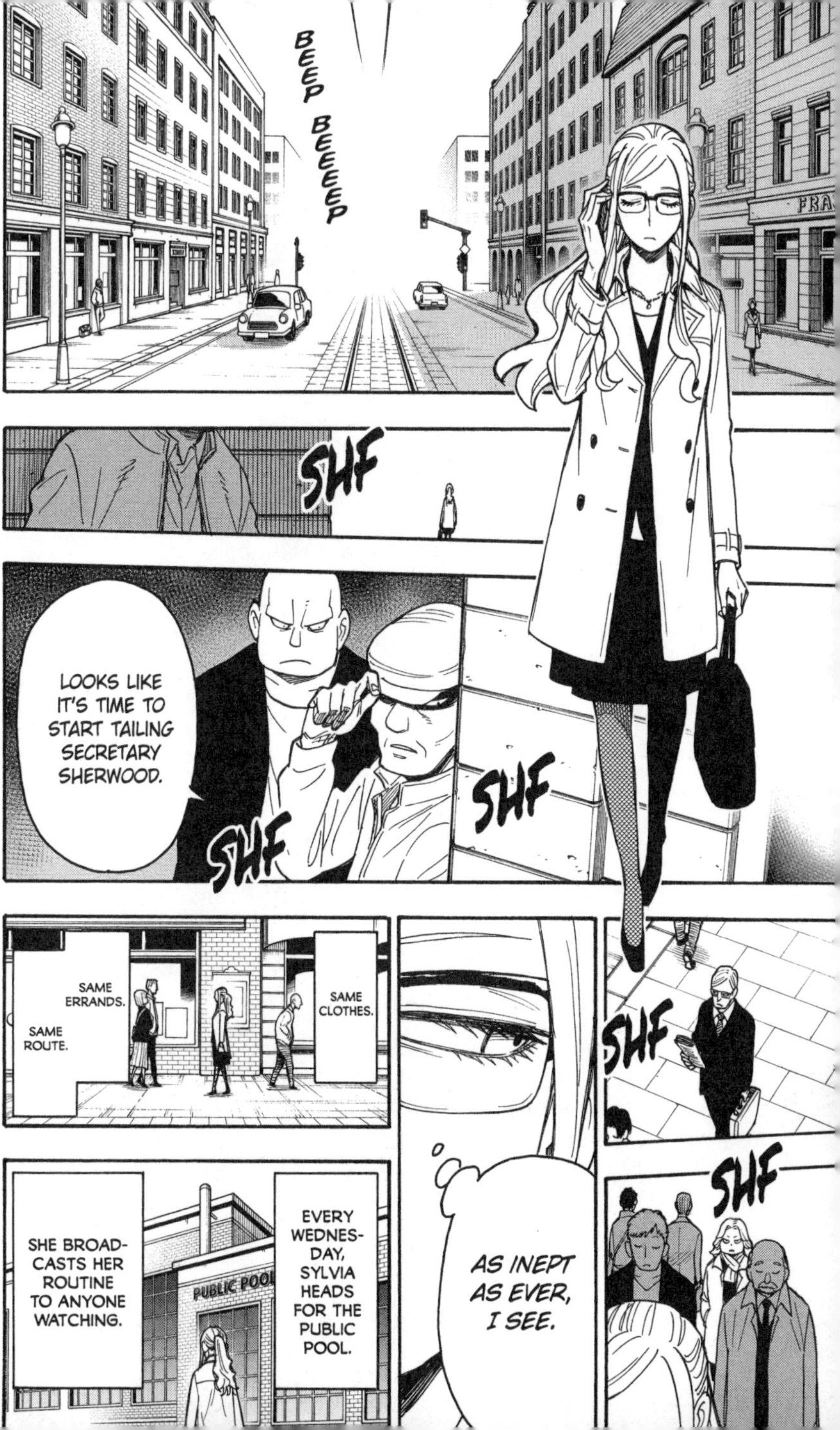
BEEP BEEEEEP
FRA
SHF
LOOKS LIKE IT'S TIME TO START TAILING SECRETARY SHERWOOD.
SHF
SHF
SHF
SHF
AS INEPT AS EVER, I SEE.
SAME CLOTHES.
SAME ERRANDS.
SAME ROUTE.
EVERY WEDNES-DAY, SYLVIA HEADS FOR THE PUBLIC POOL.
PUBLIC POOL
SHE BROAD-CASTS HER ROUTINE TO ANYONE WATCHING.

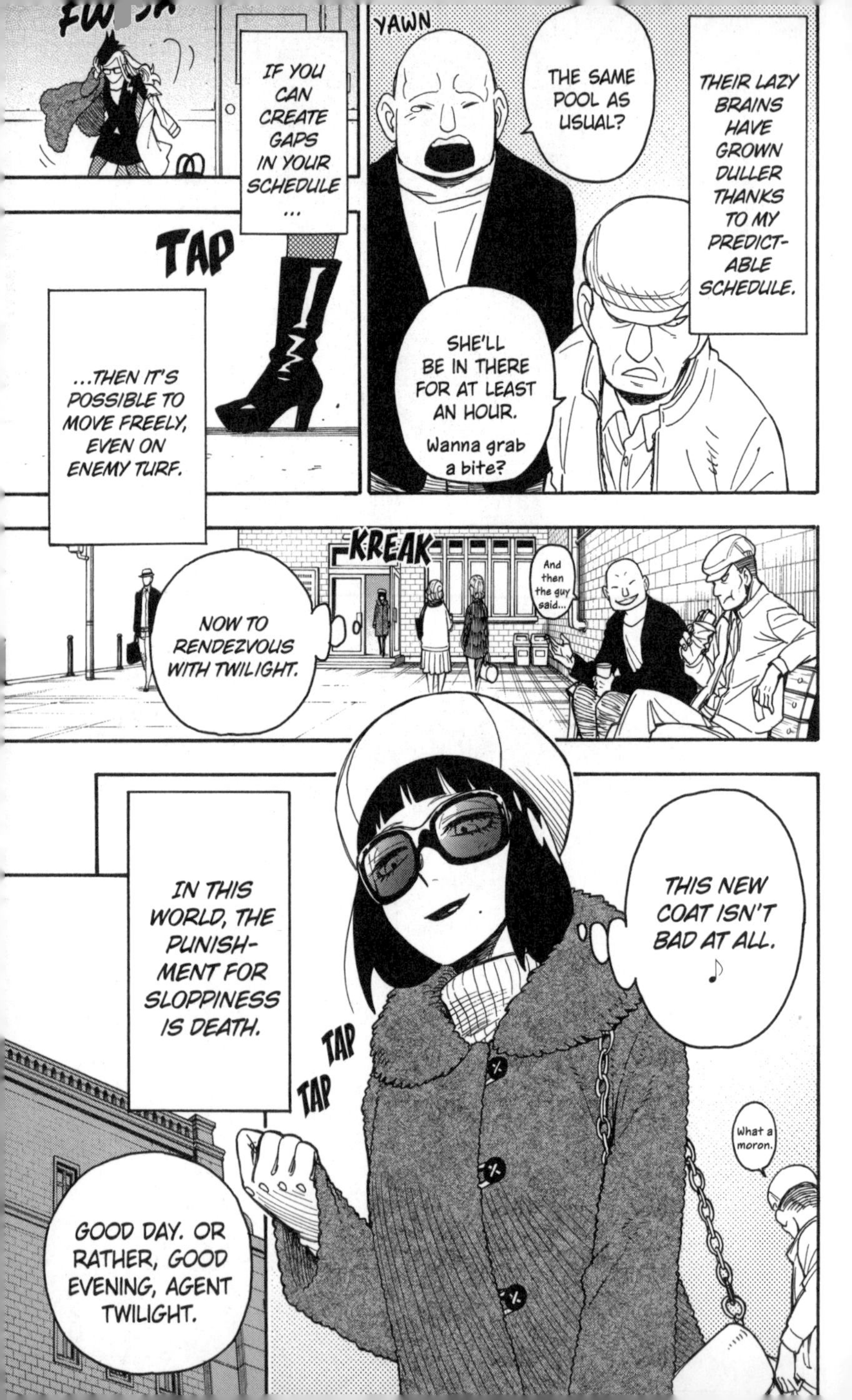
THEIR LAZY BRAINS HAVE GROWN DULLER THANKS TO MY PREDICTABLE SCHEDULE.
YAWN
THE SAME POOL AS USUAL?
SHE'LL BE IN THERE FOR AT LEAST AN HOUR.
Wanna grab a bite?
IF YOU CAN CREATE GAPS IN YOUR SCHEDULE...
TAP
...THEN IT'S POSSIBLE TO MOVE FREELY, EVEN ON ENEMY TURF.
KREAK
And then the guy said...
NOW TO RENDEZVOUS WITH TWILIGHT.
THIS NEW COAT ISN'T BAD AT ALL. ♪
IN THIS WORLD, THE PUNISHMENT FOR SLOPPINESS IS DEATH.
TAP
TAP
What a moron.
GOOD DAY. OR RATHER, GOOD EVENING, AGENT TWILIGHT.

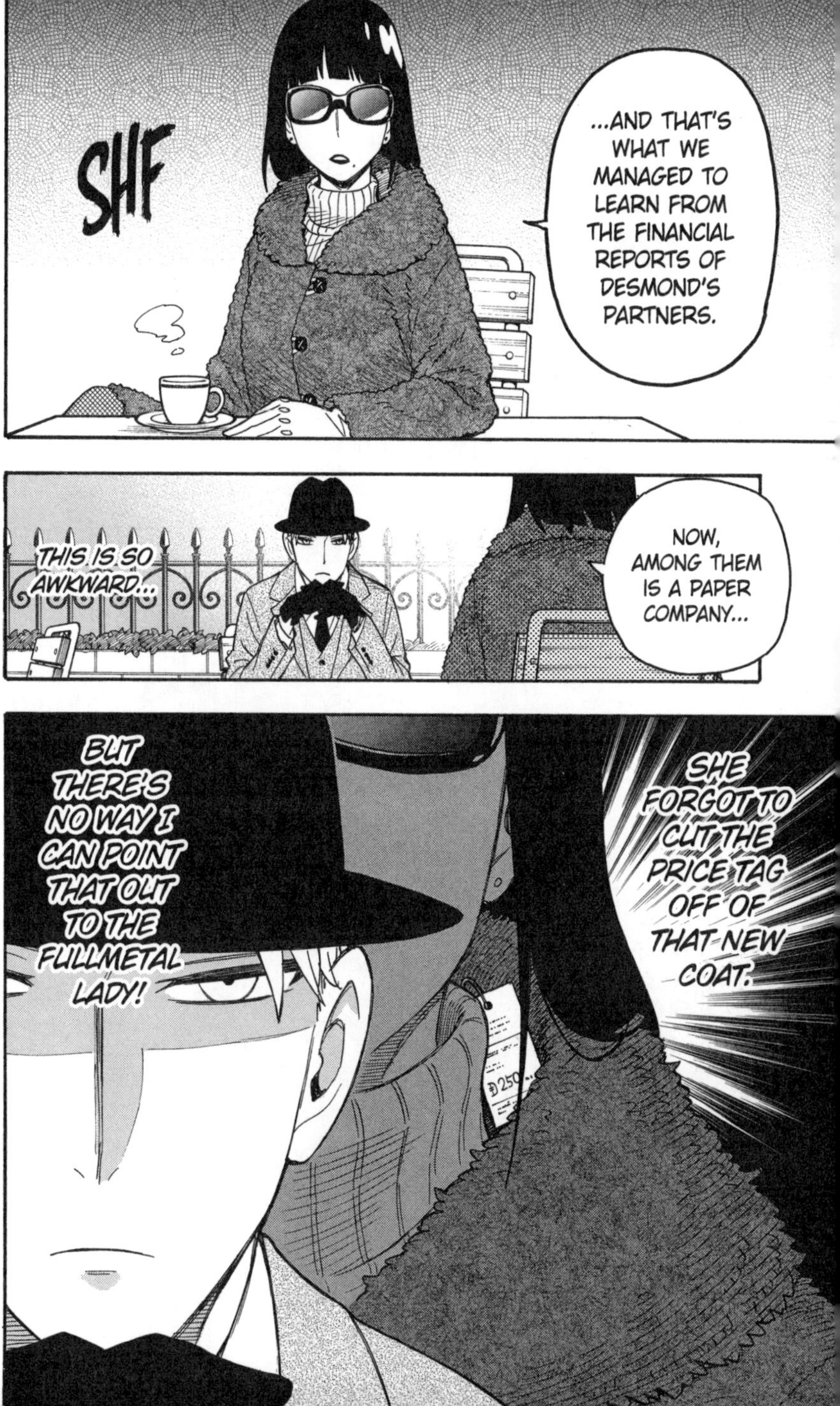
...AND THAT'S WHAT WE MANAGED TO LEARN FROM THE FINANCIAL REPORTS OF DESMOND'S PARTNERS.
SHF
NOW, AMONG THEM IS A PAPER COMPANY...
THIS IS SO AWKWARD...
SHE FORGOT TO CUT THE PRICE TAG OFF OF THAT NEW COAT.
BUT THERE'S NO WAY I CAN POINT THAT OUT TO THE FULLMETAL LADY!

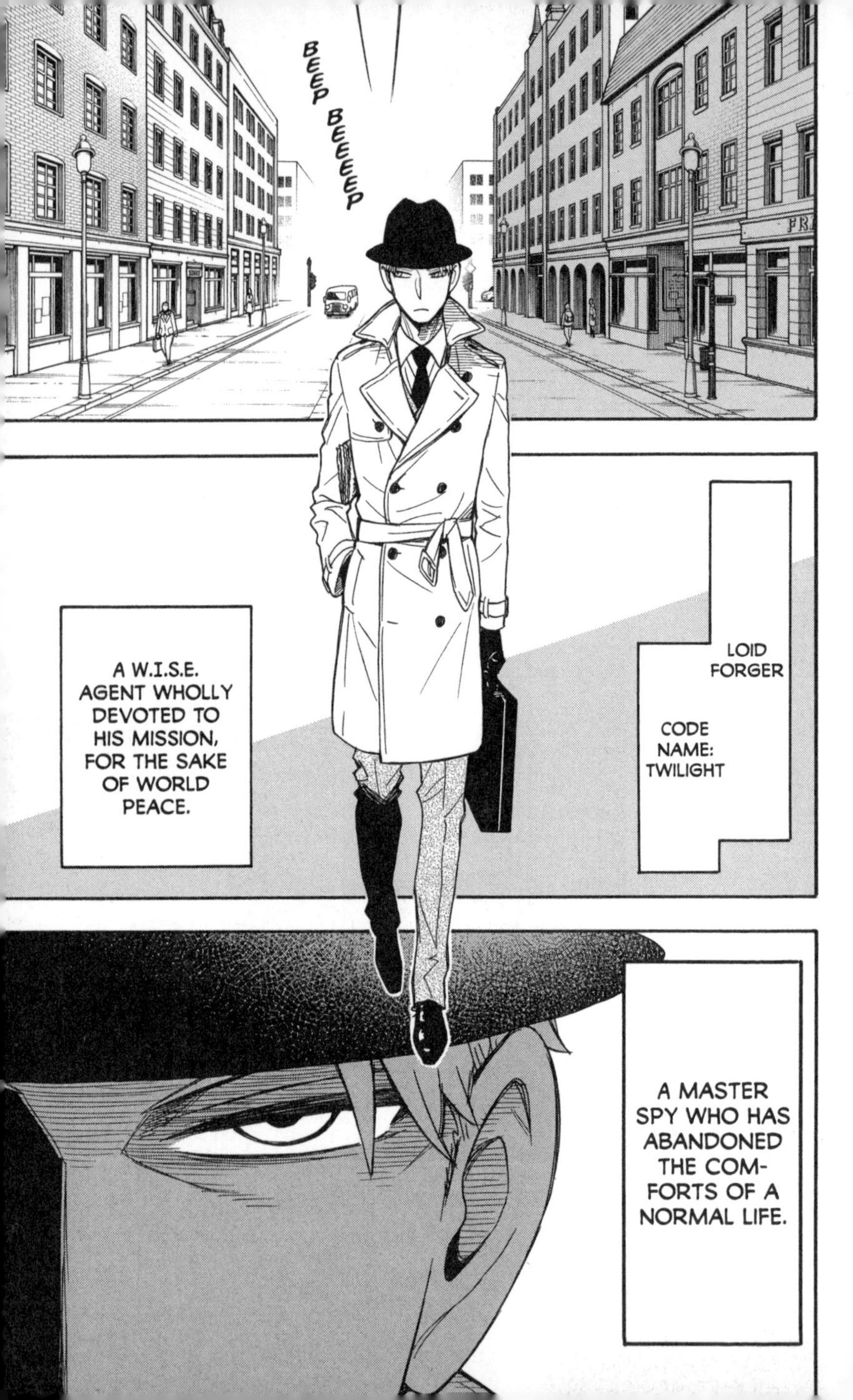
BEEP BEEEEEP
LOID FORGER
CODE NAME: TWILIGHT
A W.I.S.E. AGENT WHOLLY DEVOTED TO HIS MISSION, FOR THE SAKE OF WORLD PEACE.
A MASTER SPY WHO HAS ABANDONED THE COM-FORTS OF A NORMAL LIFE.

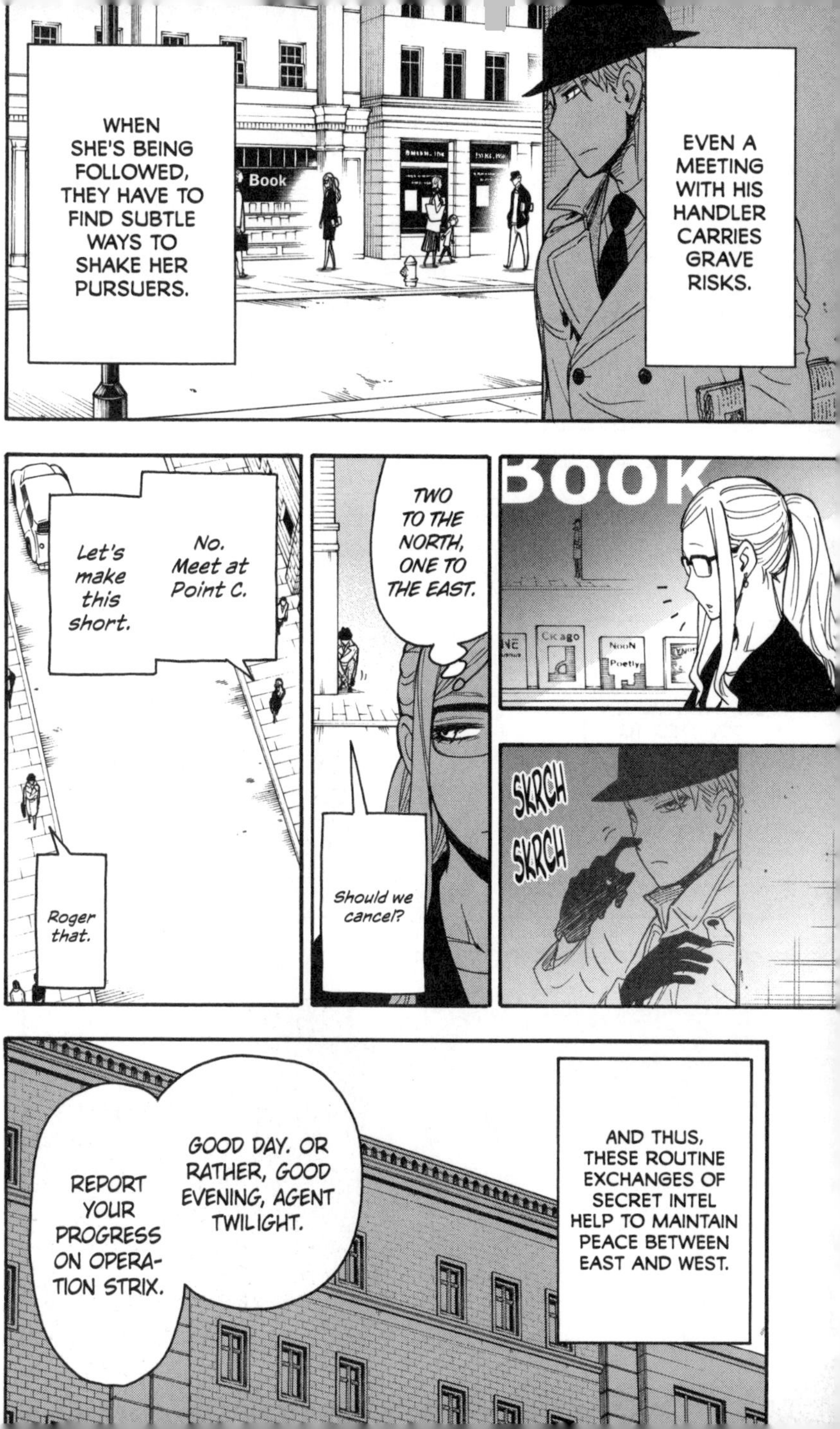
EVEN A MEETING WITH HIS HANDLER CARRIES GRAVE RISKS.
WHEN SHE'S BEING FOLLOWED, THEY HAVE TO FIND SUBTLE WAYS TO SHAKE HER PURSUERS.
BOOK
SKRCH SKRCH
TWO TO THE NORTH, ONE TO THE EAST.
Should we cancel?
No. Meet at Point C.
Let's make this short.
Roger that.
AND THUS, THESE ROUTINE EXCHANGES OF SECRET INTEL HELP TO MAINTAIN PEACE BETWEEN EAST AND WEST.
GOOD DAY. OR RATHER, GOOD EVENING, AGENT TWILIGHT.
REPORT YOUR PROGRESS ON OPERA-TION STRIX.

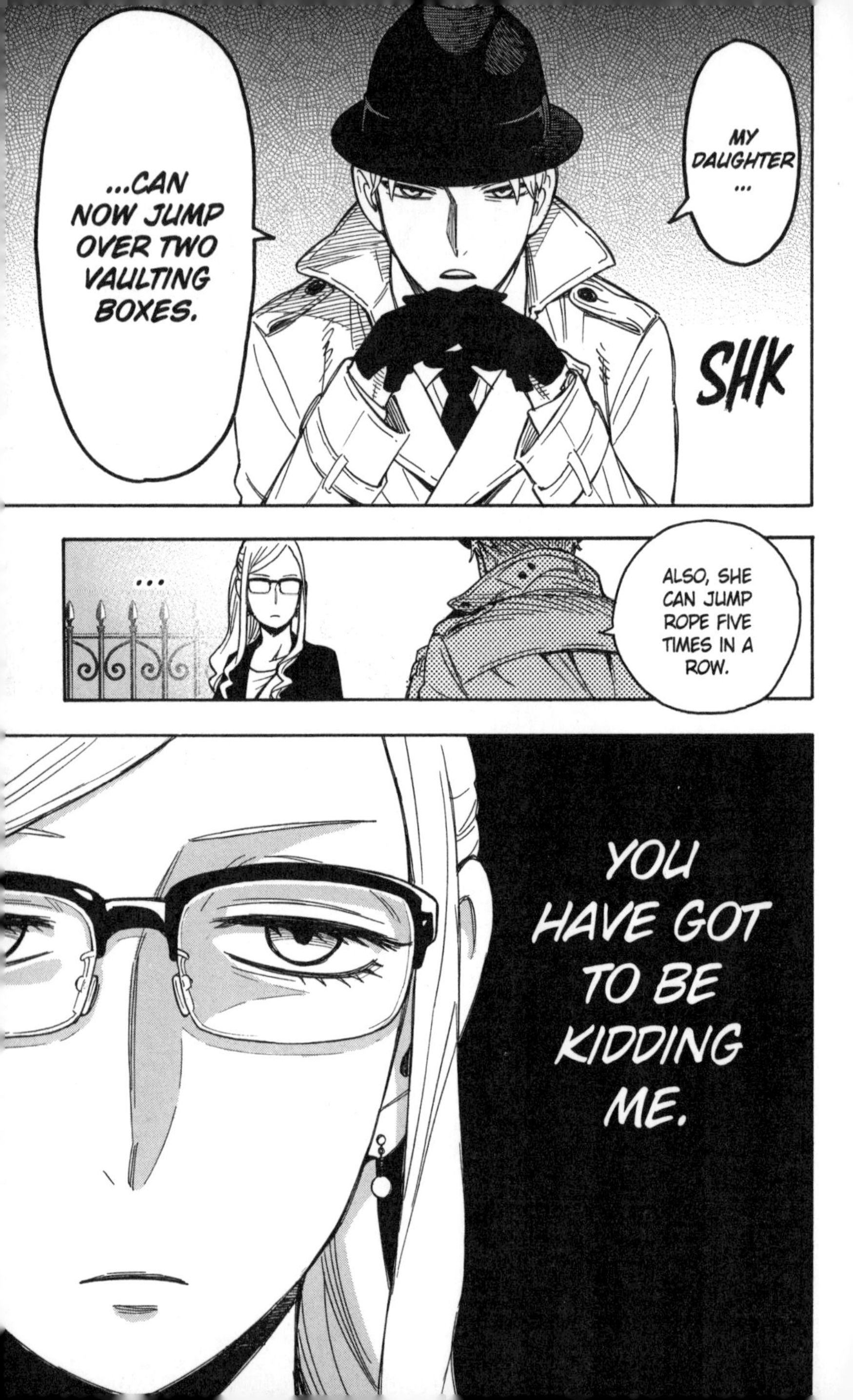
MY DAUGHTER ...
...CAN NOW JUMP OVER TWO VAULTING BOXES.
SHK
ALSO, SHE CAN JUMP ROPE FIVE TIMES IN A ROW.
...
YOU HAVE GOT TO BE KIDDING ME.

SPYxFAMILY CONFIDENTIAL FILES (BONUS)

TOP SECRET EYES ONLY

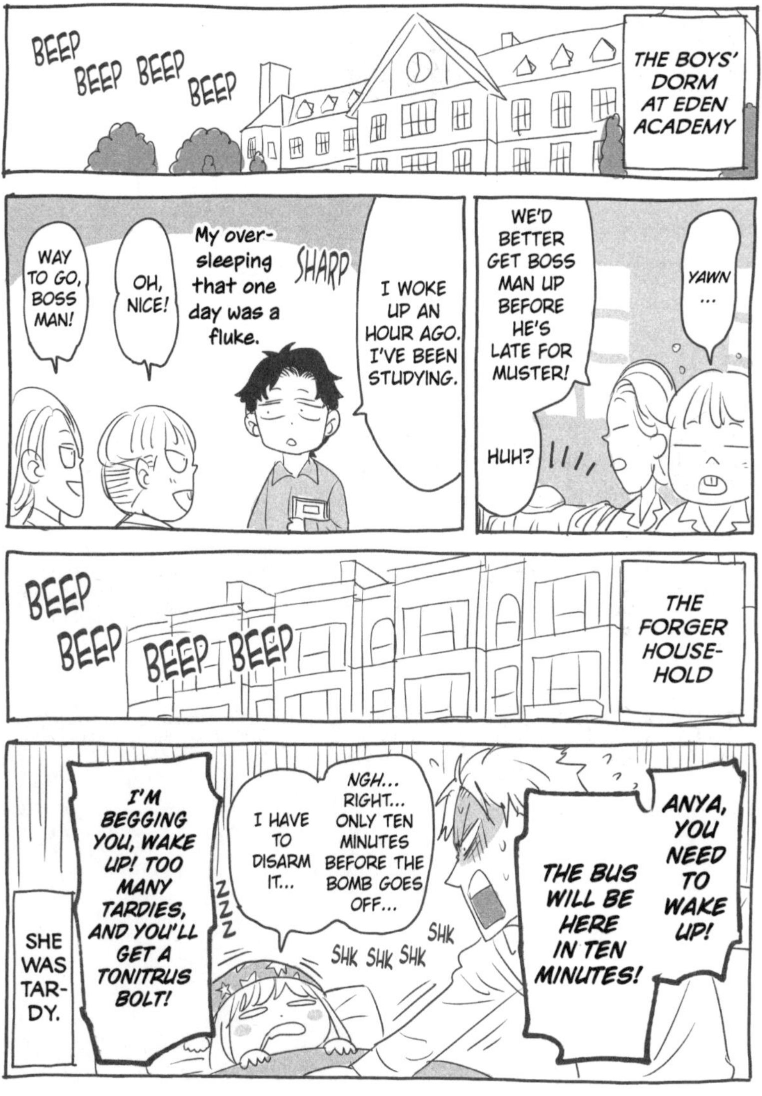
THE BOYS' DORM AT EDEN ACADEMY
BEEP BEEP BEEP BEEP
YAWN...
WE'D BETTER GET BOSS MAN UP BEFORE HE'S LATE FOR MUSTER!
HUH?
I WOKE UP AN HOUR AGO. I'VE BEEN STUDYING.
SHARP
My over-sleeping that one day was a fluke.
OH, NICE!
WAY TO GO, BOSS MAN!
THE FORGER HOUSEHOLD
BEEP BEEP BEEP BEEP
ANYA, YOU NEED TO WAKE UP!
THE BUS WILL BE HERE IN TEN MINUTES!
SHK SHK SHK SHK
NGH... RIGHT... ONLY TEN MINUTES BEFORE THE BOMB GOES OFF...
I HAVE TO DISARM IT...
ZZZ
I'M BEGGING YOU, WAKE UP! TOO MANY TARDIES, AND YOU'LL GET A TONITRUS BOLT!
SHE WAS TARDY.

SPY×FAMILY VOL. 7

SPECIAL THANKS LIST

·CLASSIFIED·

ART ASSISTANCE	
SATOSHI KIMURA	KAZUKI NONAKA
YUICHI OZAKI	MAFUYU KONISHI
HIKARI SUEHIRO	AMASHIMA
MAEHATA	MIO AYATSUKA
SOICHI OHASHI	

GRAPHIC NOVEL DESIGN	
HIDEAKI SHIMADA	ERI ARAKAWA

GRAPHIC NOVEL EDITOR
KANAKO YANAGIDA

MANAGING EDITOR
SHIHEI LIN

I LOVE CATS, BUT I'M ALLERGIC TO THEM. IT'S SO SAD.
ANYWAY, I HOPE TO SEE YOU AGAIN IN VOLUME 8.

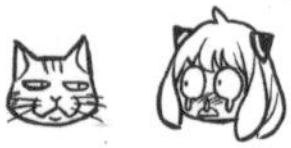

—TATSUYA ENDO

EYES ONLY READ & ~~DESTROY~~ EYES ONLY

SPY×FAMILY

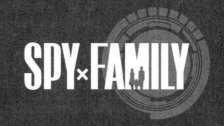

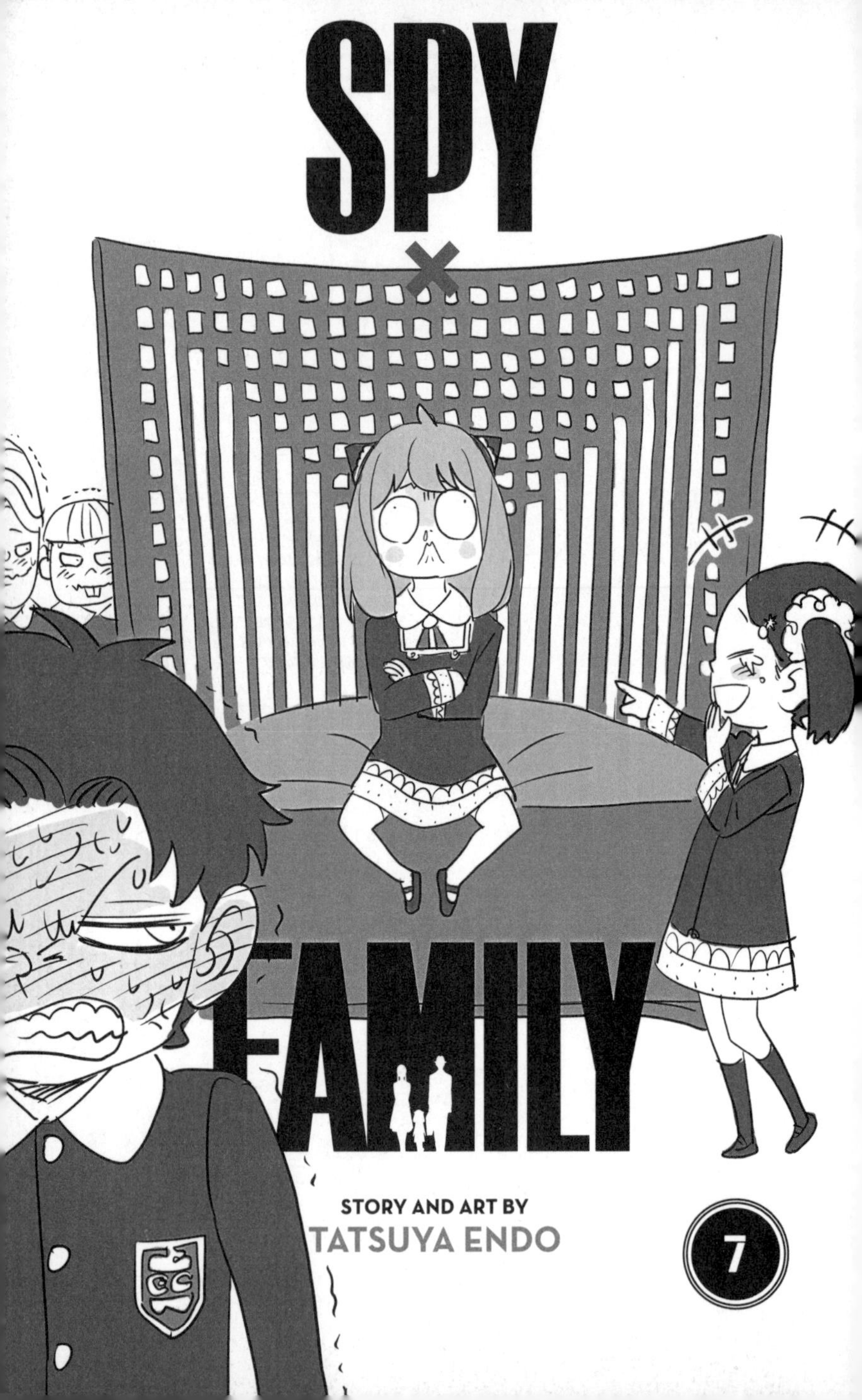
SPY × FAMILY
STORY AND ART BY
TATSUYA ENDO
7

FRANKY'S SECRET FILES

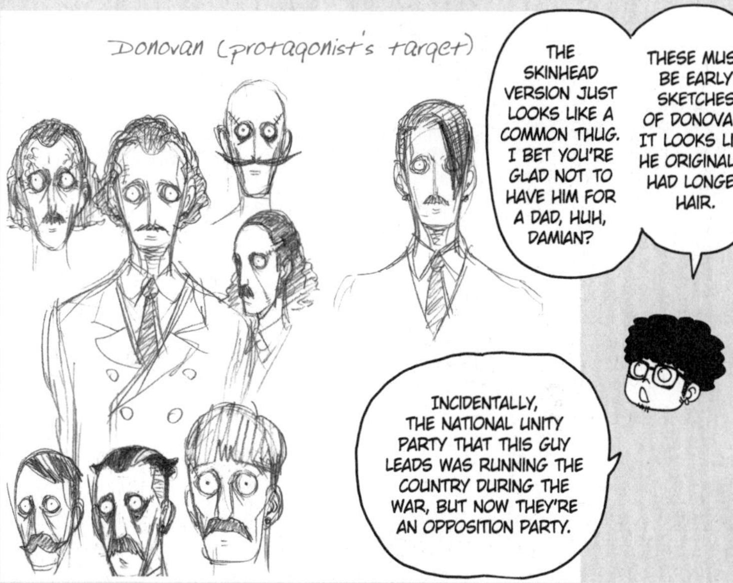
Donovan (protagonist's target)
THESE MUST BE EARLY SKETCHES OF DONOVAN. IT LOOKS LIKE HE ORIGINALLY HAD LONGER HAIR.
THE SKINHEAD VERSION JUST LOOKS LIKE A COMMON THUG. I BET YOU'RE GLAD NOT TO HAVE HIM FOR A DAD, HUH, DAMIAN?
INCIDENTALLY, THE NATIONAL UNITY PARTY THAT THIS GUY LEADS WAS RUNNING THE COUNTRY DURING THE WAR, BUT NOW THEY'RE AN OPPOSITION PARTY.

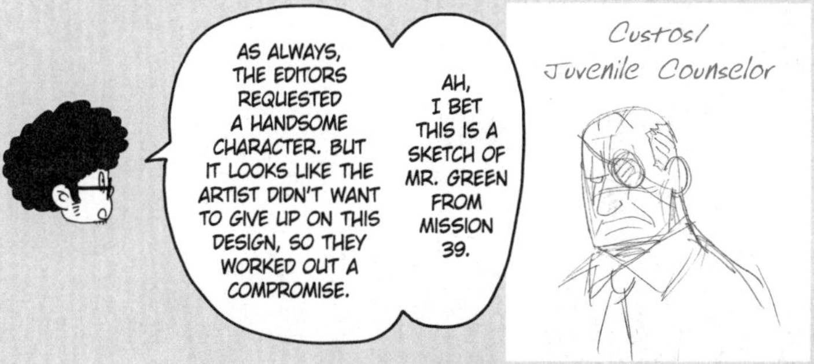
Custos/ Juvenile Counselor
AH, I BET THIS IS A SKETCH OF MR. GREEN FROM MISSION 39.
AS ALWAYS, THE EDITORS REQUESTED A HANDSOME CHARACTER. BUT IT LOOKS LIKE THE ARTIST DIDN'T WANT TO GIVE UP ON THIS DESIGN, SO THEY WORKED OUT A COMPROMISE.

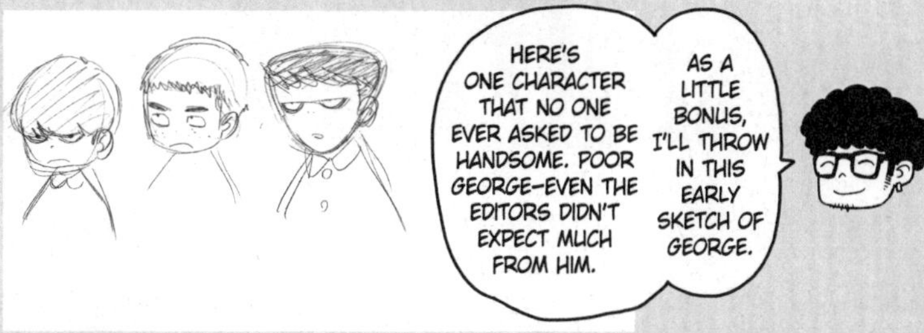
AS A LITTLE BONUS, I'LL THROW IN THIS EARLY SKETCH OF GEORGE.
HERE'S ONE CHARACTER THAT NO ONE EVER ASKED TO BE HANDSOME. POOR GEORGE—EVEN THE EDITORS DIDN'T EXPECT MUCH FROM HIM.